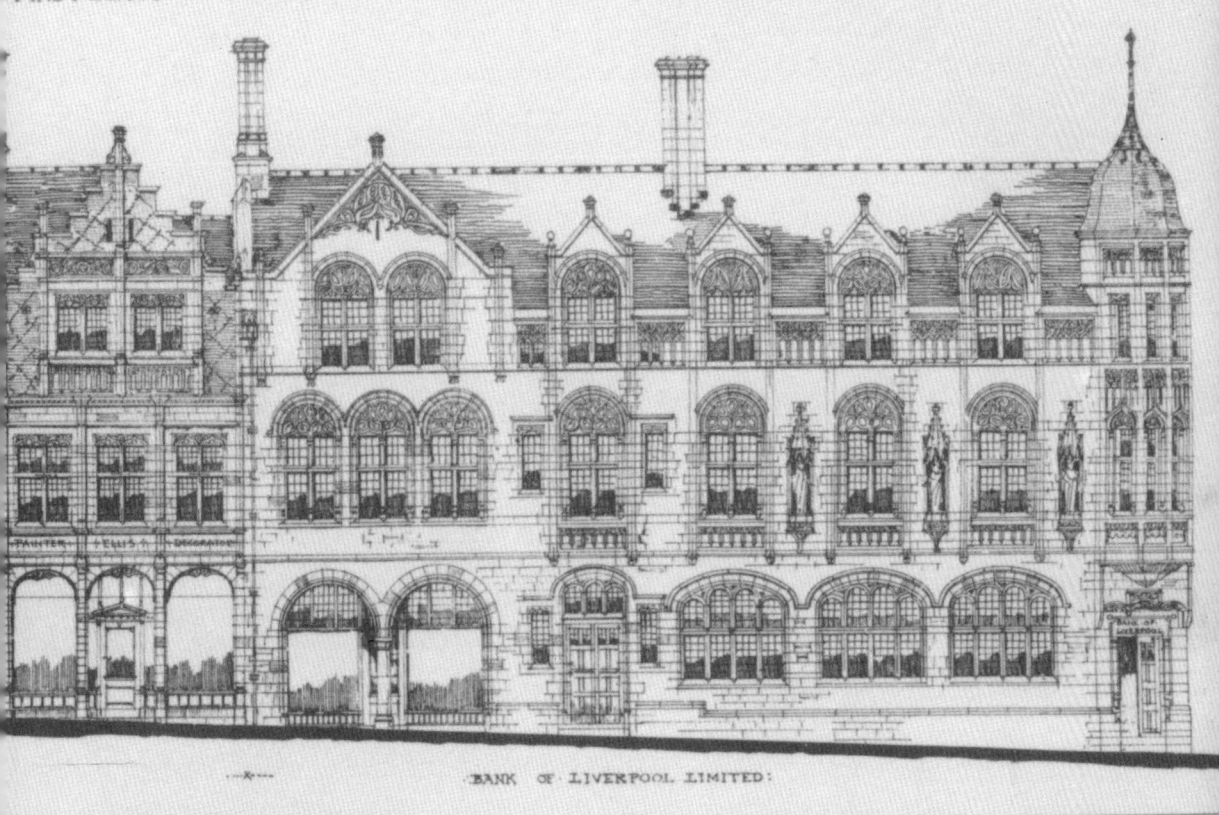

1. First design in stone and brick.
(*Building News*, 83, 1902, p. 185)

The Work of John Douglas

Eccleston Hill Lodge, Eaton Hall, Cheshire, 1881.

The Work of
JOHN DOUGLAS

Edward Hubbard

1991
THE VICTORIAN SOCIETY

Opposite: John Douglas's bookplate

This book has been published
with the aid of grants from:

The Marc Fitch Fund
The Twenty-Seven Foundation
Cadw: Welsh Historic Monuments
Cambrian Archaeological Association
Cheshire County Council
Chester Archaeological Society
Chester City Council
Chester Diocesan Advisory Committee
Clwyd County Council

ISBN 0 901657 16 6
© 1991 J. H. Hubbard

Published by The Victorian Society
1 Priory Gardens
London W4 1TT
Printed by Smith Settle
Otley, West Yorkshire

List of Subscribers

Dr Jill Allibone
Geoffrey Andrew
John H. G. Archer
John Ashdown
Stephen Astley
A. P. Baggs
John Baily
Alistair Bain, T. A. C. P. Design
Mr and Mrs J. A. Bartlett
M. N. Battersby
Joan Beck
D. A. Bell
Gilbert T. Bell
Dr J. C. G. Binfield
Peter Birkhead
L. J. Bird
Blackmoor Park Junior School, per Mr Dewsnap
Brian Blackwood
Oliver Bott
Peter Boughton
B. S. Bowden
Donald Bowe
Dr Geoff Brandwood
John N. Bray
Michael Brook
Dr Chris Brooks
A. S. Brooks
Miles Broughton
Anne and Andrew Brown
Philip Browning
Dr R. W. Brunskill
David Bryce-Smith
L. D. Butler
Donald Buttress
Canterbury City Council
R. Cavendish
M. R. Channon
Bridget Cherry
Martin Cherry
Cheshire County Council, per Ian Dunn
Chester Civic Trust, per Stephen Langtree
Chester D. A. C., per P. J. Mills
Rob Close
Clwyd Record Office, Hawarden
D. Cole
H. M. Colvin
James Conlan
G. R. Coppack
Dr P. F. Corbin
Stephen Croad
Margaret W. Cullin
Colin J. K. Cunningham
Professor James Stevens Curl
Anthea and Neil Darlington
I. A. Darlington

Dartmouth College, New Hampshire, USA
G. M. Dean
R. D. Dean
Design Group Partnership, per N. Evans
J. Dimmock
M. D. Drury
F. I. Dunn
Edinburgh College of Art
Anthony Newton Edwards, RIBA
Sheila Edwards
Dr Brent Elliott
R. R. Emanuel
Brian Evans, T. A. C. P. Design
David St John Evans, T. A. C. P. Design
Roger Evans
Stuart Evans
Dr W. Fawcett
Peter de Figueiredo
Donald Findlay
Graham Fisher
A. C. Foster
Elizabeth Foulkes
Angus Fowler
K. Geoffrey Foy
Professor R. Gardner-Medwin
Sir William Gladstone, Bt
Michael Godbee
Professor A. H. Gomme
Robert Gordon's Institute of Technology
M. Green
Dr and Mrs J. Hadley
Doreen Halewood
Jolyon Hall
Michael Hall
Neil Hamilton, MP
A. J. Hamlett
C. Hammond
Rev. Brian Harris
Richard Haslam
Jane Hatcher
E. M. Hawes
Mrs B. A. Hayes
David Heath
R. B. Heaton, B. Arch, FRIBA
A. T. Herbert
R. Herbert
Marjorie Hill
Canon D. G. Hinge
Hermione Hobhouse
W. A. Holborrow
Roger Holden
Dr Richard Holder
Graham Holland
Mrs Katherine Holland
A. S. Holliday
Dr J. E. Hollinshead
John Howard
Hamilton and Jan Howatt
Peter Howell
J. H. Hubbard
R. Huby
Vernon Hughes
A. W. Huish
Alexander Hunter
Hunterian Art Gallery
Rod Hutchinson
Keith Ingham
J. Irving
S. G. Jardine
D. H. Jennings
Bernard T. Johnson
Alan Johnson
R. Jolley
Kenneth William Jones
R. L. Jones
Eitan Karol
Thornton Kay
Denis Keeling
Rev. Canon D. C. Kelly
A. F. Kelsall
The Lord Kenyon
Celia Kinnersley
Loraine Knowles
Jonathan Knox
A. W. A. Lamont
Lancashire and Cheshire Antiquarian Society
Emily Lane
Brian Lawrence
Sheila Lemoine
Vaughan Lipscombe
Liverpool Cathedral Library
David Lloyd
Sydney Lloyd
Thomas Lloyd
Nicholas Long

David Low
Mrs Frances Lynch Llewellyn
Pauline and Tim Malcolm
Manchester Polytechnic
Mansfield Design Consultants
C. D. L. Menzies
G. R. Middleton
Gordon Miller
R. Mitchell
Trevor Mitchell
Dr Tim Mowl
C. J. Nancarrow
Dr Moira Ockrim
Julian Orbach
Rev. P. R. Owens
David O'Connor
J. R. Parker, T. A. C. P. Design
David Pendery
Jonathan Pepler
Miss E. L. Pettitt
Christopher J. Pickford
Malcolm Pinhorn
Professor Derek Poole
Dolly Potter
Ken Powell
Alan Powers
Richard Prentiss
J. D. Preston
Ven. T. W. Pritchard
David Prout
Dr A. Pullin
Rev. Noel Pyatt
Anthony Quiney
RCHAM Wales, per Sian Spink
RCHME, per Stephen Croad
RIBA British Architecture Library
RIBA Drawings Collection
P. D. Randall
J. W. Ratte
Dr R. A. Reid
A. Richardson
Margaret and Anthony Richardson
Canon M. H. Ridgway
Michael Robbins
Canon A. C. Roberts
Francis B. Roberts
John Martin Robinson
Nicholas Roe

Alan Rome
Mrs L. Salaman
Chris Sanders
J. W. G. Sanderson
L. and J. Saunders
Matthew Saunders
M. V. J. Seaborne
Dr and Mrs E. Shearing
Jeanne Sheehy
Michael Shippobottom
Teresa Sladen
Rev. Derek Smith
W. John Smith
M. R. Speak
Gavin Stamp
C. F. Stell
Timothy Stevens
Ian Stockdale
B. R. Stoner
Peter Stonebridge
Ian Sutton
T. A. C. P. Architects
Mrs M. J. Tanfield
Philip Thomas
James Thompson
Peter Thomson
Robert Thorne
Anthony Tibbles
I. Tomkinson
Alan Turner
Aidan Turner-Bishop
J. E. Vaughan
A. Geoffrey Veysey
Clive and Jane Wainwright
Chris Wakeling
David Walker
Elisabeth Walters
A. R. Warbrick
Fabian Watkinson
S. D. Webster
Alexandra Wedgwood
Ian Wells
Welsh School of Architecture, per Simon Unwin
Richard J. S. Wilcock
K. Woodward
Anthony and Susan Woolfenden
P. A. Wrather

Contents

	List of Subscribers	page v
	Acknowledgements for Illustrations	x
	Author's Preface	xi
	Editor's Preface	xiii
	Abbreviations	xix
I	John Douglas's Life	1
II	Architectural Background and Training	19
III	Chester in the Nineteenth Century	23
IV	Architectural Practice	27
V	High Victorianism	38
VI	Principal Patron	59
VII	Early Maturity: Secular Buildings	77
VIII	Early Maturity: Churches	124
IX	Douglas & Fordham: Secular Buildings	146
X	Douglas & Fordham: Churches	173
XI	Douglas & Minshull	187
XII	Conclusion	205
	References	211
	Appendix I. Correspondence from the Honourable Cecil Thomas Parker relating to the building of The Paddocks, Eccleston	230
	Appendix II. Catalogue of Works	238
	Index	281

Acknowledgements for Illustrations

Dr G. K. Brandwood   78 125 126 (both) 132 172 175 176 (both) 177 178 179 182
Cheshire Record Office   40 122
Chester Photographic Survey   120
Clwyd County Council   136
Rector and Churchwardens, Criccieth   172
Design Group Partnership   92 (Cotton Abbots) 93 (Lea Newbold) 99 (both)
Dr E. J. Diestelkamp   5 44 46 72 90 91 (School Lane) 92 (Waverton) 158 159 162 (Eccleston Lodge) 194 196
   Colour – Eccleston Hill Lodge; Over U.R. Church; Belgrave Cottages; The Limes, Pulford
Hon. M. L. W. Flower, Arley Hall   100 104 105
   Colour – Dr Willetts' House; George and Dragon Inn
Grosvenor Estate   63 66 (both) 94 95 98 (photo) 160 163 166
   Colour – Dr Willetts' House; George and Dragon Inn
Peter Howell   49 91 (Rushmere Lane) 164 193
   Colour – The Paddocks; Stud Lodge, Eaton Hall
Edward Hubbard   115
A. F. Kersting   134 135 140 199
National Museums and Galleries on Merseyside (Walker Art Gallery)   149 150 151
Neil Pike Architecture   53
Royal Commission on the Historical Monuments of England   157
Michael Shippobottom   171
Staffordshire County Council   127
Rector and Churchwardens, Warburton   103 142 144

Author's Preface

John Douglas was in practice as an architect in Chester from either 1855 or 1860 until the time of his death in 1911 at the age of 81. From *c.* 1884 he was in partnership with D. P. Fordham and from *c.* 1897 to 1909 with C. H. Minshull. From about 1860 his office was at No. 6 Abbey Square, and after his death the practice was continued at the same address, where it remained until 1974, under the style of Design Group Partnership. Despite this continuous history, the only records from Douglas's time which survive at the office are one envelope containing documents relating to Barmouth church, one photograph album, one folder of miscellaneous engravings and rough drawings, and a caricature sketch of Douglas himself by a member of the staff. The rest of the archives are reported to have disappeared during the Second World War, when the house was under government requisition. Documentary evidence of Douglas's work is thus of a scattered nature, and is that which belonged to clients' rather than the architect's side of jobs. Some has found its way into centralised safe-keeping, including sets of correspondence and accounts and some drawings in the Cheshire County Record Office. Other drawings are known to remain in buildings to which they relate, and much else still in private hands doubtless remains to be discovered. A vast quantity of material concerning the patronage of the first Duke of Westminster is at the Eaton Estate Office; the Eaton archives and the notices and illustrations of Douglas's buildings which appeared in the contemporary architectural press were the two most fruitful single sources used in the preparation of the book.

References are given at the end of each chapter, but authorities cited in connection with individual buildings by Douglas are not included with these. Instead they are collected together in the chronological Catalogue of Works in Appendix II, and recourse may be had to this for the sources of information for all ascriptions. It must be added that the Catalogue cannot be regarded as complete, for further research would without any doubt bring to light many further works for which Douglas was responsible.

Grateful thanks are due to many people (not least to the owners of a number of Douglas's houses) for help received. Although they are too numerous for each to be named, special mention must be made of Mrs. E. Berry, former Chester City Archivist and her successor Miss A. Kennett, of Mr. Brian Redwood, Cheshire County Archivist, of Mr. A. R. Mitchell of the Eaton Estate Office, of Mr. Peter Howell for the extended loan of his portfolio of illustrations and for numerous helpful suggestions, and of Mr. J. H. G. Archer for his counsel and guidance throughout the duration of the work.

Others to whom acknowledgement is due include Dr. Paul Crossley, Mrs. A. D. Edwards, Mr. Heber Fearnall, the Revd. David Hinge, Mr. Peter G. Holmes, Mr. Robert Jolley, the Revd. E. J. Basil Jones, Mr. J. E. Latham, Mr. David McLaughlin, Mr. Harold Milliken, Mr. H. Morgan, Sir Nikolaus Pevsner, Mr. Stephen Wilcockson, Mrs. N. Wild and Mrs. T. A. Williams.

Edward Hubbard
September 1974

Editor's Preface

Edward Horton Hubbard was born in Birkenhead on 2nd July 1937, and died there on 31st May 1989. All of his great-grandparents had migrated to the town during the years of its nineteenth century growth. He liked to recall that he first showed his appreciation of Victorian architecture when being pushed in his pram round the leafy suburb of Prenton, where he lived all his life. He went to Liverpool University to study architecture, but it soon became apparent that his vocation was for the history rather than the practice of architecture.

In the early 1960s an appreciation of Victorian architecture was still far from common, but Edward Hubbard had learnt to love it from his surroundings in Birkenhead and Liverpool, and, after the Victorian Society was founded in 1958, he soon became a member. He was chiefly responsible for setting up the first of the semi-autonomous regional groups which set the Victorian Society apart from the other amenity societies. He served as Honorary Secretary of the Liverpool Group for thirteen years, setting standards of efficiency and thoroughness which other groups have not found easy to match.

The speaker at the launching of the Group in 1965 was Professor (Sir) Nikolaus Pevsner, and this was Edward Hubbard's first meeting with him. It led to his working for over twenty years on Pevsner's *Buildings of England*, and later *Buildings of Wales*, series – work which Pevsner rewarded with the highest praise. He started by doing the preparation for the *South Lancashire* volume, published in 1969. For the *Cheshire* volume (1971), of which he was joint author, he again did the preparation, and contributed the parts of the book dealing with the Eaton Hall Estate, Port Sunlight, Birkenhead, and other parts of Wirral. He also did the preparation for the last volume in the series, *Staffordshire* (1974).

Following the completion of the English series, the Welsh one was launched, and Edward Hubbard undertook the new county of *Clwyd* (formerly Flintshire and Denbighshire). The book was not published until 1986. The chief reason for this was the gradual onset of debilitating illness (ankylosing spondylitis). This led to a severe crisis in 1983 in which he almost died. The determination with which he fought back astonished the doctors, for his frail body and scholarly appearance hid an indomitable courage. He tried immensely hard to regain mobility, but the odds were against him, and he had to resign himself to life in a wheelchair. The fact that the Clwyd volume nevertheless appeared three years later was a remarkable achievement. The book was rightly greeted by uniformly laudatory reviews, and was awarded the G. T. Clark Prize of the Cambrian Archaeological Association.

In 1976 he was elected a Fellow of the Society of Antiquaries.

In 1980 he was responsible, with Michael Shippobottom, for the architectural section of the Royal Academy exhibition on Lord Leverhulme, and they collaborated again on what was to be his last publication, *A Guide to Port Sunlight Village,* published by Liverpool University Press in 1988. He also collaborated, with John Vaughan, on the *Victorian Society Liverpool Walk,* published in 1986.

Apart from his scholarly work, Edward Hubbard's energies were largely devoted to conservation, and it is in no small measure due to his efforts that Liverpool has retained so much of its architectural character. The striking success of the Albert Dock as a commercial and tourist attraction could not have come about had he not struggled long and hard, for the best part of twenty years, to save it – not least by persuading the DoE to upgrade its listing from II to I.

As a committed churchman, he took his work on the Diocesan Advisory Committees for Liverpool and Chester as seriously as all his other work, serving on both for around twenty years.

He had long admired the work of John Douglas, and the preparation of the Cheshire volume of *The Buildings of England* had focussed his attention even more closely on it. When he decided to enrol at the University of Manchester for the degree of Master of Arts, the work of Douglas was the obvious subject for his thesis. The result was not only far more substantial than one would expect of an MA thesis, but showed a depth of scholarship and a capacity to write about architecture in a perceptive and enthusiastic way which were altogether exceptional. He always hoped that it could be published in some form or other, but pressure of other commitments and ill health prevented it.

On my last visit to him, a fortnight before he died, I suggested that I might edit the thesis for publication myself. Not only did he enthusiastically welcome the idea, but he even made some notes for my benefit, and, when too weak to write, dictated further notes to his father. Having been brought up in the City of Chester, I have admired Douglas's work for as long as I can remember, and this common passion was a strong link between Ted and myself. We always delighted in sharing our joy at new Douglas discoveries, and it gave me the warmest pleasure when Ted, with his customary courtesy, asked my approval for his choice of Douglas as the subject of his thesis.

It has, therefore, been in a double sense a labour of love for me to edit this book for publication. It seemed to me that it would be a fine gesture for the Victorian Society itself to publish the book in Ted's memory, and I am most grateful to its Committee for so readily approving what I now realise, in retrospect, was a bold, and even foolhardy, undertaking, considering that the Society has never before published anything so ambitious. However, the tremendous amount of practical support and enthusiasm that has enabled the project to proceed has been a source of the greatest encouragement, and a heartwarming demonstration of the affection and regard in which Ted was held.

The question of how to prepare the thesis for publication was not an easy one to resolve. Had the author been able to do it himself, he would certainly have rewritten a substantial proportion of his text, both to incorporate newly discovered information, and to take advantage of his own deeper understanding of the architecture of the period. However, although well aware that he expected me also to intervene a good deal in the text, I considered that it would be preferable to leave the text itself substantially unaltered, so that the author's own account remained unadulterated. I have occasionally made trifling alterations to the text in order to bring it up to date, but my only interventions of any weight have concerned Vale Royal, Croxteth, and Northgate Street, Chester, where recent scholarship made revision essential. In each case this has been done in such a way as to change the text as little as possible, so that it has not seemed necessary to indicate what has been done.

There remained the question of what to do with the considerable amount of new material, almost entirely gathered from the author's own files. Most of it has gone into the Catalogue of Works, but, where it related to the text, I have inserted notes, with square brackets, into what were originally merely the references for each chapter. I am uncomfortably aware that this solution is far from perfect, but it appeared the least unsatisfactory compromise.

The Victorian Society's, and my own, debts of gratitude for help with the publication of this book are many. First of all there is Mr J. H. Hubbard, the author's father, who has been a constant source of encouragement and support since I first suggested that I should undertake the task, and without whose financial backing we should have been unable to proceed. To all those foundations, public bodies, and individuals, who have made generous grants, donations, and loans, and to all the subscribers, we are deeply grateful.

My own rôle as editor has been lightened and cheered by an altogether remarkable response from those upon whose assistance I have called. These are too many to be listed in full, but special thanks are due to Mr Andrew Saint, who read the text and made many useful suggestions, and to Mr Oliver Bott, of Cheshire County Council's Environmental Planning Department, who not only supplied copies of his own lists of Douglas's works, but answered all my queries with promptness and exactitude. Mr Ian Dunn, Information Officer and Archivist at the Cheshire Record Office;

Mrs Marilyn Lewis and Miss Jacqueline Forster at the Chester City Record Office; and Mr Peter Nears, Urban Designer and Technical Manager of Peel Estates Ltd at Worsley, have all supplied not only information but copies of documents and drawings in their care. At Arley Hall I received most welcome help from Mr Charles Foster, at Croxteth Hall from Miss Andrea Ellis, and at the Eaton Estate Office from Mr Brian Bowden and Miss Rosemary Sherriff. Others who have helped include Mrs Bridget Cherry, Mr Peter de Figueiredo, Dr Tim Mowl, and Mr Michael Shippobottom. The author would, I am sure, have wished to add many names to his own acknowledgements, and these would have included Dr Ian Allan, Mr Richard Haslam, and Mr Geoffrey Veysey (Clwyd County Archivist) and his staff.

The production of a book such as this was uncharted territory for the Victorian Society, and I shall be eternally grateful to Mr John Archer for persuading Mrs Janet Allan, Librarian of the Portico Library, Manchester, to undertake the design of the book. She has done far more than just design it, for she has provided the professionalism needed for liaison with the printers, and her technical skill, wisdom, and long-suffering patience have kept the project on course. Mr Roy Stephens, Director and Secretary of the Marc Fitch Fund, gave helpful advice. At the Victorian Society, thanks are due particularly to Mrs Teresa Sladen, the Secretary, Ms Virginia Dodier, formerly Administrative Secretary, and to her successor, Ms Tamar Jeffers, whose already heavy burdens have been increased by this extra commitment, but who have gladly assisted, and to Mr Robert Thorne, Chairman of the Publications Subcommittee. All of these have shown a most noble patience in putting up with my notorious lack of business sense.

The illustrations to the author's thesis were, as his preface stated, 'without exception taken from contemporary sources'. Most were engravings, though a few were contemporary photographs. For this book, a large number of engravings have again been used, as they are fine things in themselves, and often give a revealing insight into the way the buildings were seen at the time. Some contemporary photographs (from a wider range of sources than those used originally) are included. In addition, a considerable number of modern photographs have been used. These have not been dated, because almost all were specially taken for the book, the exceptions being those of Abbeystead (taken for the Walker Art Gallery, Liverpool, shortly before the house was sold in 1980), some of those taken by Dr Geoffrey Brandwood, and those credited to the author, to Mr A. F. Kersting, to Mr Michael Shippobottom, and to the Clwyd and Staffordshire County Councils.

Gathering together the illustrations was a difficult task. Dr Edward Diestelkamp, as well as taking a large number of photographs himself, provided invaluable help in many other ways. Dr Geoffrey Brandwood not only lent me his collection of negatives, but undertook a special expedition to fill in gaps. Others whose aid is much appreciated include Mr Graham Fisher, Miss Ruth Harman, the Revd Brian Harris, Mr Julian Treuherz, and Neil Pike Architecture, of Bolton. Permission to reproduce their photographs has been gladly given by all who have been asked and all have waived their fees: their generosity is warmly appreciated.

Peter Howell
September 1990

Postscript (February 1991):
Particular thanks are due to Mr Alan Rose, for the painstaking enthusiasm with which he made the index.

Abbreviations

A.A. Academy Architecture.
A.A.H.S.C.C.N.C.J. Journal of the Architectural, Archaeological and Historical Society for the County, City and Neighbourhood of Chester.
A.S.S.B. Abbey Square Sketch Book, ed. John Douglas, Chester, 1, 1872; 2, 3, n.d.
Archt. The Architect.
B.A. The British Architect.
B.A. ob. Obituary of John Douglas in *The British Architect*, 75, 1911, pp. 362–3.
Bldr. The Builder.
Bldr. ob. Obituary of John Douglas in *The Builder*, 100, 1911, p. 697.
B.N. Building News.
B.N. ob. Obituary of John Douglas in *Building News*, 100, 1911, p. 731.
Cheshire Observer ob. Obituary of John Douglas in *Cheshire Observer*, 27th May 1911.
Chester Chronicle ob. Obituary of John Douglas in *Chester Chronicle*, 27th May 1911.
Chester Courant ob. Obituary of John Douglas in *Chester Courant*, 24th May 1911.
C.R. Census Returns. (Full references, either to Public Record Office numbers or to Cheshire County Record Office microfilm numbers, are not given.)
D.G.P. Photographs. Photograph album in possession of Design Group Partnership, 9 Abbey Square, Chester. Contains photo-graphs of Eaton Estate buildings, all apparently of 1870s, by John Douglas.
E.E.O. Eaton Estate Office. See below.
G.R. Index. Goodhart-Rendel Index of Nineteenth Century Churches, at National Buildings Record. (Compiled by H. S. Goodhart-Rendel).
Kelly. Kelly's *Directory of Cheshire*, 1914 edn. unless otherwise stated.
Liverpool Daily Post ob. Obituary of John Douglas in *Liverpool Daily Post*, 24th May 1911.
Ormerod. *History of Cheshire*, George Ormerod, 2nd edn., ed. Thomas Helsby, London, 1882.
R.I.B.A.J. Journal of the Royal Institute of British Architects.
R.I.B.A.J. ob. Obituary of John Douglas, by G. A. Humphreys, Llandudno, in *Journal of the Royal Institute of British Architects*, 3rd series, 18, 1910–11, pp. 589–90.
R.O. Record Office. (The Clwyd Record Office is at Hawarden.)
Thomas. *History of the Diocese of St. Asaph*, D. R. Thomas, 2nd edn., 1908–13.
V.C.H. Victoria County History.

Works. The Works of the Late John Douglas. Folder of loose engravings etc. in the possession of Mr. Peter Howell. [A second portfolio, bearing the title *Some Designs by the late John Douglas of Chester*, later came to light: the author bought some of its contents.]

E.E.O. Drawings. Architectural drawings at Eaton Estate Office. References to these which have been sorted and catalogued include a number, e.g. 01899. This, with in every case the prefix 122M, is the reference number for the Estate Office microfilm system.

E.E.O. Notebook. Small notebook compiled for first Duke of Westminster listing estate building works carried out. Among personal papers of first Duke at Eaton Estate Office.

E.E.O. Photographs. Photograph album at Eaton Estate Office. *Eaton Estate Photographs 1869 to 1899. Volume I*. (Volume II is missing.)

Of material at the Eaton Estate Office which has been sorted jointly by the Chester City Record Office and the Cheshire County Record Office, use has been made of Estate Papers (details of which are given in the references) and also Estate Books. The latter have been listed in *Grosvenor of Eaton (Dukes of Westminster), Volume 3, Estate Books,* List compiled jointly by Chester City and Cheshire County Record Offices, 1968–9 and revised 1972. In the references only volume numbers are given for Estate Books, and the full details of those which have been used are as follows:

Eaton Estate: Accounts to 1917: Estate Building Ledger books, fo.
  Vol. 477, 1866–75. Vol. 478, 1875–90. Vol. 479, 1889–98. Vol. 480, 1905–36.

Eaton Estate: Letter Books, each labelled SB., 40
  Vol. 689, 1881–2. Vol. 690, 1881–3. Vol. 691, 1883–5. Vol. 692, 1885–7. Vol. 693, 1887–9. Vol. 694, 1889–91. Vol. 695, 1891–2. Vol. 696, 1892–3. Vol. 697, 1893–5. Vol. 698, 1895–6. Vol. 699, 1896–7. Vol. 700, 1897–9. Vol. 701, 1899–1901. Vol. 702, 1901–3. Vol. 703, 1903–5. Vol. 704, 1905–8. Vol. 706, 1909–10.

Chester Estate: Accounts: Cash Books Etc. Vol. 1105. New Park i.e. Grosvenor Park Labour account book fo. 1865–7.

It should be added that in identifying Eaton Estate buildings which may have been designated in drawings, ledgers or letters only by the name of the then tenant, it was necessary to resort to tracing them through successive volumes of rental books (in some instances over a period of more than fifty years) until they could be identified either with the current system of estate rental numbers or with a list of properties which were sold after the First World War. The references include indications of buildings which have been identified in this way, but full details of what amounted to highly complex processes are not given.

United Reformed Church, Over, Cheshire, 1865.

The Paddocks, Eccleston, Cheshire, 1882–3.

Caricature of John Douglas by T. Alfred Williams. (Pen and wash drawing in the possession of Design Group Partnership, Chester).

1 John Douglas's Life

John Douglas, the son of John and Mary Douglas, was born at Sandiway, in Cheshire, on 11th April 1830.[1] Sandiway was at that time a small hamlet[2] in the parish and lordship of Weaverham, lying on the north side of the road from Chester to Northwich, four miles from the latter town and some two miles from the mansion of Vale Royal, then the seat of Thomas Cholmondeley, first Baron Delamere. The Chester road has now become the dual carriageway A556; twentieth century suburban housing has appeared, and the yet more heavily built-up district of Cuddington adjoins on the west, but something of the character of a scattered rural community remains. It was not until 1902–3 that Sandiway acquired a church of its own – designed and with much of the cost being met by John Douglas himself – so it was in the parish church at Weaverham that he was baptised on 16th May 1830. He was the second in a family of four, his sister Elizabeth being born in 1827, and Mary Hannah in 1832, though she was to die at the age of two in 1834, five months before the birth of the third sister, Emma. Emma herself died in 1848, at the age of fourteen.[3]

It is not known where or when Douglas's parents were married. His father, John Douglas senior, was born at Northampton[4] c. 1798–1800.[5] His mother on the other hand was a native of Cheshire. She was Mary Swindley,[6] who was born and baptised at the Eaton estate village of Aldford in 1792,[7] and who came from a family which formed a dynasty of smiths. Her father, John Swindley, was the village blacksmith at Eccleston – a village which, like Aldford, was to be the scene of some of Douglas's notable architectural activities for the Duke of Westminster. When making his will in 1839, Swindley appointed his Douglas son-in-law, John Douglas senior, as trustee and executor, though this provision was revoked by a codicil the following year. He died in 1851, a nonagenarian; at least three of his sons and grandsons were also blacksmiths at Eccleston[8] and up until the 1960s members of the family worked as smiths and ornamental metalworkers at Handbridge in Chester.[9] In the 1890s James Swindley of Handbridge was executing wrought ironwork to designs by Douglas.[10]

John Douglas senior was a builder – a joiner by trade. Described in the parish registers at the time of the respective baptisms of his children as labourer in 1827, joiner in 1830 and 1832 and builder in 1834,[11] by the late 1840s he was being styled as surveyor as well as builder and by the mid '50s as timber merchant also.[12] In 1835 he acted as architect for the pleasant stucco-faced classical house of Hartford Lodge[13] (now Whitehall) at Hartford, between Sandiway

The Work of John Douglas

and Northwich, and at the time of the 1851 Census he was reported to be employing as many as 48 men.[14] The Douglas family home at Sandiway was Park Cottage (now known as 'Littlefold') of which Lord Delamere was landlord. The building yard was here,[15] presumably at the rear, where large outbuildings exist. The house itself appears to consist of three cottages which have been thrown together to form one dwelling, though the building history is obviously complicated, and it may be that there were only two cottages, to which extensions or connecting portions were added. Enlargements have been made at the rear. Thus, although no more than two resident servants seem to have been kept,[16] and even though the rear extension may partly be of later date, Park Cottage was, despite the modest scale of its parts, quite a fair-sized house. It is therefore curious that, on his death in 1862, John Douglas senior left no more than £800. The wording of his will also suggests that larger sums would have been involved.[17] Indeed, in 1845 he had entered into an agreement (which must undoubtedly have been fulfilled) to purchase for £3,500 tenanted farmland, with farm and cottage, at Sandiway, for which he was already a mortgagee,[18] and from before 1832 he had owned land and a house in the neighbouring township of Cuddington.[19]

Thus although the designation of labourer in 1827 must have under-rated his status at that time, the picture which emerges is that of a self-made man, progressively achieving a comfortable sufficiency.

John Douglas himself was also a landowner at Sandiway, where, according to his obituary in *The British Architect*. 'His little estate ... which he inherited from his father ... was always of great interest to him, and he spent large sums of money in improving it,'[20] though he never made his home there in adulthood and he was not, as was stated in the same obituary, lord of the manor. In addition to the church, for which he gave the land as well as contributing much to the cost of its erection, work by or attributable to him includes several cottages and some larger houses. Among the latter is the so-called Sandiway Manor, which represents a remodelling (date unknown) of the farmhouse which figured in his father's 1845 agreement.[21] The only land which he is known to have owned, or on which buildings by or attributable to him are sited, extends along the south-west side of the Cuddington road, between the Chester road and the cross-roads near the church. The westernmost part of this he bought in 1900, with a portion of it being re-sold in 1906 for the erection of a house known as The Homestead (*c.* 1906–7) of which he must undoubtedly have been the architect. At the time of the 1900 purchase, the land to the east (including the site of the church) was already his, but this had been acquired at sometime subsequent to 1871.[22] Further east still the land can be identified as that which

John Douglas's Life

Douglas senior agreed to buy in 1845. As has been noted, Douglas is indeed reported to have inherited his Sandiway property from his father, but as no mention of it is made in the latter's will, details of when and how ownership passed from father to son are not clear. Illustrating cottages by Douglas (the Parsonage, 1905–6 and a pair west of the church, 1906), *The British Architect* referred to them as being on his 'inherited property,'[23] though they are in fact on land belonging to the 1900 purchase.

In 1852 Douglas's sister Elizabeth married Richard Beckett,[24] a Hartford builder.[25] Like her sisters, however, she did not enjoy a long life, for she died at the age of 34 in 1862,[26] the same year as her father. The death of the mother, Mary Douglas, occurred the following year.[27] A stained glass window with Latin inscriptions, presented by John Douglas[28] to the church at Weaverham (which he restored in 1877), commemorates his parents and his sisters.

Besides nieces (children of Richard and Elizabeth Beckett),[29] Douglas had a number of Swindley cousins,[30] and also a cousin named Walter Douglas Edwards whom he employed as an assistant in his office.[31] Over a period of years Richard Beckett was contractor for a number of Douglas's buildings,[32] and the architect Richard Thomas Beckett, who was a son of Richard by a second marriage,[33] seems to have worked for a while in his office.[34]

Nothing is known of Douglas's school education. The records of the King's School at Chester, Sir John Deane's Grammar School at Northwich and the Boteler Grammar School at Warrington for the relevant period are all either non-existent or inconclusive. Nevertheless, Douglas was, at an early stage in his career, responsible for new buildings for the Boteler Grammar School (1862–4) and the possibility of his having received this commission as a result of being a former pupil cannot be dismissed. It may also be imagined that from an early age he would have frequented his father's yard or workshops, and it is tempting to attribute to the influence of these years some of the masterly use and understanding of building materials which characterise his work as an architect. It may certainly be supposed that he received instruction in joinery from his father, for his timber detailing is of an exceptionally high order, suggesting a real love and feeling for the material, and it is said that he could himself make a six-panel door in one day.[35]

However, the first fact which, after his baptism, is definitely known of his life, is his being articled to the Lancaster architect E. G. Paley (1823–95)[36] whose office he would presumably have entered in the mid or late 1840s. After the completion of his articles he remained with Paley and became his chief assistant. *The British Architect* noted, at the time of Paley's death, that, 'Mr. John Douglas, of Chester, was his pupil, and afterwards his chief

The Work of John Douglas

assistant, and looks back on the association with the happiest recollections.'[37]

There is confusion as to the date at which Douglas established his own practice in Chester, with it not being clear if this was in 1855 or 1860. If the former date, it is not known where his office was situated, for it was in or about 1860 that he moved into No. 6 Abbey Square,[38] the house in the cathedral precinct which he continued to occupy for the rest of his life. At first it served both as his home and his office (except possibly for a short period in the mid 1860s when he seems to have had an office in Eastgate Street)[39] and later as an office alone. To the north-west of the cathedral church and the monastic buildings of the predecessor Benedictine abbey, the square is the site of the abbey's outer courtyard. The Abbey Gateway in the south-west corner may possibly date from 1377; two of the four cottages built by Bishop Bridgman in 1626 remain, but much of the square is now lined with eighteenth and early nineteenth century brick houses. The best are Nos. 7–10 on the north side, dating from between 1754 and 1761. Nos. 3–6 on the west are smaller, but have similar stone quoins and rusticated lintels, and must be of like date, and although lacking the handsome classical doorcases of their neighbours they possess enriched fanlights. Unlike those on the north side, they are not all the property of the Dean and Chapter, and Douglas seems to have owned No. 6.[40] In the north-west corner of the square, it has irregular fenestration and is of five bays on the ground floor and three above. It is surprisingly small, being shallow on plan, due to restrictions of the site. Internally, much alteration seems to have taken place in the Douglas era. Its windows look across Abbey Square to the cathedral, and the square, which retains its cobbled paving, has changed little since Douglas knew it, though during his period of occupancy he witnessed the replacing of the old Bishop's Palace on the south side by Sir Arthur Blomfield's buildings for the King's School, and the transformation of the cathedral tower in the course of Sir Gilbert Scott's restoration.

On 25th January 1860, John Douglas married Elizabeth Edmunds, of Bangor Is-coed, Flintshire. The ceremony took place in the church at Bangor (which he restored, 1868 and 1877) and was witnessed by John Douglas senior, Richard Beckett and one Mary Edmunds, who was probably Elizabeth's mother. Her father, who had been a farmer, was no longer alive.[41] Douglas was then 29 years old, and his bride some two or three years his senior.[42] At the time of the 1861 Census they were living, with one servant girl, at the house in Abbey Square,[43] and the following year their first child, John Percy Douglas, was born. There followed the births of Colin Edmunds in 1864, Mary Elizabeth in 1866 and Sholto Theodore in 1867,[44] but in 1868 Mary Elizabeth died of scarlet fever, and the following year there occurred the birth of Douglas's last child,

Nos. 31–3, Dee Banks, Chester, 1869.

Jerome, who lived for only three days.[45] Thus in 1871 the household consisted of the parents and John Percy, Colin and Sholto, as well as two servants.[46] It seems likely that, sometime before 1870, the family had moved into No. 4 Abbey Square,[47] with No. 6 presumably being given up entirely to office use. Later in the '70s they moved out to a house in Dee View (soon to become Dee Banks)[48] at Great Boughton, a mile or so from the centre of Chester, but not before John Percy Douglas had died, at the age of twelve, shortly before Christmas in 1873.[49]

The house at Great Boughton is one of a semi-detached pair – the present Nos. 31 & 33 Dee Banks – sited on high ground above the River Dee, with fine views across meadowland towards the city centre. Though the block is of fairly massive appearance, the houses are not particularly large internally, and their fittings and woodwork are quite simple. Douglas was from time to time involved with aspects of property ownership in Chester, and he had been in possession of land at Dee View as it then was since at least 1865, in which year he was ordered by the Improvement Committee of the City Council to enclose it with a fence.[50] Though obviously built by Douglas with the intention that one of the houses would be for his own occupation (they carry the initials JD and carved representations of architects' instruments) the pair was probably planned as an investment as well as a home. No. 33 was the one in which he lived, but No. 31 seems also to have remained in his ownership.[51]

The Work of John Douglas

Also, some years elapsed between the building of the houses and his taking up residence, for the pair is dated 1869 and the move from Abbey Square did not take place until about 1876.[52] The house may possibly have been let until such time as the move became financially practicable, but whatever the circumstances John and Elizabeth Douglas were not to enjoy their new home together for long, for she died there, of laryngitis, in 1878, after a year's illness, and he thus began his life of more than 30 years of widowhood. Still further bereavement came in 1887, with the death from consumption, at the age of 23, of his son Colin, who had himself become an architect.[53]

Colin's illness had been of some three years standing,[54] that is, dating from 1884, which was apparently the year Douglas took into partnership D. P. Fordham (*c.* 1846–99) – the earliest noted record of the firm of Douglas & Fordham is dated 22nd January in that year.[55] Is it possible that the formation of the partnership was prompted by a tragic realisation that there might be no secure future for a partnership of John Douglas & Son? If so, there is a sad irony in the fact that Fordham himself contracted consumption,[56] and that this led to his premature retirement and death.

Little is known about Daniel Porter Fordham. He was born in about 1846;[57] was a good pen and ink draughtsman, as certain published sketches show,[58] and was an assistant in Douglas's office at the time of his being taken into partnership.[59] He was, in fact, by 1872 already associated with the office,[60] though it was not until after the partnership was formed that he became a member of the Chester Archaeological Society.[61] Neither did Fordham, who remained a bachelor, seem to establish his own household in Chester until this time, first at No. 14 Chichester Street, and after about 1890 at No. 19 Raymond Street.[62] He was succeeded as Douglas's partner by C. H. Minshull (1858–1934). The Douglas obituary in *The Builder* stated that Fordham's retirement took place in 1898, and that it was on his death in 1899 that Minshull was taken into partnership. Other obituaries also refer to the new partnership being formed following the death of Fordham.[63] This would seem to be borne out by an article on 'John Douglas, Architect,' in *The British Architect*, in 1898, which sympathised, 'with his able partner Mr. D. P. Fordham in his present enforced retirement,' but still referred to the firm as Douglas & Fordham.[64] References to Douglas & Minshull occur in 1898, however, including one in the same issue of *The British Architect*,[65] and the earliest such reference noted is dated 25th November 1897.[66] It must thus have been on Fordham's retirement that the firm was reconstructed, with both events taking place in 1897. Following his withdrawal from the practice, Fordham went to live in Bournemouth, with his unmarried sister, and died there, intestate, in April 1899 at the age of 53.[67] On his death, the office in Abbey

Square assumed for a period the use of mourning paper.[68]

Charles Howard Minshull was born in 1858. The son of a Chester bookseller, he was educated at the King's School and became articled to Douglas in 1874. He was an active member of the Chester Archaeological Society and other local organisations,[69] and contributed a chapter on 'The Half-timbered Architecture of Cheshire,' to *Memorials of Old Cheshire* – the Cheshire volume of P. H. Ditchfield's *Memorials of the Counties of England* – which appeared in 1910.[70] His home was in Lorne Street, Chester.[71]

It is said that in the later years of the Douglas & Minshull partnership Douglas himself became less active in the firm, visiting the office less regularly and acting in more of a consultative capacity.[72] The likelihood of this is borne out by the evidence presented by some of the buildings of the 1900s. It is thus inexplicable that in 1909 – at a time when in view of his advanced age the help and support of colleagues would surely have been all the more necessary for him – the Douglas & Minshull partnership should have been dissolved.[73] Minshull set up independently with one E. J. Muspratt, as Minshull & Muspratt, in Foregate Street, and for the last year or two of Douglas's life the Abbey Square practice reverted to the style of John Douglas, Architect.[74] It may be noted that some new works undertaken in this period were in collaboration with others. Relations with Minshull may not have been entirely severed, however, for on Douglas's death he immediately reappeared on the Abbey Square scene, and continued the practice, as senior partner, under the style of Douglas, Minshull & Muspratt.[75]

With his wife and four children dying during his lifetime, Douglas was survived only by his son Sholto Theodore who, there is reason to suppose, may have been the cause of disappointment or anxiety to him. Sholto, who seems to have remained unmarried, is not known ever to have adopted any profession or form of employment and he was, at the very least, a heavy drinker. He could be seen pacing the Rows in Chester, waiting for the pubs to open. In his defence mention has been made of his gentlemanly demeanour, and of his being well dressed and capable of walking straight on his way home, though this is the least which could have been expected of a son of John Douglas.[76]

For many years Douglas continued to live in the same house in Dee Banks, but in the 1890s he built a new one for himself. It bears the date 1896, though he may possibly not have moved in until 1901.[77] It also is in Dee Banks and commands a similar view. He seems to have previously owned the site, for it must presumably be the land referred to in a letter of 1874 to the Improvement Committee of the City Council, in which he stated that, '. . . I am building a wall round my Property at Wallmere Hill, Dee Banks. . . .'[78] His earlier house was known as Walmer House [79] and (apart

The Work of John Douglas

from the further variant spelling in the 1874 letter) the later one was referred to as both Walmer Hill and Walmoor Hill,[80] the latter being the name by which it came to be known and which at any rate by 1906 Douglas himself was using on his red die-stamped letter head.[81] Walmoor Hill dramatically exploits a steeply-sloping site, above the river. Although never completed (the service wing was obviously intended to extend further) it is quite large and, compared with his earlier house, represents a considerable departure in terms of size and grandeur. Doubtless the building of the house resulted from increasing affluence, yet it was a strangely ambitious undertaking for a widower well advanced in his 60s, and the circumstance seems to be reflected in two names by which it was popularly known in the locality – 'Douglas's Castle' and 'Douglas's Folly.' However, besides the initials and monograms 'JD' which appear on and in the building, there are also those of 'STD.' The house was thus built with his son in mind, perhaps, it may be conjectured, to some degree with the intention of instilling into Sholto a sense of pride or responsibility. A pair of cottages at Sandiway, dated 1907, also carries the initials of both father and son.

Douglas had been in failing health for some months prior to his death, under the care of Dr. Giffen of Boughton. The last professional task with which he was concerned was the addition of

Walmoor Hill, Dee Banks, Chester, 1896. (*British Architect*, 58, 1902, p. 442).

John Douglas's Life

the tower to St. Paul's church at Colwyn Bay (1911) and he had expressed the hope, which remained unfulfilled, that he would live to see it completed.[82] He must thus have known that his life was drawing to a close when he made a new will, signed at Walmoor Hill on 21st April 1911 and witnessed by his housekeeper and a housemaid[83]. Nine days later, on 30th April, there occurred his 81st birthday and, after, several days of unconsciousness, he died at nine o'clock on the morning of Tuesday 23rd May.[84] The funeral took place on 25th May in what had by then become the Old Cemetery at Chester, and the body of John Douglas was laid in the family grave, the first burial in which had been that of his daughter more than 40 years before.[85] The following Sunday a memorial service was held at Sandiway.[86]

Douglas left £32,088:17:6. His will, made so shortly before his death, made no specific bequests, but he left all his property to Sholto, with varying degrees of restriction. Walmoor Hill and its contents came to him immediately. The remainder, other than the Sandiway property, was to come to him after being held in trust for five years provided that during this period (and here seems an indication that Douglas did not altogether trust his son) he had neither mortgaged Walmoor Hill nor become bankrupt. As for Sandiway, this was to remain perpetually in trust, with certain restrictions upon its sale, and with Sholto and his successors receiving the income. Provision was made for successors in the event of Sholto dying childless and failing to appoint a successor by will, and any successor becoming entitled to the property was to be obliged to take the name of Douglas.[87] For a while Sholto continued to live at Walmoor Hill, but – alas for the monograms – did not do so for much longer than his five years probationary period if at all, for he had left Chester by the end of the First World War,[88] and the house became a girls' school, Walmoor College. It is now the administrative headquarters of the County Fire Brigade.

Sholto Douglas may, it is thought, at some time have patronised a home for alcoholics in the Midlands, but the next authenticated sighting after his departure from Chester is at the Queens Hotel, Abingdon, where he signed his will on 20th November 1940. On 5th January 1943 he died, in Oxford, at the age of 75, his body being returned to Chester for burial in the family grave.[89] If he had been living a hotel sort of existence, it might be expected that the Oxford address at which he died was that of a guest house or nursing home. It seems, however, to have been a private house[90] at which he was thus perhaps a lodger. Of his father's £32,000, he left £7,893:9:11, and much of his will is concerned with the circumstances of departures from the terms of his father's will, and of the trust relating to the Sandiway property having been broken. Some specific bequests were made, and a gentleman in Edgbaston was

The Work of John Douglas

John Douglas in 1890. (*Building News* 58, 1890, p. 686).

named as residuary legatee.[91]

Despite the extensive and tangible legacy which John Douglas has left in terms of architecture, and despite a certain amount being established about his family and background, he himself remains a remarkably obscure figure, with little definitely known about his private life and his character and personality. There is but scanty record even of his physical appearance. A photograph published in 1890[92] portrays him in late middle age, bearded, with a long but not thin face and with the suggestion of a keen and alert expression. He is remembered later in life as looking 'squarer' and with his hair probably much whiter. He is also remembered as being tall and well-

John Douglas's Life

built (as was Sholto)[93] and the photograph does seem to be that of a broad-shouldered man. The only other representation which has come to light is a pen and wash caricature sketch,[94] incorporating two little parodies of Douglas buildings, and depicting him in old age, slightly bowed and bent, with steel-framed spectacles and with less hair than in the photograph. He carries a portfolio and a tubular ear trumpet – effectively symbolising his having continued to work throughout the years of advancing age. The drawing was made by T. Alfred Williams, an assistant in the office, who used to refer to Douglas (as did perhaps the rest of the office staff) as 'Old John.'[95] The ear trumpet is authentic, for he is remembered being seen with it in church[96].

The church at which Douglas worshipped, and in the parish of which Dee Banks is situated, was that of St. Paul, Boughton, for the rebuilding of which in 1876 he was himself the architect. The church choir would visit Walmoor Hill when carol-singing at Christmas, and be provided with refreshments by the housekeeper. Sholto was never seen in church.[97]

A further item of information relates to the church at Sandiway (1902–3) and to his having continued to work in old age. Unable, in his 70s, to climb ladders in order to inspect the construction in progress, he would peruse the roof timbers through binoculars.[98]

Douglas's career seems to have been one of thorough devotion to architecture, a dedication which may well have been intensified by the death of his wife and other domestic sorrows. 'John Douglas lived heart and soul in his profession,' wrote the *Chester Chronicle* in its obituary, adding that he had no time to indulge in public life.[99] Other than matters relating to his property, nothing is indeed recorded of active interests or concerns beyond the spheres of architecture and the Church. In December 1869 he wrote to the Town Clerk of Chester, on behalf of the Chester Diocesan Open Church Association, requesting the use of the Town Hall for a meeting;[100] at the time of his death he was reported to be the president of a recently-formed Chester and North Wales Architectural Society[101] (of which no record has been found), and was a member of the Chester Archaeological Society from 1861 until his death.[102] The name of this society has varied from time to time, but its nature was best expressed when it was known as the Chester and North Wales Architectural, Archaeological and Historic Society. Although at one time frequently attending its meetings, and occasionally exhibiting drawings and photographs of his work, in later years Douglas was seldom if ever present,[103] and he never addressed the society, read a paper or contributed to its journal.

Indeed Douglas left no record of his thoughts and views on architecture, and his only publication – the *Abbey Square Sketch Book*, produced under his editorship – is of a very self-effacing

The Work of John Douglas

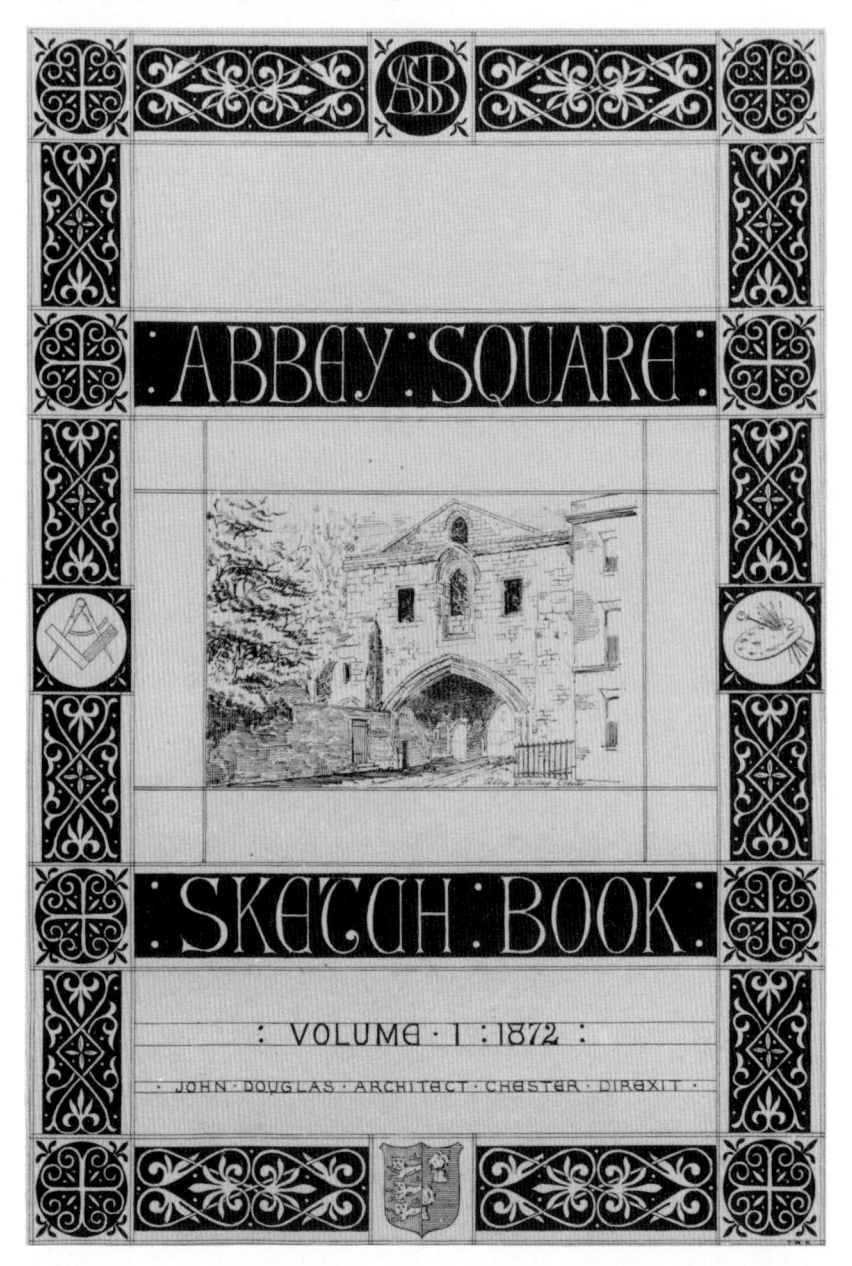

Frontispiece to *Abbey Square Sketch Book*, Volume I, 1872.

nature. It appeared in three folio volumes, the first dated 1872, the second and third undated but, on the evidence of dated illustrations, not earlier than 1876 and 1889 respectively.[104] The work consists of sketches and measured drawings by many contributors (though there are also some photographs in the third volume) illustrating buildings and furniture, mostly late mediaeval and of the sixteenth

John Douglas's Life

and seventeenth centuries, and mostly in Cheshire and the northwest. A number of the plates are the work of persons who are either definitely known, or are likely to have been, Douglas's pupils or assistants, and the *Chester Chronicle* obituary confirms that many of the drawings were by members of his staff, with Douglas himself being the originator and inspirer. His own contribution was confined to one jointly-ascribed plate in the third volume,[105] but it may be supposed that he also designed the title pages or was at least responsible for the drawing of the Abbey Gateway which they incorporate. Although telling nothing of his theories or opinions on architecture, *Abbey Square Sketch Book* indicates certain styles and details which he liked, as comparison between some of the plates and some of his own buildings makes clear.

Of Douglas's character, it may be supposed that he possessed a sense of family pride, and perhaps wished to establish a dynasty. Such seems to be the evidence of the terms of his will regarding the Sandiway property, and of the building of Walmoor Hill, with its initials and monograms, and where a stained glass window on the staircase commemorates one Captain Richard Douglas, who died in the Peninsular War. It may also be of significance that his son (though admittedly not his eldest son) was given the traditional Douglas name of Sholto. Yet the personal modesty which characterises *Abbey Square Sketch Book* may have been typical of him. In conducting the memorial service at Sandiway on the Sunday following Douglas's death, the vicar of Weaverham recounted that, 'When it was proposed that a tablet should commemorate his work and [that of another benefactor of Sandiway church], he remarked that that was not the way of "the old fellows" whose faith is embodied in the great cathedrals and parish churches they reared, but their names are unknown to man.' The vicar added that Douglas spoke often of the love of God being the motive of all abiding work.[106] A tablet was nevertheless placed in his Chester church of St. Paul, Boughton, after his death, commemorating him as, 'A generous contributor to the funds of this parish.'[107] Thus a faithful Churchman, evidence of his devout nature is provided by the existence of a little oratory at Walmoor Hill.

It may be surmised that Douglas was endowed with a more than usually strong sense of national loyalty. Statues of the Queen were placed in niches both at Walmoor Hill and in the range of buildings which he designed, as his own client, in St. Werburgh Street, Chester (1896–7) (see page 191). Admittedly both specifically commemorate the Diamond Jubilee, but such action on the part of an individual citizen was rare even in 1897. Rare also is a reference to patriotism among qualities chronicled in an obituary, but that by G. A. Humphreys of Llandudno, in the *Journal of the Royal Institute of British Architects*, praised Douglas as, '. . . a true architect, a hero

The Work of John Douglas

in his work, a cultured gentleman, counting no personal sacrifice, looking for no reward save the honour of his Art and the uplifting of his country.'[108]

An anecdote is related by Maurice B. Adams. 'He had just completed an exceptional house in which every detail followed the solid thoroughness of mediaeval building. Meeting the client on the job the employer said, "Very nice and all that, but damned expensive, Douglas." "True," replied the architect, "I found it so; I spent more than my commission on my clerk's wages looking after the work, and I don't think the builder has made a five-pound note out of his contract; but I'm glad you think it nice."'[109]

An interesting indication of personal opinion is provided by a letter to the Town Clerk of Chester on the subject of seats in Grosvenor Park, the entrance lodge and other structures for which (1865–7) he had designed under the patronage of the second Marquess of Westminster. The seats to which he objected – apparently on associational as much as aesthetic grounds – were of a type still occasionally seen, though none remain in Grosvenor Park.

> 6, ABBEY SQUARE,
> CHESTER
> 15th April 1868
>
> Dear Sir,
>   I have just been through the Public Park and am really sorry to see such a frightful standard adopted to support the Seats. – in all 24 Serpents the most hateful reptile human beings can look at used in the most unpractical manner. if a prize had been offered for the the [sic] vilest idea whh. could be turned into a support for seats those at the Park would have had it before all others. –
>   I am sorry to see so successful an effort to Churchwarden the park & hope you will use your endeavours to prevent further this is my only excuse for troubling you with this Note.
>   Yrs. Faithfully
>   John Douglas
>   P.S. Rather than such Seats shd. have been adopted I would have given the Seats myself. J.D.[110]

With Douglas remaining such a shadowy figure, it is all the more notable that there happens to survive a scrap of paper on which is his rough draft, with erasures and alterations, for a letter of condolence to a former client, but which strikes a note of deep personal sadness. Dated 23rd December 1899, it was written during the disasters of the Boer War and on the day following the death of the Duke of Westminster whom Douglas had served for 30 years. 'Dear Mrs. Williams,' he wrote, 'I am very sorry indeed to hear of the death of

John Douglas's Life

Mr Williams & beg to offer you my sincere sympathy. What with the national Calamities & the death of friends this Xmas to a [great] many including myself will be a very miserable one. All Cheshire is mourning the death of the Duke of Westminster who has been so universally beloved and respected. . . .'[111]

An indication of another loss which grieved him may be provided by an earlier letter to the same lady in which, apparently unrelated to the subject in question, he wrote that 'Mr. Fordham whose health broke down died in the early part of this year.'[112]

'A good architect but a poor hand at accounts!' So wrote Colonel David Scotland, the Duke of Westminster's secretary, in 1884.[113] There is evidence that Douglas discharged routine professional responsibilities with assiduity, but that he was indeed deficient in financial acumen. The patronage of the Duke of Westminster and Douglas's relations with the Eaton estate office will be considered in a later chapter, but it may at this point be noted that he was at times slow in presenting his accounts, and that in one instance ten years or more elapsed before he made a claim for fees to which he considered himself entitled,[114] and two episodes relating respectively to the church of St. John the Divine at Barmouth (1889–95) and to St. Werburgh Street, Chester, were both characterised by either delay or confusion. The Barmouth church is one of Douglas's finest, though its history is marred by the fact that in 1891, during construction, the tower collapsed, bringing down much of the rest of the building with it. The donor of the eastern portions of the church was the Mrs. Williams (previously Mrs. Dyson Perrins) to whom the letter of condolence was written in 1899. Earlier in that year, and sometime after her agreed contributions had been made, Douglas presented her with an account for £2,460:9:9 (or £1,678:12:0 if payments which he considered were due from the parish rather than from herself were excluded) consisting of expenses incurred in the reconstruction and completion of the church, and £700 for his fees. Mrs. Williams expressed herself as being 'very much surprised,'[115] and in the hands of her solicitor, Edward Nevinson, of Nevinson & Barlow of Malvern, the claim was largely rejected. Although conceding that his client might be liable for payment of a certain amount of money, Nevinson succeeded in reducing the £2,460:9:9 to one pound thirteen shillings. The principal point which emerges is that the reimbursement which Douglas was seeking included £1,550 which he had himself agreed to contribute towards the reconstruction costs. Papers relating to the matter include a communication from Nevinson, on the reverse of which has been written, presumably in connection with the office filing system, 'Letter from Mr. Nevinson,' and to this Douglas has added, 'in which he says it is preposterous for me to receive payment for my services as Architect.' In fact, the letter states that the claim for

The Work of John Douglas

commission is repudiated on Mrs. Williams's behalf,[116] and it is in an accompanying set of notes that he states, 'The attempt to charge Architect's Commission is preposterous,' maintaining that adequate remuneration had already been provided in the form of an earlier payment or payments.[117] These notes have in turn been annotated by Douglas – one apparently reasonable statement being dismissed as 'Mere quibble' – but the solicitor's case (with the possible exception of the question of commission which a further note says was never paid) seems to have been unassailable. Douglas's own statements of account moreover contain an extraordinary reference to designs for the lectern and organ case, not included in the accounts, '& as neither appeared to be appreciated no bill sent.'[118]

As for St. Werburgh Street, the full saga is something from which Douglas emerges with the greatest credit, both as architect and – with his having bought up the land and built the property in order to enhance Chester and prevent unsuitable development – as citizen. This enterprise of the 1890s was not, however, free from tribulation, and certain of its complications involved the Dean and Chapter of the cathedral and the then Ecclesiastical Commissioners. In 1906, some ten years after the events in question, he made renewed but belated and unsuccessful attempts to obtain, through the Chapter Clerk, £100 to which he considered himself to be entitled from the Commissioners.[119] Tribulation even dogged his Sandiway benefactions, presumably in connection with his gift of the land on which the church was built, for in this same correspondence with the Chapter Clerk he made mention of, '. . . what I may almost say the merciless treatment of the Eccl. Commrs. at Sandiway. . . .'[120]

Whatever his limitations as a businessman, Douglas was nevertheless active within the field of property ownership, in addition to his Sandiway interests and his land at Dee Banks. Between 1885 and 1889 he owned the Royal Oak Inn in Foregate Street, Chester;[121] in 1900 he purchased, and re-sold to the Corporation for road-widening purposes, some houses in Hamilton Place, though in doing so he was acting on behalf of a syndicate[122] and was thus perhaps a party to a scheme enabling the city to acquire the property quietly and painlessly, and a syndicate was also involved[123] with his ownership between 1896 and 1899 of land and cottages in Union Street. This also was purchased by the Corporation, as a site for Public Baths (1898–1901), for which the firm of Douglas & Minshull had by then already been appointed architects.[124] In 1902 a small further area of adjoining land was conveyed by Douglas to the Corporation.[125] Instances of Douglas acting as his own client or developer, and erecting buildings to his own designs on his own land included houses in Grosvenor Park Road (c. 1879–80), houses in Bath Street (1903), shop premises at Boughton Cross (1898–1901), and, above all, the east side of St.

John Douglas's Life

Werburgh Street. It is fitting that it should have been this masterpiece of half-timbered design that was chosen to carry a commemorative plaque[126]. Placed on the wall of the Bank at the foot of the street, its inscription reads as follows:

TO RECORD THE WORK AND SERVICES OF
JOHN DOUGLAS
BORN 1830 DIED 1911
ARCHITECT OF THIS SIDE OF S. WERBURGH ST.
& OF NUMEROUS OTHER BUILDINGS INCLUDING
MANY CHURCHES, IN THE COUNTY PALATINE &
IN THE PRINCIPALITY, THIS TABLET IS PLACED BY
A FEW OF HIS OLD PUPILS & ASSISTANTS. AD. 1923
'USUI CIVIUM DECORI URBIUM'
DURAT OPERE IPSE

Pair of cottages, Wrexham Road, Belgrave, Cheshire, *c.* 1871.

The Limes Farmhouse (now Green Paddocks), Pulford, Cheshire, 1872.

II Architectural Background and Training

It must have been in the mid or late 1840s that John Douglas was articled to E. G. Paley (1823–95). The long saga of the largely ecclesiastical practice in which Paley was at that time junior partner is one of the most remarkable in the history of the Gothic Revival. In 1836 Edmund Sharpe (1809–77) set up in practice in Lancaster and in 1845 took into partnership Edward Graham Paley. Although he handed over most of the work to Paley in 1847, the Sharpe & Paley partnership was not formally dissolved until 1851, when Sharpe withdrew.[1] The firm then continued under E. G. Paley alone, until H. J. Austin (1841–1915) was taken into partnership in 1867. Diverse mutations of title followed, including changes from Paley & Austin to Paley, Austin and Paley and to Austin & Paley, and the practice continued well on into the twentieth century.[2] The buildings for which it is best remembered are splendid late nineteenth century churches of the Paley & Austin and Austin & Paley periods, providing evidence of the quality and quantity of work which a provincial office was then capable of producing. Yet the earlier years of the practice – including the years during which Douglas received his training – are of significance within the context of Early Victorian Gothic development.

The architecture of the late 1830s and the 1840s was largely a matter of romantic and superficial taste on the one hand and ecclesiology on the other, with few architects sharing the degree of commitment to classicism displayed by C. R. Cockerell (1788–1863). The stream of free revivalism ran strong, exemplified by the Jacobethan mansions of Edward Blore (1787–1879), the *palazzi* of Charles Barry (1795–1860) or the picturesque eclecticism of J. C. Loudon's publications, though the distinctive character of Early Victorian architecture is no less due to the more intransigent Gothic which emanated from A. W. N. Pugin (1812–52) and from the Oxford Movement. The first of the *Tracts for the Times* appeared in 1833, Pugin's *Contrasts* (following his conversion to Rome) in 1836, his *True Principles of Pointed or Christian Architecture* in 1841 and his *Apology* in 1843. In 1839 the Cambridge Camden Society was formally organised (becoming the Ecclesiological Society 1845–6) and the first issue of *The Ecclesiologist* was published in 1841.[3] Under the influence of Pugin's fanatically-held belief of Gothic being not an acceptable alternative style but the only correct and Christian way to build, and of the Cambridge Camden Society's dictatorial insistence on 'Middle Pointed,' there emerged Gothic which was archaeologically correct, honest in its construction, and moral and religious in its inspiration.

The Work of John Douglas

Outstanding among the contributions made to mediaeval scholarship in this generation were those of Edmund Sharpe. In his *Architectural Parallels* (1845–7), *Decorated Windows* (including *A Treatise on. . . . Decorated Window Tracery in England*, 1849) and *The Seven Periods of English Architecture* (1851) he continued the tradition of archaeological study established by Rickman, with whom he had been acquainted.[4] 'Sharpe, E., Esq., M.A. S. John's College; Architect; Lancaster,' first appeared in the list of Cambridge Camden Society members in 1842,[5] and he is included among the select band of 'Architects Approved' given in volume three of *The Ecclesiologist*.[6] As for E. G. Paley, his background was ecclesiastical, being the son of a clergyman and grandson of the theologian Archdeacon William Paley.[7] Moreover, his brother, Frederick Apthorp Paley (1815–88) was friendly with Sharpe at St. John's.[8] F. A. Paley was himself a writer on the subject of Gothic architecture; by 1841 he was a committee member of the Cambridge Camden Society;[9] he served as its joint honorary secretary, with Benjamin Webb, from 1841 or '42 until 1845,[10] and he corresponded with Pugin, who wrote to him as follows: –

> My dear Sir, – I was truly gratified by the receipt of your kind letter. There are few men whose appreciation I should desire more than your own. In fact I have never met with any one who entertains more correct views of Church Architecture than yourself and our friend Mr. Webb. *The Ecclesiologist* does an infinity of good, and I am the more reconciled to its not being quite so strong as you and I could wish, as it is therefore better received by a host of intermediate men who could not swallow strong drink but are exceedingly useful to the cause as far as they go. . . .[11]

F. A. Paley seceded to Rome in 1847 and later devoted himself largely to classical literature,[12] but architectural publications in his Camdenian days included the text of *Illustrations of Baptismal Fonts* (1844), *A Manual of Gothic Architecture* (1846) and the didactic *The Church Restorers: A Tale*, in addition to his widely used *Manual of Gothic Mouldings*, which first appeared in 1845. An indication of E. G. Paley's degree of involvement and of his own archaeological studies is provided by a contribution which he made to the 1891 fifth edition of *Mouldings*, the first to appear after F. A. Paley's death: –

> I well remember going home to my father's Rectory at Gretford, near Stamford (about 1839 to 42), and taking with me, amongst other architectural books, Rickman's 'Attempt to discriminate the styles of Architecture in England.' My brother, I recollect well, read this work with avidity, and became extremely

interested in the subject of English Architecture, and frequently accompanied me in my visits to examine and sketch the neighbouring churches. . . . As a young student of Church Architecture, I measured and sketched mouldings as one important part of my studies, and I like to think that my brother's early interest in this work . . . fortunately eventuated in the publication of his book on Mouldings. I had the pleasure to send him from time to time several of the examples that appear in the book. . . .[13]

Strangely, E. G. Paley seems never to have joined the Cambridge Camden or Ecclesiological Societies. Certainly his name does not appear in the membership lists during the crucial 1840s, and neither does that of John Douglas.

Despite the connoisseurship of the Decorated style displayed in *Decorated Windows*, Sharpe's own buildings include churches of decidedly thin and pre-archaeological character. In fact, although mentioned among 'Architects Approved' he by no means escaped the strictures of *The Ecclesiologist*, his remarkable terra-cotta churches at Lever Bridge, Bolton (1842–4) and Platt, Manchester (1844–6) being duly lambasted. The unique enterprise reflected by these two buildings provides an indication of Sharpe's versatility and of his technical interests and expertise.[14] Active in public life in Lancaster, he became a town councillor in 1841, was mayor in 1848, and from 1845 onwards espoused the cause of sanitary reform in the town. He had, however, been involved with railway work, as a contractor, since 1838, and after his final abandonment of architectural practice in 1851 he devoted himself to civil engineering, to further writing and to his business concerns.[15]

E. G. Paley was also capable of straying from the straight and narrow path of Camdenianism. It is no surprise that his sketches include a copy of the view of St. John's Hospital at Alton given in Pugin's *Present State of Ecclesiastical Architecture in England*, but he also copied a towered Italianate extravaganza from Charles Parker's *Villa Rustica*; in Cambridge he sketched the Fitzwilliam Museum,[16] and his Ince Hall, Cheshire[17] (1849),[18] now demolished, was Italianate. Nevertheless, his predominantly ecclesiastical practice was an overwhelmingly orthodox one. Remaining largely faithful to the styles of the thirteenth and fourteenth centuries, Paley was little affected by High Victorianism and continued within the Puginistic mainstream through the 1850s and '60s. His churches were solid, competent and dull, and only with the coming of H. J. Austin did the production of the Lancaster office spring brilliantly to life.

It may thus be supposed that, entering the office of Sharpe & Paley as a pupil of Paley, Douglas would have received a sound ecclesiological training, rich in knowledge of Gothic scholarship and construction, but perhaps with little from Paley which would have

The Work of John Douglas

stirred his imagination as a designer. His own early independent works are consistent with such a supposition.

Douglas may not have joined the office until after Sharpe had handed over the bulk of the work to Paley in 1847. Certainly any overlap which he may have had with Sharpe's active participation in the practice is not likely to have been long. With there being uncertainty as to whether it was in 1855 or 1860 that he established his own practice in Chester, the date at which he left Lancaster is unknown. It can, however, be said that during the years he would have been with the firm, as pupil and assistant, he must have witnessed the progress of at the very least a dozen ecclesiastical commissions, both nominally by the Sharpe & Paley partnership and by Paley alone after 1851. Notable among these was the rebuilding of Wigan parish church, Lancashire (1845–50, initiated by Sharpe), but whatever degree of responsibility Douglas may have had in them, it would obviously have been likely to have been greater in the case of later work such as the church at Rylstone, Yorkshire (1853), Thwaites, Cumberland (1854) and Christchurch, Bacup, Lancashire (1854) and the nave at Penwortham, Lancashire (1855).[19]

It may be noted that in 1847 the firm was responsible for the partial rebuilding of Davenham church, Cheshire,[20] barely three miles from Sandiway. In the absence of contrary evidence, it may be wondered if John Douglas senior was the contractor for the work. If so, could the contact thus established have been the reason for it being Paley's firm to which his son was sent? Alternatively, if Douglas was by then already at Lancaster, could he have been instrumental in obtaining the Davenham commission for his mentor?

To the late 1850s belong churches at Garstang, Lancaster and Barrow-in-Furness[21] which would have been among the further jobs which Douglas may have been concerned with had he stayed with Paley until 1860 rather than leaving for Chester in 1855. Before considering this question of the confusion of dates and also the fruits of Douglas's early independence, something must be said about the city in which he chose to settle.

III Chester in the Nineteenth Century

The second half of the nineteenth century was a period generally propitious for provincial architectural practice. Not only major cities and towns of the Industrial Revolution but also medium-sized county and market towns enjoyed a considerable degree of autonomy, and something of a balance existed between their independence both of London and of each other, and the sustenance which they derived from improved communications, particularly in the form of railways. For architects, their services in demand to fulfil requirements of a changing and expanding society, improved communication also took the form of the professional and technical press, particularly from 1842 onwards with the appearance of *The Builder*. Week by week the journals provided a compendium of nation-wide and sometimes international news, together with illustrations and descriptions of new buildings, keeping the provinces informed of what was going on in the capital and *vice versa*.

A cathedral city, a county town and, from the 1840s, an important railway centre, Chester was and is a flourishing local capital for most of its county and for North Wales. With its riverside setting, with the tangible remains of its past dating to Roman times, its City Walls, its unique raised covered walkways (the Rows) lining the principal streets, and with it being one of only two British towns of any size to retain extensive evidence of timber-framed building, it is also a place of exceptional charm, character and archaeological importance. Its abundance of ancient buildings would have had special appeal to a nineteenth century architect, not least to John Douglas, with the background of mediaeval scholarship which he would have imbibed under Paley's tuition.

It may also be assumed that in choosing to live and work in Chester, rather than in establishing himself in Liverpool or Manchester, Douglas was further attracted by the prospects which it offered of a largely rural and largely domestic and ecclesiastical practice in (as the St. Werburgh Street tablet records) the County Palatine of Chester and the Principality of Wales. Douglas's houses and churches do range from Surrey to Scotland, and there is a sprinkling of works in the Midlands and a number in Lancashire, but most are in North Wales, in Chester itself and (although there is a thinning out west of Chester in the Wirral peninsula where the influence of Liverpool architects is encountered) in the western part of the county of Cheshire. Yet despite its limited geographical coverage, Douglas conducted a practice which achieved national renown.

The Work of John Douglas

With the work of Thomas Harrison (1744–1829) and in particular his masterpieces in the form of the Grosvenor Bridge and the county buildings at the Castle, Chester is of significance within the field of English Neo-Classicism, but it also holds a distinctive place in the history of Late Victorian architecture. This is largely due to three separate but closely-related factors – half-timber revivalism, the patronage of the Grosvenor family, that is, of the second Marquess of Westminster and the first Duke of Westminster, and the numerous architects who practised in the city in the second half of the nineteenth century. Foremost in giving a special character to the Late Victorian architecture of Chester and its region, particularly as a result of his work for the Duke of Westminster, Douglas was also pre-eminent in ability and reputation among the architects involved, though a degree of national reputation was gained by his contemporary Thomas M. Lockwood (1830–1900) and his pupil E. A. Ould (1852–1909). Both Lockwood and Ould also included the Duke among their clients, and both, like Douglas, made some significant contributions to half-timber revivalism. Although not originating in Chester, and with isolated examples dating back to the *cottage orné* era, this *genre* became a speciality in the city, where it was well established as a movement before becoming nationally widespread and fashionable. In view of its interest and importance, the early history of its adoption is worth recounting in some detail, especially as this throws light on ideas and attitudes prevailing in Chester at the time that Douglas was establishing his practice.

With the successive piecemeal rebuildings of the Chester Rows, survivals of any work earlier than the seventeenth century are rare, and the predominance of brick in early nineteenth century illustrations shows how extensive Georgian rebuildings and refacings had been.

The continuing loss of ancient timber buildings was deplored by the Chester Archaeological Society, founded in 1849 as the Architectural, Archaeological and Historic Society for the County, City and Neighbourhood of Chester. An appendix on 'Street Architecture in Chester' in the volume of its *Journal* published in 1857 deplored that 'Instead of the rich and lively *facades*, (and) the curiously carved fantastical gables . . . the eye sees nothing but miserable brick, and incongruous piles of heavy Athenian architecture!'[1]

The anonymous writer, whose implied contempt for Harrison is not unexpected in an antiquary of the period, went on to note that, 'Exceptions there are, it is true, – precious springs in the weary desert, – and refreshing it is to turn to them. A few houses yet exist here and there about the city, little picturesque bits for the artist's pencil; and a few, yet far *too few*, restorations of later years have sprung up as indicative of the dawn of a more appropriate taste. But

Chester in the Nineteenth Century

we earnestly warn our fellow-citizens, that if Chester is to maintain its far-famed celebrity as one of the "wonder cities" of England, – if the great European and Transatlantic continents are still to contribute their shoals of annual visitors to fill our hotels, and the not too plenteous coffers of our tradesmen, one course only is open to us. We *must* maintain our ancient landmarks, we must preserve inviolate our city's rare attractions, – our quaint old Rows, unique and picturesque as they certainly are, must not be idly sacrificed at Mammon's reckless shrine!'[2]

After further emphasis, interestingly enough, on the importance of the tourist trade, the writer referred to '. . . the number of strangers, drawn by curiosity from all parts of the world to see this city of the past. It behoves us all, therefore,' he continued, as 'as best we may, jealously to watch over its precarious renown, by arresting, where possible not only the devastating hand of time, but also the frequently less cautious and so infinitely more dangerous fingers of the arch spoiler, Man! Remember, too, that every old house preserved or judiciously restored, or every new one erected after the same distinguishing type, will tend to raise the importance and perpetuate the fair fame of our venerable city!'[3]

Such advice was already in the process of being taken in the form of work by Thomas Mainwaring Penson (1818–64), a Chester architect, though other members of his family practised in Oswestry and Wales. The story of the black-and-white revival in Chester begins with his restoration of a shop in Eastgate Street (*c.* 1850–52) for Mr. Platt, a pharmacist. The work won the approval of the Archaeological Society[4] which, at a meeting in 1852, drew attention to the dilapidated condition of timber houses in Northgate and Watergate Streets, which 'might easily be restored with as much effect as had that of Mr. Platt.'[5] A contemporary guide book considered it to be, 'a most successful and elegant illustration of the manner in which the antique character of our domestic architecture can be preserved, with every regard for modern requirements and comforts,' and added the 'hope that the good sense and intelligence, as well as public spirit, displayed by Mr. Platt in this judicious work of restoration, will give an impulse to other improvements in the right direction; while at the same time it excites a regret that alterations have been previously effected, in such utter disregard of the architecture of the Rows. . . .'[6]

In fact the work was a 'restoration' in the sense then current, and seemed to involve a rebuilding, or at least a refacing, with little regard to correct re-instatement or historical precedent. The doctrine of anti-scrape which Ruskin had already advanced in the *Seven Lamps*[7] and which in 1877 became the creed of the Society for the Protection of Ancient Buildings found little following in Chester. Mr. Platt's building has been demolished, but nearby in Eastgate

The Work of John Douglas

Street there survive two shops (1856) which represent the first entirely new building of the revival. Echoing local sentiment, *The Builder* observed that, 'The substitution of ugly brick fronts and sash windows for the old gables whenever repair or alteration has become necessary, has done much injury to the appearance of the streets, and should not be encouraged. We are glad, therefore, to see that in two fronts recently put up under the direction of Mr. T. Mainwaring Penson, the old style has been adhered to, and to good effect.'[8] A short distance away is another restoration which Penson carried out in 1859 with the Marquess of Westminster as his client.[9] In 1861, while a grocer's shop on the opposite side of Eastgate Street was being built in fanciful half-timber style by T. A. Richardson,[10] the Archaeological Society was expressing disquiet at the threatened destruction of one of the remaining old timber-framed buildings. This was God's Providence House of 1652 in Watergate Street. In the event the Society was satisfied when in the following year it was rebuilt, on an enlarged scale, and to a new half-timbered design by James Harrison (1814–66), with certain of the old wood worked into the facade.[11] A spirit not dissimilar to that of Camdenian church restoration thus seemed to prevail, with a new building 'erected after the same distinguishing type' an acceptable alternative to, or possibly almost synonymous with one 'judiciously restored.'

Half-timbering was also carried out by the firm of Kelly & Edwards, under which style James Harrison's practice was continued after his death. None of its exponents worked exclusively in the manner, however, and by no means all of the building work which so transformed Victorian Chester was black-and-white. One of Penson's best works is the Gothic stone Crypt Buildings, Eastgate Street (1858),[12] notable as introducing into the street a new scale and height which was to set the pattern for much of the subsequent redevelopment. The scale became gargantuan with the partially half-timbered Grosvenor Hotel (1863–6), begun by Penson for the Marquess of Westminster and completed after his death in 1864 by the firm of Kyrke Penson & Ritchie.[13]

Among the wealth of black-and-white work which followed, even the genuinely old timber-framed buildings owe much to the nineteenth and twentieth centuries, with most of them undergoing heavy restoration and with the Georgian sash windows which had been almost universally inserted being almost equally universally removed. The early seventeenth century Bishop Lloyd's House owes its present fenestration and apparent completeness to a Lockwood restoration;[14] the cathedral is one of Sir Gilbert Scott's most thorough restorations; and, indulging in the hyperbole employed by David Lloyd in dubbing it 'An English Carcassone,'[15] Chester may be described as a Victorian city.

IV Architectural Practice

John Douglas's first known independent work was a garden ornament, no longer extant, erected in 1856 for the Honourable Mrs. Cholmondeley at her house of Abbots Moss, Oakmere, Cheshire. Mrs. Cholmondeley was the sister of Sir Tatton Sykes, of Sledmere, Yorkshire, a builder of churches and patron of G. E. Street. She was, moreover, the sister-in-law of Lord Delamere – Hugh Cholmondeley (1811–87) who had in 1855 succeeded his father as second Baron.[1] With Abbots Moss being less than three miles from Sandiway (where, as has been noted, the elder Douglas's house formed part of the Delamere estate), the garden ornament may have been commissioned to provide opportunity for a young local man at the outset of his career. It must have given satisfaction, for Douglas's next recorded work, and what is known to have been his first major commission, is the rebuilding of the entire south side of Lord Delamere's seat of Vale Royal. A very considerable part of a not inconsiderable house, the wing is dated 1860 and 1861, and the work thus overlapped with the building of his first church – that of St. John the Evangelist, Over (1860–63) (see page 42) built at the expense of Lord Delamere as a memorial to his first wife. Further work for the Baron followed in later years, but this early aristocratic patronage and the encouragement which Douglas is reported to have received from his noble client[2] must have been invaluable in helping to establish his practice and reputation.

With regard to the question of whether it was in 1855 or 1860 that he set up in practice, an article on 'John Douglas, Architect,' in *The British Architect* in 1898 is inconclusive, for before specifically mentioning Douglas it refers only in general terms to what an architect may accomplish during, 'a busy practice of some 30 to 40 years.'[3] In support of the early date are explicit references in obituaries in 1911 to his having lived and worked in Chester for 56 years[4] and to having commenced work there at the age of 25.[5] Also, the Abbots Moss garden ornament was of 1856 and it would seem likely that the south wing of Vale Royal was conceived before 1860, the earlier of the dates inscribed upon it. On the other hand he could have designed the garden ornament while still in Paley's employment; as has been noted, it was in or about 1860 that he first occupied 6 Abbey Square; no reference has been found indicating his presence either as householder or architect in Chester earlier than that date, and he does not appear in White's *Directory of Cheshire* published in 1860. Indeed, an item on Douglas in the series 'Contemporary British Architects,' in *Building News* in 1890 gives 1860 as the date he began practice.[6] As this appeared during his

The Work of John Douglas

lifetime, he presumably supplied the information himself, though the article is not completely accurate, for it confuses some of the works which it lists. A possible explanation might be that he left Lancaster in 1855 and did indeed then begin work in Chester, but in the employment of another architect such as T. M. Penson or James Harrison; and that he established his own practice, in Abbey Square, in 1860 (the year of his marriage), perhaps on the strength of having received or been offered the Vale Royal and Over commissions.

Douglas's output was by no means confined to single jobs for individual clients, and Lord Delamere was but the first of many steady patrons for whom a succession of commissions was executed. Others included, in Cheshire, the landowner R. E. Egerton-Warburton, and W. H. Lever, later Lord Leverhulme; in Wales the family of Lord Kenyon, the Gladstone family (including the G. O. M. himself), Alexander Balfour, and the Dyson Perrins family, of the Lea & Perrins Worcester Sauce firm, for whom work was also undertaken in Worcestershire. In Lancashire he was employed by the Earl of Sefton, and, further afield by the vicar of Tamworth and by John Joseph Jones, of Abberley, Worcestershire. Chief among his clients, however, was the first Duke of Westminster, and his practice was dominated by work for the Duke's Eaton estate. The first recorded instances of employment at the hands of the Grosvenor family are the entrance lodge and other structures at Grosvenor Park, Chester (1865–7) and the church at the Eaton estate village of Aldford (1865–6) (see page 49), for the second Marquess of Westminster. T. M. Penson, by whom the Marquess had previously been served, had died in 1864, and the choice of Douglas as a local architect to replace him may perhaps have owed something to the influence or recommendation of Lord Delamere, with whose family the Grosvenors had long been on terms of close friendship.[7] The Marquess's son, who was created Duke of Westminster in 1874, succeeded as third Marquess in 1869, and from then on began the flood of work which for thirty years flowed unabated through Douglas's office.

The country practice conducted by John Douglas thus owed much to the landed interest, and, although it also benefited from the infusion of new wealth into the field of architectural patronage, most of the building types which had been rare or unknown in the eighteenth century, and which a growing population and an increasingly industrialised society were now demanding, found little place within it. Yet the age made new demands even from traditional building types, and Victorian requirements and ideals are reflected in Douglas's intricately planned country houses (some of them for newly-affluent middle class clients) and in his banks, shops, schools and model farms, rural cottages and industrial housing, while his numerous churches and church restorations reflect Victorian religious and ecclesiological zeal. Predominantly domestic and ecclesiastical, the practice included only the occasional hotel, factory extension, workhouse chapel, market hall, cottage hospital or swimming bath. Designs for a town hall (Bootle, 1880) and railway station (Liverpool Exchange, 1881) never advanced beyond the stage of competition entries, and only with St. Deiniol's Library, Hawarden (1899–1902 and 1904–6) (see page 199), as part of the National Gladstone Memorial, did anything approaching a major public work emerge.

Just as the absence of family papers preserves the veil of obscurity over Douglas's personal life, the loss (despite the continuation of the practice at the same address until 1974) of virtually all the office documents means that activities within 6 Abbey Square are equally unknown. Nothing is recorded of the office organisation or the number of staff employed; only hints exist as to the roles and responsibilities of respective personnel, and the roles and responsibilities of the two successive partners remain matters for conjecture.

The most complete record of any one job which has so-far come to light is a set of letters, written by Douglas, relating to the building of the master's house at Witton Grammar School, Northwich. He had been the architect for a new building for the school itself (1869, but later altered and enlarged) on a site near St. Helen's church – the ancient parish church of Witton – and the new commission was for a master's house with which accommodation for boarders was to be combined. The correspondence was addressed to Messrs. Black & Trafford, a firm of Northwich solicitors acting for the school governors, and covers a period from December 1874, following the commissioning of the work, to its completion in December 1878. It consists of 44 items, all in Douglas's own hand, except for one letter and a telegram sent in his absence by his assistant, George Smith. Three of the four last letters, written after the death of Mrs. Douglas, are on mourning paper.[8]

Some of the letters refer only to arrangements for appointments, or to drawings being despatched in the post, and few were written after building work commenced, but the series indicates the principal stages in the progress of the commission and in the discharging of an architect's responsibilities. At first, Douglas had difficulty with the plan, considering the site to be unsuitable for the purpose required. Presumably in deference to his advice, the site was changed, enabling him to produce a design which satisfied him. Alterations and amendments were made to suit the wishes of the clients, though they were warned, perhaps in answer to calls for economy, that, '– for the amount of accommodation it is impossible for the building to be simpler otherwise it will be a small factory whh. I am sure you would not like to see built.'[9] With the design

The Work of John Douglas

agreed, working drawings and specifications were prepared and tenders sought, allowing for alternative types of roofing slate, as Douglas understood there to be difficulty in obtaining the ones he preferred. In fairness to a builder who had tendered, he later drew attention to circumstances concerning the relative costs of these alternatives. Advising that quantities would probably have to be supplied if more than one or two tenders were to be expected, he explained that, 'I do not take them out myself but employ a surveyor whose charges are included in the Building Tender.'[10] He had, perhaps characteristically, seemed a little vague on the question of costs, and, although his estimate was for £2,500 to £3,000, the lowest tender was in the region of £3,600. As a result, the project seems to have fallen into abeyance for some months, but in due course a revised design, estimated for £2,500, went out to tender. The process was lengthy, for Douglas wrote, '. . . you would hardly believe it has taken about 5 weeks to get them (the tenders) in – I am very sorry for this delay but it has certainly not been on my account for I have done all I could in the matter.'[11] Evidently the prices were still in excess, or else the governors were bent on further economy, for although this was in July 1876, by November Douglas was declaring himself in favour of the last set of plans and considering the price a fair one. In December, it was agreed that William Leicester, one of the builders who had tendered, should go through the scheme with a view to reducing his price, and in January 1877 he submitted an amended estimate. 'I have had considerable difficulty in getting him down to this figure,' wrote Douglas. 'He positively refused to stand by his original tender & considering the time it has been sent in and the advance that has since taken place in the price both of Labour & materials I am not surprised that he should want more money. . . .'[12]

Being in the days before standard forms of contract, the agreement was drawn up by Black & Trafford and approved by Douglas, who suggested the inclusion of additional clauses to avoid certain (unspecified) difficulties which were then troubling him on another job. It was not until May 1877 that the contract was signed, but from then on things seemed to go smoothly, with construction supervised by Reece, Douglas's clerk of works. Although pointing out that it was usual for the client to pay the clerk of works direct, Douglas undertook to pay Reece's weekly wage of £1, on the understanding that this would be refunded to him, in addition to his own commission which, he confirmed, was the usual 5% on outlay. Subsequent letters refer to requests for payment on account of his commission and to his visiting the site. On one occasion, although he had issued to the builder a certificate for £500, only part of this was met, and he wrote asking that the remainder be paid. Finally, when dealing with the last accounts, he expressed the hope that the

Architectural Practice

building would give satisfaction, and the last letter mentions his sending, for future reference, a drainage plan to be kept in Black & Trafford's office and a tracing of it to be kept by the schoolmaster at the house itself.[13]

It was at about the time that the Witton master's house was under way that the Douglas family vacated 6 Abbey Square (*c.* 1878 if they went straight to Dee Banks, or earlier if there was an intermediate sojourn at No. 4). With the house thus being apparently devoted entirely to office use, it suggests the existence of a considerable staff of 'clerks' (or draughtsmen) and assistants; the busy nature of the practice is indicated by Douglas having employed his own clerk of works, and during the four years with which he was concerned with the master's house well over 40 other commissions were handled by the office. Although many of these were comparatively small Eaton estate buildings, they also included three or four fair-sized houses and some dozen churches and church restorations. The Witton correspondence shows that Douglas was himself nevertheless fully involved with design and administration, even in connection with what was not a particularly large or distinguished building.

A certain though obviously limited degree of responsibility was delegated to his then assistant George Smith. When a telegram was received requesting an estimate of cost, for it to be laid before a meeting of the governors of Witton Grammar School, Smith replied, 'Mr. Douglas away should say estimate would be from two thousand five hundred to three thousand write tonight.'[14] It was Douglas himself who, on his return to the office later the same day, wrote confirming these figures, and at a later date Smith acknowledged receipt of a communication from Black & Trafford, stating that Douglas, away for a few days, would give attention to it on his return. In 1877 Smith wrote to the Town Clerk of Chester confirming arrangements for a site meeting which he was to attend,[15] and in 1872, in submitting two schemes to the Improvement Committee of the City Council, Douglas wrote, 'I will thank you to lay before the Committee the accompanying plans which my assistant Mr. Smith will explain to you.'[16] The projects in question were for houses in Grosvenor Park Road (a scheme which remained unexecuted and was superseded by a new design built *c.* 1879–80 with Douglas as his own developer (see page 112), and for St. Werburgh Chambers, an office block (1872–3) in St. Werburgh Street. Douglas's own close involvement with the productions of the office is further shown by the fact that plans for an adjacent row of shops for the same client (St. Werburgh's Mount, 1873–4) were delayed in being submitted to the Improvement Committee due to Douglas having been unwell.[17]

Although Douglas is open to criticism for faulty estimating, the Witton correspondence suggests that, in advising his employers and

The Work of John Douglas

fulfilling their requirements (and displaying some firmness in doing so) while at the same time safeguarding the interests of the builder, he performed his professional duties in an assiduous and otherwise admirable manner. The job was untypical in extending over so long a period, but is interesting as illustrating the nineteenth century phenomenon of a client in the form of a committee, and the letters also reflect something of the increasing complexity and responsibility which characterised architectural practice. In *Architect and Patron*[18] Frank Jenkins has drawn attention to the significance of the decline in standards of craftsmanship, the advent of new materials, the rise of the general contractor and the growth of lump sum competitive tendering as factors which led the architect to greater involvement in financial and legal considerations in the form of arbitration, contract procedure or the issuing of certificates. Similarly they rendered necessary careful site supervision and fuller instructions embodied in working drawings, details and specifications, and they led to the emergence of the quantity surveyor as an increasingly important individual in building contracting.

The extension of the architect's duties was accompanied by the movement for the establishment of professional reputation, with the aspirations of professional status and integrity, as conceived by Sir John Soane (1753–1837), embodied in the ideals of the Institute of British Architects. Founded in 1835, this became the Royal Institute of British Architects in 1866. Although registration and a closed profession formed the logical and inevitable eventual culmination, the idea provoked antagonism on the part of those who saw in it a threat to the ideal of the freedom of the architect as artist. Opposition to a registration Bill promoted by the Society of Architects in 1891 led to the submission to the R.I.B.A. of a Memorial objecting to the principle of registration and to the production of a set of essays, *Architecture, A Profession or an Art*, under the editorship of Norman Shaw and (Sir) T. G. Jackson. Published in *The Times* accompanied by a letter signed by Sir Arthur Blomfield, J. D. Sedding, Jackson, Shaw, Alma-Tadema and Burne-Jones, the Memorial itself carried the signatures of many of the most distinguished architects and artists of the day. Among the forty-six architects, and one of the few practitioners outside London to add his signature, was John Douglas. The architects included non-members and also members of the R.I.B.A. (though some of the latter resigned at this time) and Douglas was listed among the members.[19] This was erroneous, for he never joined the Institute.[20]

That Douglas should have been included among the Memorialists is proof of the standing and recognition which he achieved in his lifetime. The year after its consecration, his first church, St. John's Over (1860–63) (see page 42) was illustrated and described in

Building News;[21] his work came to be frequently featured in that publication (which in 1890 included him in its series on 'Contemporary British Architects')[22] and in *The Builder*, *The Architect* and *The British Architect*, while a number of his works exhibited at the Royal Academy appeared in *Academy Architecture*. Although *The Builder's* features on 'Architecture at the Royal Academy' included mild and reasonable criticism, such comments as the journals offered on Douglas's buildings were favourable in tone.

It was, however, *The British Architect*, under the editorship of T. Raffles Davison (1853–1937), and with northern interests and progressive and perceptive policies, which emerged as the most enthusiastic admirer. This was largely or entirely due to Davison, whose pen-and-ink 'Rambling Sketches' appearing weekly with accompanying comment, gave generous coverage to Douglas, and the hand of Davison may also be detected in editorial comment lavish in its praise. Over the years *The British Architect* was little short of eulogistic. 'As simple, pleasing, and effective domestic architecture, such examples as we have lately given of Mr. Douglas's designs are unsurpassed,' it wrote in 1877[23] of Lea Hall Farmhouse (1873) (see page 99) and a pair of cottages (*c*.1874) at Aldford. In reviewing the 1886 Royal Academy show, it singled out Abbeystead, Lancashire (1885–7) (see pages 149–51), built for Lord Sefton: 'The Palm for domestic English is certainly this year to be awarded to Mr. John Douglas, for his drawing of a nobleman's mansion . . . This design exhibits a power possessed by few English architects in the combination of variety and picturesqueness together with dignity and breadth.'[24] For Raffles Davison in 1884, Plas Mynach, Barmouth, Merioneth (1883) (see page 110), 'very nearly realised to me the idea of a perfect country house,'[25] inside which he found, 'one of the most charming little halls I have seen.'[26] He felt that, 'The pyramids, the Egyptian temples, and the monoliths are the sort of work to hold their own with the broad country and the limitless sky, and suggest some nobility of feeling and aspiration amongst their builders. This house of "Plas-Mynach" seems to carry on something of such a feeling, owning the value of simplicity and unostentation. Where it stands, isolated and prominent, bounded on one side by the hills and on the other by the sea, such qualities as these seem to bespeak for men and their work some place of dignity in the world . . .'[27]

Referring to Abbeystead in 1893, Davison commented that, 'There are few country houses in England so altogether excellent as those which have their birth at 6, Abbey Square, Chester,'[28] and in 1897 he described 'a red-letter day' of 'an inveterate sketcher,' in the form of a train excursion from Chester to Bala with the church at Maentwrog, Merioneth (remodelled 1896) (see page 183) as objective. He had enjoyed, 'a mixture of good companionship, fine weather, lovely scenery, and sketching . . . a compound of perfect delight. Add to these attractions a little country church by Messrs. Douglas & Fordham, as a subject for a sketch, let the weather be a brilliant July sunshine, the scenery that of North Wales, and Mr. John Douglas for a companion, and what could mortal wish for more!'[29]

Somewhat less emotive (and containing a disclaimer of any 'wish to indulge in any undue panegyrics') and thus more convincing, is the article on 'John Douglas, Architect,' in *The British Architect* in 1898, 'when,' as it noted, 'after a long and honourable career, Mr. John Douglas is leaving a whole street in Chester [St. Werburgh Street] with the hall mark of his artistic work.' It states that, as must long have been apparent to readers of the journal, 'no other country practice had made an equally substantial appeal on our sympathies,' and it provides a valid and discerning summary of the nature of Douglas's achievement: 'There has been no practice of the art of architecture in this country more consistent in its general excellence of aim and attainment than that carried on for many years by Mr. John Douglas, of Chester. Ranking high in quality above the average level of architecture, either in London or the provinces, it has been a pattern and example to us all. Though the practice carried on at 6, Abbey Square, Chester, has not often had the stimulus of "great occasion" or glittering circumstance, such as is associated with great town halls, museums, palaces or cathedrals, it has always been guided by the determination to live up to every occasion and make every building characteristic of its purpose, and expressive of the best art the firm could supply. Whether it be a row of cottages or a nobleman's house, a large academy or a village school, a country church or the most elaborate effort possible, the same level of thoroughness and high level of accomplishment has followed through all'.[30]

In its obituary, *The British Architect* referred to Douglas as having, 'achieved a reputation which has long since placed him in the front rank of living architects,' and stated that, 'Of its kind, we do not believe that this country has ever seen a more admirable professional life.'[31]

It was thus not mere local chauvinism which led the *Chester Chronicle* to describe him as, 'the doyen of provincial architects,'[32] and, praised by both Sédille and Muthesius, he can be considered as having achieved international recognition.

Hermann Muthesius (1861–1927), attached to the German Embassy in London between 1896 and 1903 for the purpose of studying English housing, made the significance of late nineteenth century English architecture (and particularly domestic architecture) known in Germany. *Academy Architecture* had,

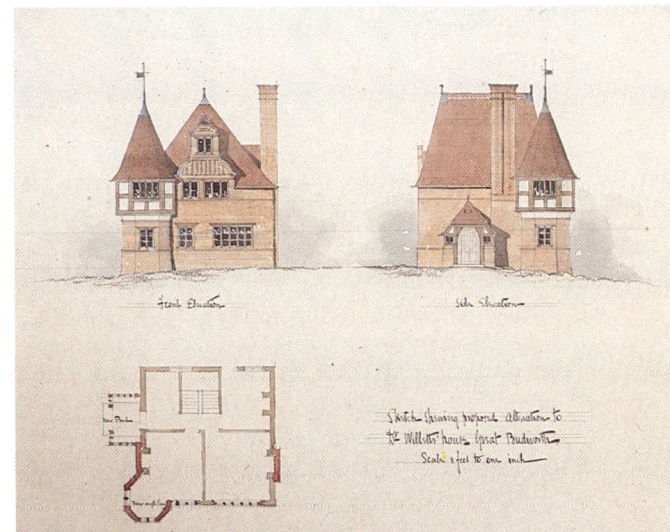

Top left: Stud Lodge, Eaton Hall, Cheshire, 1881–2.
Top right: Unexecuted design for alterations to Dr Willetts's house, Great Budworth, Cheshire, 1874. (Drawing at Arley Hall)
Middle: First scheme for remodelling George and Dragon Inn, Great Budworth, Cheshire, 2nd March 1874. (Drawing at Arley Hall)
Bottom: Unexecuted design for Luncheon Room, Eaton Hall, Cheshire, 1877, with annotations by the Duke of Westminster. (Drawing at Eaton Estate Office)

The Work of John Douglas

however, from 1889, already done something to make English design known abroad, and in writing about developments in England Muthesius was predated by the French architect Paul Sédille (1836–1900). Published in 1890, Sédille's *L'Architecture Moderne en Angleterre* is a slight work in comparison with Muthesius's lengthy and more influential writings. It nevertheless showed awareness of the best domestic architecture of the period, and it is within this context that Sédille referred to Douglas. Reproducing material which he had published in *Gazette des Beaux Arts* as early as 1886 and 1887,[33] he provided four illustrations and made special mention of Douglas's work on the Eaton estate.[34] 'It is impossible to remain unmoved,' he wrote, 'at the sight of the beautiful buildings of all kinds which Mr. John Douglas has built in and about Chester. The various small houses he has built in Eaton Park for the Duke of Westminster are no less charming.'[35]

In Muthesius's *Die Englische Baukunst der Gegenwart*, 1900, six buildings or groups by Douglas are described and generously illustrated,[36] and although *Die Neuere Kirchliche Baukunst in England*, 1901, contains only a passing reference,[37] the three-volume *Das Englische Haus*, 1904–5, illustrates Abbeystead, an Eaton estate building (the Aldford Cheese Factory, Bruera, 1874–5) and a plan of Barrowmore Hall, Great Barrow, Cheshire (c. 1881).[38] It contains also a appraisal of Douglas, which, prefacing consideration of Sedding's domestic work, places him in distinguished company. 'Although in effect Norman Shaw considerably dwarfed his contemporaries', Muthesius conceded, 'he was not an isolated figure. There were a number of skilled and extremely efficient fellow-architects, who shared his aims. One thinks first of John Douglas in Chester. . . . His houses gave the newer parts of Chester its character and he also built many large country-mansions and smaller houses round the outskirts of the city and up and down the country. Like the triple constellation Webb-Nesfield-Shaw, he closely followed the traditional native style, remaining constant to it throughout his life,'[39]

Yet despite his fame, the only form of official recognition ever extended to Douglas seems to have been a medal, awarded for Abbeystead when it was shown at a Paris exhibition.[40] *The British Architect* noted that he, 'lived and died without a letter of distinction to his name,' and considered that, 'his full life's record of practice as an architect received a totally inadequate record [*sic*: ? reward], both in money and honours,'[41] Maurice B. Adams commented more tersely, 'John Douglas, neglected by the Royal Academy, created quite a school of his pupils, and well deserved the Royal Gold Medal which he did not get.'[42]

Turning to detailed consideration of Douglas's architecture, it may for convenience be analysed in terms of five separate categories.

Architectural Practice

The first, which may be called High Victorian, is a chronological as much as a stylistic distinction, and extends from the outset of his practice until the end of the 1860s. The remaining four categories are stylistic, and for want of better names may be termed Vernacular, Germanic, Gothic and Elizabethan. Their respective demarcations are not always distinct, for they co-existed simultaneously, and elements of more than one are frequently found together in the same building, Throughout these stylistic categories can be discerned a consistent vocabulary of detailing, with its origins within the period of the High Victorian category.

It is to Douglas's earliest works – those of the High Victorian category, that attention must now be given.

v High Victorianism

High Victorianism in English architecture can be considered as a phenomenon which flourished during the two decades following 1850; which although something of a spent force continued to manifest itself in the 1870s, and which, although influential in America, had little parallel development on the continent of Europe. Largely, though not exclusively, expressed in terms of Gothic, it accompanied the acceptance of that style for universal adoption and the virtual, if temporary, emancipation of Gothic from strong ecclesiastical overtones. This vigorous new life into which the Gothic Revival entered was characterised by broad eclecticism in the choice of architectural sources; by a remarkable freedom in the use and adoption of elements and (within limits) of styles; by concern for surfaces and materials as illustrated in the use of constructional polychromy, and, most obviously, by sculptural and intensely dramatic architectonic qualities. Paradoxically, the results could mean either extreme richness and elaboration, or sheerness and severity, but with the common factors being inventiveness, boldness and a sense of massiveness. Seen in its context within the development of the Romantic Movement, and thus tracing its ancestry to the 18th century, High Victorian architecture partakes of the sublime as much as of the picturesque. Like a swift transition to Wagner from the gentle unclouded romanticism of Mendelssohn, High Victorianism erupted from the era of Pugin, Barry and Loudon, and ran its tempestuous course before subsiding with docility into the age of Shaw, mature Pearson and the Aesthetic Movement.

Although High Victorianism as a movement can be considered as dating from 1849 with the publication of *The Seven Lamps of Architecture* by John Ruskin (1819–1900) and the inception of All Saints' Church, Margaret Street by William Butterfield (1814–1900), earlier seeds and sources are discernible. Among these the picturesque utility of Pugin's and Butterfield's domestic buildings not only provided precedent for sculptural massing, but led, via Street, to Phillip Webb (1831–1915) and provided inspiration for Late Victorian domestic architecture.

Ruskin followed *The Seven Lamps* with the first volume of *The Stones of Venice* in 1851 and the second and third in 1853. His advancing of the claims of North Italian Gothic when advocating the general adoption of a chosen precedent had obvious and momentous influence. Also, the diversity and variety which characterised Mid-Victorian stone carving may in large measure be traced to the passionate eloquence of 'The Nature of Gothic' in the second volume

High Victorianism

of *The Stones*, anticipated in its concern for craftsmanship and spontaneity by 'The Lamp of Life.' Although direct correlation between cause and effect cannot be proved, it may be noted that further suggestions of High Victorianism found in Ruskin include appreciation of massiveness and the distinguishing of sublimity as a separate element from beauty, and the condemnation of curvilinear tracery with its substitution of line for mass. His 1853 *Lectures on Architecture and Painting* (published in 1854) contain much on the emotional importance of the roof – with the plea that it be made steep – and the symbolic significance of the tower. That in 1850 the design of All Saints', Margaret Street, underwent dramatic change can only be explained in terms of a direct response to Ruskin's espousal of the cause of constructional polychromy in the Lamps of 'Truth' and 'Beauty.' That this building, conceived as the model church of the Ecclesiological Society should, moreover, have become an aesthetic battleground between Butterfield and Alexander Beresford Hope is symbolic of the freedom from archaeological convention which distinguished High from Early Victorian Gothic.

With the 1850s the relationship between cause (in the form of publications), effect, and general ethos cannot be properly distinguished, but writings symptomatic of the movement are *Brick and Marble in the Middle Ages: Notes of a Tour in North Italy*, 1855, by G.E. Street (1824–81) and *Remarks on Secular & Domestic Architecture, Present & Future*, 1857, by George Gilbert Scott (1811–78). Despite Butterfield's long career, it was to Street and Scott that the leadership of High Victorianism had passed by the mid-1850s, and they were soon joined by William Burges (1827–81) and Alfred Waterhouse (1830–1905). Continental influence other than that of Italy may previously be traced in the movement, but impetus to the French contribution was given by the Lille Cathedral competition of 1855 (won by Burges and Henry Clutton with Street as runner-up) and by the appearance of Viollet-le-Duc's *Dictionnaire Raisonné de l'Architecture* from 1854. Partly French in inspiration, and one of the latest and one of the greatest expressions of High Victorianism was Waterhouse's remodelling of Eaton Hall for the Duke of Westminster, and as this was carried out while John Douglas was engaged on estate work for the Duke, subsequent mention will be made of it.

As already noted, E. G. Paley was little affected by High Victorianism and until the coming of H. J. Austin his practice remained within the Puginistic, Camdenian tradition of the Gothic Revival. It is thus no surprise that Douglas's own earliest works do not uniformly partake of High Victorian character. His best buildings of the 1860s can, however, be considered as belonging to the movement; its influence can be further traced in work of much later date, and something of its character can be discerned in the

The Work of John Douglas

heaviness and elaboration of his first known design – the now vanished garden ornament at Abbots Moss, Oakmere (1856) for the Honourable Mrs. Cholmondeley. Octagonal, font-like and somewhat top-heavy, this was raised on steps and had a sundial on one side of the bowl (which served as a flower vase) and a carved griffin motif (inspired by the family crest and supporters) between stem and bowl. It had the mark of an earnest and over-done effort on the part of a young man anxious to please and impress. Work on a very different scale came with the second recorded job – the south wing of Vale Royal (1860–61) for Mrs. Cholmondeley's brother-in-law, the second Lord Delamere.

Founded by Edward I, the abbey of Vale Royal was the largest Cistercian house in England, and had a unique 14th century *chevet*. Nothing of the church remains visible above ground, though the present house is partly on the site of the conventual buildings and incorporates monastic remains.[1] In 1860 Douglas recased the centre of the south range, which until then had been timber-framed, to match Edward Blore's south-east wing of 1833, and the next year he added the south-west wing, altering the dining room at about the same time.[2] It was a task of a scale and nature for which his training with Paley could hardly have prepared him, and the result is immature and lacking in confidence, The Elizabethan style was borrowed from Blore, and the material was brick with stone dressings. The asymmetrical south front has a gabled block projecting at either end of a lower connecting range, and this latter, with a gable in the centre, is unresolved in its elevational treatment. The shorter north front, where less is attempted, is simpler and better. Hints of High Victorian inventiveness are restricted to oriel windows, an arcaded conservatory (now bricked up), a slender clock

High Victorianism

tower with short pyramid spire and, near it, a small hipped roof recessed behind a parapet. The spire and this roof, and tiny dormered louvres in the spire, may be seen as forerunners of elements which Douglas was later to develop. Similarly, a gabled projection on the north front has corners which change from rounded to rectangular in a detail which, in its incipient wilful individualism, suggests the freedom which he was later to apply to the design of corbelling.

Construction at Vale Royal overlapped with that of Lord Delamere's church of St. John the Evangelist, Over (1860–63). Again in accordance with what might be expected as a result of Paley's teaching, this is a competent church and, even if lacking in great originality, is (in contrast with Vale Royal) done with consistency and conviction. It is fully articulated in its parts, and has a clerestorey and a south-west tower and spire. The style is Early Decorated, with a variety of window shapes and Geometrical tracery. The exterior is of sandstone, rockfaced, and the interior is plastered, with stone dressings. Quite lively carving includes stiff-leaf capitals, angels as internal hood-mould stops (which occur in other of Douglas's early churches) and the heads of a bishop (presumably Bishop Graham of Chester) and Queen Victoria as porch hood-mould stops. The nave roof is curious, with principals and common rafters all trussed, scissor-wise, and foreshadows the great variety of roof structures which later Douglas churches were to embody. The font, with a central shaft surrounded by four colonnettes, is of a form which was later to be used, and the roundels which, containing emblems of the Evangelists, decorate the sides of the bowl, are features which were to be of importance in Douglas's decorative detailing. Small roundels occur also on the churchyard gatepiers. The pitchpine stalls, although not yet in a recognisable Douglas joinery style, are typical of him in the care which has been lavished on their detailing, and elements which were later to be developed include free-standing colonnettes, conventionalised poppyheads and bench-ends incorporating curved outline. Nailhead ornament also occurs, contributing to the feel of High Victorian chunkiness, though it is not something which Douglas used in his maturity. Free-standing shafts bifurcate the clerestorey windows externally, and are another feature which was to recur, but perhaps the most obvious detail in terms of future development is that of the corbels of the tower arch at the west end of the south aisle. A Douglas characteristic is a corbel which can be described as an inverted semi-cone, and which was subject to varying forms of scale, shape, profile and enrichment. The feature occurs at Over as a semi-octagon. Although St. John's does not display the power and individuality of which Douglas was later to be capable, to visit it is a moving experience. The embryonic hints of many churches yet to

South front of Vale Royal, Cheshire: east wing by E. Blore, 1833, rest J. Douglas, 1860–61. Photograph, c. 1910)

41

The Work of John Douglas

come are discerned, and it can be realised how important this, his first ecclesiastical commission, and quite a lavish one, must have been to the architect.

While St. John's, Over, was still under construction, Douglas restored the chancel at St. Mary's church, Eastham, Cheshire (1862–3). Subsequent alterations and enrichments (in part attributable to him) have overlaid the work, but the chancel roof, and probably also that of a north-east chapel, both of which rest on versions of the semi-cone corbel, can be ascribed to this period. The client was a Miss White, who possessed proprietary rights over the chancel and who, living in Abbey Street, Chester,[3] was Douglas's neighbour in the cathedral precinct.

It has already been suggested that his designing of a new building for the Boteler Grammar School, School Brow, Warrington (1862–4) might indicate that he was a former pupil, though this can only be speculation. In reverting in this building to secular architecture, the lack of assurance which was apparent at Vale Royal is again in evidence. The school possesses none of the confidence of St. John's, Over, though Douglas was sufficiently satisfied to exhibit the design at a meeting of the Chester Archaeological Society in 1862.[4] In a minimal and functional sort of Gothic, the building is of brick with

EXTERIOR AND INTERIOR OF ST JOHN'S CHURCH · OVER · CHESHIRE. JOHN DOUGLAS ARCH*.

High Victorianism

stone dressings and some polychromatic use of brick, in yellow and purple, for voussoirs and banding and diapering. It can never have been really attractive, and, used for the Corporation Works Department, now looks grim and forlorn. There is little hint of future maturity, with one remarkable exception. The principal external feature is a broad, square tower, rising as part of the main elevation, and on the front of which a sundial from the predecessor building was formerly placed. The tower has a low pyramid roof recessed behind a parapet, and although the quiet simplicity of form must have been diluted by a corner bell turret (now destroyed), this anything but High Victorian form was used by Douglas in later years, and with its crowning vane, the tower must have presented a piquantly *fin de siècle* appearance.

Related to the Boteler Grammar School in being of brick with some polychromy and of an immature but obviously experimental nature, were two houses in Upper Northgate Street, Chester, now demolished – Nos. 21 (1865) and 23 (1865–6). The owner of the former was a builder, from whom the site of No. 23 was bought by the doctor who attended Mrs. Douglas at the time of her death thirteen years later.[5] The first had a single-gable frontage with some arcaded Gothic fenestration. The second, larger and more varied, had sash windows and few historicist trappings, and can stylistically only be described as Victorian. The roof was hipped, of low pitch. Hipped roofs provide a recurrent theme in Douglas's work, and other features which foreshadowed later usage were windows rising through the eaves and terminating in hipped dormers, and heavy brick corbel tables – big chunky corbels, with rounded unmoulded brackets, sometimes in more than one stage, re-appeared in his detailing as well as the inverted semi-cones. Forest Hey, Sandiway, stands on land which Douglas almost certainly owned, and represents a remodelling (1882), doubtless by him, of an earlier villa. Remaining low-pitched roofs and polychromatic brick suggest the latter to have been similar in character to the Chester houses, and it may thus also be attributed to Douglas, and dated in the 1860s.

The Congregational Chapel at Over (1865, now United Reformed church), half a mile from St. John's, may also be considered with these buildings in being brick, polychromatic and experimental, even though possessing a very different and positive character. Stylistically it is a hybrid, being a very High Victorian combination of Gothic and round-arched forms, and with pyramidal pinnacles of great elaboration. It is, however, the polychromy which is most memorable, with zig-zag patterns in the slating of the roof, alternate bands of yellow and red brick relentlessly encircling the walls, and with some red sandstone in the form of diapering. There are also granite columns and some carved stonework. The latter includes foliated capitals and heads which (whereas the Establishment along

Church of St John the Evangelist, Over, Cheshire, 1860–3. (*Building News*, 11, 1864, p. 169. Drawing by R. W. Mallett)

The Work of John Douglas

United Reformed Church, Over, Cheshire, 1865.

the road was given the bishop and the queen) are those of Calvin and Luther. At the side of the building is a small single-storey projection of semi-octagonal plan but having a free-standing pointed octagon roof. Also, a semi-octagonal roof projects at the rear, and quadrant blocks with sweeping roofs flank the main gable end. Here is already clearly recognisable an inclination for distinctive steep roofs and turret forms which provides one of the most notable characteristics of Douglas's later work. As for detailing, this is largely characteristic of the date, with much use of nail-head ornament in the woodwork, but incised roundels within the otherwise wildly High Victorian stone pinnacles may be noted. Jangling away in bright sunshine, the building presents an astonishing sight. Yet the octagon roof and the roundels show that amid the cacophony there is evidence of an architect of refinement and sensitivity as well as of resourcefulness.

And these qualities had already become fully apparent in a furniture shop at Nos. 19 & 21 Sankey Street, Warrington (1864). Douglas's first building of real and outstanding quality, it is indeed in its way one of the best things he ever did, and it would be difficult to better it as an example of Mid-Victorian street architecture. The shop front has been destroyed, but had piers and arcading with stone carving both in relief and in incised patterns, and there were interesting corbels and stumpy semi-octagonal colonnettes. Not only pre-occupation with corbel and bracket forms, but also interest in

High Victorianism

Nos. 19–21 Sankey Street, Warrington, Cheshire, 1864. (*Works*)

shafts or posts, including octagonal ones, may frequently be encountered in Douglas's work. Above ground floor level the frontage remains. It is of red sandstone with lighter dressings, and both stones alternate in voussoirs. Fenestration is in the form of Gothic arcading, articulated by free-standing polished columns and disposed asymmetrically with proportions and rhythm of great subtlety. There is much stone carving of exceptional quality and refinement in the form of foliated patterns, some of it within roundels. The facade is crowned by an elaborately corbelled cornice (again displaying Douglas's interest in such detailing) and recessed behind the parapet is a steep hipped roof.

The general North Italian character of this building and the polychromy (albeit restrained) is strongly Ruskinian. To what

The Work of John Douglas

extent Douglas may have derived this direct from source and to what extent from prevailing ethos cannot be known. However, the possibility of his having been influenced by Scott's *Remarks* – which provides a logical and rational working out of much that is to be found in the writings of Pugin and Ruskin – is suggested by the close approximation of the Sankey Street building to some of Scott's suggestions for commercial street architecture. He noted that '. . . the Gothic street fronts in Italy look well with horizontal cornices. . . . A bold block cornice, with or without a corbel table, and carrying a parapet pierced or otherwise, will always be an effective element in street architecture; and if backed by a high-pitched roof, so much the better;'[6] that shop fronts should incorporate piers so as to prevent the impression of the building being carried on plate glass,[7] and that 'A lofty roof rising boldly from behind the parapet . . . will give individuality to our building. . . .'.[8] Moreover, in reiterating a plea for polychromy he specifically suggested polished granite window shafts and voussoirs of alternate stones.[9] Also, in 'Notes on the Uses to be Made of the Mediaeval Architecture of Italy,' forming an addendum to the book and consisting largely of material reprinted from *The Ecclesiologist* of June 1855, Scott laid stress on polychromy and on the use of the detached shaft in windows and arcading.[10]

As already noted, the first known instances of Grosvenor patronage are work at Grosvenor Park, Chester (1865–7) and the rebuilding of Aldford church, both for the second Marquess of

Lodge, Grosvenor Park, Chester, 1865–7.

High Victorianism

Westminster. Grosvenor Park, presented to the city by the Marquess and opened in 1867, was designed by Paxton's pupil Edward Kemp, Douglas being responsible for the entrance lodge, a canopy over a spring known as Billy Hobby's Well, the gates and railings, and a retaining wall with balustrade along the bank of the River Dee. A large octagonal shelter shed, though commenced, was not proceeded with (its base being converted into a seat) when it was decided to site nearby a statue of the Marquess, which would have been dwarfed by it.

The original ironwork at Grosvenor Park has gone, but the gatepiers remain – single blocks of granite, developing from chamfered squares into fuller octagonal forms at the heads. This, and a square developing into a pyramid are characteristic gatepier shapes used by Douglas. The entrance lodge is a picturesquely-composed little building with stone ground storey and half-timbering above – Douglas's first known use of black-and-white. The lodge is, however, fully High Victorian, with the masonry detailing being Gothic, and including a central shaft dividing a two-light window, and stiff-leaf enrichment to the moulded caps of circular chimney shafts. The half-timbering includes much ornamental carving and some pargetting, but all of so spiky a nature as to render the High Victorian character indisputable. The timber-framed porch is prophetic of certain details yet to come, though what can be seen as the most recognisable Douglas-like feature is a window rising through the eaves and ending in a hipped dormer roof – a development of those at No. 23 Upper Northgate Street. Billy Hobby's Well is a small octagonal structure, with a turret-like roof, rising to a big lead finial, and the enrichment includes roundels and stiff-leaf ornament. In miniature, crystalline fashion it represents the clear-cut refinement of the Warrington shop, as well as Douglas's now fully recognisable *penchant* for steep roofs and slender verticality.

The progress of work at Grosvenor Park is quite fully documented, and it is, for instance, recorded that Douglas arranged for stone for the construction of the river embankment to be supplied from the Permanent Way Stores Department of the London & North-Western Railway at Watford, and that Benjamin Owens, one of the contractors, was able to wangle irregular payments. Writing to Mr. George Allen at Eccleston (acting for the Marquess) he pleaded, 'I am very sorry to trouble you this morning, but I *really* had expected Mr Douglas to have been able to give us £*321*, this morning [in connection with work elsewhere], but he has not done so being so very much out of town, am therefore obliged to ask you for £*100*.'[11] Then later, 'Could you please advance £40. Upon the Park account until we bring that matter to a forward state? as I am very short this morning.'[12] Then again, 'I am very much

The Work of John Douglas

pained to trouble you. Mr. Douglas has gone away somewhere – and I am short of £45.0.0. Can you please let me have it on the Public Park account.'[13] At least two of these three appeals were successful,[14] and at a later date a letter was sent from Douglas's office, signed by one William Bakewell, stating that, 'I am desired by Mr. Douglas to say that a/cs shall be sent to you either tomorrow or the day after. Be good enough not to give Mr. Owen (sic) a cheque without a certificate from Mr. Douglas.'[15] On the occasion of the ceremonial opening of the park, Douglas was among those invited to join the procession and attend a dinner.[16]

The church of St. John the Baptist (1865–6) at the Eaton estate village of Aldford (replacing that in which Douglas's mother Mary Swindley was baptised) is a developed version of St. John's, Over, and represents a stage in Douglas's emancipation from Paley in ecclesiastical architecture. Douglas's scheme succeeded an abortive design for rebuilding the church by Paley himself, made in 1861.[17] The church as built still owes much to conventional ecclesiological precedent in form and style, and is similar in its elements to Over, the chief difference being its having an axial west tower rather than an asymmetrically placed steeple. It does, however, possess a degree of individuality and heaviness which endows it with something of the High Victorian flavour apparent in the secular buildings just discussed but absent at Over. It is also more expensive, with greater use of Geometrical tracery and with ashlar interior and marble columns. Free-standing shafts again bifurcate the clerestorey openings, but inside instead of out, and large angel hood-mould stops punctuate the length of the nave. The expense lavished is further apparent in furnishings and fittings (such as the pulpit with marble inlay) and the extensive use of Maw encaustic tiles. The stalls are similar to those at Over. The most remarkable feature is the tower, which has a balustrade of pierced quatrefoils on a heavy corbel table and a south-west vice carried up as a high and prominent conical-roofed turret. Goodhart-Rendel considered the 'effect more baronial than ecclesiastical,'[18] and its eccentricity must have seemed all the greater before the present spire was added (c. 1872–6).

Contemporary with Aldford church is St. Bartholomew's, Sealand, Flintshire (1865–7). Here again the style is Early Decorated, and although it is a small church (there are no aisles) it is not impoverished (the interior is ashlar). Douglas himself paid for the stained glass of the east window. The exterior is rock-faced, but with an ashlar course providing a horizontal stripe. The most distinctive feature is the south-east tower, with heavy corbel table and short pyramid spire. Although the vice is not used to such spectacular effect as at Aldford, its lower stages have (and this occurs in other Douglas churches) some free sculptural emphasis, here internally as well as externally. Again there are angel hood-mould

Church of St John the Baptist, Aldford Cheshire, 1865–6; spire c. 1872–6.

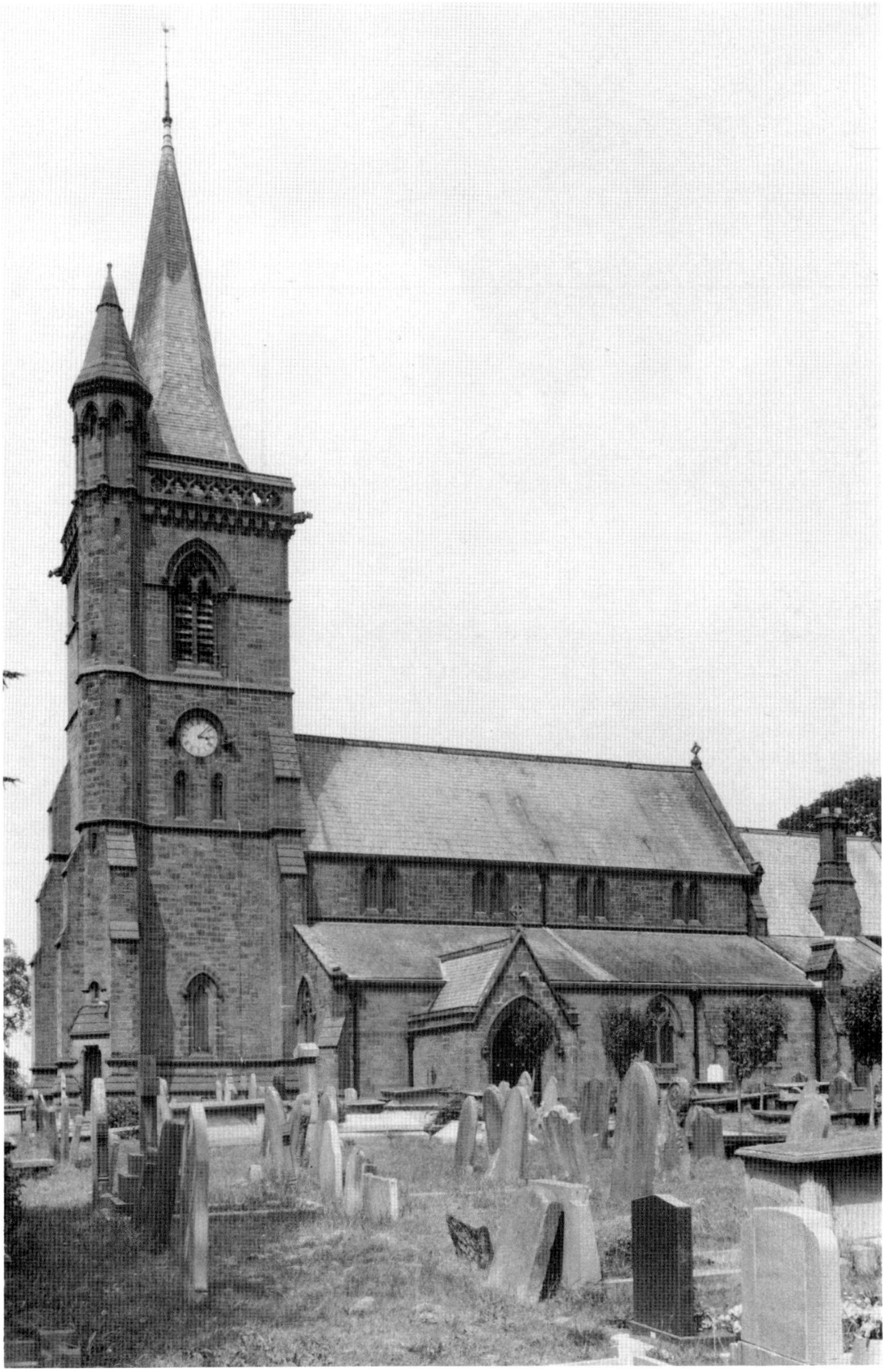

Oakmere Hall, Cheshire, 1867. (*Works*)

stops, and use is made of shafts, including free-standing shafts in the sedilia and a chancel window. The stalls display curved ends, conventionalised poppyheads, pierced patterns, and crosses in roundels. Roundels occur also in the font, and there is a single one (containing a flower pattern) in the tympanum over a small window in the tower.

The most ambitious building of Douglas's High Victorian period, and one of the largest houses which he ever designed, is Oakmere Hall (1867), quite near to Sandiway, built for John Higson, a Liverpool merchant. Although on a large scale, it can stylistically be related to the Warrington shop, Billy Hobby's Well and, to a lesser extent, the Sealand tower.

In considering the factors which shaped a High Victorian mansion such as Oakmere, the Ruskinian concept of mass and of the emotional significance of the roof form must be to the fore, and, echoing 'The Lamp of Power,' Scott, in his *Remarks*, considered 'Actual dimensions, and especially *height*,'[19] desirable for a dignified country house. In addition, and in addition to the contribution of continental Gothic, a usual element in High Victorian domestic architecture is the irregularity of massing, integral to the dramatic and inventive nature of the mode, but equally an expression of the logical concept of picturesque utility in planning. Expressed by Pugin as 'raising an elevation from *a convenient plan* into so many *picturesque beauties*,'[20] the concept of the building being an

High Victorianism

expression of functional arrangement was elaborated by Scott, who acknowledged the debt owed to Pugin for the idea, drew attention to the adaptability of Gothic as emphasised by Ruskin, and advocated 'A full development and bold, generous treatment both of the whole design and of its parts, according to the requirements.' Similarly, he wished 'each part to express as distinctly as possible its use and destination.'[21]

Scott himself dealt only briefly, if philosophically, with detailed social and planning aspects, but contemporaneously with the building of Oakmere the functional requirements of such a house were recorded in the three successive editions, 1864–71, of *The English Gentleman's House*, by Robert Kerr (1823–1904). Providing instruction, according to the sub-title, on 'How to plan English residences, from the parsonage to the palace', the treatise deals with the nature and needs of individual rooms and with principles of aspect, orientation and arrangement, with the segregation of family and servants seen as an over-riding objective. Presenting rules and recommendations for the accommodating of medium-sized and large Victorian households, the book remains a valuable social document.

An early example, indeed probably the prototype, of a particular plan form is provided by Waterhouse's Hinderton Hall, Cheshire, dated 1856 though not illustrated in *The Builder* until 1859.[22] Exhibiting principles expounded by Scott, it received fair commendation from Kerr.[23] The plan form, well suited to High Victorian expression, is that which Douglas adopted at Oakmere Hall, and as it reappears in other of his houses, it may conveniently be referred to as the Hinderton-Oakmere type. It consists of a *corps de logis* or main block containing reception rooms occupying a long garden front and returning along a shorter end. These enclose on two sides the entrance, hall and staircase, and the entrance elevation exploits the combination of porch, high staircase window and (as an optional extra and one which Douglas used in this position only at Oakmere) tower. Beyond the main block extends a service wing, usually prolonging the entrance front, and the dining room, at the end of the main block on the garden side, has direct service communication.

With this rigid plan form being to a certain extent adaptable for individual conditions of orientation, prospect and approach, at Oakmere Douglas gave southern and eastern aspects to the main rooms, in a setting of attractively landscaped grounds. The complicated requirements which the customs of the time demanded of a house of this size are well provided for, and the plan includes, for instance, a cloakroom near the main entrance and what would seem to have been a 'gentleman's room' or business room on the entrance front in easy communication with both entrance and service quarters. The service quarters themselves are neatly and

The Work of John Douglas

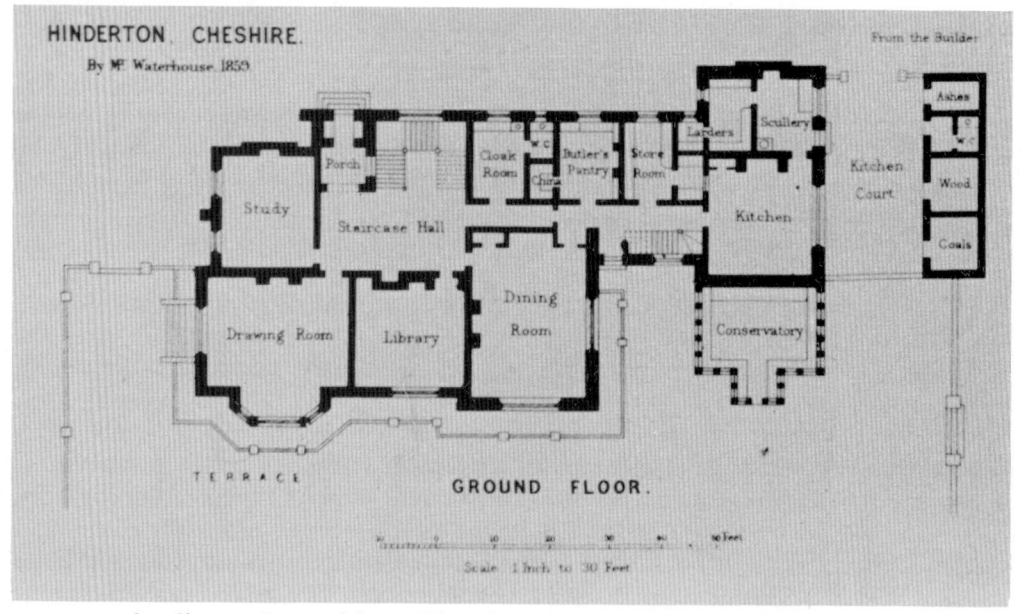

competently disposed on either side of a central spine corridor. There seems, however, to be some ambiguity regarding service to the dining room, though this may result from later alterations. Also, although traceried windows duly express the staircase on the entrance front, the hall which lies behind rises through two storeys and has gallery and rooflight. Interesting spatial effects result, though there is illogicality in introducing into this plan form a strong element of the central hall type.

The exterior is handled with gusto, and rock-faced masonry with ashlar dressings emphasises the lively and rugged drama, as does the random (though doubtless carefully considered) arrangement of many of the windows. At the end of the service block on the garden side rises a high tower, its steep roof recessed behind a parapet, and at the junction of main and service blocks on the entrance front is a smaller tower, also with recessed roof, and with tourelles, above a *porte-cochère*. The main roofs are also recessed, that of the main block neatly hipped, and at the two corners of the main block are round turrets, their conical roofs again recessed behind parapets. There are hipped dormers, and a number of miniature gabled dormers, and the stone carving includes, in tympana, the familiar roundels. The circular turrets at first suggest French inspiration, but the miniature dormers (previously hinted at at Vale Royal) and the steep hipped roofs (seen at Vale Royal and in the North Italian context of the Warrington shop) must be regarded as manifestations of the Germanic influence which became more strongly and overtly apparent in Douglas's work in later years.

The long entrance and garden fronts are not completely successful

Plan of Hinderton Hall, Cheshire, by Alfred Waterhouse, 1856. (*The English Gentleman's House*, Robert Kerr, 3rd edition, 1871, p. 443 from *Builder*, 17, 1859, p. 42–3)

High Victorianism

**OAKMERE HALL
GROUND FLOOR PLAN**

a PORTE COCHÈRE
b ENTRANCE HALL
c CLOAKROOM
d STAIRCASE HALL
e ⎫
e ⎬ DRAWING ROOMS
e ⎭
f DINING ROOM
g GARDEN ENTRANCE
h GENTLEMAN'S ROOM
i SERVICE WING
j BILLIARD ROOM OVER

Ground floor plan of Oakmere Hall, Cheshire, as in 1990. (Neil Pike Architecture)

as coherent and balanced elevations, though they are admirable in their individual groups and parts, and the house can be seen as a key building in Douglas's development. It is the largest commission which he had up until that time received, and in its turrets and steep roofs and its miniature dormers clearly marks not only his propensity for verticality and dramatic skylines, but also the emergence of a consistent and personal interpretation of Gothic along these lines.

With Oakmere Hall being of such significance within Douglas's *oeuvre* and with it in any case being so notable an example of a High Victorian country house, it is all the more regrettable that its interior should have undergone drastic alteration in an all too thorough de-Victorianisation, presumably early in the twentieth century. No original woodwork or chimneypieces seem to survive in the principal ground floor rooms; the hall has been remodelled, and even the staircase, though at first sight reliable, has also probably been interfered with. Of original features which do remain, the respective ceilings of the dining room and two drawing rooms are instructive. The former is Gothic in character, with heavy beams, doubtless originally dark, whereas those in the drawing rooms have lighter though still elaborate treatment with plaster cornices and centre roses. Such imparting of contrasting character was advocated by Kerr, who considered that a dining room should be in 'conformity with the substantial pretensions of English character and English fare. . . .the whole appearance of the room ought to be that of masculine importance.'[24] The drawing room on the other hand should possess 'lightness as opposed to massiveness,' and 'be comparatively delicate . . . entirely *ladylike*. The comparison of Dining-room and Drawing-room, therefore, is in almost every way one of contrast.[25] Douglas continued to observe such differentiation in the fitting up of domestic interiors.

An unexecuted design – probably a competition entry – for Whitchurch Town Hall, Shropshire (undated) was also High Victorian, and happens to be similar in its massing to the garden front of the main block at Oakmere. Also, it had arcaded windows with circular shafts, and polychromy in the form of occasional courses of contrastingly dark stone. It moreover had a steep hipped roof (again recessed behind a parapet) and miniature dormers, and the development of Douglas's interest in distinctive roof forms and skylines along Germanic lines is shown at St. Paul's church, Helsby, Cheshire (1868–70). Here there is a western bell turret in the form of a flèche. It is broached, and its profile is broken at the base by tiered articulation in two stages, and it has what may conveniently be described as 'slit' dormers – apertures covered by a flap of roof of slightly shallower pitch than that of the surroundings. There is a

St Paul's Church, Helsby, Cheshire, 1868–70. (*Building News*, 25, 1873, p. 194)

St Ann's Church, Warrington, Cheshire, 1868–9. Exterior. (*Building News*, 17, 1869, pp. 28–9. Drawings by J. H. Metcalfe)

certain High Victorian, and perhaps something of a French, feel about the body of the church, which has lancets, plate tracery and a polygonal apse. Except for the belfry, however, the church is conventional, and illustrates the general conservatism of Douglas's ecclesiastical design, within which High Victorian traits are limited, and which are less adventurous than much of his contemporary secular work.

The great and remarkable exception to this generalisation is St Ann's church, Warrington (1868–9). Quite startlingly bold and

The Work of John Douglas

original, this constitutes a prodigy church in Douglas's output. The nave is broad, high and aisleless, and is spanned by an arch-braced roof, though the chancel and a semi-circular apse are rib-vaulted in stone and brick. The nave walls are in effect panels between buttresses which project both inside (where arches span between them) and out. There is hardly any masonry, brick being used almost exclusively, and with mouldings, blank arcading and even plate tracery built up in brick. Externally, there are lofty buttresses to nave, apse and (perhaps with less structural justification) the outer corners of the south-east tower. As at Aldford, the tower has a corbel table and conical-roofed vice turret, and there is a recessed spire, or steep hipped roof, which, like the Helsby belfry, has tiered breaks at its base. There is a sense of magnitude and solidity – in fact the High Victorian attribute of massiveness. The apse would seem to owe much both to French precedent and perhaps also to the influence of G. E. Street. However, it may be noted that a local writer, presumably prompted by the un-English use of brickwork and the outline of the spire, commented of the building, significantly if not altogether accurately, that, 'Its design and appearance remind the spectator of the quaint churches seen on the banks of the Rhine.'[26]

In his *Church Design for Congregations*, James Cubitt observed that, 'A not unfavourable specimen of recent aisleless churches with wooden roofs is St Anne's [sic] Warrington by Mr John Douglas. Its buttresses are partly internal, though their chief projection is outside. The detail is bold and simple but,' and here follows quite unjustified criticism, 'scarcely atones for the lowness of the proportions, and the awkwardness of the general form.'[27]

Among other of Douglas's buildings of the late 1860s, a number incorporate half-timber. Although these obviously relate to the Grosvenor Park entrance lodge, they also belong to a stream of development which reached fruition in the 1870s and which can be seen as a reaction to High Victorianism. Mention will thus be made of them in a later chapter, within the context of Douglas's early maturity and the Vernacular Revival. The last of his secular buildings of the 1860s not to display the influence of these trends are Witton Grammar School, Northwich, Cheshire (1869, later altered and enlarged, and a very minor work), and the pair of houses (Nos. 31 & 33) Dee Banks, Chester (1869), which he built for himself and in one of which he lived for so many years.

Though sharing something of the quality of massiveness, and quite imposing on their prominent site above the River Dee, these houses are internally quite modest in their scale and their fittings. A detail worth noting is the garden railings, which, set on a wall, had widely-spaced uprights with forked bases – a feature which reappeared in work of the 1870s. Of the houses themselves, the features most characteristic of Douglas are the porches, though these

St Ann's. Interior (see p. 55)

THE BUILDING NEWS, JULY 9TH 1869

ST ANNE'S CHURCH

WARRINGTON
JOHN DOUGLAS
ARCHITECT

The Work of John Douglas

are probably later additions, and the block is otherwise of brick, with large sash windows and some polychromy, stone dressings and Gothic detailing. It is unassumingly High Victorian, and the only evidence of the new spirit which was abroad, and which was already apparent in Douglas's work elsewhere, is in the form of ribbed brick chimneystacks redolent of the seventeenth century and English vernacular traditions. The pair of houses must be regarded as Douglas's last High Victorian work, and that one of them must, from the first, have been destined for his own occupation, suggests quite a strong belief in, and commitment to, the Gothic cause at a time of aesthetic transition and uncertainty. If 1870 can be considered as the turning point between the Mid and Late Victorian eras, it can, in terms of Douglas's work, be seen even more clearly as the point of transition from his High Victorian phase to a period of early maturity.

In the 1870s, it was in work for the third Marquess (later Duke) of Westminster that Douglas's newly-developed maturity found greatest opportunity for expression. Some consideration may thus now appropriately be given to the great estate which Douglas so worthily improved and adorned, and to the great nobleman who for thirty years remained his principal patron.

VI Principal Patron

The Cheshire family of Grosvenor traces its ancestry to Gilbert le Grosveneur, nephew of Hugh Lupus, the Norman Earl of Chester and himself a nephew of the Conqueror. The manor of Eaton was acquired by marriage in the fifteenth century, and the first house on the present site was that built in 1673–85 for Sir Thomas Grosvenor, third baronet, with William Samwell as his architect. 'It was as a result of Sir Thomas's marriage to the heiress of the manor of Ebury that the family acquired its London property which, with the developing of Mayfair and Belgravia, was to bring fabulous wealth to subsequent generations. The seventh baronet was created Baron Grosvenor in 1761, and Viscount Belgrave and Earl Grosvenor in 1784. He was in 1802 succeeded by his son, who in 1831 became first Marquess of Westminster and who employed William Porden to rebuild the house, *c.* 1803–12. Porden was assisted by Benjamin Gummow, and in 1823–5 wings were added by Gummow. The result was the spectacular Gothic mansion which, with its delicate battlements, pinnacles, iron tracery and plaster fan-vaults, remains recorded in Buckler's illustrations. A heavy-handed attempt to convert this into something more acceptable to the next generation was made in 1845–54 by William Burn for the second Marquess (succeeded 1845), and the house in this state of compromise has sometimes been misleadingly illustrated (e.g. by Eastlake) as being by Porden.'[1]

The second Marquess of Westminster (1795–1869) was of austere character and unswerving devotion to duty as family man, politician and landlord.[2] Of parsimonious disposition, he nevertheless displayed liberality in so far as it was incumbent upon him to do so in discharging the responsibilities of his station. He gave close and conscientious personal attention to the administration and improvement of his estates, including his London property, where the development of the southern portion of the Grosvenor land, initiated in the time of the first Marquess, continued, with Thomas Cubitt as lessee in Pimlico. The Marquess's Cheshire estate, in addition to that of Eaton itself, included property in Chester. Strong ties of politics and patronage linked the family and the city, and although it was not uncommon for a great family and a great estate to dominate a set of villages or even a market town, the close association which existed (and to some extent still exists) between the Grosvenors and so large a place as Chester is exceptional.

William Burn (1789–1870), besides altering Eaton for the Marquess, designed Fonthill House for him, on his Wiltshire estate, contributing a Scottish baronial mansion to the complicated story of

The Work of John Douglas

successive buildings on Beckford's domain. On the Eaton estate, the Chester architect Edward Hodkinson (d. 1909) rebuilt Saighton Grange,[3] retaining its mediaeval gatehouse, and as a parallel to Burn's superficial Victorianisation of the Hall, carried out a similar process at Porden's Eccleston church.[4] As already noted, T. M. Penson was also employed and, after his death, Douglas was responsible for Aldford church (1865–6) (see page 000) and buildings at Grosvenor Park, Chester (1865–7). It may be added that the Grosvenor Arms, Aldford, though in its present form representing a Douglas & Fordham remodelling (1891–3), incorporates a datestone of 1867, and work may perhaps have been done there by Douglas at that time. The designer of the Marquess's village improvements has not been identified, though attribution could be made to Hodkinson or Penson. They include farms, schools and numerous cottages, many of them bearing dates of the 1850s and '60s. In a recognisable and uniform style, they provide a good example of extensive model estate building on the part of a benevolent landlord, but are completely overshadowed by the quantity and quality of work undertaken in the next generation. At Eaton Hall itself, in Chester, and throughout more than a dozen villages and hamlets on his vast Eaton estate, the architectural endeavours of the first Duke of Westminster were among the most extensive and admirable of all instances of Victorian aristocratic patronage. Moreover, there can surely have been few cases in the history of architecture in which a designer has executed for a private patron more works than John Douglas undertook for the Duke.

Hugh Lupus Grosvenor (1825–99) succeeded his father as third Marquess in 1869, was created Knight of the Garter in 1870 and Duke of Westminster in 1874. Devout churchman, philanthropist, politician, model landlord, enlightened patron and devotee of the turf (he bred and owned two winners of the Triple Crown), the picture presented is that of the *beau idéal* of a great Victorian nobleman, and it is difficult not to endorse the eulogistic terms in which his life and character have been extolled. Possessing seriousness and a stern devotion to duty to no less an extent than did his father, these qualities were tempered by humanitarianism, personal charm, and the ability to enjoy himself. *The Times* in its obituary noted that, 'He could pass from a racecourse to take the chair at a missionary meeting without incurring the censure of the strictest. The Nonconformist conscience, which was so much disturbed by Lord Rosebery's racing successes, never, so far as we know, resented those of the Duke of Westminster. . . . His piety was so sincere, his active benevolence so great, his sympathy with all branches of philanthropic endeavour so genuine, that criticism was disarmed.'[5] George Wyndham described the Duke not only as, 'that kind heart and chivalrous gentleman,' but also as, 'the nicest man I

Principal Patron

have ever known,' and, as Mark Girouard commented when quoting him, Wyndham was no fool.[6]

Like his father and grandfather before him, the Duke (as third Marquess) initiated alterations to Eaton Hall immediately on inheriting it. He found it in the state of compromise wrought by Burn, but, 'There was no suggestion of compromise in the transformation effected by Alfred Waterhouse in 1870–83, at a cost of £600,000. . . . The work of encasing, rebuilding and extending was carried out in a style which, though owing something to the C13 and something to France, was an outstanding expression of High Victorian originality. This Wagnerian palace was the most ambitious instance of Gothic Revival domestic architecture anywhere in the country, and to approach the W . . . front . . . up the 1¾m. length of the Belgrave Avenue was an unforgettably dramatic experience.'[7]

The year 1874 saw not only the conferring of the Dukedom, but also the coming of age of Lord Grosvenor, the Duke's eldest son, and the event was celebrated in a way consistent with the scale and magnificence of Eaton and with the Duke's status as a great landed magnate and the richest man in England. Five-thousand people were entertained in the grounds; for five days Chester was *en fête*, and the heir's birthday itself was observed as a public holiday in the city and for miles around. Yet the state and splendour which over the years was maintained at Eaton and in London at Grosvenor House arose not so much from personal inclination as from a sense of duty that the dignity, obligations and significance of his rank should be adequately sustained. Conscientiously discharging the responsibilities which the Duke saw as a necessary accompaniment of privilege, the public offices which he accepted included the Lord Lieutenancies of Cheshire and (following the creation of the L.C.C. in 1888) of London; Grosvenor House was the centre of philanthropic enterprise on a colossal scale, though it was perhaps in Chester that his generosity was most consistently felt.

The park at Eaton was open to the public, and a concern for the well-being and recreation of the working classes was displayed in many of the social and moral causes (by no means all of a conventional or predictable nature) which he espoused both in and outside Parliament. Although never accepting ministerial office, he continued the tradition of political service of a great Whig family, and was active in Parliament throughout his adult life, having represented Chester in the Commons, as Earl Grosvenor, before taking his seat in the Lords. Despite being a leading 'Adullamite' at the time of the abortive 1866 Reform Bill, he and Gladstone remained political allies besides being neighbours in the country – Hawarden across the Flintshire border being virtually contiguous with the Eaton estate. Almost alone among the aristocracy, the Duke supported Gladstone's passionate anti-Turkish campaign at the time

The Work of John Douglas

of the Bulgarian Atrocities in 1876. A breach came in 1886, however, over the issue of Irish Home Rule, with the Duke among those instrumental in precipitating the parting of the ways for the Liberal party and the ancient Whig families. Characteristically, the personal friendship of the two men was renewed as a result of the sense of outrage which they shared over the Armenian massacres of 1894–5. In 1898, the year of the death of the statesman, the Duke became Chairman of the Gladstone Memorial Fund, and less than three months before his own death in 1899 he laid the foundation stone of St. Deiniol's Library – the Gladstone Memorial Library at Hawarden, designed by Douglas & Minshull (1899–1902 and 1904–1906).

Of the Duke's Cheshire building projects, a few individual jobs were, in addition to Eaton Hall itself, entrusted to London architects.[8] St. John's School, Chester, is by E. R. Robson (1836–1917);[9] F. B. Wade and R. W. Edis (1839–1927), both of whom worked on the London Grosvenor estate, were responsible respectively for the church of St. Mary-without-the-Walls, Handbridge, Chester,[10] and the Overleigh Lodge at Eaton;[11] and towards the end of his life the Duke turned to the youthful Lutyens for garden designs[12] and to G. F. Bodley (1827–1907) for the superb church at Eccleston.[13] In general, however, the estate buildings were the work of Chester architects. Some were designed by Lockwood, and some by erstwhile pupils and assistants of Douglas. It was, however, to Douglas himself (whose humble Swindley relatives remained domiciled on the estate at Eccleston Smithy during the greater part of the time he served his noble patron) that the vast majority of the buildings were entrusted.

With the Duke exercising close personal interest in his London, Flintshire and Cheshire estates, it is characteristic that at or about the same time that Waterhouse was instructed to remodel Eaton Hall, Douglas received his first commission for estate buildings. This initial group included fifteen separate items, and although construction seems to have spanned from 1870 to 1872, Douglas's original account covers the years 1869–72[14] and suggests that he was first consulted immediately after the third Marquess entered his inheritance. The future Duke was similarly prompt in putting in hand the revival of the Eaton Stud, and although over the years various works were carried out by Douglas in connection with this, and although the Duke was ready to commence breeding and racing by 1875,[15] an ambitious scheme of 1870 by Douglas for a completely new Stud and Stud Groom's House was, curiously enough, never executed.

There was, however, no abatement in the mighty flood of estate building, rebuilding and improvement which flowed throughout the rest of the Duke's life. Not only did it include model farms and

Central Gateway, Eaton Hall Stud, Cheshire, 1870. (Drawing at Eaton Estate Office)

cottages, but also schools and reading rooms, the building and restoration of churches and, in Chester, urban cottages and tenements as well as commercial premises. All this was pursued oblivious of the agricultural depression of the last quarter of the nineteenth century which wrought such havoc elsewhere. Pastoral farming was, in any case, less affected by the depression than arable, and the dairy-farming county of Cheshire, with its ready market of neighbouring commercial and industrial centres, suffered less than any other. Even though rents were nevertheless reduced on the Eaton estate in the mid 1880s,[16] the Duke of Westminster was exceptional among landowners in continuing ambitious schemes of improvement, and in the 1890s, while over much of the country the depression entered its second devastating stage, the flood of building at Eaton became a torrent. The economics of this and the evidence of the relevant estate archives would be worthy of investigation, but it would seem likely that the creating of larger farms with increased accommodation for stock rendered them more economically viable, and it should not be assumed that the improvements were subsidised from the Duke's steady urban rents.[17]

It has been stated that the results of the Duke's activities included 48 farmhouses, 360 cottages, 11 lodges, 8 schools and school houses and 7 institutions and village halls.[18] This number of cottages seems impossibly high, and, correlating the extensive though not thoroughly comprehensive estate archives with the evidence provided by existing buildings, the following would seem to be a more accurate list of new buildings and major remodellings and enlargements, for most of which Douglas was architect: Four churches and chapels, 8 parsonages and large houses, *c.* 15 schools and institutions, *c.* 50 farms either in whole or part, *c.* 300 cottages, lodges, smithies, gamekeepers' houses etc., 2 factories, 2 inns and *c.* 12 commercial buildings. These figures relate only to the Eaton

The Work of John Douglas

estate and to Chester, and do not include the Flintshire Halkyn estate, with its leadmines, where a church was built. Neither do they include restorations or minor alterations, and they are in addition to all that was accomplished in the time of the second Marquess.

The continuous building programme was but one facet of a system of efficient estate management in which progressive agricultural policies were pursued. The latest methods were employed on the home farm (Woodhouse Farm at Aldford, with its farm buildings attributable to Douglas); tenant farmers were encouraged to do likewise, and the Aldford and Balderton cheese factories (1874–5) were among the first twenty or so to be established in Britain, following the importation of the idea from America in 1870 as an alternative to the system of farmhouse cheese-making.[19] Eaton Hall had its own gas supply (with a gas-works designed by Waterhouse) and an early electric lighting installation. In addition, the village of Eccleston was also supplied with gas (Gas Works Cottage, 1897, being by Douglas & Fordham) and in 1895–6 the estate acquired its own railway system, with a miniature goods railway linking the G. W. R. sidings at Balderton with Eaton Hall and the estate works department.[20]

Besides their quantity and their functional utility, the architectural achievements of Douglas and the Duke are characterised by attractiveness and ambition well beyond the unassuming neatness with which much model estate building is endowed. Writing in *The British Architect* in 1881, Raffles Davison referred to, 'that happy union of wealth and artistic skill which would make many a fine estate one great picture without a blot from end to end,' and continued, 'Towards the knowing how fine a thing such may be, a visit to the Eaton Park and estate, near Chester, may be some help, for two generations of noble owners have there been adding points of interest and beauty to the landscape in a princely manner, in many a picturesque lodge, farmhouse, and village church and school, to say nothing of Eaton Hall itself.'[21] Later, the same journal, in an item on 'The Duke of Westminster as a Patron of Architecture,' commented that, 'the buildings erected on the Eaton Estate in way of lodges, farmhouses, cottages, etc. were so admirable in design and execution that the whole Eaton Estate is a model of its kind and full of interest to the architect from the great palace itself and its gorgeous chapel, erected by Mr. Alfred Waterhouse, R.A., down to the tiniest cottage designed by Mr. John Douglas.'[22]

Yet the very perfection of such an estate can cloy. The visual charm of the buildings and villages at Eaton is such as to override such danger, but there remains an oppressive quality in the immaculateness of Aldford, Eccleston or Saighton, providing a reminder that being subject to the enlightenment and benevolence of a model Victorian landlord meant being subject to his paternalism.

Principal Patron

Villagers may have been free from the horrors of rural slums (which, however picturesque the hovels might have been externally, could rival their more publicised industrial counterparts in terms of squalor), but farmers and labourers alike would find the Duke and his agent as concerned about their morals as about their rents or their drains.

There can be no doubt that the Duke took a personal interest in his tenantry, and was fully conversant not only with broad questions of policy, but with all details of estate management and building work. The only letter from Douglas to the Duke which has come to light takes the form of a detailed report of some 700 words, prepared in 1878 in response to instructions from the Duke, on progress made at Wrexham Road Farm, Eccleston (see page 94). Dating from 1877–84, this was the first entirely new farm, comprising both house and farm buildings, which Douglas built for the estate. Besides giving details of the state of advancement of the farm buildings, Douglas compared them with, and referred to having visited, a farm at Tattenhall – presumably Tattenhall Hall Farm, with its buildings designed by James Harrison. He also reported that, 'I have at Your Grace's request studied plans by John Birch for a farmstead at Grafton, Cheshire, for Lord Stanley' – doubtless that known as The Wetreins – and that as a result he had made certain alterations to the plans, including those of the farmhouse scullery and cheeseroom. He added, perhaps somewhat ruefully, 'All this I have done in accordance with Your Grace's wish to achieve a layout similar to Grafton. While the massing of the building seems now less satisfactory than in its original form, I am confident that the plan must now meet with your approval.'[23] During the prosperous years of high farming of the third quarter of the century which preceded the disastrous years of the fourth, numerous books on the design and construction of farms appeared. One of the soundest and most comprehensive was J. B. Denton's *The Farm Homesteads of England*, in which both the Tattenhall and Grafton farms were illustrated.[24] The latter appeared also in one of Birch's own publications in 1874.[25] and it was perhaps this, rather than the building itself, to which the Duke drew Douglas's attention.

Drawings for an unexecuted scheme by Douglas for Aldford Hall Farm show the Duke's concern for aesthetic as well as practical matters. A set of drawings dated 30th and 31st July 1876 carry many pencilled notes, sketches and amendments by him. In particular, an elevation is annotated, 'string courses bolder/ red *stone* up to lower windows/ 3 small windows closer together/ gables rather more important/ W.' Sketches were made to these effects, including a set of Dutch gables being made larger. The amendments, as drawn out in a new set of plans and elevations in Douglas's office on 8th August, were undeniable improvements, and apparently met with approval, the only pencilled addition to the set being the initial 'W.'[26]

SOUTH ELEVATION

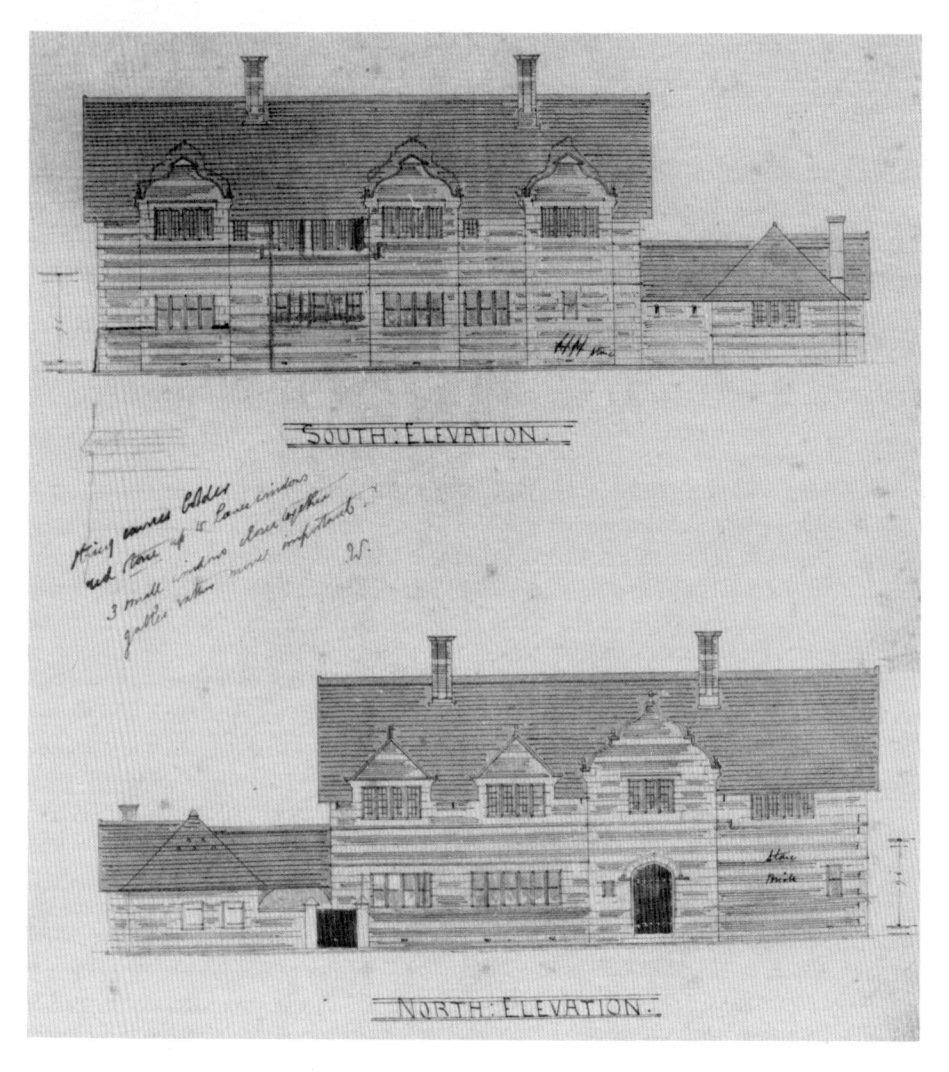

NORTH ELEVATION

South Elevation

Principal Patron

Elevations, Aldford Hall Farm, Cheshire, with annotations by the Duke of Westminster, 30th/31st July 1876. (Drawing at Eaton Estate Office)

Close and active attention is similarly apparent in letters sent to Douglas by the agent. Typical of many such comments are, 'The Duke does not like the ornamental brickwork, so it had better be plain,'[27] or, 'His Grace *does* object to slates for the covered yards,'[28] or, 'His Grace has made several alterations which kindly notice,'[29] or again, 'you will perceive that His Grace has approved of Plan A with some slight alterations,'[30] and, 'The pencil notes on the *house* plan are His Graces.'[31]

It is not known to what extent or with what degree of regularity there were direct communications or personal meetings between Douglas and the Duke. The Wrexham Road letter is an isolated survival, and although there exist references to meetings and appointments, Douglas's dealings seem for the most part to have been with the estate office, the agent acting as intermediary between him and the Duke. The post of land agent was held successively by Samuel Beckett and the Honourable Cecil T. Parker.

Cecil Thomas Parker (1845–1931) was the second son of the sixth Earl of Macclesfield, a nephew of the Duke of Westminster himself, and son-in-law of the Archbishop of Canterbury, and he served as agent to the first and second Dukes from 1881 until his retirement in 1911.[32] He was a strict and meticulous estate manager; the first Duke considered him to incline to harshness and would intervene in favour of leniency;[33] village children would curtsey as he rode by on his white horse,[34] and he emerges from the pages of the estate office letter books as a most formidable figure. Together with the ledgers, rentals and other documents, the letter books (with the letters written by Parker or on his behalf by members of the office staff) provide a fascinating and historically important record of the day-to-day running of the estate and the Duke's affairs. The hundreds of letters which over the years were sent successively to John Douglas, Douglas & Fordham and Douglas & Minshull, merely supplemented what must have been innumerable regular meetings between Parker and Douglas and members of the Abbey Square staff, and thus do not form a complete record of communication. They nevertheless cast light on building work, on procedure and on personalities.

Amended elevation, Aldford Hall Farm, Cheshire, 8th August 1876. (Drawing at Eaton Estate Office)

They indicate, for instance, that despite the lavish building programme, expenditure was carefully controlled and value for money was demanded. At Eccleston Smithy (being rebuilt 1896–8 when no longer tenanted by the Swindleys), Parker, 'was just in time to stop the men laying a 4″ drain to the shed where the horses are shod – This would have been a *wilful waste of money* & should never have been ordered or even contemplated.'[35] The cutting down of estimates was a regular procedure. Of Churton Heath Lodge, Bruera (1891–2), Parker wrote, 'I have received the tenders for the above; the lowest is about 200£ too much. You had better revise the quantities and specifications & get fresh tenders by Monday next.'[36]

Or again, of Broad Hey Farm, Lower Kinnerton, (1892–3), 'The Kinnerton Farm estimates came out as the Poulton one did much too high nearly $^1/_3$ too much./ Some curtailment must be made the cost should not exceed £2300.'[37]

Typewriting began to replace hand-written letters in the 1890s, and that the running of the estate office was on modern lines is indicated when, as early as 1892, Parker commented, 'I wish you were on the Telephone Exchange!'[38]

Eccleston Hill (1881–2), a large house, virtually a mansion, was designed by Douglas for the occupation of the Duke's secretary, then Colonel David Scotland. Scotland had previously resided at The Elms, Pulford, remodelled by Douglas (1871), and Eccleston Hill was altered (1892–4) for his successor, Arthur Lawley. Similarly, another house of considerable size was built nearby, as the agent's residence with estate office adjoining, for Cecil Parker. This was The Paddocks (1882–3).

All Parker's letters to Douglas relating to The Paddocks are given in Appendix I. They are cold and imperious in tone, and although Parker seems never to have been a particularly effusive correspondent, his attitude to Douglas was markedly deficient in courtesy, and suggests not only coldness but actual hostility. On first taking up his post, when Douglas had already been established in the Duke's favour for some twelve years, he wrote in terms of 'Dear Sir . . . Yours Faithfully.' Before long this developed to 'Dear Mr. Douglas. . . . Yours Truly,' but this degree of informality (which is embodied in the Paddocks correspondence) was short-lived, for he soon reverted to 'Dear Sir' and, after the formation of the Douglas & Fordham partnership, 'Dear Sirs.' Throughout the entire correspondence from 1881 until 1909 when (two years before

The Paddocks, Eccleston, Cheshire 1882–3. (*Building News*, 45, 1883, p. 288. Drawing by E Hodkinson)

Principal Patron

Douglas's death and Parker's retirement) the last letter was written, there is not one word of satisfaction or praise, and whenever comment or opinion was expressed, it was in order to complain. Departures from the routine and the factual in the letters take the form of protests over alleged or implied negligence, excessive costs, or delay in sending in drainage plans of completed buildings and accounts. Whether due to inefficiency within his office, or to Douglas's own lack of business-sense, this grievance at least seems to have been justified. A particular source of irritation was Parker's Buildings, Foregate Street, Chester (1888–9), a block of tenements in connection with which Parker complained of poor construction and materials and delay in rectifying the results. 'Smoky chimnies are an intolerable nuisance & I know His Grace would be very much displeased if he knew that no attempt had been made to overcome the nuisance,'[39] he wrote, and again, 'I am *much vexed* to find the work executed here far from satisfactory.'[40]

It may be significant that when obliged to convey approbation, Parker once resorted to the use of inverted commas. 'The Duke thinks that the plan sent herewith seems to be "an exceptionally good one". Please proceed with the necessary work in order to get tenders from builders without delay.'[41] No such refinement was employed in another letter which consisted of one sentence only: 'I have submitted your sketch to the Duke who, you will be sorry to hear, does not at all approve of it.'[42]

The rather less than gracious terms in which the Duke's views were transmitted include a letter on the subject of the iron gates (executed by Douglas's cousin James Swindley) at the Eccleston Lodge of Eaton Hall (1893–4) (see page 162). 'You had better not give any orders about the painting of the Gates. . . . the Duke gave the order himself to have them painted white; has seen them several times, & likes them. It would take a bold man to give any order now, in opposition to his Grace.'[43] It may be surmised that Douglas wanted them black, which would have looked better, but white they remain to this day. Or again, 'I am desired by His Grace to write to you & *strongly protest* against the *absurd* system which you have of over windowing all the plans of cottages & houses wh. you send for his approval. For the past 13 plans in every plan that has been submitted; His Grace has cut out several lights & this has become monotonous. . . .'[44]

Illustrating also the attention to detail exercised by the Duke is a letter relating to the Eaton Hall Gardeners' Bothy (1893–4): 'I find that a great amount of work has been put into this building without either His Grace's sanction, or my knowledge. I am desired to say that this does not meet with His Graces approval. No detail has been furnished of the interior work, and provision has been made for lining the sides of the passage without ever consulting the Duke's

Gardeners' Bothy, Eaton Hall, Cheshi[re] 1893–4. (*British Architect*, 69, 1908, 206)

wishes on the subject. I must ask you at once to furnish me with all details of interior work which you propose to put in the above in order that they may have His Graces sanction. A wood block floor is to be laid in the lower passage. Tiles of a chocolate or buff colour must now be put *on* the walls, but a sample tile must first be placed in order that His Grace may decide which he prefers; there is to be no Scrafito work in the Gables.'[45]

All this, however, is but one side of the picture, and indeed only one side of the correspondence. It also tells nothing of whatever direct dealings Douglas may have had with the Duke or his successive secretaries. So steady a stream of dissatisfaction inevitably suggests deficiencies or incompetence on the part of Douglas. He must, however, be exonerated from such charges, not only on the evidence of the brilliantly-designed and soundly-constructed buildings which still remain to be used and admired, but also on account of the high regard in which he was held by the Duke. The Duke of Westminster, for whom almost every architect in England would have been glad to work, would not over a period of 30 years have given such steady and extensive employment to one in whom he did not have confidence, and of whose abilities he could have been in doubt.

With the respective roles of Douglas and Parker necessitating prolonged and close association between them, the existence of any personal animosity must have made the situation difficult for them both. The degree of animosity on Parker's side is suggested by the fact that after almost 20 years of collaboration, he should have written, not to the firm but to Douglas personally, in such terms as these: 'With reference to our conversation this morning I beg to enclose you the Account for Dodleston Cottages showing the items about which I complained marked in blue pencil. I also complain of the charges throughout for the extra works.'[46] That forms the complete text of the letter, and in the next he stated, 'I am obliged for your letter which I regret to say does not satisfy me. . . .The extras are all charged as the *very highest price*. I decline to pay £15 for the dry rubble stone walls to sides of paths 4s/6d is an outrageous price 2s/6d is the utmost it is worth & the £9:6:0 must be erased from the bill for "coping set in cement. . . ."'[47]

This was in 1900, after the first Duke had died. At the time of his death in December 1899, the new church at Eccleston was still under construction, and this is what Parker then wrote to its architect:

29th Decr. 1899

Dear Mr Bodley,

Eccleston Church,

I am desired by the Executors of the late Duke of Westminster to write to you and ask you to be good enough to let me know what sums will be required to complete the above; also to say that no fresh work is to be put in which was not sanctioned by the late Duke.

I understand that you are preparing drawings for the cutting down of the four windows on the North side and for making a new one on the South near the Entrance porch.

I presume you are considering the question of gas lighting?

Yours very truly
Cecil T. Parker

P.S. If any additions or alterations beyond the windows are considered necessary, the consent of the Trustees must first be obtained.[48]

Douglas, who, as the already-quoted note to Mrs. Williams suggests, was personally afflicted by the death of the Duke, received something rather different in tone to mark the end of his 30 years of service:

29th Decr. 1899

Dear Sirs,

It is no use going on with any plans or specifications for buildings contemplated by the late Duke of Westminster, as no works can now be carried out for which estimates have not been accepted by His Grace.

Yours Faithfully
Cecil T. Parker

Messrs Douglas & Minshull[49]

Most of the estate building work was put out to competitive tender, with a small circle of local builders being habitually employed. Some work was done by Douglas's brother-in-law Richard Beckett, but being dilatory in the execution of the shop at Saighton (1882–3) he incurred the wrath of Parker[50] and was never

The Work of John Douglas

St Mary's Church, Pulford, Cheshire, 1881–4.

heard of again. The estate building ledgers, as well as references in the letter books, show that others employed were Thomas Hughes of Aldford (up until the late 1880s), George Parker (whose business at Eccleston and Chester was carried on from c. 1890 by his sons as Parker Bros.),[51] Peter Edwards of Dodleston (from the late '80s onwards) and, in the '90s, W. W. Freeman of Chester. It is interesting to note the standard and size of work which these local firms were capable of. The Paddocks, with brickwork, masonry and joinery of considerable elaboration and quality, was built by Thomas Hughes, and Parker Bros. were the contractors for St. Deiniol's Library, Hawarden. The Duke would direct which builders were to be invited to tender, and only occasionally was departure made from this small group for external contracts, though building was also done directly, through the estate works department at The Cuckoo's Nest, Pulford. The estate's own staff were in fact responsible for the timberwork (the actual woodcarving being by Edward Griffiths of Chester) at Douglas's church at Pulford (1881–4), though George Parker contracted for the masonry.

Jobs carried out by the works department do not appear in the building ledgers (which in any case are rendered not wholly reliable by curious gaps and omissions). Certain of the buildings which are not documented by references to builders or architects are of inferior standards of design. Including a farm at Pulford and some cottages at Handbridge, Chester, it may be inferred that these which (unlike other undocumented works such as Guy Lane Farm, Waverton) cannot on stylistic grounds be attributed to Douglas, were designed without benefit of architect in the estate office or works department and executed by the latter.

A dispute arose in the 1890s concerning responsibility for cottages. Three almost identical pairs by Douglas & Fordham were built, 1887–8, at Balderton (immediately south of Cheese Factory), Belgrave (¼ mile north of Belgrave Lodge on west side of Wrexham Road) and Eccleston (Wrexham Road Cottages), and a further near-identical set of three, to a different Douglas & Fordham design, seems to have been built, 1889–91, at Aldford (south of Grosvenor Arms), Pulford (at north end of village on east side of Wrexham Road) and Waverton (southernmost of two blocks north of church on east side of village street) (see pages 163–4). Although the two types were built of similar plan, comprising the three bedrooms, living room and scullery, with some form of storage and E. C. or W. C. usual in model rural cottages of the period, the elevations differ – the earlier are of brick and terra-cotta with two small gables on the front, and the later have larger gables with some half-timber. These two sets became the prototypes for certain standard designs which were frequently repeated during a period of extensive cottage building in the '90s. Most or all of the small gable derivatives, including some in which the gables were omitted altogether, were designed and supervised by Douglas & Fordham in the normal way, and comprised some fourteen pairs, built *c.* 1893–9. However, plans were also adapted by the staff in the estate office, where a standard large-gable type was evolved, reminiscent of the 1889–91 original, but simplified and with no half-timbering. Eleven of these plagiarised pairs were built, with Peter Edwards as contractor, 1891–4, and during the course of this operation protest was made by Douglas, who considered himself entitled to fees. It had previously been agreed that when in the course of estate building, a design was repeated and quantities supplied and superintendence given, a commission of 2½% would be forthcoming. Interpretation of this, in connection with another building, led to disagreement with Cecil Parker in August 1892,[52] and in October Parker wrote, 'the Cottages have been so much altered and amended that no commission could rightly or legally be claimed; but, as Mr. Douglas seems somewhat aggrieved, I will shortly have a statement made showing a lump sum on which the Duke will pay 2½% commission.'[53] The result was an offer of £96, being a rate of 2½% on £350 for each pair, the average cost of which may be calculated to have been £754:3:5. This

The Work of John Douglas

evidently failed to satisfy Douglas, for in 1893 a payment of £100 was made,[54] of which Parker commented, 'You will please understand that this payment is to settle the question, and no further payment will be made should any more cottages be built on similar lines.'[55] More were built. At least five further pairs of this type can be identified among cottages erected by Peter Edwards and Parker Bros. between 1893 and 1896.[56] It may have been these to which Douglas referred when making a further claim in respect of repeated cottage designs as late as 1909 – a claim repudiated by Parker[57] who was in any case doubtless correct in adding that, 'had you wished to make such a claim it should have been sent in years ago to the Exors of the late Duke of Westminster. No liability attaches to the present Duke.'[58]

The making of so belated an application seems to have been prompted by the fact that Douglas was at the same time seeking payment of fees for work done in the designing of an unexecuted project for a Children's Home, at Pulford (*c.* 1903). Unexecuted schemes had, over the years, also been the cause of difficulties and negotiations. In the pre-Parker days it was, it seems, the question of fees for the unrealised design for the Eaton Stud which led the then agent, Samuel Beckett, to write, and, incidentally, in more reasonable and conciliatory terms than Parker would have done, 'if you consider the matter *has not* been settled satisfactorily the matter *must* be, as I said before, referred to The Duke & perhaps you will consider that it will be well for you to mention the subject to His Grace personally. It has been a most unfortunate affair & I do not feel disposed to re-open it but at the same time can offer no objection to your doing so if you consider that you are not properly compensated.'[59]

It is interesting to note that, although prepared to bow to the dictates of the Duke on detailed matters of design, and despite his financial vagaries, it was on questions relating to scales of remuneration – a subject vital to the status of the still precariously established architectural profession – that Douglas attempted to stand firm. His having done so, and the degree of determination displayed in connection with the Schoolmaster's House at Witton Grammar School, Northwich (1874–8) suggest some strength of character, the existence of which would make a clash of personalities between himself and Parker all the more likely.

There can be no doubt that, had he lived longer, the first Duke would have continued the estate building programme, adding new farms and cottages and rebuilding old, presumably until such time as everything which preceded the second Marquess's improvements had been replaced. It can be expected that he would also have completed the systematic elimination of early nineteenth century Gothic. Not only did he purge Eaton Hall itself of all visible traces of

Porden, but Bodley's Eccleston church replaced Porden's and Edis's Overleigh Lodge replaced a Perpendicular confection of the 1830s by Thomas Jones. The Douglas & Fordham Belgrave Lodge (1889–90) took the place of something similar, and their Iron Bridge Lodge (1894–5) and Eccleston Ferry House (1887–8) succeeded simple Gothic houses of a type doubtless once widespread but of which only one survives west of Eccleston church. This latter house, another near Dodleston, William Hazledine's Iron Bridge of 1824 which carries the Aldford Approach of Eaton Hall across the Dee, and some iron balustrading are all that remain to be seen of Georgian Gothic, against which Victorian taste had so strongly rebelled. Their survival may be attributed only to the death of the Duke.

In singling out (as did Sédille) Douglas's Eaton estate work for special mention, Muthesius wrote that, 'His most charming creations include a whole series of small buildings (lodges, farm-buildings, workmen's houses, schools, etc.) in the vicinity of Eaton Hall, the Duke of Westminster's seat in Cheshire, where', he added, 'their fresh and natural character shows them up to great advantage against Alfred Waterhouse's main house'.[60] The High Victorian remodelling of the Hall was indeed something of an anachronism even at its commencement, with the Vernacular Revival buildings which Douglas was erecting in the park and surrounding villages being more in accord with the spirit of the '70s. These were obviously to the Duke's liking, and it is said that he was never satisfied with the results of Waterhouse's work,[61] though even if he had embarked upon the remodelling later and employed, say, Ernest George, it is difficult to see how the scale of Eaton could have been interpreted in Late Victorian terms.

A comment on the Duke's interest in building was made by Douglas's former partner C. H. Minshull. Writing on the subject of Cheshire half-timbering he added, 'Among the patrons of the building arts none was more susceptible to the peculiar charm of this "nogging-work" than the late Duke of Westminster, who caused to be erected on his Eaton estate numerous buildings faithfully reproducing the forms and features of the Cheshire prototypes. In this work his Grace was fortunate in having at command the services of an architect, Mr. John Douglas, than whom no one has been more successful in recapturing the spirit of the old timber-work.'[62] It was at the Duke's instigation that Douglas's own redevelopment scheme in St. Werburgh Street, Chester (c. 1895–7 and 1898), was carried out in black-and-white instead of stone, but Minshull's comments are an exaggeration. By no means all of the Douglas estate buildings use half-timber, and with one exception those which do utilise it in combination with other walling materials and in ways inconsistent with local historical precedent. What the Duke obtained was a Late Victorian Vernacular Revivalism in which half-timbering formed a

The Work of John Douglas

picturesque ingredient, and the significance of which will be considered in the next chapter. The stables of Eaton Hall, although built as a structural continuation of the house itself, and although originally designed by Waterhouse in similar style and materials,[63] were built in a gentler manner, using half-timber, red stone and brick, and with red tile roofs. They do not seem to have formed part of the earliest stage of the building operations, and it is not difficult to believe that the change was made on the orders of the Duke, perhaps after having had time to acquire doubts about Waterhouse's Gothic and to acquire a taste for Douglas's vernacular.

The first Duke was succeeded by his grandson, the colourful and flamboyant Bend'Or, by which heraldic and equine nickname he is still remembered. Although very different in character from his grandfather, he too was a conscientious landlord. Nevertheless, with the death of the first Duke the building programme ceased; Douglas & Minshull were in the 1900s responsible for only occasional and minor jobs, and it is a matter of regret that, although in Bend'Or's time the Grosvenor possessions were expanded enormously on a global scale, the western part of the Eaton estate itself was sold off to tenants and other individual purchasers shortly after the First World War. Much of what the first Duke and Cecil Parker had nurtured and Douglas had embellished thus fell victim to the flood of land sales which in those years resulted in the break-up of so many historic estates. Though some of the farmsteads are still scrupulously maintained, unsuitable new development, the caprices of individual owners and dilapidation have wrought their toll. Balderton, Bretton and Pulford in particular present a tatty picture in contrast to the spotlessness of the villages which still form part of the present Duke's estate.

It was in 1961, with the commencement of the demolition of Eaton Hall itself in the time of the third Duke, that the very heart was torn from the first Duke's architectural achievements. Although a new house has now risen on part of the site, and although the gardens and minor attendant buildings remain, all that survives of the vast Waterhouse mansion are the chapel and stables. The seeds of its destruction were already sown in the time of the first Duke, with the era witnessing, from the 1868 Reform Act onwards, acceleration of the forces which eroded the ascendancy of the landed interest and the traditional ruling classes. Yet despite the loss of the house, there still remains a unique record of Victorian aristocratic patronage. A glorious legacy from the Indian summer of the wealth, power and prestige of the great landed families survives in the chapel at Eaton, in Eccleston church resplendent in its spacious grounds, in the scores of buildings in the villages and in those which, with glowing brick and sparkling timber nogging, adorn Eaton park, and the banks of the Dee, and the verdant Cheshire pastures.

VII Early Maturity: Secular Buildings

The death of the second Marquess of Westminster in 1869 came at a time of architectural transition, and the commissions which flowed from the third Marquess (later first Duke) gave Douglas ample opportunity to show himself aware of, and receptive to, the new spirit which was abroad. In 1870, Leyswood, designed two years previously by R. Norman Shaw (1831–1912), was exhibited at the Royal Academy; Bodley's church at Tue Brook, Liverpool, was completed and that at Pendlebury begun, and Hoar Cross was commenced but two years later. Thus, when Waterhouse's High Victorian remodelling of Eaton Hall was only being commenced, Late Victorian architecture had already arrived in its maturity and perfection. Yet 1870 can be seen as a watershed. On the one hand was a more solemn age, with Gothic of strongly religious affinity pursued as a crusade by its serious-minded proponents. On the other was an age more redolent of the social graces – the age of the Aesthetic Movement, in which pleasure as well as duty found acceptance and whose moral earnestness was that of William Morris (1834–96) and the Arts & Crafts Movement rather than that of the ecclesiologists. E. W. Godwin (1833–86), the lover of Ellen Terry, and W. Eden Nesfield (1835–88), a member of the Whistler-Rossetti circle and described by Simeon Solomon as, 'a fat, jolly hearty fellow, genuinely fond of smoking, and I deeply grieve to say of women. . . .'[1] form curious but symptomatic links in the chain from Pugin to Lethaby.

The development from Godwin's Congleton Town Hall to his Dromore Castle illustrates how readily severe and chunky Burgesian Gothic could melt into refinement and the cult of what, to use the catchword of the time, may be called the 'artistic.' Cloverley Hall, though designed as early as 1865, in character teetered on the borderline between High and Late Victorian. Although this house by Nesfield was Gothic, its freedom and freshness of plan and ornament were such as to suggest that, given encouragement, it would have begun to break out in half-timbering, and it was from the mid-1860s that Nesfield and Shaw began separately (though in partnership together) to produce buildings in what they termed the 'Old English' style.[2] Although preceded by George Devey (1820–86) in using vernacular materials of the south-east, and although building on the tradition of functional planning established by earlier Gothic Revivalists, their houses were nevertheless revolutionary. With irregular outward-thrusting plans, and highly picturesque amalgams of varying materials and styles, the houses of Nesfield and Shaw exemplify the re-appraisal of principles of design, the departure from scholarly standards of historicism, and the

The Work of John Douglas

Stowford Cottages, Crewe Hall, Cheshire, by W. E. Nesfield, c. 1864–5.

awareness of the English rural tradition which characterise the Domestic Revival of the late nineteenth century. Audacious eclecticism brought together differing period elements with the use of brick, half-timber, tile-hanging and pargetting, and with embellishments in the form of 'artistic' touches such as the decorative roundels which Nesfield called 'pies.' This style, no less than their closely-related 'Queen Anne' manner of brick and white-painted timber, they carried out with a charm and a zest and an absence of doctrinaire overtones which were lacking in the more austere work of Philip Webb (1831–1915).

Something of their showmanship appears even in Nesfield's *Specimens of Mediaeval Architecture* (1862) and Shaw's *Sketches from the Continent* (1858). Although these include measured details, the fanciful spirit of the brilliant sketches foreshadows the authors' unceremonious approach to domestic design and contrasts with the greater sobriety of the *Abbey Square Sketch Book*. Although the selection of the examples in Douglas's volumes is apparently arbitrary, and although many perspective sketches are given, the high proportion of measured drawings (including plans) suggests a seriousness of purpose and, while not completely eschewing the romantic and the picturesque, a concern to present antiquarian material for study or emulation.

Douglas's own espousal of the Vernacular Revival stems from the Penson-founded resurgence of half-timbering in nineteenth century Chester, and his lodge at Grosvenor Park (1865–7) belongs to this movement. Yet in developing, from these local origins, along the lines of the newly-fashionable 'Old English' manner, it is likely that

Early Maturity: Secular Buildings

he was directly influenced by Nesfield, and it may be wondered if he was familiar with the latter's estate cottages at Crewe Hall, Cheshire (c. 1864–5), with their tile-hanging, pargetting, tiled roofs of broken outline and massive ribbed chimneystacks of brick.

Douglas's first Eaton estate buildings of the early 1870s include some in a distinctive vernacular manner of his own, though others are less personal and are of an apparently more experimental nature. At this time he used tile-hanging and (more rarely) incised pargetting. Both are native to the south-east and not to Cheshire, but pargetted patterning in relief, which he also used, occurs in the county, and a house of 1658 in Whitefriars, Chester, thus embellished is in *Abbey Square Sketch Book*.[3] Tile-hanging and pargetting, with black-and-white half-timbering occur at the Park Keeper's Cottage, Eaton Hall (1870–71), and, with brick-nogging, in the strongly Nesfieldian St. Werburgh Chambers (built as offices, 1872–3) and St. Werburgh's Mount (shop premises, 1873–4) in St. Werburgh Street, Chester.

A most thoroughly Nesfieldian Douglas building is a pair of cottages, dated 1868, at Great Budworth, Cheshire, for R. E. Egerton-Warburton of Arley Hall. Arley itself was by George Latham of Nantwich, and in addition to Douglas, the galaxy of talent employed by Warburton on his Cheshire estate included Butterfield, Edmund Kirby, Nesfield, Salvin, Street, T. H. Wyatt and William White. The cottages are neat and 'artistic', with a ribbed chimneystack and large panels of sunflowers and other

Park Keeper's Cottage (now Deer Park Cottage), Eaton Hall, Cheshire, 1870–72. (*Architect*, 10, 1873, p. 120)

: Park Keeper's Cottage : Eaton Park : Cheshire :   John Douglas Architect Chester 1878

The Work of John Douglas

patterns in incised pargetting. The ascription to Douglas is in an article on the village by Raffles Davison in *The British Architect* in 1884, which also ascribes a similarly vernacular cottage to Nesfield and states that this was built 22 years previously.[4] Although there is no reason to question the respective Douglas and Nesfield attributions, this date is impossibly early, for the researches of Mr. Andrew Saint have shown that it was a tour in Kent and Sussex made by Nesfield and Shaw in September 1862 which prompted the evolution of the 'Old English' style, and that the earliest example of it must be Nesfield's lodge of 1864 in Regent's Park. As Davison must thus have been in error, there remains the possibility that Douglas and Nesfield worked at Great Budworth at the same time. Uncertainty and a link with Nesfield are to be found also at Croxteth Hall, Lancashire, where Nesfield designed a Gothic dairy (1861–2) and a vernacular laundry (1864), as well as making unexecuted designs for the remodelling of the house (1863), and Douglas designed kennels, for the fourth Earl of Sefton. The kennels are in a heavy High Victorian style.[5]

The Great Budworth cottages indicate a phase of extreme experimentation or uncertainty, bearing in mind that the cottages predate his High Victorian pair of houses in Dee Banks, Chester (1869). The ribbed brick chimneystack – a Nesfieldian motif of seventeenth century and south-eastern association – is the only significant feature which the Great Budworth and Dee Banks buildings have in common. A more comprehensible and logical pattern of transition from High Victorianism to the vernacular manner of Douglas's Late Victorian maturity is provided by a series of buildings which, though preserving some hardness and Gothic character in their brick and masonry, incorporate half-timber of a less spiky nature than at the Grosvenor Park lodge. These include the Rectory, Bangor Is-coed, Flintshire (1868); Weaver Bank Farm, Minshull Vernon, Cheshire (c. 1869); Burford Lane Farm, Heatley, Oughtrington, Cheshire (c. 1869); the enormous unexecuted scheme for the Eaton Stud (1870); and an unexecuted scheme for the Eccleston Lodge at Eaton Hall (1871).

The Eaton Stud project, however, was still strongly Gothic, both in masonry and timber detailing. Nevertheless, with half-timbering and with turrets and high hipped roofs, it provides a reminder that the secular buildings of Douglas's maturity cannot be understood in terms of the Vernacular Revival alone. Although in his work the mutation from High to Late Victorian is clear, it was never complete, and there remained throughout his career certain traits – particularly with regard to the design of roofs – which can be discerned in his work of the 1860s and which can indeed be considered as remaining High Victorian in character. This is the element which may be termed the Germanic.

Early Maturity: Secular Buildings

The Eaton Stud with its steep roofs and half-timber provided a meeting point between Douglas's High Victorianism of the 1860s and both the Germanic and vernacular elements of his maturity. The same applied to a remarkable temporary structure – its black-and-white timbering was only painted on – in the form of a Triumphal Arch in City Road, Chester, erected on the occasion of the visit of the Prince of Wales to open the Town Hall in 1869. 'Welcome Earl and Countess of Chester' it loyally proclaimed, though unfortunately for the inscription His Royal Highness was not, as had been expected, accompanied by Princess Alexandra. Worse, the scheme proved over-ambitious and was not ready in time for the great event. However, with its tourelles, steep hipped roof (actually a pyramid) of concave profile, miniature dormers (hipped in this case) and bold finials or terminal vanes, with two exceptions it displayed all the principal features which Douglas was so resourcefully to exploit in the design of roofs. One exception was the pitched roof recessed behind a parapet which is not specifically Germanic but in combination with all these other roofing elements had appeared at Oakmere Hall (1867) (see page 50). The other was the spire or turret articulated by tiered divisions in its lower stage, and this also had already appeared, being used at St. Ann's church, Warrington (1868–9) (see pages 55–6), and Helsby (1868–70) (see page 54).

With central and northern Europe being less thoroughly rifled for precedents than were Italy and France, Douglas was exceptional in his use of features which were obviously derived from the German states and from the Netherlands of the middle ages – a house by Godwin at Northampton, illustrated in 1871,[6] is a rare instance of something which approximates to his Germanic manner at its more intense – and it may be wondered from what sources his knowledge was derived.

Being restricted to English and Welsh examples, *Abbey Square Sketch Book* does not help. The shingled belfries of Essex, which might be considered as having affinities with Douglas's Germanic manner, find no place in the work, though Marton church, the nearest Cheshire equivalent, is included.[7] Both his partners travelled on the continent – Fordham at any rate sketching in Germany and Belgium,[8] and Minshull many times visiting Germany[9] – and he himself may well have done so. Before his work coalesced into recognisably Germanic form at Oakmere and, yet more strongly, in the Triumphal Arch, details from earlier schemes can be seen as constituting Germanic elements. They include the clock tower on the south wing at Vale Royal (1860–61), the turret roofs at Over Congregational Chapel (1865), and Billy Hobby's Well at Grosvenor Park (1865–7). It may be that these indicate an innate liking for pointed roof forms, and that this found expression in mediaeval German features after Douglas had become acquainted with such

The Work of John Douglas

precedents. Among the examples which appeared in the architectural press, *The Builder* published a series illustrating Franconian town halls, domestic architecture of the Rhine, and the gates of Prague, in 1866-7.[10] Although these alone cannot have provided sufficient information or inspiration for his adoption of the *genre*, they may perhaps have confirmed his interest in it, and thus have had immediate influence on Oakmere and St. Ann's, Warrington. In any case, Douglas must have viewed with interest a series of new buildings in related style by A. Guldenpfennig, at Paderborn, Westphalia, featured in *The Builder*, 1870-73,[11] and he may have seen with pleasure some views of Nuremberg in *The Architect* in the '70s.[12] German examples in Shaw's *Sketches from the Continent* are mainly ecclesiastical rather than secular, though they do include one of the Prague gateways.[13] Some relationship may be traced between Douglas's work and a town gate at Soest, Westphalia,[14] but it may be noted that with a fair, if limited degree of accuracy, the Chester press reported his Triumphal Arch to be similar to one of the gateways of Prague.

Before considering more buildings of vernacular and Germanic character, something must be said about Douglas's detailing. Some features and decorative motifs are largely confined to specific periods or phases – for instance in the late 1860s and 1870s cylindrical chimney shafts with mouldings sometimes enriched with waterleaf ornament, gatepiers which turn from squares to octagons or diminish to pyramids, and railings with forked bases. In addition, however, there can be recognised a consistent and highly distinctive

Above and below left: Triumphal Arch, City Road, Chester, 1869 (temporary structure). (Engraving after a drawing by J. H. Metcalfe)

Below right: Gateway at west end of bridge, Prague. (*Architectural Sketches from the Continent*, Richard Norman Shaw, 185?, plate 91)

Early Maturity: Secular Buildings

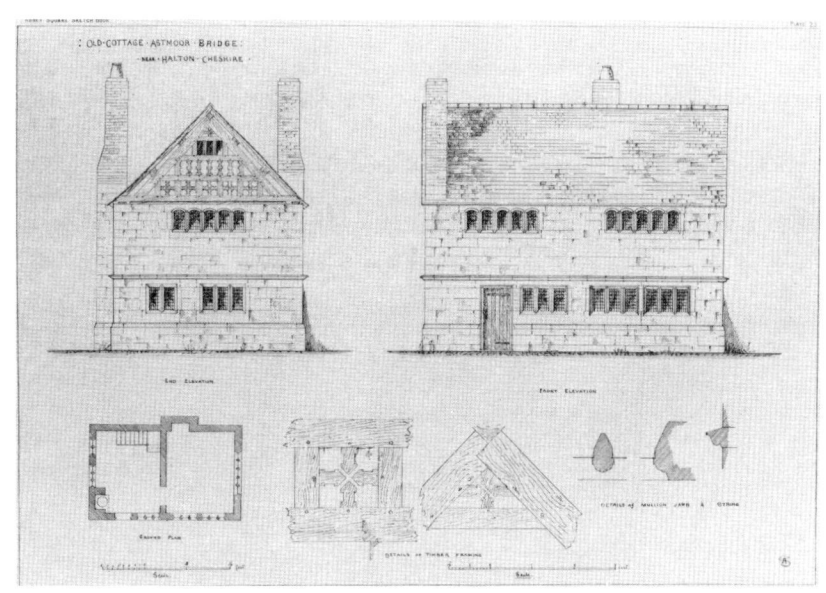

Old Cottage, Astmoor Bridge, near Halton, Cheshire. *Abbey Square Sketch Book*, I, plate 23. Drawing by A. Schofield)

vocabulary of detailing which had its roots in the 1860s, matured in the '70s and pervaded Douglas's buildings of every type throughout the remainder of his life. Derived from a variety of sources and developed with scrupulous regard for the nature and qualities of the materials employed, Douglas's detailing and the care which was lavished on it is a major factor in endowing most of his buildings with so strong a feeling of quality, and in rendering them so instantly attractive and instantly recognisable.

Mention has already been made of heavy corbels, corbel tables and corbels of inverted semi-cone form, but a more readily discernible Douglas characteristic is his treatment of the heads of mullioned window lights in the form of curves – either segmental, three-centred or, more rarely, semi-circular. These Tudor shapes belong mainly to the 1870s, and subsequently a more elaborate and Gothic treatment was adopted, with cusping or depressed ogees. Although in buildings with brick walling stone dressings might be used, the capabilities of materials were also logically exploited in the form of moulded brick for mullions and straight, curved and shaped heads, or of terra-cotta for the latter. In *Abbey Square Sketch Book* precedent for the use of rows of low mullioned windows with curved-headed lights is illustrated by a cottage near Halton, Cheshire[15] (see above), and for moulded brick mullions and heads by Pooley Hall, Polesworth, Warwickshire.[16] Cusped or depressed ogee lights might appear in wood in half-timbered work, but whatever the framing material, Douglas window detailing frequently includes elaborate patterns of lead-work in the glazing. Lead was also called upon to show what it could do in the form of heavy ornamented finials for Germanic turrets and roofs.

The Work of John Douglas

It is, however, Douglas's joinery that displays the greatest consistency, quality and mastery of medium, and makes the exploring of a well-fitted house or church such a delicious experience. This, as already suggested, could be attributable to early practical instruction received in his father's workshop. The chief sources for his style are English Late Gothic architectural woodwork and seventeenth century furniture, welded together in a manner which, though distinctly personal, is closely bound up with advanced taste of the 1870s.

Characteristic – indeed virtually the hallmark of Douglas's joinery

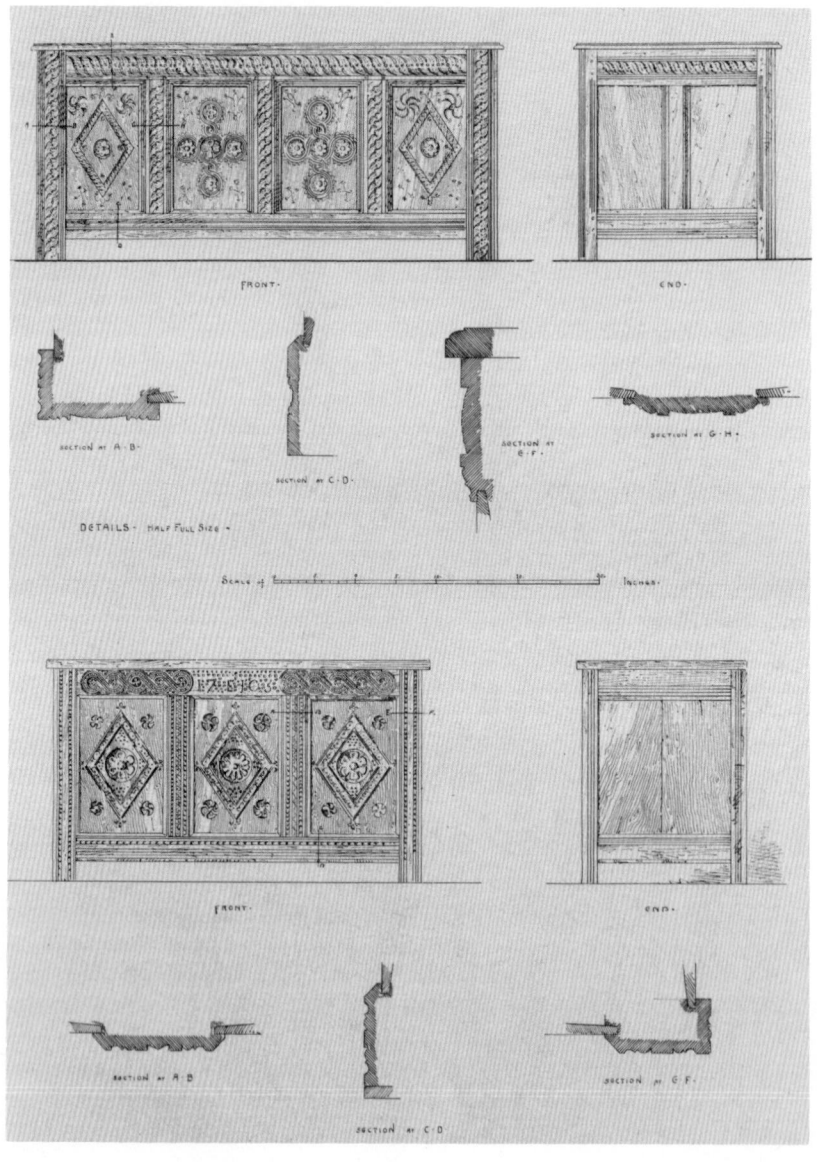

Oak Chests. (*Abbey Square Sketch Book* I, plate 5. Drawing by E. Hodkinson)

Early Maturity: Secular Buildings

Old Cabinets at Calveley, Cheshire, and Chester. (*Abbey Square Sketch Book*, plate 72. Drawing by T. W. Haigh)

detailing – is a feature which, although common in Jacobean furniture, had its origin in panelling of earlier date and which, in the apparent absence of an accepted term, may be called 'unmitred moulding.' In this, no scribing of either the edge or surface mouldings of framing members occurs at the joints. Edge moulding for horizontal and vertical members simultaneously being impossible, one or both remain plain or merely splayed. The character of the system is, however, emphasised by surface

85

The Work of John Douglas

moulding, usually in the form of plain incised lines or channels, with those of the short members stopping at the edge of the continuous members into which they are tenoned, and with those of the latter carried through oblivious of the junctions. The result is a clear exposition of the system of framing with, for instance, the separate stiles, rails and muntins of a door being expressed. It may be wondered if the inherent logic and structural honesty had particular appeal for Douglas and his obvious love and feeling for wood, for a similar putting of functional form to aesthetic use is displayed in the design of staircases. Instead of cladding the soffit of a flight with panelling or plaster, he would frequently expose the underside of the steps, and would mould and make into a decorative feature the glued wedges traditional in staircase construction.

That English furniture provided inspiration for joinery is shown by the numerous examples which appear in *Abbey Square Sketch Book* and which include not only unmitred mouldings but also turned balusters and incised lozenge, roundel and other patterns[17] which also figure in Douglas's work. Such patterns have some relation to the 'pie' discs of Nesfield and Shaw, and happily co-habit with them in Douglas's ornamentation, though the origin of pies is more exotic. Mediaeval precedents for the stone-carved roundels which Douglas so frequently used in a Gothic context in the 1860s appear in Nesfield's *Specimens*[18] but their translation into Late Victorian terms – as used by Nesfield at Kinmel (1868–74) – seems, however, to have been through the influence of Japanese prints and

Detail from interior elevation of cloister Mont St Michel. (*Specimens of Mediaeval Architecture*, W. Eden Nesfield, 1862, pl. 51)

Early Maturity: Secular Buildings

porcelain. Thus partially a product of the interest in things oriental which helped to mould Late Victorian taste, pies might contain geometrical patterns, whorls or flowers, particularly sunflowers. With sunflowers in any case a fashionable decorative device by the 1870s, they are to be found in Douglas's work both in and (as at the Great Budworth cottages) out of pies. Another Nesfield and Shaw device is a bracket of curved profile – either concave or ogee – such as occurred in the dining room inglenook at Leyswood with pies in the spandrels. Douglas also made use of this, in timber porches for instance, though also on a smaller scale internally. It might appear in chimneypieces which, either with or without the fashionable overmantel, would have shallow curved brackets breaking forward into the room, their undersides enriched with reeding or incised lines. Similar freedom of design, with selective use of derivative details and a sure sense of craftsmanship, characterises the staircases of Douglas's larger houses. Although differing considerably in detail, typical examples have, as well as exposed wedges, heavy turned balusters, simple in profile and of late sixteenth or seventeenth century type; newels more thoroughly Victorian with ball finials, and incised linear ornament on both balusters and newels. His large staircases moreover nearly always have a landing or gallery with an arcade on timber posts. Gothic ornament occasionally creeps into the more elaborate domestic woodwork, but as this fusion of seventeenth century with late mediaeval detail is more fully developed in church furnishings, it will be considered in the following chapter.

Although undoubtedly derived by Douglas direct from furniture, the unmitred moulding is found also in the work of Nesfield and Shaw and, together with pies, is an element in the decorative art and massive jointed furniture of the Bruce Talbert era. The evolution of this style from High Victorian Gothic design (just as Godwin's work displays a similar though more complete transition in terms of architecture) may be illustrated by Waterhouse's timber detailing (not least by some which was at Eaton Hall) and by successive editions of *Hints on Household Taste* by Charles L. Eastlake (1836–1906). In particular, the 1878 fourth edition substituted several 'artistic' furniture designs with unmitred mouldings and pies for more austere Gothic pieces which still remained in the third edition of 1872.[19] Douglas's High Victorian church fittings, as at St. John's, Over (1860–63) and Aldford (1865–6) may be compared with Eastlake's earlier designs, and his mature joinery detailing with those in the fourth edition. However, whatever the factors and influences which determined his assimilation of the new style and the ethos which produced it, his transition preceded that displayed by Eastlake. He had sought out, or been attracted to, seventeenth century furniture before the time of the publication of *Abbey Square*

The Work of John Douglas

Newton Hall, Newton Bridge, Lancashire. (*Abbey Square Sketch Book*, I, plate 31. Drawing by F. J. Thorne and T. W. Haigh)

Sketch Book in 1872, and the principle of unmitred mouldings is utilised at St. Ann's, Warrington of 1868–9 and in mature form at St. Alban's church, Tattenhall, Cheshire of 1869–70.

At Oakmere Hall virtually the only principal interior to retain fittings intact is the billiard room at the extremity of the service wing on the first floor. Its chimneypiece, besides having pictorial panels carved in relief, has unmitred mouldings and curved brackets, and an adjoining corridor is spanned by a set of curved brackets with pies. This seems impossibly early for 1867, and is inconsistent with what can be deduced of the original detailing elsewhere in the house. The possibility of the room being the result of later alteration cannot be ruled out, and its exterior is consistent with the idea of a Douglas remodelling of the '70s. However, curved brackets no less than unmitred mouldings and pie-like roundels date from the 1860s, for they are to be seen in the timber porch of the Grosvenor Park entrance lodge. Thus although Douglas's joinery detailing, as well as his Vernacular Revivalism, emerged as part of, and fully abreast of, a broad movement of advanced taste, it too had origins in his High Victorian phase.

Although in due course depressed ogee and cusped window lights generally superseded the three-centred sort, on a larger scale the latter form remained a feature in Douglas's work by way of elliptical or basket arches, particularly for doorways. He also used, though less frequently, the decorated stone lintels of north Lancashire and the Pennines, selections of which appear in *Abbey Square Sketch Book*.[20] They were used at Green Lake Farmhouse, Aldford (1870) and Dodleston School (1870, altered) though it was not until the 1880s that they were at all widely adopted. What in any case is a more widespread motif and which, like curved window lights and half-timber, forms an important ingredient in Douglas's vernacular manner, is the use of patterns formed by brick headers. An obvious

Early Maturity: Secular Buildings

development of his interest in the enriching of the wall surface displayed in the polychromy of the 1860s, such patterns include the Tudor system of dark diapering (rare in his work before the 1880s) and (used particularly in the '70s) projecting headers arranged in diaper lozenge patterns against a background of either similar or different coloured brick or white plaster. A Cheshire or, apparently, more commonly a south Lancashire contrivance, lozenge patterns at Newton Hall, Lancashire, are to be found in *Abbey Square Sketch Book*.[21] Square panels formed in brick were also used, and, together with a staircase window with brick mullions and patterned leadwork, such lozenge and rectangular patterns in the gables are the only distinguishing features of the Master's House at Witton Grammar School, Northwich (1874–8), where, as has been noted, cost restrictions were so stringent. They occur also at a set of cottages at Great Budworth (Nos. 54–57 High Street, *c.* 1870) and, with ranges of windows with curved-headed lights and some pargetting, at a cottage on Douglas's own land at Sandiway (on Chester road, north-east of Blue Cap Hotel, *c.* 1879). The patterns are also to be seen at an asymmetrical pair of cottages at Belgrave (west of Belgrave Lodge on west side of Wrexham Road, 1871), on the Eaton estate, which in addition shows evidence of Douglas's short-lived tile-hanging period. A complicated mixture of materials and elements, including two types of curved window head, combine in a pair of

Colour plate page 18

Cottage, Chester Road, Sandiway, Cheshire, *c.* 1879. *British Architect*, 11, 1879, p. 204. Drawing by R. Davison)

The Work of John Douglas

Pair of cottages, Wrexham Road, Belgrave, Cheshire, c. 1871.

cottages which forms the Aldford Lodge of Eaton Hall (1877–9).

Of other Eaton cottages, a pair at Pulford (west of the Cuckoo's Nest on road to Oldfield's Farm, c. 1872–6) with plain brick walling and straight-headed stone mullioned windows has few distinguishing Douglas-like features, though a number of cottages in similarly anonymous style derived from it. Also outside the general mainstream of his vernacular development is a pair at Aldford (south end of west road in village on east side, c. 1874) with incised pargetting and which, with timber casement windows and two plastered gables, has a twentieth century look, and only timber porches with curved brackets which meet to form Gothic arches hint at its date and authorship. Nearby, an asymmetrical block of four (south end of centre road in village on west side, c. 1874) is of similar style and materials, though another block of four of identical plan (west end of south road in village, 1874) is rendered more typical of Douglas in being of brick with timberwork in the gables. A cottage near Cotton Farm, Waverton (c. 1872–6) with an unmoulded brick Gothic arch is also an unusual work, but the most remarkable departure from Douglas's usual repertoire is Church Farmhouse, Waverton (1882–3) which is an exceptional instance of Vernacular Revivalism carried to the point of period imitation. With coped gables, diapered brick and stone dressings, its proportions and detailing look authentically seventeenth century.

Of similar date, and indicating that at least up until this time Douglas was still interested in occasional experiment and in doing

Right: Pair of cottages, School Lane, Aldford, Cheshire, *c.* 1874.
Below: Block of four cottages, Rushmere Lane, Aldford, Cheshire, 1874.

The Work of John Douglas

George and Dragon Inn, Great Budworth Cheshire, c. 1875. The insert shows the inn before remodelling. (*Architect*, 14, 1875, p. 318. Drawing by E. Hodkinson, 1875)

the unexpected, is an asymmetrical pair of cottages at Eccleston (west end of village, 1881–3) which, in its combination of raised pargetting, white-painted wood and pebble-dash rendering, looks distinctly Edwardian. Its window frames with mouldings standing proud of the wall surface recur in later work.

Belying its date in its use of large areas of plain white rendering is (away from Eaton) the George and Dragon, Great Budworth, which was remodelled from a simple three-bay Georgian inn (1875), as part of Mr. Egerton-Warburton's campaign to restore the village and render it picturesque in Victorian eyes. The inn has ribbed

Below left: Church Farmhouse, Waverton, Cheshire 1882–3.
Right: Cotton Abbey Farmhouse, Waverton, Cheshire 1873. (Photograph c. 1880)

Early Maturity: Secular Buildings

Above left: Lea Newbold Farmhouse, Bruera, Cheshire, c. 1873. (Photograph c. 1880)

Right: Wettenhall Hall, Cheshire. (*Abbey Square Sketch Book*, I, plate 24. Drawing by A. Schofield)

chimneys, moulded brick mullions, an elliptical-headed doorway and a steep pyramid turret of Germanic character and, it may be noted, the hanging sign was brought from Nuremberg.

Returning to the Eaton estate, a further building for which no exact parallel exists is Lea Newbold Farmhouse, Bruera (c. 1873). Although having a timber porch, a pyramid turret roof and timber casement windows below elliptical arches, the principal feature is a set of enormous shaped gables, fancifully decorated with finials. These gables may have been derived from Stretton Lower Hall and Stretton Old Hall, Cheshire, and although they remained exceptional in Douglas's work, smaller pedimented Dutch gables hold a more secure place in his vernacular output. His adoption of them provides another instance of being in accord with contemporary ideas, with their figuring in the 'Queen Anne' mode of Nesfield and Shaw and in its development by E. R. Robson and J. J. Stevenson (1832–1908) for London Board Schools after 1870. Again, however, precedent is found in *Abbey Square Sketch Book* in the form of Dutch gables on both principal fronts of Wettenhall Hall, Cheshire.[22] Similar gables appear at Aldford Hall Farm (1881–2), in an unexecuted scheme for it (1876), at Cotton Abbots Farmhouse, Waverton (1873), and Wrexham Road Farm, Eccleston (1877–84). The last two are rare among Douglas's secular buildings (except for his semi-detached houses and cottages) in having symmetrical elevations.

Although Douglas had previously been responsible for the rebuilding or remodelling of a number of farmhouses and sets of

The Work of John Douglas

farm buildings for the Duke of Westminster, Wrexham Road was his first complete farmstead for the Eaton estate, with house and buildings designed together as a whole, as well as being the subject of Douglas's only known surviving letter to the Duke. The group is a particularly attractive one, and it gave satisfaction, for when giving instructions for a new farmhouse in 1885 (probably Brookside, Pulford, 1885–6), Cecil Parker wrote that the Duke, 'likes the Wrexham Road Farm, design.'[23] Although the Eaton farms differ in the disposition and arrangement of their parts, the nature of the accommodation originally provided at Wrexham Road was typical of that embodied in subsequent plans, and also similar in its elements to that previously built (away from Eaton) at Weaver Bank and Burford Lane Farms. The bulk of the buildings were those for the housing of cattle, with shippons (their longitudinal feeding passages served from one root house or feed store), houses for young stock and a bullock shed and yard. Subsidiary accommodation included the barn (demoted from its status as giant and king of farm buildings), stables, carthouses and piggeries. In common with all Douglas's farms, the layout is informal, with none of the elements of axiality which characterised Georgian and many Victorian pattern book model farms, and the buildings are grouped loosely round four sides of a yard. The buildings are brick and the house, which stands a little apart at one corner and is dated 1880, is of brick with stone dressings. With Dutch gables having ball finials and both triangular and segmental pediments, it is elaborately treated, though this degree of display is restricted to two elevations, those facing towards the yard being more utilitarian. This tendency to 'show fronts' is marked among Eaton farmhouses and cottages, with plain brick and timber casements frequently appearing at the rear, irrespective of the fenestration and architectural character of the front.

Wrexham Road Farm, Eccleston, Cheshire, 1877–84. (Drawing at Eaton Estate Office, as engraved for *Building News*, 54, 1888, p. 838)

Early Maturity: Secular Buildings

Nevertheless, Wrexham Road Farm is of considerable quality, with the studied simplicity of the farm buildings highlighted by a little dovecote turret in an angle of the yard and with a gatehouse containing a delectable touch of half-timber in its gable.

Half-timber is indeed the most important and consistently-used element in Douglas's vernacular buildings. With certain notable exceptions he used it for individual parts, as did Nesfield and Shaw, and not for the entire walling of a building, thus obtaining artistic effect and picturesque variety. Both the cottage near Halton and Newton Hall, as shown in *Abbey Square Sketch Book*, have half-timbered gables above masonry and brick walling respectively, producing a Victorian, not to say Douglas-like appearance. Among the first of Douglas's buildings for the Duke (then third Marquess) of Westminster, was a coach house near Eccleston church (1870, converted to a reading room by Douglas & Fordham, 1892). Its timberwork includes concave lozenge patterns formed by quadrants in square panels, of a type which occured at Newton Hall. Of all the decorative motifs of the local timber framing of the Welsh border and the north-west, this is the only one which Douglas used consistently, though the presence of any such device in his work at this time is exceptional, and more typical is the gable end of the nearby Church Cottage (1870). This is plain and simple and has an unusually high proportion of white plaster to dark timber. Although such meagreness of timber in the hands of lesser architects seems thin and ignorant, Douglas's treatment has a convincing and distinctive character which is difficult to define.

Although closer to the square panels of the border and north-west rather than to the close-studding common in the south-east, what may conveniently be called Douglas's 'light' half-timbering has little clear English historical precedent, and German influence can again

Wrexham Road Farm, Eccleston, Cheshire. (Album of photographs of *c.* 1899 at Eaton Estate Office)

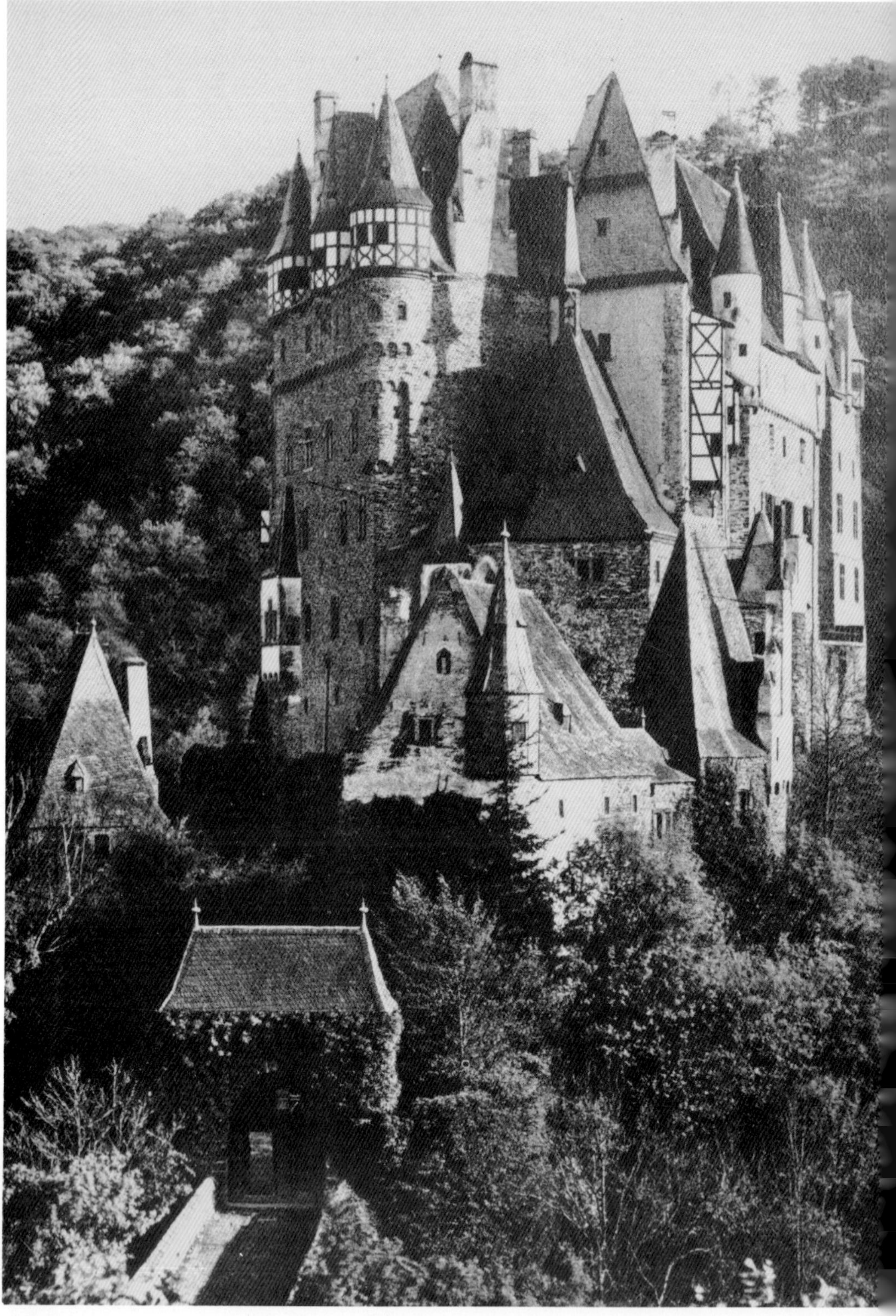

Right: Dunsdale, Frodsham, Cheshire, 1876. A striking example of Germanic influence. (*British Architect*, 8, 1877, p. 66. Drawing by R. Davison)

Opposite: Schloss Eltz an der Mosel, Rheinland.

be detected. The importing to Cheshire of an alien visual tradition in timberwork, and the seeking of inspiration on the Rhine or the Moselle for use on the Dee, would be an exercise in the nature of coals to Newcastle. Yet comparison of Douglas's timberwork of this period, as well as his roof forms, with such buildings as the Marksburg, Braubach, or the fairy-tale castle of Eltz on the Moselle, suggests beyond doubt that such was the case. The roofs, towers and timberwork of Eltz are particularly telling in relation to Douglas's work.

Varying degrees of adaptation and of infusion of local details and character mark Douglas's use of 'light' half-timbering, and buildings in which it appears include a number with moderately pitched roofs and otherwise innocent of Germanic features, such as the block of four cottages at Aldford already mentioned (page 91). Away from Eaton they include Polesworth Vicarage, Warwickshire (*c.* 1870), which has concave lozenges, herring-bone bracing and an early instance of diapered brick, the former Sessions House, Northop, Flintshire (1877), a coffee house at Rossett, Denbighshire (1881, now National Westminster Bank) and a farmhouse at Mount Alyn, Rossett (*c.* 1881, now Yew Tree).

However, in the 1870s half-timber was usually combined with more adventurous roof forms. At a set of loose boxes built in connection with the Eaton Stud in paddocks at Eccleston (1871) play is made with hipped gables which, although familiar from Butterfield and Street as well as from Nesfield, relate equally to the interest in roof shapes, and particularly hipped roofs, inherent in Douglas's Germanic manner. The Gamekeeper's Cottage and Kennels in the park at Eaton (1870-71, now Eaton Lodge and

97

Above: Gamekeeper's Cottage and Kennels (now Eaton Lodge), Eaton Hall, Cheshire, 1870–1.
(*Architect*, 10, 1876, p. 120)

Below: Gamekeeper's Cottage and Kennels (now Eaton Lodge), Eaton Hall, Cheshire, 1870–71.
Photograph *c*. 1899 at Eaton Estate Office)

Early Maturity: Secular Buildings

Above: Cheaveley Hall Farm, Huntington, Cheshire, 1875–8. (Photograph *c.* 1880)
Below: Lea Hall Farm, Aldford, Cheshire, 1873. (Photograph *c.* 1880)

altered) with which a luncheon room for shooting parties was combined, is of stone and half-timber and has a great diversity of hipped roofs and a conical-roofed staircase turret, though the timberwork is, in this case, quite heavily enriched. Less elaborate instances of half-timbering (mostly 'light') with Germanically-related roof forms abound on the Eaton estate, and are seen also at Hill Bark Farm, Frankby, Cheshire (1875) – a beautiful group of red sandstone, half-timber and dark tiled hipped and gabled roofs. At Eaton a similar flavour pervades farm buildings at Manor Farm, Pulford (1871), extensive buildings at Cheaveley Hall Farm, Huntington (1875–8) with gables, steep hips and a dovecote turret, and, to a lesser extent, the Aldford (near Bruera) and Balderton Cheese Factories (1874–5). Lea Hall Farmhouse, Aldford (1873) presents

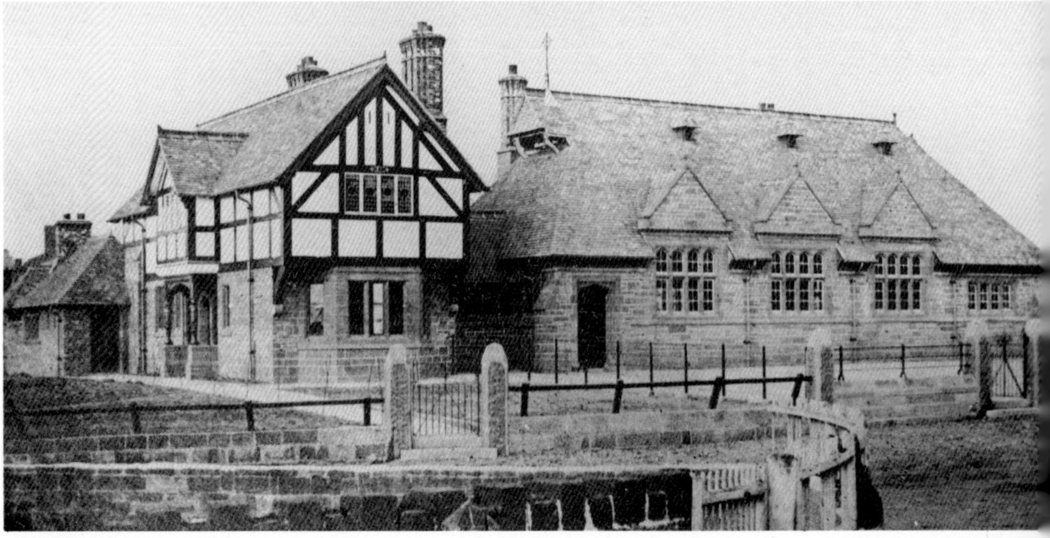

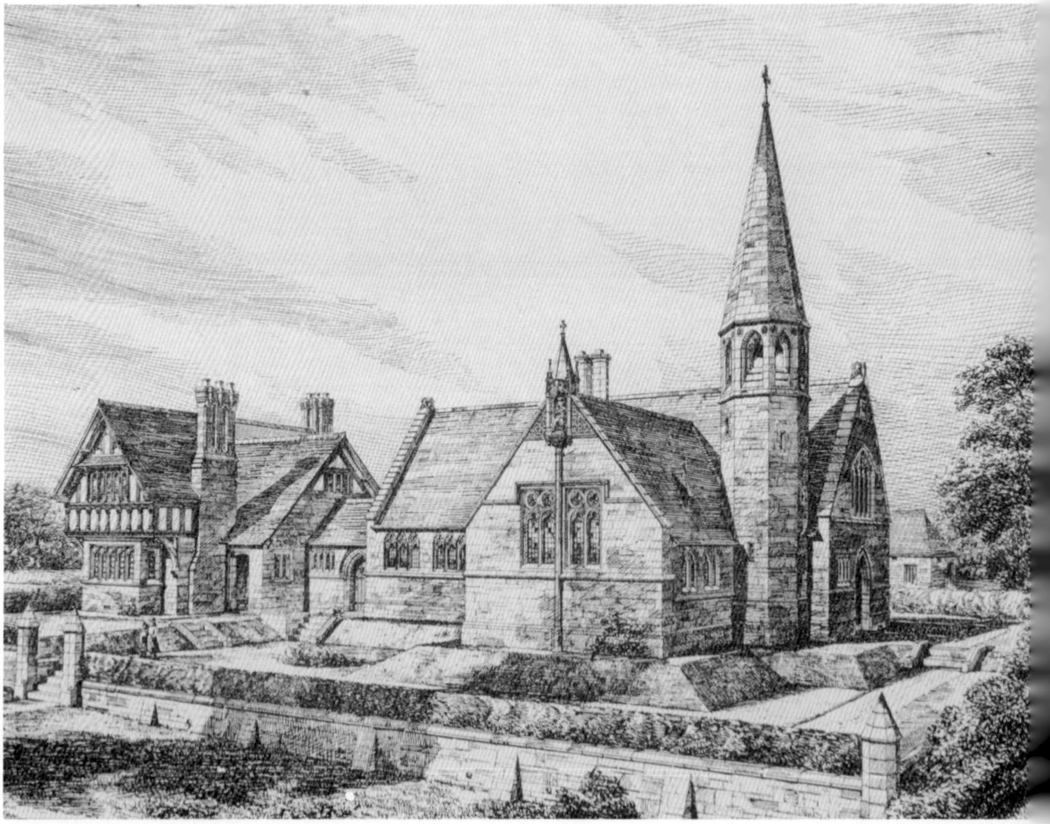

Early Maturity: Secular Buildings

brickwork (including moulded brick mullions), 'light' half-timbering, a timbered porch with curved brackets, carved bressumers consistent with local precedent, gables at the front and hipped roofs at the rear.

School, Waverton, Cheshire, 1877–8. Photograph c. 1880

Although Gothic windows were used in the school at Dodleston (1871) and two schools at Aldford (1870), these buildings (all of which have been altered) were of predominantly vernacular character, with the only hints of Douglas-like roofscape being in hipped gables at Dodleston and in bellcotes. At Waverton school (1877–8) the school house is partly half-timber with a jettied upper storey, while the school building proper has an enormous hipped roof, with hints of Germanic miniature dormers and gables with ball finials above the windows. Similar articulation between school house partly of half-timber and school entirely of stone occurs at Eccleston (1874–81), though here the school itself can only be described as Gothic, and is more thoroughly so than any other secular building of Douglas's maturity. The contrast in style between school and school house, and something of a disparity in scale between the Gothic minutiae of the one and the quite large jettied gable of the other is endearingly toy-like. Waverton and Eccleston are outstanding among Douglas's village schools, and though both are attractive, Eccleston is the more delightful of the two.

Colour plate page 35

An unexecuted scheme for a luncheon room in the park at Eaton (1877) had a Germanic roof form, as has the pumphouse at Eccleston (c. 1874) and also the Dutch Tea House in the gardens at Eaton Hall (1872). Formerly with decorations by Stacy Marks, the Dutch Tea House has steep hipped roofs, sprocketed to give a concave profile, and rising to a point with an enormous lead finial. Although a chimney is of the heavily ribbed 'Old English' sort, the framing of the verandah and black-and-white walls is exceptional among Douglas's timberwork in having small-scale carving of decidedly continental character.

Colour plate page 18

Also exceptional is The Limes Farmhouse, Pulford (1872, now Green Paddocks), which is remarkable even among the Eaton estate buildings for the care and expense lavished on it. The windows contain leadwork, a feature which by no means all of them possess, and the interior is unusual among the farmhouses in that the architect has given attention to its appearance, with unmitred mouldings used and with Douglas's hand evident in the detailing of the staircase. The roof is an enormous hip (with a small turret-like roof at the rear) and the symmetrical frontage has a pargetted gable. It is, however, virtuosity in the use of brick which makes the building memorable. Not only is purpose-made brick (produced on the estate) used for moulded stringcourses, sills, mullions and curved heads, but for the complex finials and moulded copings of curly Dutch gables. The gables have wall shafts on corbels, and

School, Eccleston, Cheshire, 1874–81. British Architect, 11, 79, p. 26. Drawing by D. P. Fordham

Dutch Tea House, Eaton Hall, Cheshi[re] 1872. (*British Architect*, 11, 1879, 194. Drawing by R[.] Davison)

Douglas's liking for enriched wall surfaces is also displayed in panels formed of moulded brick ribs in the gables and in friezes between the ground and first floor windows. Brick is also used resourcefully at the Upper Servants' Houses, Eccleston (1875–8, now Morris Oak), though contrary to the original intention some stone was also introduced. Semi-octagonal wall shafts rise into finials; wall panelling is enriched with cusped heads, and wall surfaces are further enlivened by isolated courses of stone. The original occupants of these three

Early Maturity: Secular Buildings

cottages included the Duke of Westminster's butler and chef.

Regarding the colour and texture of materials of buildings so far discussed, masonry was for the most part executed in local red sandstone. Brick, which figures more prominently in the appearance and character of most Eaton estate works, included different types – in the 1870s both commons and dull warm reds. In combination with dark brown roofing tiles effects were produced which, though striking in colour particularly when contrasted with half-timbering, are generally of a soft and harmonious character. However, with The Limes and the Upper Servants' Houses, in which the qualities and capabilities of brick are so notably exploited, an increased redness and hardness is apparent, and with the prominent roof of The Limes being of bright red tile, there is foreshadowed a delight in extreme ruddiness which re-emerged at the end of the 1870s. Whether of the hard or more gently-textured character, however, natural colour plays an essential part in Douglas's buildings, to which monochrome illustrations seldom do justice. That this should be so, presents another aspect of his mastery of materials and their potential, and Sédille made special mention of the colouring of Eaton estate

Scheme for remodelling Mill, Warburton, Cheshire, 1872. (Drawing at Warburton New Church)

The Gelli, Tallarn Green, Flintshire, 1877. View from north-west. (Photograph c. 188[...]

buildings: 'Of brick and wood construction, with artistic touches of stone, here and there, roofed with tiles, almost completely in red, but in a red which is both light and delicate, they stand out most pleasantly against a background of verdant countryside.'²⁴

An unexecuted scheme (1872) for remodelling a water mill for R. E. Egerton-Warburton, at the village of Warburton, Cheshire, provides a fascinating instance of the Germanic manner. It involved the giving of variety and Douglas-like character to a 'functional tradition' structure by the cosmetic touches of buttresses and a half-timbered loop-hole gable, and by a steep hipped roof with which a large decorated Netherlandish gable was combined.

Germanic also, with turret and hipped roofs, and again making extensive use of purpose-made brick, is a house at Ruloe, Cheshire (c. 1873), built for the agent of George F. Wilbraham's Delamere estate. Of curiously fragmented plan, it leads to consideration of the design and planning of the larger houses of Douglas's early maturity and this, in turn, involves the noting of a development in his use of half-timber.

Occupying a remote and elevated position on the border of Cheshire and the Flintshire Maelor, The Gelli (1877), a mile or two from the Flintshire village of Tallarn Green, was built for the Honourables Georgina and Henrietta Kenyon, daughters of the third Baron Kenyon, of Gredington. This modest country house consists of three ranges, arranged domino-fashion at right angles to each other along the edge of a hill top. Contemporary standards of convenience and propriety were not met in so far as the entrance severed communication between kitchen and dining room. Moreover, the principal rooms face north, though this was doubtless to take advantage of a view, and south light was also contrived for the drawing room. Of a free, outward-thrusting nature, and generated by the conditions of the site, the plan indeed belongs to the Late Victorian Domestic Revival, and although Douglas never indulged

The Gelli, Tallarn Green, Flintshire, 1877. View from south-east. Photograph c. 1880)

in the interlocking L-shaped rooms of Nesfield and Shaw, and only rarely designed inglenooks (something of a cliché of their style), The Gelli smacks of the radicalism of Nesfield, Shaw and Webb, and the picturesque Old Englishery of the two former.

Shavian is the long drawn out composition of Tudor and vernacular elements executed in brick, stone and half-timber. The detailing of brick mullions, curved-headed lights and brick lozenge patterns is, however, immediately recognisable as Douglas's, and equally characteristic are the hipped roofs and dovecote turret of the stables and a large square tower-like block with pyramid roof and against one side of which is a smaller bell turret. This tower occurs above what was originally the kitchen, and the provision of some form of tower, with or without pyramid roof, in the region of the service quarters (as at Oakmere Hall) occurs in several of Douglas's larger houses. The fittings of the Gelli, although simple and with the joinery in pine rather than oak, are an early instance of a typical and consistent Douglas interior – six panel doors with unmitred mouldings, chimneypieces with curved brackets, newels and balusters with incised linear ornament, and the landing in the form of an arcaded gallery with turned posts. The convention of different character for dining room and drawing room is perpetrated (though this had been ridiculed by Eastlake) with the former having a panelled ceiling of timber ribs and the latter a plaster cornice.

Entirely vernacular in character (except for a Germanic hint in the turret-like roof of a canted bay window) is Whitegate Vicarage, Cheshire (1878) built at the expense of Lord Delamere. Consisting of a happy mixture of brick and partly-jettied half-timber, it also has at right angles to the entrance front a small stable building, which gives the sense of a partially-enclosed court.

Before considering further houses of the late '70s, and Douglas's development of the use of half-timber, something must be said about an earlier work – Broxton Higher Hall, Cheshire (c. 1872). This in-

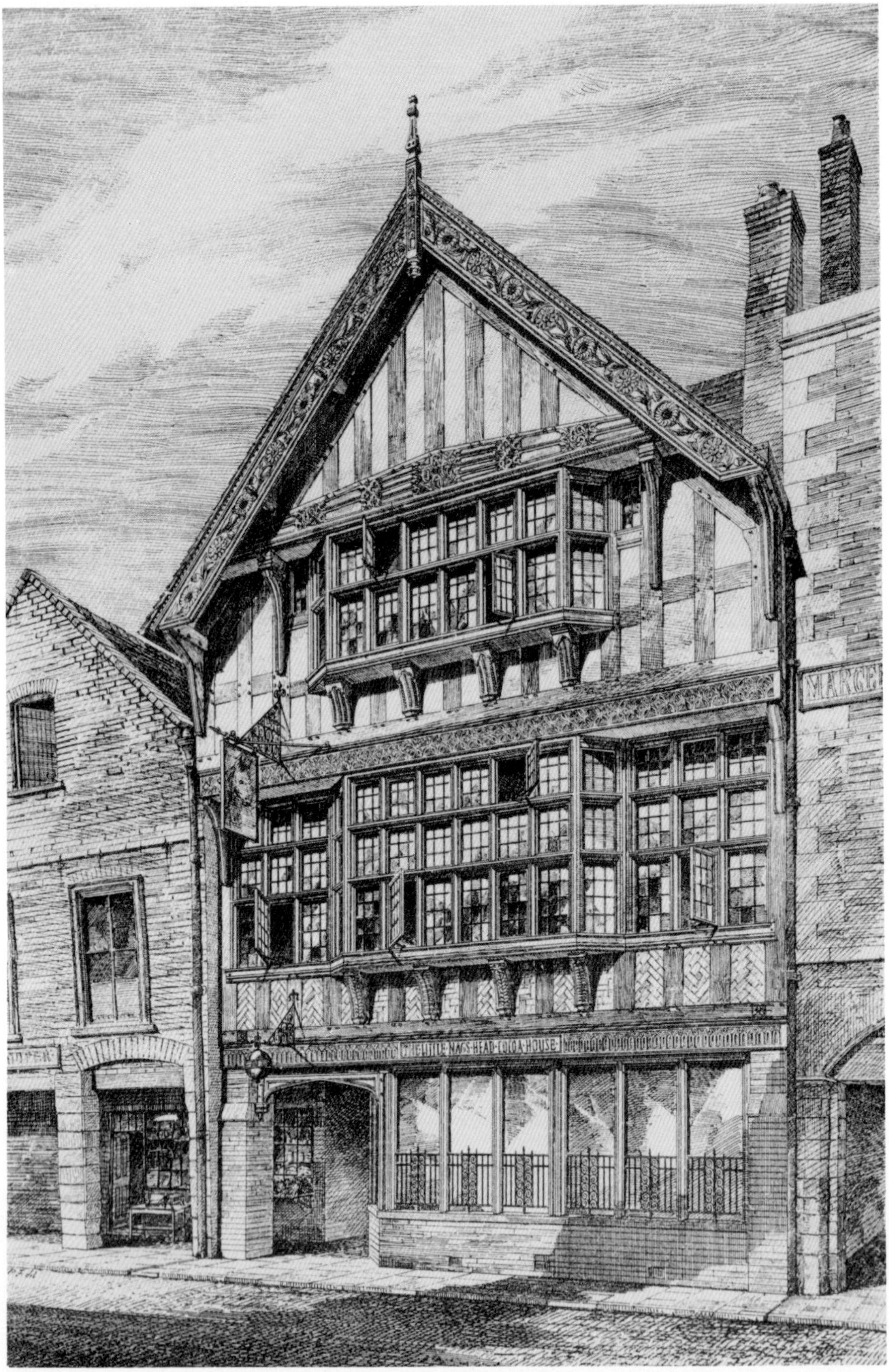
THE LITTLE NAGS·HEAD·COCOA·HOUSE

Early Maturity: Secular Buildings

corporates earlier parts, notably a length of timber-framed walling, which has two gables and the concave lozenge patterns and which found its way into *Abbey Square Sketch Book*.[25] Reconstructed using the old wood, Douglas made this the centre of the entrance front, and designed the entire walling of the remainder of the main block in half-timber. So ambitious an attempt at half-timber at this stage in the Vernacular Revival was unusual for any architect, but (even allowing for later alterations) the result is thin and unconvincing, and shows that Douglas's 'light' half-timbering was incapable of maintaining so sustained an effort. The same applies to the rear entrance lodge at Oakmere Hall which, with its walls entirely black-and-white, is attributable to Douglas.

The frontage of the Market Hall at Northwich, Cheshire (1874, demolished) seems also to have been entirely half-timbered. It was, however, with the remodelling of a former inn in Foregate Street, Chester, to form the Little Nag's Head Cocoa House (1877, demolished) that a significant new departure in Douglas's half-timbering became apparent. The place was promoted by the Duke of Westminster as a working men's coffee tavern, and was the forerunner of several sets of premises established by the Chester Cocoa House Co. Above the ground floor the walling was entirely half-timbered – with some brick nogging. No 'light' half-timbering here, however, and the enthusiasm for wood already apparent in Douglas's joinery here found expression in external carpentry. There would seem to have been a sense of glorying in the solidity and power of the oak, and in the ability to enrich it with moulded mullion and transom and heavily-carved bracket, bressumer and barge-board. The top-most beam had Gothic cusping in roundels and horizontal panels, but the jetties were carried on curved brackets and the barge-boards boasted sunflower pies linked by trailing foliage. Thus a re-interpretation of Chester's ancient architecture in terms of Late Victorian artistry and sophistication, the Little Nag's Head was understandably described by *The British Architect* as, 'one of Mr. Douglas's happiest efforts.'[26]

Equally competent in its handling of timberwork is Llannerch Panna, Penley, Flintshire (1878–9, now Tudor Court), built for the Honourable George T. Kenyon, younger son of the third Baron. Its main block (Douglas's service wing, planned as part of a scheme for replacing a smaller Georgian house, remained unexecuted) is entirely half-timbered. There is, though, little carving, and decoration is otherwise restricted to diagonal and herring-bone bracing and strutting and the concave lozenges. In terms of form, the only element not in accordance with local historical precedent is a polygonal bay-window with turret-like roof, similar to that at Whitegate Vicarage. There are ribbed chimneystacks not appropriate for the region, though herring-bone brick patterns in

The Little Nag's Head Cocoa House, Foregate Street, Chester, 1877. Building News, 33, 1877, p. 508. Drawing by D. P. Fordham)

The Work of John Douglas

another are a complex version of a Cheshire feature represented in *Abbey Square Sketch Book* by Lower Carden Hall [27] and Marton Hall. [28] The knowledge, consistency and restraint of the timbering endow it with the true spirit of its prototypes, but although the house is unusual among Douglas's works in so closely approaching period imitation, the bright red tile roof and hard Ruabon brick of the plinth and chimneystacks brand it immediately as Victorian.

In so far as the centre of Llannerch Panna is occupied by a large hall, the plan is consistent with the type of house which inspired the elevations, and it has none of the spreading freedom of The Gelli. Yet equally it belongs to the rationalism of the Domestic Revival, and in having living rooms at either end of the central hall anticipates a form used by Guy Dawber (1861–1938), and the hall itself, rising through two storeys with a gallery, has some affinity with the living-halls advocated by M. H. Baillie Scott (1865–1945). Earlier panelling is worked into all the principal rooms except the drawing room, which thus preserves its feminine grace. The front door, with ribs, iron studs and hinges and two little slit windows is glorious, and similar to many such which Douglas designed. Yet despite the usual characteristics Douglas's joinery is otherwise fairly subdued, perhaps in deference to the old work, and it is the half-timbering, the light and spacious galleried hall and the wealth of mellow panelling which give a haunting air of timelessness to the house, and make it special within Douglas's *oeuvre*.

The question arises as to the form of construction of the half-timber buildings, and whether the patterning is genuine framing or a superficial veneer such as Norman Shaw is known to have used. There seems to have been variation in practice among Douglas's Cestrian contemporaries.[29] As far as his own work is concerned, the evidence is incomplete, but he would sometimes, and perhaps

Llannerch Panna, Penley, Flintshire, 1878–9. (*Building News*, 36, 1879, p. 198. Drawing by D. P. Fordham)

Early Maturity: Secular Buildings

always, use a solid system of oak framing but with a brick backing sharing the load-bearing function. Under a coat of cement rendering (not lime plaster) the infill of the timbers would also be of brick, thus diluting still further the principle of framing. At the same time it is possible that only rectangular framing members are solid, with braces and struts (and perhaps even rectangular members in gables) being applied to the brick infill and corresponding in depth only with the thickness of the rendering. Despite Douglas's ecclesiological training and the survival of High Victorian characteristics in his work, his having been prepared (as seems at least at times undoubtedly to have been the case) to countenance sham framing in this way represents a characteristically Late Victorian cavalier rejection of Puginistic and Ruskinian doctrine. What happens in the case of jettied construction is not clear, though the brick inner lining must presumably be omitted.

Jettying, though absent at Llannerch Panna, occurs in plenty at Rowden Abbey, Herefordshire (1881). This is another entirely black-and-white house, but with complicated roof forms (including hips) and such features as a canted bay window slotted beneath a jettied gable, it is a varied design, lacking the historical authenticity of Llannerch Panna. It is also more heavily ornamented, having curved bracing and concave lozenges and also Gothic detail in heavily-cusped window lights and carved barge-boards and bressumers. To the following year belongs another Kenyon commission – the Parsonage, Tallarn Green (1882, now Vicarage) built largely at the expense of the Misses Kenyon of The Gelli. Intended for the occupation of a curate, it is very tiny – smaller than the Eaton estate farmhouses – but being nevertheless the residence of a gentleman is carefully fitted up, and has a singularly perfect Douglas interior in miniature. Displaying 'light' half-timbering, it is a late instance of Douglas's use of this, and the elaboration of the Rowden Abbey carpentry was to be of significance in terms of future development.

Vernacular, but outside the mainstream of development, is Plas Mynach, Barmouth, Merioneth (1883), the qualities and siting of which moved Raffles Davison to such eloquence. Built largely of local stone it has a strength and austere simplicity unusual in Douglas's work. There is a low spreading tower with vice turret, again over the kitchen, though stepped gables form the most distinctive feature. Welsh precedent for their use includes Dolaugwyn Hall, Towyn, recorded in *Abbey Square Sketch Book*.[30] The hall, staircase and landing provide a classic example of Douglas's domestic joinery, executed in pine. It may be noted that the door knocker at Plas Mynach, like the Great Budworth inn sign, came from Nuremberg.

Also demanding consideration within the vernacular context is a

The Work of John Douglas

further Egerton-Warburton commission – the restoration (1880) of the timber-framed Bent Farm, Warburton of 1600, in the course of which Douglas-like features and character were given to the house. Douglas was a member of the Society for the Protection of Ancient Buildings from its foundation in 1877 until 1882,[31] but the uncompromising and at times self-assertive domestic and ecclesiastical restorations which he performed owe more to the Camdenian zeal likely to have been absorbed from Paley than to the Society's principles of 'anti-scrape.'

If Mid-Victorian attitudes continued to colour Douglas's approach to restoration work, the tenacity of High Victorian character which persisted in his maturity reached a notable climax in the late 1870s and early '80s, but consideration of this must be preceded by mention of an earlier work – the Colwyn Bay Hotel (*c.* 1872). Colwyn Bay, Denbighshire, began to be developed as a resort from about 1865, and over the years Douglas was responsible for a number of buildings in the town, not all of which have been identified. With dozens of bedrooms approached by a spacious staircase, a large suite of public rooms and complicated service quarters, the hotel was one of the largest buildings which Douglas ever designed, and provides an instance of Victorian requirements transforming traditional building types – the inn expanded beyond recognition to provide seaside holidays for the affluent middle

Plas Mynach, Barmouth, Merioneth, 1883. Staircase and Hall. (*British Architect*, 2 1884, p. 230. Drawing by R. Davison)

Early Maturity: Secular Buildings

classes. It was opened in 1872 and may thus have been conceived some years previously, and with its plate glass sash windows, sparing Gothic detail and high steep roofs, it partakes of High Victorian character. The High Victorianism is, however, of the sort from which emerged Douglas's mature Germanic manner, elements of which are apparent in hipped roofs with receding tiers of hipped dormers and some turret-like forms. The elevations are interesting in their variety and in so far as they express internal arrangement, and although they do not emerge as fully-resolved compositions, there is a unifying element in the very strength and solidity of the somewhat lumpish massing.

The climax of High Victorian character referred to is provided by a series of buildings which, built within a few years of each other in the late 1870s and early '80s, form a coherent stylistic group and mark the zenith of Douglas's Germanic manner. They are also marked by a number of features which were foreshadowed earlier in the '70s at The Limes (with its high Germanic roof) and the Eaton Upper Servants' Houses – the use of hard, bright red brick, and the extension of Germanic elements from the roof to the wall, particularly by the use of blank panelling and attached shafts. All this may be seen as development of Douglas's concern for the wall surface and his interest in its enrichment. Panelling with Gothic cusped heads is directly related to windows of like ilk. Wall shafts

Plas Mynach, Barmouth, Merioneth, 1883. Staircase Gallery and Hall Fireplace. *British Architect*, 21, 1884, p. 242. Drawing by R. Davison)

(which with stringcourses can provide a system of larger panels) may be semi-hexagons or semi-octagons, and perhaps ribbed, and rise through gables to emerge in the round as finials, often with broadly-projecting castellated caps. These may be seen as a facet of the liking for posts and shafts dating from those which divide the clerestorey windows at St. John's, Over (1860–63) (see page 42). Likewise the curved and ogee corbels and brackets which accompany this motif (including arcaded corbel tables and unmoulded curved corbels of more than one order) may be seen as evolving from his inclination for distinctive and at times heavy corbels, and also from his taking up of the Nesfieldian and Shavian concave or ogee bracket. Yet the panelling and wall shafts as they had by this time evolved have German or Netherlandish (and perhaps more specifically Flemish) parallels. Moreover, there is close similarity between Douglas's big chunky corbels and corbel tables, both as used at this time and earlier, and those at the castle of the Teutonic Knights at Marburg and the palace of the Grand Master of the Order at Marienburg.[32]

As for the redness of buildings in this group, most of them are

Nos. 6–11, Grosvenor Park Road, Chester c. 1879–80. (*Die englische Baukunst d Gegenwart*, H. Muthesius, 1900, plate 80)

Early Maturity: Secular Buildings

executed in pressed Ruabon brick. Exceeding even its Accrington counterpart in the fiery intensity of its colour, this was first produced by the brick and tile manufacturer J. C. Edwards, a leading figure in the Late Victorian revival of the use of terra-cotta. Although he had been in business previously, and made sanitary ware at his works at Trefynant, near Ruabon, Denbighshire, it was in about 1870 that Edwards first opened up the red clays of the district and commenced the making of bricks,[33] and extensive though not exclusive use was made of his products by Douglas.

Of work of the Germanic climax, a terrace of houses on the east side of Grosvenor Park Road, Chester (Nos. 6–11, c. 1879–80), is, like the Colwyn Bay Hotel, an amorphous mass of great solidity and bulk. It is, however, a fully disciplined and resolved composition of considerable power and tension. It has high, steep roofs and several gables. With one of these an enormous hipped gable, and with slender octagonal turrets of concave profile at either end of the range, the character is strongly Germanic. Yet there occur not only rectangular panels with ribs of moulded brick, but the vernacular motif of lozenge patterns in headers, their white background providing a sparkling contrast to the red brick walls and roofing tiles. The resourceful use of brick and (in small quantity) terra-cotta is among the chief wonders of these houses, being brought into service for ribbed chimneystacks, moulded mullions, straight-headed, curved and cusped window lights, wall panelling (some of it also cusped) and (in the richly-treated northernmost house with its hipped dormers) wall shafts, corbelling and corbel tabling. Among other details, a timber porch with curved brackets, and a lead finial and iron vane respectively terminating the turrets, provide characteristic touches.

The terrace (for which an unexecuted scheme was prepared in 1872) was built with Douglas himself as developer and landlord. Leading as it does to the main entrance of Grosvenor Park (with its lodge by Douglas, 1865–7), the road was laid out with railings on both sides and a shrubbery behind those on the west, as part of the second Marquess of Westminster's laying out of the park, and provision was made for the retention of railings and shrubbery should development take place behind them.[34] The Marquess's concern for the maintenance or improvement of the approach to the park was shared by the first Duke, for Douglas noted that he had, 'promised the Duke to keep an eye on the Grosvenor Pk. Rd.,' which he considered that, with the building of the terrace, 'as far as one side is concerned has been faithfully performed.'[35] On the opposite side, St. Werburgh's Roman Catholic church was built to designs by his former assistant Edmund Kirby (1873–5), and although interested in acquiring the remaining land behind the shrubbery, he failed to do so,[36] and proposals for buildings (1903–6)

The Work of John Douglas

and the cutting through of a road to link up with houses he had built (1903) nearby in Bath Street were never implemented.

However, his activities on the east side were not confined to the houses, for built at the same time, and grouping with them, is Grosvenor Park Baptist Church (1879–80). With octagonal turrets flanking its gable end, it relates well with its neighbours, and the flêche which formerly rose from the ridge must have given the finishing touch to the exciting skyline of Grosvenor Park Road. Doubtless it was Raffles Davison who wrote in *The British Architect* of, 'a picture, which for effect, I have seldom seen equalled in street architecture . . . this little side street, with its new bright red brick church and houses . . .well illustrates what an architect can do when he has a whole street to go at . . .'[37]

In the Grosvenor Park Road houses, Gothic detailing is virtually confined to cusping, and the use by Douglas of vernacular elements and shining red materials places the work firmly within his Late Victorian output. Yet with dramatic skyline, massiveness, and the elaboration of wall surfaces, the terrace is at the same time strongly High Victorian in nature, and speaks of the sublime as much as of the picturesque. Even when used more or less in isolation and assimilated in a vernacular context, as with the roofs and staircase turret of the Gamekeeper's House and Kennels at Eaton, or the hipped roofs at Cheaveley Hall Farm, Douglas's Germanic elements can be seen as emanating from his High Victorian period. As used with the consistency and intensity of Grosvenor Park Road, the phenomenon of the Germanic manner can only be seen, not just as a continuation of, but as a sudden and sophisticated revitalisation of High Victorianism.

Shotwick Park, Cheshire, *c.* 1879. Entrance front. (*British Architect*, 1879, p. 36. Drawing by R. Davison)

Tobacco Factory for Cope Bros. & Co., Liverpool, c. 1880. (Demolished)

It may be noted that at this time Douglas reverted to the stereotyped though functional and adaptable Hinderton-Oakmere plan form for three of the four large houses which belong to this short-lived Germanic eruption. The fourth – Shotwick Park, Cheshire (c. 1879), has been altered and extended, but it would seem from the first to have been closely related to this form. Shotwick Park is similar to the Grosvenor Park Road terrace in its massive solidity and indefinable form, its heavy hipped and gabled roofs and its elaborate use of brick. Windows rise through the eaves into hipped dormers, and the service wing extends at right angles, thus defining an entrance court, as hinted at on a smaller scale at Whitegate Vicarage. The Shotwick roofs include turret forms, though none of the slender octagonal sort found at Grosvenor Park Road. Two such did occur at the extension to the Tobacco Factory of Cope Bros. & Co. on the corner of Lord Nelson and St. Vincent Streets, Liverpool (c. 1880, demolished). This was a taut, compact design, with strong vertical emphasis, and with a riot of red steep hipped roofs, turrets, lead finials, miniature dormers (some hipped and having their own massive finials) and with a lower gatehouse having its own hipped roofscape. Common brick was used, but dressings in hard purpose-mades and some stone included moulded mullions, cusped panelling, wall shafts, arcaded corbel tables and – to complete a veritable treasury of Douglas detailing – curved brackets. The highly picturesque result was all the more potent on

115

account of the building being perched on a cliff edge above the platforms of Lime Street Station.

Also belonging to this group on account of their turret roof forms, though the materials are more subdued, are St. Oswald's Vicarage, Parkgate Road, Chester (1880), and the attributable remodelling of Forest Hey, Sandiway (1882).

Like the Colwyn Bay Hotel and Copes' building, an unsuccessful competition entry for Bootle Town Hall, Lancashire (1880) represents for Douglas an unusual building type, and included municipal offices, council and mayoral suites and assembly room. Although the design was irregular in its massing, and also broken up by buttresses, something of an overall grid effect resulted from the rhythm of mullions and transoms, panelling (some of it cusped) and the larger panels resulting from wall shafts (some of which rose up into finials with projecting caps) and stringcourses. Being intended for execution in stone rather than brick, some greater elaboration of detail was indicated in the form of carving, a set of heavy unmoulded corbels, and window tracery. As for the roofs, they included turrets and a tall clock tower ending in an octagonal spire with tiered breaks at its base. This tower and the large windows of the assembly room helped to pull the composition together, though it remained somewhat disjointed, and another unsuccessful competition design dating from the following year indicates the limitations both of Douglas's Germanic manner and of himself as a designer.

This scheme, prepared jointly with the civil engineer C. F. Findlay, was for Exchange Station, Liverpool, the terminus of the Lancashire & Yorkshire Railway, and represents a yet more unusual departure for Douglas in terms of building type. With a range of offices fronting the station sheds, it presented to Tithebarn Street a long and ambitious frontage in the Germanic manner, with steep roofs, towers and turrets. Well-handled individually, the long drawn-out series of events failed to coalesce, and although capable of

Above and right: Barrowmore Hall (Barrow Court), Great Barrow, Cheshire, c. 1881. (Demolished) (*Building News*, 41 1881, p. 494. Drawing by E. Hodkinson)

Early Maturity: Secular Buildings

sustaining the length of the Grosvenor Park Road terrace and the varied grouping of Shotwick Park, the Germanic manner seems inappropriate for so long a façade as this. Irrespective of style, the apparent inherent liking for vertical emphasis and closely-grouped masses which found expression in the Germanic manner would in any case seem to have militated against the successful handling by Douglas of a long elevation. The unexecuted scheme for the Eaton Stud was exceptional in being a lowish spreading group which vertical emphases were able to unite, but the Colwyn Bay Hotel and, at the outset of his career, the south wing of Vale Royal (1860–61) show this limitation.

To judge from the published engraving, there may also have been some lack of cohesion about Barrowmore Hall (or Barrow Court), Great Barrow, Cheshire (c. 1881, demolished), though this cannot have obscured the merits of what must have been a fascinating building of outstanding importance. Built for H. Lyle Smith, a Liverpool grain merchant, it was one of Douglas's largest country houses, and expanded the Hinderton-Oakmere plan to a quite considerable scale. An additional room (a school room, with children's staircase adjoining) was placed beyond the dining room on the garden front; the hall was two-storeyed with a gallery, and the service quarters included such refinements as a luggage entrance and a laundry with adjoining drying ground. Here again an entrance court was defined, with the service wing projecting and being continued by stable buildings. The entrance front at least had no Germanic hipped roof forms, but the heaviness of mass which it shared with Grosvenor Park Road and Shotwick Park, and the detailing and use of brick, place the house firmly within the

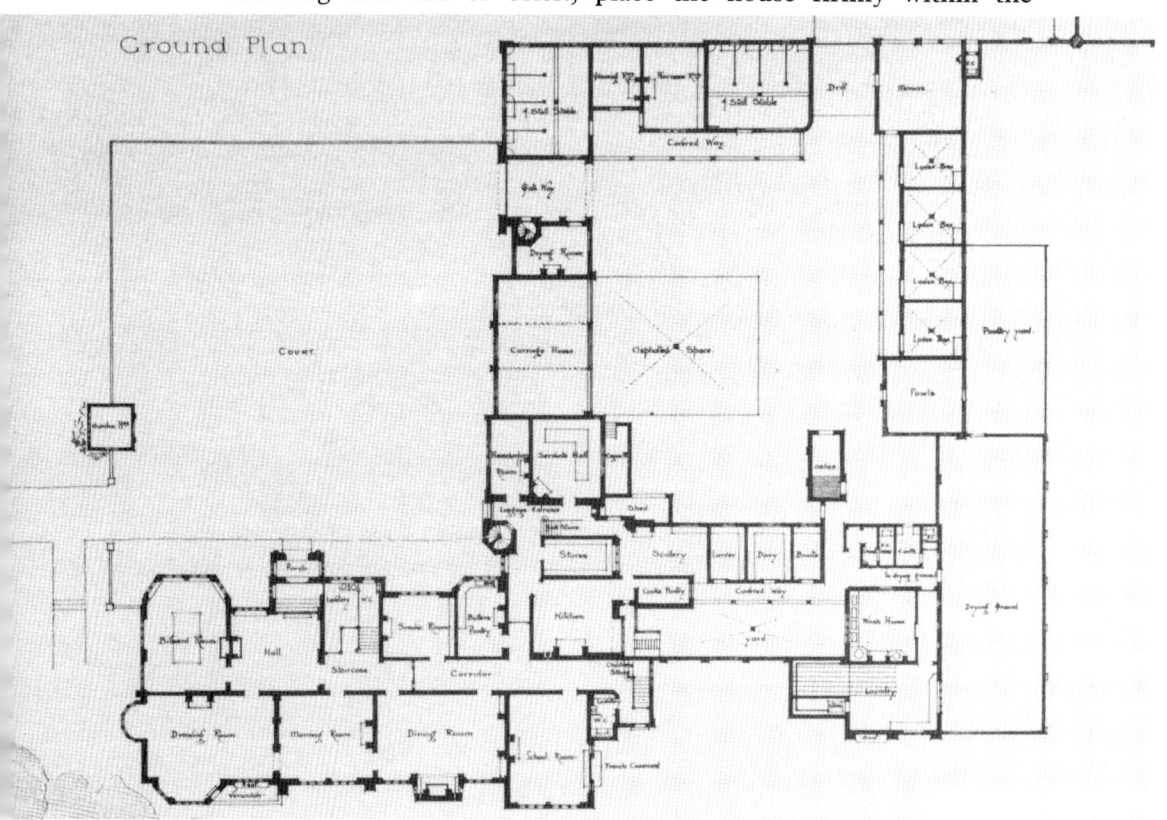

The Work of John Douglas

Germanic climax. The free, sculptural treatment of craggy masses included particularly a canted bay window which, below a gable, was transformed to rectangular plan by two sets of brick corbelling, one recessed behind the other. Despite the main block being 'double pile' it was spanned by a single pitched roof, and the enormous gable end which resulted, and another gable on the entrance front, were elaborately ornamented with panelling (much of it cusped) and wall shafts rising from corbels and ending in finials with broad caps. Thus although the gables themselves were straight-sided, they had something of the Netherlandish character of that of the Warburton Mill scheme. Equally massive but simpler in detail was a castellated tower, with vice turret, forming a focal point at the junction of main and service blocks. A more ambitious version of the tower which was to appear at Plas Mynach, it resembled it and that at The Gelli in having risen above the kitchen. Cusped window lights abounded, but particularly attractive and Douglas-like was the gatehouse between entrance court and stable yard. It had a pyramid roof with clock turret, cusped panelling, and a window rising through the eaves to end in a gable and flanked by wall shafts which emerged as ball finials. The brick and terra-cotta for the house was supplied, not by J. C. Edwards, but by Henry Bowers of Ruabon. It would seem that in addition to the three-dimensional decorative brickwork, extensive use was made of blue diapering.

Such diapering appeared with frequency in Douglas's buildings from this time onwards, particularly on the Eaton estate and particularly as patterning on Ruabon brick. It may be seen as related to the polychromy of his High Victorian phase, and its use at this date may perhaps have been prompted by a desire to exploit the colourful properties of Ruabon products. It may be supposed to have found special favour with the Duke of Westminster, for it also appears in most work done for him by Lockwood, and in Edis's Overleigh Lodge at Eaton, and its use was so widespread as almost to constitute a distinctive stamp for estate work of the 1880s and '90s.

Built for the Duke's secretary, then Colonel David Scotland, Eccleston Hill, Eccleston (1881–2) is another version of the Hinderton-Oakmere plan, though the service quarters are disproportionately large, due to the alterations made by Douglas & Fordham (1892–4) when Scotland was succeeded by the Honourable Arthur Lawley. Despite the Mid-Victorian plan, the exterior is quieter and less dramatic than other buildings considered in this group. The brickwork is tempered by extensive use of stone dressings; Germanic and related elements are confined to one turret-like roof and restricted use of cusped panelling and wall shafts, and enrichment of the wall surface depends largely upon blue diapering. There is something of the amorphous blockiness of the Colwyn Bay Hotel or Grosvenor Park Road, but the vocabulary of gable, hip and

Early Maturity: Secular Buildings

canted bay window is handled with restraint; the end of the main block has a sensitively-contrived grouping of a chimneystack and gable with ball finials and wall shafts on inverted semi-cone corbels, and the difference in character between this building and others of the Germanic group is further marked by the use of half-timber for the entrance porch and the gable of the stable gatehouse. Eccleston Hill has undergone alteration, but the oakwork of the hall and staircase remains as an outstanding example of Douglas's domestic joinery – panelling, unmitred mouldings, curved brackets, incised patterned and linear ornament, exposed staircase wedges and arcaded gallery.

Colour plate page 35

More Germanic is the contemporary Stud Lodge at Eaton Hall (1881–2), a little building whose main part turns from being circular and brick to octagonal and half-timber and ends in a pointed roof. Though remarkable, it is eclipsed by the marvellous Eccleston Hill Lodge (1881) (frontispiece), built where the former main approach to Eaton from Chester enters the deer park. Compared with Waterhouse's mansion, Douglas's vernacular lodges and cottages in the park tend towards tameness, but here he showed himself capable of rising to the occasion in terms of ducal grandeur. It is a three-storey gatehouse, with rib-vaulted gateway, and its outline owes much to the Chester Triumphal Arch. So intense is the concentration of Germanic and other characteristic forms and details that it appears almost as a Douglas self-parody. A red hipped roof with chamfered corners, so tall and steep as to be virtually a spire, rises between four tourelles; on the outer side a central vertical panel contained within wall shafts includes armorial bearings and ends in its own spirelet; hipped roofed blocks abut against either side of the tower, and one of these has its own conical-roofed staircase turret. Materials include stone, half-timber and diapered brick, and there are miniature hipped dormers, lead finials, cusped panelling, cusped and traceried windows, cusped corbel tables and curved brackets and corbels.

Despite the vehemently Germanic character, the half-timber is not of the 'light' variety (neither is it at Stud Lodge), but is rather a system of close-studding with cusp-like decoration to diagonal bracing. Masonry is interspersed with occasional courses of darker stone. Striation of this sort appears elsewhere in Douglas's work at this time and later, but may be seen as another feature with roots in his High Victorian phase by reason of the bands in the Whitchurch Town Hall scheme, the continuous ashlar course at Sealand church

Colour plate page xix

(1865–7) and the cruder brick stripes at Over Congregational Church (1865). Such polychromatic horizontal emphasis had been advocated by Ruskin as an expression of construction.[38]

Only one other building achieved comparable dramatic impact and facility to amaze. The Paddocks, Eccleston (1882–3), something

119

The Work of John Douglas

of a companion piece to Eccleston Hill in being built as a residence for the Duke's land agent, was put in hand for Cecil Parker soon after his having assumed the post. A compact version of the Hinderton-Oakmere plan in that almost all the accommodation was contained within one block, the external massing of which did not clearly distinguish between principal and service parts. The service end has been demolished, thus wrecking Douglas's fantastic composition, though what remains is spectacular enough. Materials are pressed brick with diapering, and red stone dressings with much carving. As at Eccleston Hill Lodge there are horizontal bands of stone, here set within brick, including some in the chimneystacks. Set against enormously high red hipped roofs are steep coped gables and dormers, all with finials which have their origin in wall shafts which enclose vertical panels of windows, and there are miniature hipped dormers, cusped panelling and cusped corbel tables. Two conical-roofed corner turrets occur in similar relation to the plan as those at Oakmere (1867) (see page 50); a projection containing front door and staircase has canted corners corbelled at a higher stage into rectangles, as occurred at Barrowmore Hall; adjoining this is a conical-roofed staircase turret, and the demolition involved the loss of three further turrets. Yet again an entrance court was defined by a projecting range with gatehouse, the latter having pyramid roof, gabled dormer with wall shafts and another conical turret. This range also is partially destroyed, but the end which remains contained the estate office, where Parker held sway for almost 30 years.

Colour plate page xix

A great heavy front door, surrounded by elaborate stonework, prepares the visitor for riches within, though the interior does not represent a complete Douglas fitting-up. Earlier doors, chimneypieces and woodwork were incorporated, and certain puzzling features may date from a redecoration when Basil Carr succeeded as agent in 1911. Douglas's contributions, however, include a good chimneypiece in the dining room and the staircase which, with variations and refinements beyond the usual, exceeds expectation in its scrumptiousness.

Although girt in the full panoply of Douglas's Germanic manner, The Paddocks is unique among his buildings in having some quite strong French character, derived from the corner turrets and steep coped dormers and from crocketed ogees over the front door and some of the windows. Although mentioning the house of the Duke's secretary, it must have been The Paddocks rather than Eccleston Hill which Sédille had in mind when exclaiming, 'C'est un petit château!'[39]

Mention must finally be made of two buildings in Chester. The brick and stone Grosvenor Club and North & South Wales Bank (1881–3, now Midland Bank) was later extended by Douglas &

120

Midland Bank, 1881–3 and 1908, and Diamond Jubilee Memorial Clock, 1899, The Eastgate, Chester.

Minshull (1908) but as first built the street frontage consisted of a tall narrow four-storey gable and a hexagonal Germanic turret above a corbelled oriel. In an early design, revised in execution, the gable was of stepped form; there was the familiar cusped panelling, and also a system of wall shafts which were intersected by string courses, incorporated corbels and brackets, and ended in broad-capped finials. Moreover, there was sinuous and wiry tracery (some of it in spandrels below elliptical arches) suggesting Hanseatic or Flemish origin. The building adjoins the Eastgate of the City Walls (an arch of 1768–9 which replaced the mediaeval gateway) and in connection with the scheme it was proposed to erect a clock turret spanning the walkway over the centre of the arch. Although the idea was revived at a later date, nothing came of it at this stage, just as a scheme by Douglas for alterations to the arch sponsored by the Duke of Westminster (as third Marquess) in 1872 proved abortive. Besides the elimination of the clock, departures from the original design included detailed changes of fenestration and wall enrichment (though the use of wiry tracery remained), the inclusion of a prominent chimneystack, with stone bands, as at The Paddocks, and, most notably, the substitution of a gable with curved shapes for the stepped version.

The idea of a large shaped or otherwise enriched gable embracing

The Work of John Douglas

a whole facade dates back to the scheme for Warburton Mill, and this Netherlandish feature (which may be seen as something separate from the more vernacular-inspired shaped gables used for farmhouses) made its brief re-appearance in the 1880s with Barrowmore Hall, the Grosvenor Club and, in strongest and purest form, the former Cheshire County Constabulary, Chester (No. 142 Foregate Street, 1884). This presents a broad and high gable frontage of brick and terra-cotta, more specifically Flemish in design than any other of Douglas's buildings, but with characteristic detailing such as cusped window lights.

It may be wondered to what extent Douglas's use of these gables was stimulated either by the 'Queen Anne' style or by the more strongly Flemish work of Sir Ernest George (1839–1922). If he did not already know George & Peto's Harrington Gardens and Collingham Gardens, London (*c.* 1881) their respective publication in 1883[40] and 1884[41] might at least have had some effect upon the County Constabulary. The question of relationship between the Grosvenor Club and County Constabulary and a large ornamented gable design by one of Douglas's chief admirers for one of his regular suppliers is also intriguing. Published in 1881 and presumably intended to display the properties of terra-cotta, this was a 'Suggestion for a Riverside Terra-Cotta Warehouse adapted from an old design by T. Raffles Davison for J. C. Edwards Esq. Ruabon.'[42]

This chapter has dealt with Douglas's secular buildings from the emergence of a mature manner of expression up until the time of his entering into partnership with D. P. Fordham. Good as are many of the buildings of his High Victorian phase, there is a hesitancy and a seeming lack of purpose in the disparities of style and quality which they display, contrasting with the masterful confidence apparent from 1870 onwards. While aware of and receptive to contemporary architectural thought and ethos, he produced buildings of highly individual stamp with the English vernacular and German secular Gothic precedents providing the dominant themes. In varying and developing these themes, consistency of quality and detail was maintained, and even buildings which stand alone as stylistic departures from the main body of his work are no less endowed with conviction and distinctive character.

Vernacular and Germanic played their part in Douglas's churches, also, along with what may be thought of as Late Victorian ecclesiastical Gothic. Consideration must now be given to the churches of his maturity, and the evolution of this style in his work be traced.

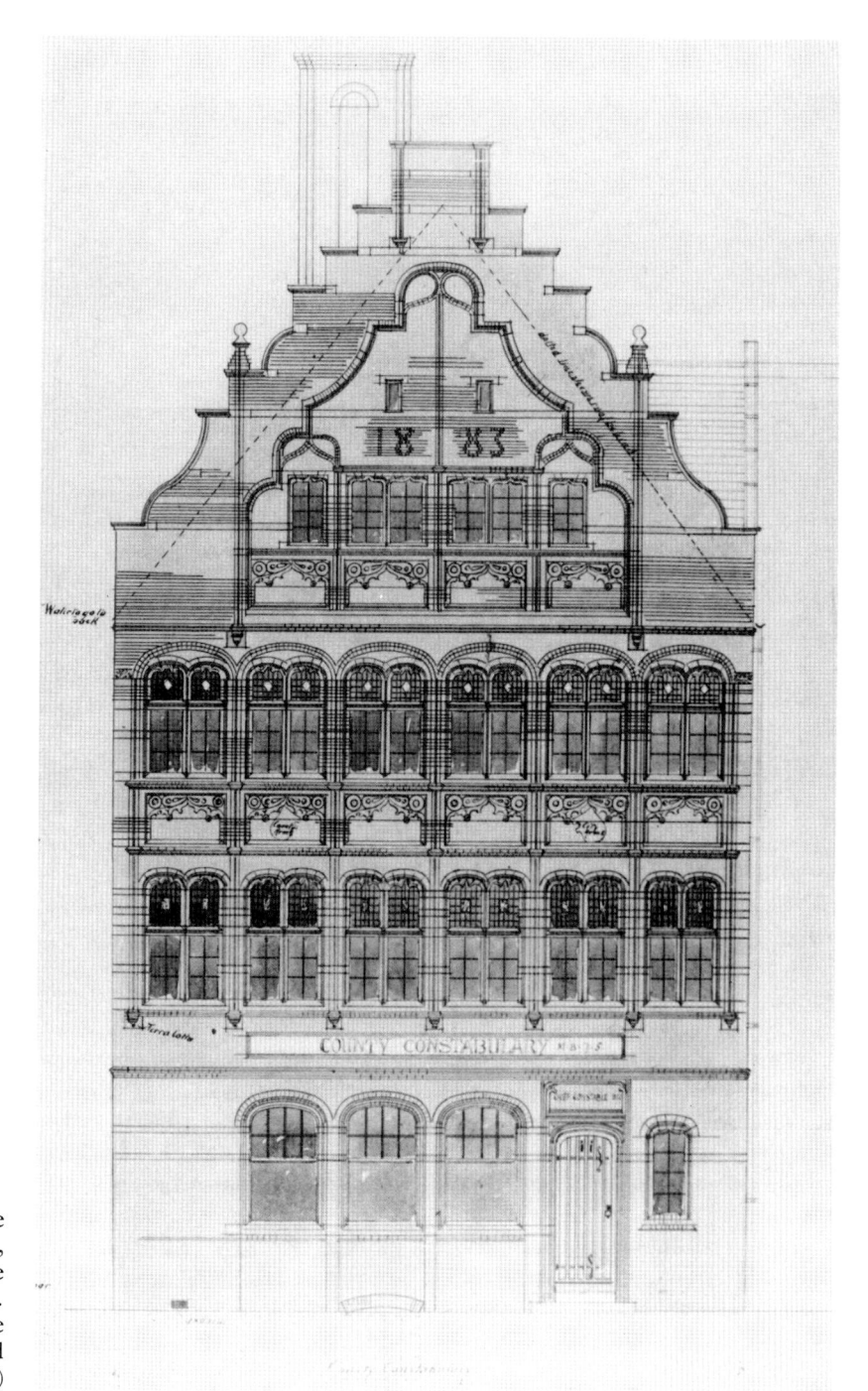

Former Cheshire County Constabulary, No. 142 Foregate Street, Chester, 1884. (Drawing at Cheshire Record Office dated 6th February 1884)

St Mary's Church, Whitegate, Cheshire 1874–5. (*Architect*, 14, 1875, p. 318. Drawing by E. Hodkinson)

VIII Early Maturity: Churches

In the years 1874–5 the church of St. Mary at Whitegate, Cheshire, was remodelled, largely at the expense of Lord Delamere, and with John Douglas as architect. Opposite the lodge gates of Vale Royal, the church was the 'capella extra portas', without the gates of the Cistercian abbey, and although the body of the building dated from 1728, it incorporated the oak posts of the arcade of what had been a timber-framed church, probably of the fourteenth century. The Georgian building – a brick box with parapets, round-headed windows, west tower and apsidal east end – was not such as to commend itself to Victorian ecclesiological sentiments, and it would have been entirely replaced were it not for the old woodwork and the fact of the eighteenth century bricks being considered attractive ones. In the event, a remarkable transformation was effected whereby not only the mediaeval arcading but much of the eighteenth century walling was retained, though the exterior was given a completely Victorian and Douglas-like appearance. A short chancel was added; the parapets were removed and the roof carried down to new coved eaves; traceried windows with straight heads (a feature which Douglas used on other occasions and which appears at Eccleston School, conceived at about the same time) were inserted; the tower was reduced in height and given buttresses and a short Germanic shingled spire, broached and with miniature 'slit' dormers; a half-timbered porch was added and the aisles and new chancel given half-timbered gables. Some old wood was worked into

Early Maturity: Churches

the roof; the new chancel arch was built in timber and, needless to say, the Georgian box pews and other fittings were swept away.

With its use of half-timbering the church partakes of Douglas's vernacular manner. The use of wood was doubtless suggested by the ancient arcading, and it may be supposed that the ideas and experience gained at Whitegate influenced the introduction of timbering in three churches which belong to the years immediately following.

St. Paul's Boughton – Douglas's own parish church in Chester – is a rebuilding (1876) incorporating parts of an 1830 predecessor by William Cole. With lancets and an uncompromisingly stark exterior of red pressed brick (one of Douglas's earliest uses of it), the church dramatically occupies a steeply-sloping site above the River Dee. A brick-nogged and hipped-roofed aisle is a later addition (1902) and the original nave and aisles are under one roof span and embraced by a huge three-sided apse extending their full width. With posts and pointed arches entirely of timber, the high arcading of the 1876 nave is an enlarged version of what, when entire, doubtless existed at

St Paul's Church, Boughton, Chester, 1876; south aisle 1902. Interior.

St Michael's Church, Altcar, Lancashire, 1879. Exterior.

Whitegate and for which the closest surviving Cheshire precedent is at Marton. Black-and-white framing fills the spandrels; the roof construction is heavy and complex, and the internal timberwork at St. Paul's has both an awesome sense of strength and a sensitivity and feel for the material which is in accordance with the 'artistic' tenor of the age. In its big-boned simplicity of plan and in its use of structural timberwork on so bold a scale, St. Paul's is exceptional among Douglas's churches, and if St. Ann's, Warrington (1868–9) (see page 55), is his prodigy church of the 1860s, this is the prodigy of the '70s.

Exceptional also is St. Michael's, Altcar, Lancashire (1879), built at the expense of the Earl of Sefton, and which Raffles Davison considered, 'should increase the respect which is felt for the vigour and dignity of Mr. Douglas's work throughout the country.'[1] Here the scale is tiny, and the building is unique in Douglas's output in being entirely half-timber, and with the framework exposed inside

St Michael's Church, Altcar, Lancashire, 1879. Interior.

St Chad's Church, Hopwas, Staffordshire, 1881.

and out. Although the detailing marks it as his own, it is his nearest approach to a complete historical pastiche, and it overlapped in date with the building of the convincingly-timbered Llannerch Panna (1878–9). At Altcar the oak is handled with a verve and assurance which makes most Victorian Vernacular Revivalism seem pallid, and inside this exquisite little building one can wallow in the sheer beauty of the wood, and sense the intense enthusiasm which Douglas must have felt in designing for it.

The Revd. W. MacGregor, vicar of Tamworth, who employed Douglas on other occasions, was closely involved with the building of St. Chad's, Hopwas, Staffordshire (1881), with its complicated build-up of elements above the chancel, culminating in a steep octagonal flêche. The external walling is of brick and half-timber and here the solid framing has (in accordance with Douglas's apparent usual custom) a brick backing, with the internal walls being of exposed brick. The porch is timber-framed, and there are straight-headed traceried windows.

The Work of John Douglas

Although external half-timbering and internal wooden posts and framing were occasionally introduced in later churches, they never recurred with the same frequency or with equal virtuosity as in this group of churches which, it is reasonable to suppose, took its impetus from the early fragments found at Whitegate. Whether or not any additional impetus could have been derived from Norman Shaw's chapel at Peplow, Shropshire (1877–8) must be a matter for conjecture.

That Douglas should have departed from conventional ecclesiastical design by introducing such strong elements of the vernacular was in any case unusual, and for the most part his churches of the 1870s onwards may be classified as being Late Victorian Gothic. Although within this context always incorporating recognisable forms or detailing, they tend to be less idiosyncratic and to display a lesser fund of originality than does his contemporary secular output, just as (with the exceptions of Over Congregational Chapel, 1865, and St. Ann's, Warrington) his churches of the 1860s are less inventive than High Victorian secular buildings of the same period. In this continuing tendency to conservatism may be detected further confirmation of the strength and durability of the ecclesiastical discipline of Paley's office. The appearances of the Vernacular and the Germanic were limited and occasional, and a complete kicking over of the traces, as at St. Ann's, Warrington, and St. Paul's, Boughton, was exceptional.

Within a national context, the maturing of Late Victorian ecclesiastical Gothic may be exemplified by the big brick churches of the 1860s by James Brooks (1825–1901), which are High Victorian in their boldness and massiveness but forward-looking in their simplicity and refinement, and in the work of J. L. Pearson and G. F. Bodley, whose quiet, sober and sensitive churches provide the late nineteenth century ecclesiastical counterpart to the Domestic Revival. Pearson's vaulted church of St. Peter, Vauxhall (1860), is but a short step from his fully developed St. Augustine's, Kilburn (1871–7); in 1863 Bodley changed his High Victorian design for All Saints', Cambridge, to something quieter and more English and thus paved the way for Tue Brook (1868–70), Pendlebury (1870–74) and Hoar Cross (begun 1872). The involvement of William Morris and his circle with Bodley churches of the '60s foreshadows, moreover, the Arts & Crafts connection with the free and eclectic churches of J. D. Sedding (1838–91). Varying elements of what under Camdenian dictate had been the forbidden fruit of Perpendicular occur at Tue Brook, Pendlebury and Hoar Cross, or at Sedding's church of St. Clement, Boscombe (1871–3). Perpendicular contributed nothing to Pearson's cool and lucid lancet style, and Bodley retained a respect for flowing tracery, but it nevertheless played a profound part – not least in the hands of the Paley & Austin partnership – in the refined

Early Maturity: Churches

and unpedantic but nonetheless scholarly Gothic of Late Victorian church architecture.

Just as Douglas's pair of cottages at Great Budworth (1868) in Nesfieldian vernacular style appeared, with dramatic suddenness, as his first Late Victorian secular building, so two Cheshire churches of 1869–70 – St. Alban's, Tattenhall and St. Mary's, Dodleston – may be considered as his first Late Victorian churches, with Helsby (1868–70) as the last one of his High Victorian phase. The change is immediately apparent by reason of the use of Perpendicular motifs, exceptionally *avant-garde* for the date, and their presence may be explained by neither of the churches being entirely new. Earlier – apparently fifteenth century – parts were in both cases incorporated. With the tower and most of the aisle walls, Tattenhall retains the more extensive mediaeval remains, and Douglas's impeccably Perpendicular nave arcade with octagonal piers, and five-light east window with rectilinear tracery, may owe something to their predecessors. Much freer, but free in a fresh, Late Victorian way, are shallow and unmoulded segmental arches to the clerestorey windows internally, while the hand of Douglas of the 1860s is still apparent in foliated corbels and angel hood-mould stops. Despite Dodleston being an Eaton estate village, the Duke of Westminster (as third Marquess) paid only for the lych-gate and churchyard wall, and the rebuilding of the church may have been put in hand prior to his succession. Old work includes only the lower stage of the tower and some reused windows, and to Douglas can be ascribed reticulated

St Mary's Church, Dodleston, Cheshire, 1869–70. (*Works*. Drawing by G. Smith, 1871)

The Work of John Douglas

tracery, straight-headed windows with cusped lights, and the upper stage of the tower. To this he gave Perpendicular character by means of two-light cusped and traceried bell openings and a band of quatrefoils in lozenges, though his own distinctive touch appears in a short spire recessed behind the parapet. The quatrefoil frieze appears elsewhere in his work, and there is precedent for it in Cheshire towers. His use of the feature is particularly close to those at St. Chad's, Over and Weaverham (which he restored in 1877). Other churches where it occurs include Tarvin (illustrated in *Abbey Square Sketch Book*)[2] and at Northop, Flintshire (also restored by him in 1877 and also in *Abbey Square Sketch Book*[3]) there are quatrefoils not in lozenges but in squares.

Both Tattenhall and Dodleston have timber-framed porches, a feature sufficiently unusual at the time for *The Builder* to consider that at Dodleston 'rather quaint.'[4] Interesting in introducing vernacular into Gothic churches, they nevertheless do not compare in significance with the later more extensive woodwork of Whitegate and its progeny, and precedent for timber porches attached to masonry churches may be found, not so much in Cheshire, as in the examples of Herefordshire and its region.

Tattenhall and Dodleston in their use of Perpendicular are special cases, explicable, like Whitegate, in terms of what was retained of earlier work. Also an isolated instance was the addition (*c.* 1872–6) of a tall shingled spire, of Germanic character, tiered at the base and broached, to the tower of Douglas's earlier (1865–6) church at Aldford (see page 49). A more consistent and Gothic development can be discerned in a series of churches which begins with that of St. John, Hartford (1873–5), a short distance from Sandiway. Although intended to have a west tower and broached spire, the present tower was added at a later date (1887–9) to a revised design. There is a clerestoreyed nave and lower transepts which are attached not to the nave or to a crossing proper, but to the chancel. That on the north was for the accommodation of children; that on the south houses organ chamber and vestry, and the treatment of their respective openings on either side of the chancel differs. Equally free are the stylistic motifs. The arcade with alternating octagonal and circular piers is the most archaeologically correct feature, and although the windows are for the most part plain or cusped lancets, there is a little bar tracery, including a curious subdivision within the central light of the east window. Characteristic Douglas traces include inverted semi-cone corbels, free-standing columns bifurcating the aisle windows internally, wall shafts (here in the form of miniature buttresses) between the lights of the east window externally, and timber-framed porches with their openings framed by brackets of curved profile.

The most notable feature of Hartford is the masonry. The walling,

Early Maturity: Churches

both outside and in, is of yellowish stone in small rock-faced blocks, with smooth dressings largely of local pink Runcorn stone. The resulting contrast of colour and texture shows a continued liking for polychromy, but in terms of a sophisticated exploration of the use of stone. Inside, the rough surfaces produce a striking effect, particularly where the light falls on them in the region of the clerestorey, the arches of whose window openings die simply into splayed reveals. Thus although within a conventional Gothic framework, Hartford church is endowed with much freshness and freedom, and that this is accomplished in an unostentatious and harmonious way, with none of the heaviness or aggressiveness of High Victorianism, marks it out as belonging to the Late Victorian era.

There followed several churches to which similar comment applies. St. Paul's, Marston, Cheshire (1874, demolished), was small, with much moulded brick, lancets, and a miniature west tower and spire not unlike that which contemporaneously evolved at Whitegate. Rossett Presbyterian Chapel, Denbighshire (1875), has lancets and a Germanic flêche tiered at its base. St. Stephen's, Moulton, Cheshire (1876), is more surprising, with a variety of fenestration and the interior in two kinds of brick despite the exterior being stone. Also to these years belongs the commencement (1876) of the rebuilding of Christ Church, Chester, replacing a predecessor of 1838 by Thomas Jones, and carried out in stages, apparently to progressively amended designs, up until 1900. A tower and spire intended at one time never materialised, and it is not clear which parts of the present church date from 1876. Another building which never received its intended spire is the former Welsh Church of St. John the Evangelist, Mold, Flintshire (1878). Churches in this group, including Hartford, have various forms of sheer and unmoulded battered buttresses. This feature, closely associated with late nineteenth century architecture of Arts & Crafts affinity, occurs in bold form at the east end of St. John's, Mold, where together with a set of five stepped lancets grouped under one hood-mould, it imparts a decidedly advanced, *fin de siècle* flavour. The building of St. John's overlapped with that of the important church at Halkyn, but before this is considered, something must be noted of the detailing of churches.

Consistent and recognisable features occur in the design of ecclesiastical fittings. A font bowl carried on a central column surrounded by a cluster of subsidiary shafts is, for instance, frequently encountered, but it is the joinery detailing of church furnishings which merits special study. The unmitred mouldings and incised lozenges and pies familiar from domestic interiors are all there, sometimes along with ball finials and miniature turned balusters of seventeenth century derivation. Allied with these are Gothic motifs, such as cusping similar to that already noted in

The Work of John Douglas

bressumers at the Little Nag's Head, Chester (1877) (see page 106) and Rowden Abbey (1881). Closely related are cusped and depressed ogee heads (as used for window lights and wall panelling) both in solid panels and open screenwork. English fifteenth century ancestry is here obvious. Such precedent exists also for cusped patterns within a roundel (a bench-end with one at Silk Willoughby, Lincolnshire, is in *Abbey Square Sketch Book*[5]), though Douglas also developed the idea inherent in this into freer spiky and swirling tracery patterns, which likewise sometimes appear in the carving of half-timber. Something of its wiry complexity is hinted at in an illustration in *Abbey Square Sketch Book* of a fifteenth century German cabinet at the South Kensington (that is, Victoria and Albert) Museum,[6] and it would seem to relate also to the Flemish or Hanseatic tracery of the Grosvenor Club, Chester (1881–3). Included in the same plate as the German piece is an English cradle, dated 1641, with unmitred mouldings and round finials similar to those which Douglas sometimes used.

Another decorative element is tracery in the form of thin vertical miniature panels, an inch or two wide. When terminated with a single cusp (something also shown in the Silk Willoughby illustration) a key-hole effect results, but a more distinctive form consists of closed heads surmounted by one or more tiers of circles.

Left: Pew at Church of St John the Evangelist, Sandiway, Cheshire, 1902–3.
Right: Stall ends, Astbury Church, Cheshire. (*Abbey Square Sketch Book*, I, plate 60. Drawing by F. J. Thorne)

Early Maturity: Churches

This occurs in the late mediaeval screens and bench-ends at Astbury, Cheshire, liberally illustrated in *Abbey Square Sketch Book*,[7] which also gives an example from Plemstall, Cheshire.[8] It furthermore shows the great hall screen at Haddon Hall, which with its cusped, ogee and varyingly traceried panels would seem likely to have provided direct influence on Douglas's detailing.[9]

Other forms and elements include conventionalised poppyheads, sometimes of diamond or lozenge shape (also seen in the Silk Willoughby plate) and posts or shafts related in feeling to the external attached wall shafts. Also often with broad castellated caps, these can be either square (placed straight or diagonally) or octagonal, and occur particularly in reredoses (sometimes in stone rather than wood) and organ cases, and octagonal or circular shafts also have obvious application in the design of lecterns. Bench-ends, either for clergy, choir or congregational seating, are frequently of curved profile. The forms of tracery already noted, as well as incised lozenge and disc patterns, are applied to solid surfaces, and the tracery appears not only in open form, as in screens, but as patterns in pierced panels. Such patterns appear, for instance, in pulpits, but more frequently in the continuous kneeling desk at the front of nave seating. Yet again this is an aspect of Douglas's maturity which is traceable to the 1860s, with pierced circular patterns as well as proto-

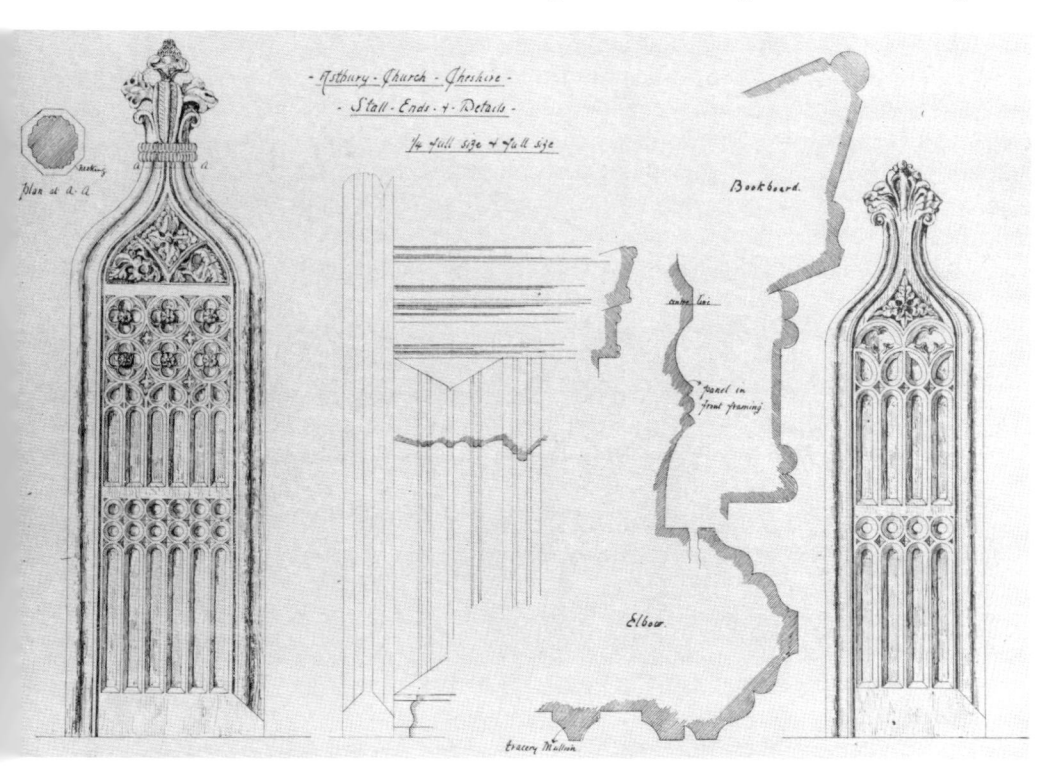

The Work of John Douglas

Church of St Mary the Virgin, Halkyn, Flintshire, 1877–8. Exterior.

pie roundels used in the furnishings at Sealand (1865–7).

At Hartford, the oak pulpit has unmitred mouldings and incised sunflower patterns, and the chancel and nave seating, of pine, displays unmitred mouldings, curved bench-ends and conventionalised poppyheads. Thus although the fittings of this church are in no way outstanding among Douglas's comparable work, they illustrate basic elements of the consistent and coherent style which formed his medium of expression for ecclesiastical woodwork. With contributions from a greater range of sources, this style produces results of even greater richness – though of equally restrained and disciplined richness – then does his domestic joinery.

The miniature circular tracery of the Astbury screens was sometimes inflated to the scale of full-sized architecture, for instance at Eccleston School (1874–81) (see page 100), and small circles also figure, together with other shapes, in tracery design, particularly within windows with straight heads. This is to be seen in the Bootle Town Hall design (1880), at Rowden Abbey, Eccleston Hill Lodge (1881) (frontispiece), or at Hopwas. At the latter church there are also tracery bars or mullions rising from the centres of the cusped heads of lower lights. A distinctive feature of Douglas's tracery design, this appeared in compressed form in the Bootle design and is the principal pattern in the straight-headed windows at Whitegate.

The church of St. Mary the Virgin, Halkyn (1887–8), was built for

Early Maturity: Churches

the Duke of Westminster on his Flintshire estate. It consists of nave, chancel, north aisle, south-west porch and north-east tower in the angle between chancel and aisle with its base forming a vestry. The style is a mixture of Early English and Decorated with lancets and Geometrical bar tracery but also with much cusping. The chancel south fenestration is in the form of an arcade of lancets separated by shafts both outside and in, where they are free-standing and of marble. There is a faint mid-Victorian whiff about this arcade and its shafts, about the piers of the nave arcade which are granite, and about clusters of marble or granite shafts (with which the inverted semi-cone corbels occur) around the chancel arch. There is, however, an overall smoothness and sense of quiet assurance which gives to Halkyn a place of special significance in Douglas's Late Victorian Gothic development, and sets the tone for virtually all his subsequent churches.

Church of St Mary the Virgin, Halkyn, Flintshire, 1877–8. Interior.

The Work of John Douglas

A semi-hexagonal wallshaft divides the two windows of the west front, and what was also to become a frequently-used Douglas feature is the porch gable which, like those of the main roof, is coped, and also has a short horizontal extension of coping on either side. Specifically Late Victorian character is apparent in the repose and broadness thus suggested, but more strongly so in the squat square character and refined detailing of the tower. Particularly notable is the treatment of the north-west vice turret. Projecting only slightly from the tower wall faces and raised only slightly above the battlements of the parapet, this has a blocky rectangular feel, and the light apertures – vertical slits in the lower stages and quatrefoils above – are artily placed and have tiny leaded lights. Below the parapet of the tower runs a frieze of quatrefoils in lozenges, as at Dodleston, and the authorship is unmistakably proclaimed by a square pyramid roof which rises behind the parapet, crowned with a big lead finial and elaborate iron vane.

As much as any of Douglas's churches, Halkyn breathes a spirit of spontaneity and enjoyment, and in all its mellow fulness his ecclesiastical woodwork can be appreciated at its best. The nave bench-ends are of curved elevation between posts with incipient octagonal finials. Those in the choir have traceried panels and end, not in poppyheads, but in circles containing conventionalised ornament – three-dimensional pies, no less. The reredos has diagonal square shafts with broad caps, and panels with sunflowers and pierced circles. Sunflowers also adorn the choirstalls, and shallow diaper patterns the pulpit; unmitred mouldings are everywhere, those of the choirstalls heavily enriched, while the stalls, the front desk of the

Church of St Mary the Virgin, Halkyn, Flintshire, 1877–8. Choir stalls.

Early Maturity: Churches

nave seating and the vestry screen display a diversity of pierced panels with traceried patterns.

It may be added that the completeness and consistency of the church owes something to stained glass by Heaton, Butler & Bayne, who were responsible for work associated with the Duke of Westminster elsewhere.[10] Other than J. C. Edwards, Douglas does not seem to have consistently patronised any particular manufacturers or craftsmen, though Hart, Son & Peard, who supplied the original light fittings at Halkyn, provided metalwork for some of his other buildings.[11]

Halkyn was followed by the vernacular-inspired churches at Altcar and Hopwas, but the mainstream of Gothic development continued with those at Pulford and Warburton, the former the only other complete church which Douglas designed for the Duke of Westminster.

St. Mary's, at the Eaton estate village of Pulford (1881–4) (see page 72), is aisleless, but has a north-west tower and spire (accommodating the porch) and chancel transepts planned for the same respective purposes as those at Hartford. The interior is of ashlar in local reddish sandstone, presenting, with the heavy timbered roof, an effect of warm richness. The same stone appears outside, but interspersed with occasional lighter courses, forming horizontal bands as at Eccleston Hill Lodge and The Paddocks (1882–3) (see page 68). Though here applied to a quieter and more unassuming building, vitality is nevertheless imparted to the wall surface, and resourcefulness in the handling of masonry and its capabilities thereby displayed. A band of traceried panels in the tower further illustrates Douglas's command of the properties of materials in that, when executed in stone, such panels frequently display greater elaboration or variety than when carried out in less tractable brick or terra-cotta, as with the cusping at Grosvenor Park Road (c. 1879–80) (see page 112). The spire is one of Douglas's most thoroughly Germanic – a shingled octagon, with tiered breaks, miniature hipped dormers and four clustering pinnacles, and with all these elements having hints of concave profile. The side windows of the nave have tracery below straight heads, and others display great stylistic variety with plate, bar and reticulated tracery. A diagonal passage linking nave with north transept burrows through a sham buttress, and great chunky unmoulded corbels flank the transept openings. Yet despite all this wilfulness, an air of quiet sobriety and harmony, even of simplicity suffuses, attributable perhaps to sureness of proportion and scale, equal sureness in the use of materials, and consistency of detail.

R. E. Egerton Warburton paid for St. Werburgh's (New Church) at Warburton (1882–5) which, with nave, chancel, north aisle, north-east tower and south-west porch is identical in plan form to

The Work of John Douglas

St Werburgh's Church, Warburton, Cheshire, 1882–5. (*British Architect*, 2 1884, p. 234. Drawing by E. Hodkinson)

Halkyn. At the latter church an ancient carved stone was built into a large south buttress at the junction of nave and chancel, and this must have suggested the sundial in identical position at Warburton. There is, however, greater refinement and a tighter discipline than at Halkyn, and greater stylistic unity than either there or at Pulford. Neat, broad and strong, it is a thorough-going Late Victorian church of Perpendicular character. As such, a certain, though only a very limited amount of Douglas's individuality has been submerged, and his hand is readily discernible. This is not least the case with the quite steep roof, which shows no inclination either towards the (admittedly somewhat later) fashion for low pitches or to bow to the precedent of fifteenth and early sixteenth century Cheshire churches in this respect. There is, on the other hand, a Late Gothic, not to say Tudor feeling about the two-light windows under shallow segmental heads and hood-moulds on the south side of the chancel, closely related to Douglas's completely straight-headed traceried windows. The porch gable coping with short horizontal extensions is here repeated, and Late Victorian squatness and horizontality are here further suggested by flanking buttresses, while a canopied niche in the gable adds an extra touch of sensitivity and refinement. The sturdy pinnacled tower is, with its paired two-light bell openings,

Early Maturity: Churches

quatrefoil frieze, pinnacles and battlements, fully fledged Neo-Perp. Throughout the building the tracery is Perpendicular in its conventionalised patterns. In places curvilinear members suggest an earlier period, but it is everywhere unpedantic and is characteristic of the architect in such features as small circles, apertures with single cusps of 'key-hole' effect, and mullions or tracery rising from the centres of lower lights.

By the time Warburton New Church was completed, the Douglas & Fordham partnership had been formed, and Pulford and Warburton are the last two churches of John Douglas's independent practice. Possessing greater suavity than Halkyn, with them he reached the full maturity of his Late Victorian Gothic manner. With occasional vernacular contributions, the conventional Neo-Perpendicular of Warburton and the more free ranging but no less harmonious idiosyncracies of Pulford (with which may be included the continued use of Early English lancet forms) from this time onwards provide the ingredients for churches.

Turning to restorations, the 1870s opened with an attempt to transform St. Peter's, Little Budworth, Cheshire, of 1798, into something ecclesiologically acceptable (1870–71). This 'restoration' of a Georgian church to a condition which had never existed did not involve a complete remodelling as at Whitegate, but included the removal of pews, gallery and ceiling, and, apparently, the insertion of a sort of tracery into the round-headed windows. Well may *The Builder* have commented, on what to a later generation seems an unnecessary mauling, 'The restoration of this structure has been attended with considerable difficulty.'[12] In contrast the largely fifteenth century church of St. Chad, Holt, Denbighshire, must have presented a more congenial subject. Work on the chancel was carried out by Ewan Christian for the Ecclesiastical Commissioners, but the remainder was Douglas's responsibility (1871–3). Whitewash was removed and the under-tower vaulted where only springers had existed, and sympathetic and self-effacing repair was effected. Only in inverted semi-cone corbels and in the tracery and conventionalised poppyheads of surprisingly subdued nave seating is his hand detectable.

St. John's, Burwardsley, Cheshire, received a distinctive tiered bell turret in an otherwise unremarkable scheme (1871), and for the most part church restorations fall between the extremes of Little Budworth and Holt, and involved repair and varyingly drastic scrapings and refurbishings. A series of the 1870s and early '80s provides a vintage crop of fittings and furnishings.

Work at Eastham, where Douglas had previously restored the chancel (1862–3), has been confused by further restorations and embellishments by other architects, but work of 1874–5 includes stalls with unmitred mouldings, traceried bench-ends and miniature

The Work of John Douglas

attached octagonal shafts, and must be by Douglas. Similarly a new vestry, organ chamber and organ case (1881–2) can be attributed to him, with the organ case having octagonal posts, unmitred mouldings and traceried panels. St. Peter's, Northop, Flintshire, restored by Douglas (1877), has inverted semi-cone corbels and a stone reredos with diagonally-set finials with castellated caps. Of the oak fittings the altar table has stumpy octagonal shafts and unmitred mouldings; the organ case has octagonal posts with castellated caps; unmitred mouldings and solid traceried panels occur in sanctuary panelling, stalls, organ case, pulpit and nave seating (which has differing panels in the bench-ends) and there are pierced patterns in the organ case, stalls and the front desk of the nave seating. Sunflowers in the stall bench-ends and wavy running patterns with demi-sunflowers along the stall fronts give a further touch of freshness and artistry.

The Halkyn and Northop furnishings together probably provide the best examples of Douglas's joinery of the 1870s, but that dating from the restoration of St. Mary's, Weaverham (1877) is also of interest, particularly the nave seating with a traceried panel and pair of turned finials to each bench-end, pierced panels in the front desk

St Eurgain and St Peter's Church, Northop, Flintshire, restored 1876–7. Altar table c. 1876- enriched 1879. Reredos panels painted by Hardman & Co., 1877.

Early Maturity: Churches

and armrests with miniature shafts and incised carved linear ornament. Douglas also designed a new font to replace the one at which he himself was baptised, though the early one has since been re-instated. Work at St. Mary's, Tilston, Cheshire (1877–9) amounted almost to a rebuilding, though old work retained included the nave walls, which have straight-headed windows. Whether or not these previously contained tracery (the present tracery is undoubtedly Douglas's), the feature would have appealed to him, and he repeated it in the chancel, which appears (except for re-used roof timbers) to be entirely his. Appropriately for what is quite a small and unpretentious church, the furnishings are simple, though they include conventionalised poppyheads and curved bench-ends.

Good furnishings date from the 1877 restoration of St. Dinoth's, Bangor Is-coed, Flintshire. The stalls are of Douglas's restoration of 1868, but to the later date belongs the nave seating with the usual features. Particularly attractive is the pulpit, which has not only pierced traceried panels but free-flowing incised sunflower patterns. The porch has a half-timbered gable which may be compared with the contemporary Little Nag's Head, Chester, as its bressumer is enriched with cusped carving and there are sunflower pies in the barge-boards and in the spandrels of ogee brackets which flank the opening.

To the 1880s belongs a thorough scraping, stripping and refitting at St. Garmon's Llanfechain, Montgomeryshire (1883), and also what, as at Tilston, may be considered as a remodelling, at the tiny and remote church of Betws Gwerfil Goch, Merioneth (1881–2). Of the refenestration, the east window has distinctive features of Douglas's Perpendicular tracery and the furnishings typical joinery details. More remarkable is the west bell turret which, although having a broached spirelet of familiar form, is flanked by buttresses so broad and tall as virtually to amount to screen walls. Of battered profile, and innocent of historical precedent, they have something of an early twentieth century Arts & Crafts feel – a quality shared by the lych-gate – and would seem to represent a response to the primitive and timeless aura of the existing structure.[13]

A further remodelling is that of St. Bartholomew's Great Barrow, Cheshire. Some work was done in 1871, but in a later, more extensive scheme (1883) the partly domestic and partly Gothic survival character of the chancel of 1671, which Douglas must have found most congenial, was taken up in what almost amounted to a rebuilding of the nave. He used straight-headed windows with hood-moulds and tracery with the 'key-hole' motif above curved-headed lights, and the porch, with four-centred doorway and hood-mould, is a simple and rustic version of that at Warburton. The roofs of nave and chancel were made spick and span with red Ruabon tiles.

In his restorations and remodellings, Douglas displayed

Warburton Church · S·W·View ·

Left: Scheme for remodelling St Werburgh's (Old) Church, Warburton Cheshire, *c.* 1880. (Drawing at Warburton New Church)

Camdenian thoroughness in his attacks on galleries, box pews, whitewash and plaster, and in his efforts to restore or create Gothic character, and here, as already noted, the influence of Paley would seem apparent. With the range of styles and periods which he himself drew upon as a designer being so wide, and with single-minded commitment to 'Middle Pointed' no longer advocated as an article of faith in the age in which he worked, he would seem to have been sympathetic to all phases of Gothic architecture, and so far as can be ascertained, to have effected self-effacing repair or correct re-instatement of mediaeval work. At the same time he had no compunction in using his own recognisable forms and details when work of new design came to be introduced. Similarly he would redress internal masonry or strip plaster from rubble walling (practices anathema to the S.P.A.B.), and with the employment of alien materials, such as the Great Barrow roofing tiles, did not hesitate to assert newness. This combination of respect for selected aspects of the past with confidence in the worth of modern contribution is apparent in the remodellings as well as the less extensive restorations. Whitegate, with inspiration taken from the internal timbers is an extreme case, but with the building having otherwise been Georgian the work was exceptional in its ruthlessness. Tilston, Betws Gwerfil Goch and Great Barrow suggest a more sensitive appreciation of the style, scale or *genius loci* of the buildings, from which distinctively personal treatment in each case developed.

This is particularly true of an unexecuted scheme similar to Whitegate in so far as being a remodelling, partly in vernacular terms, of a church which retained ancient timberwork. St. Werburgh's, Warburton (Old Church) is a mixture of fifteenth century timber framing, seventeenth century masonry and

Right: St Mary's Church, Betws Gwerfil Goch, Merioneth, remodelled 1881–2 (*British Architect*, 1881, p. 416. Drawings by E. Hodkinson)

142

Saint Mary's Church · Bettws·Gwerfil·Goch · Corwen · John Douglas · architect

Longitudinal Section
looking South:

Old Church

Part of North Elevation:

Scale of Feet

George Edmund Street R.A.
14 Cavendish Place
London W

Early Maturity: Churches

Part of longitudinal section and north elevation of scheme for rebuilding St Werburgh's (Old) Church, Warburton, Cheshire, by G. E. Street, October 1880. (Drawing at Warburton New Church)

eighteenth century brick. The scheme retained the timber and stone nave, but replaced the higgledy-piggledy brick eastern parts with a new and enlarged east end. The small scale and simple rustic character was continued in the new work, and half-timbered gables introduced. The most notable feature was a low crossing tower with depressed ogee bell openings and a short broached spire. The unexecuted design for Hartford spire had broaches, but here they were so broad and low and the contrast between them and the steeper spire proper so striking as to introduce a new aspect of Douglas's interest in distinctive skylines. As such (and especially as it here had miniature 'slit' dormers) it may be classified among his Germanic forms, and some (though not exclusive) German precedent may be noted.

Additional interest attaches to this Warburton scheme on account of an alternative one having been prepared by G. E. Street. The two form a remarkable contrast, for Street, while also retaining the nave and its timberwork was less conservative than Douglas in his treatment of it, and his new east end was vaulted, of great splendour and elaboration, and quite astonishingly inappropriate for the nave in terms of style, character and scale. Street's proposals are of 1880, and Douglas's perhaps of about the same time and must in any case have predated his Warburton New Church of 1882-5, built as the alternative to these abortive schemes. The old merely underwent repair, under Douglas's supervision.[14]

The ecclesiastical buildings of Douglas's early maturity belong unmistakably to their age, but they also (as with his secular work) display the development of bold and confident personal modes of expression. His new churches and his restorations and remodellings show a conviction and a consistency of purpose in the evolution of Late Victorian Gothic with special vernacular and Germanic contributions, while at the same time he showed himself capable of greater sensitivity in the handling of ancient work than did George Edmund Street.

IX Douglas & Fordham: Secular Buildings

The nature and degree of responsibility shared by John Douglas's successive partners is a matter for conjecture. So little is known about the running of the office that virtually the only recorded activity on the part of Daniel Fordham is his having ordered an iron sign, supplied in 1890 by Douglas's cousin James Swindley, for a shop in Chester belonging to the Duke of Westminster. With the Duke and the estate office in ignorance of this, it called forth one of Cecil Parker's epistolary broadsides.[1] As far as designing is concerned, it may be noted that, after setting up on their own, a number of Douglas's former pupils and assistants produced recognisably Douglas-like buildings. Thus while still in his office, they had become imbued with at least some of the forms, details and character of his work. The close personal attention which Douglas is shown to have given to such a comparatively minor job as the Witton Schoolmaster's House (1874–8) indicates that he is unlikely to have delegated much or any basic planning and designing to subordinates. Nevertheless, the prolific output of the practice suggests that he himself could hardly have taken responsibility for each and every aspect of the creative processes. Despite its overall consistency and quality, at least some of the detailing, and perhaps even some resolving of plans and elevations from Douglas's sketches, must surely have been entrusted to staff working either under his general influence or direct supervision.

With Fordham having been associated with the office for at least a dozen years prior to the formation of the partnership in about 1884, he would have had ample opportunity to assimilate the spirit and peculiarities of Douglas's work and, again bearing in mind the evidence of the independent work of erstwhile pupils and assistants, might well under the continuing influence of the master have been capable of producing reasonably Douglas-like results. To what extent he did so, or to what extent his rôle was an administrative one, or to what extent the two partners may have collaborated on design cannot be known. However, as will be explained, it is possible that Fordham alone was responsible for the firm's work at Port Sunlight. It may thus tentatively be supposed that, during the period of partnership, Fordham (the case of Minshull is rather different) can be credited with having done at least some designing but that this was largely in the manner of Douglas and subservient to his influence.

If this supposition is correct, no immediate change in character of work or style would be expected to follow the creation of the partnership. Nevertheless, changes did occur in the early 1880s, that is,

Douglas & Fordham: Secular Buildings

just before the partnership was formed and at a time when Fordham must already have occupied a senior position in the office. The changes do, however, relate naturally and happily to Douglas's own stylistic evolution, and their occurring at this date may be seen as coincidence. At the same time it must be borne in mind that D. P. Fordham's role could have been greater than these suppositions permit, and that although the work of the firm of Douglas & Fordham will be considered largely in terms of John Douglas alone, there remains the possibility that in doing so Fordham's contribution is underestimated.

The changes referred to are several. They include a growing degree of elaboration in the enrichment of half-timber, as at Rowden Abbey (1881), and the combination of bright red pressed brick with blue diapering, as at Eccleston Hill Lodge (1881) (frontispiece) and, apparently Barrowmore Hall (c. 1881). Both developments have an inherent tendency to hardness, and this became more apparent later in the 1880s and in the '90s. Another change was the virtual though not complete abandonment of the Germanic manner, after its concentrated use in the late 1870s and early '80s. In contrast this was succeeded by a quieter and less dramatic manner, the emergence of which coincided with the latter stage of the Germanic climax, and which forms the last of the stylistic classifications of Douglas's work. Its buildings are nearly always asymmetrical, and its elements include mullioned and transomed windows, canted bays, moderately pitched roofs and coped gables with ball finials. Its historical precedent is late sixteenth and seventeenth century vernacular building of the limestone belt and the north-west, and it may conveniently be referred to as 'Elizabethan.'

Quite apart from the isolated instance of Neo-Elizabethan at Vale Royal (1860–61) the style is rooted in Douglas's earlier work. The use of mullioned windows had been ubiquitous, and such details as the ball finials of the coped Dutch gables at Wrexham Road Farm (1877–84) (see page 94) provide an obvious link. The sober informality of Eccleston Hill (1882–2), as contrasted with the Germanic swagger of its brick contemporaries, also foreshadows the style, and something of a mid-point between Eccleston Hill and the full Elizabethan manner is provided by a scheme for the remodelling or rebuilding of Cornist Hall, Flint (c. 1884, different from that executed). It was of diapered brick with stone dressings, and irregular in form and vertical in emphasis, though the main roof was recessed behind a parapet and gables with ball finials were prominent. Characteristic detail included cusped window lights and an elliptical entrance arch. There was also a pyramid roof on a tower-like square block, as at The Gelli (1877) (see pages 104–5), and this tower is the only portion of the published design to have been executed, the remainder of the frontage being in inferior and simpler

Elizabethan style. The rebuilding was never completed, and the interior has been cruelly altered. Bronwylfa, St. Asaph, Flintshire, has been no more fortunate. The original design (*c.* 1883) apparently preceded that of Cornist, but represents the first full instance of the Elizabethan manner. It had straight-headed mullioned and transomed windows, and the garden front, symmetrical in mass only, had projecting end wings with canted bay windows and coped gables with ball finials. As in the case of Cornist, the building as executed was to a different design, and only the lower part now remains, reconstructed after a fire.

The revival of the Mid-Victorian Hinderton-Oakmere plan form was restricted to the Germanic climax, and although its influence continued to be apparent, it never re-appeared in its full form. What must have been the next Elizabethan domestic design – Wigfair, Cefn Meiriadog (1882–4) – is particularly free in its planning. Here again is a pyramid-roofed tower, its outline providing a vestigial Germanic touch among the Elizabethan elements. The latter include the corner of a canted window being corbelled out to produce a rectangular plan below a gable. The historical precedent for this must be the hall oriel at Hoghton Tower, Lancashire. Yet archaic or tentative versions have already been noted at Barrowmore Hall and The Paddocks (1882–3) (see page 120), and one occurred also in the Bronwylfa design. It could be supposed that Douglas was aware of the Hoghton example but adapted and developed the idea before using it in the form of a close copy. On the other hand it may be wondered (just as it may be wondered in connection with his use of Germanic elements) whether he seized upon a historical precedent

Wigfair, Cefn Meiriadog, Denbig shire, 1882–4. (*Bri Architect*, 24, 1885, 200. Drawing by F Hodkinson, 1885)

Douglas & Fordham: Secular Buildings

which happened closely to coincide with forms or ideas which he had already independently espoused.

The finest of Douglas's Elizabethan houses, and one of the finest and largest which he ever designed, is Abbeystead, Lancashire (1885–7). Extolled by Raffles Davison and *The British Architect*, it was built for the Earl of Sefton on his Over Wyresdale estate. It is L-shaped, with a main block and service wing at right-angles to each other defining an entrance court. In this it conforms to Douglas's frequent practice, and although there is no stable gateway (the stables were built away from the house) the service wing does incorporate a tower. With castellated turret, this is tall, but broad rather than aspiring. With Abbeystead being an irregular gabled house grouped round such a tower, it brings to mind Borwick Hall, further north in Lancashire, a late sixteenth century house built round a mediaeval pele tower and illustrated in *Abbey Square Sketch Book*.[2] The Abbeystead tower suggests comparison with that at Borwick, but those at Barrowmore and Plas Mynach (1883), which are its immediate ancestors in Douglas's *oeuvre*, do not. Thus, as in the case of the Germanic style and the Hoghton bay window, there exists the curious situation of Douglas developing from tentative beginnings an idea which, in its final form, emerges as something for which archaeological precedent already existed.

The central portion of the garden front at Abbeystead is of five bays punctuated by three canted bay windows rising to gables, all of them different and one of the Hoghton type. Smaller blocks extend on either side, that on the right forming a bridge over a stream and having two further canted bays, one of them ending in Douglas's

Abbeystead, Lancashire, 1885–7. Entrance front.

The Work of John Douglas

device of a pitched roof recessed behind a parapet. There is much liveliness in the careful asymmetry and in the detailing which (as throughout the house) includes straight-headed and depressed ogee window lights. The canted bay windows and their gables hold the elevation together and provide the vertical accents expected in any extensive Douglas design. They nevertheless remain subordinate to the horizontal lines of the roof ridges and to the relaxed spreading nature of the general massing. Douglas's Elizabethan manner has a greater sense of occasion and grandeur than can be achieved with half-timber, while at the same time it is free from the tensions of High Victorianism and the Germanic manner. At Abbeystead it enabled him satisfactorily to resolve a long and monumental elevation.

In using an Elizabethan style, not with the rigidity of Blore or Salvin in an earlier generation, but within the free context of the Domestic Revival, Douglas may be compared with, and may well have been influenced by, Ernest George and Norman Shaw. Shaw never attempted really large houses in either vernacular 'Old English' or 'Queen Anne' and for important commissions such as Adcote (1876–81), Flete (1878), and Dawpool (1882–4) evolved his stone-built Neo-Tudor or Neo-Elizabethan style. It would have been no surprise had Douglas's first departure along these lines been for Abbeystead, as an answer to the aesthetic and associational problems posed by providing a mansion (even though not a principal seat) for a great landed nobleman. Abbeystead was, however, preceded by the abortive Bronwylfa scheme, by (it would seem) Wigfair, and by their progenitors. He thus already had to hand the stylistic means with which he fulfilled – and fulfilled with a high degree of accomplishment – the opportunity presented by Lord Sefton's commission.

Abbeystead, Lancashire, 1885–7 Garden front.

Douglas & Fordham: Secular Buildings

Contemporaneously with Abbeystead, Elizabethan was used for additions to Jodrell Hall, Cheshire (1885, where shaped gables were used, perhaps, with their Renaissance associations, as concessions to the existing Georgian house) and to Halkyn Castle, Flintshire, for the Duke of Westminster (1886). It was also used, with happy effect, for Home Place, between Oxted and Limpsfield, Surrey (1894), which, with the exception of one ecclesiastical design, is the only instance of Douglas penetrating further south than the Midlands. Chosen by Raffles Davison for his book *Modern Homes* as 'one of the best of the many admirable domestic buildings designed and carried out in many parts of England by its architects,'[3] Home Place is of brick and stone and is a small and very free version of the Hinderton-Oakmere plan, with the service quarters contained within the one block, as at The Paddocks. There is a variant of the Hoghton bay window, an entrance court with covered gateway leading to the stables, an oriel above the porch, and play is made with shaped heads of window lights.

Home Place is a medium-sized house, belonging to the prosperous

Abbeystead, Lancashire, 1885–7. Hall.

The Entrance Court

Above: Home Place Oxted, Surrey, 1894 (*British Architect*, 50 1898, p. 220)

Home Counties commuter country, and Elizabethan is also displayed in an interesting group of yet smaller houses in and around Colwyn Bay, Denbighshire. Llety Dryw Hall (1893) is a simple stone-built villa, having a genuinely seventeenth century air in at least its asymmetrically disposed gables and decorated lintel. Outside the town, Bryn-y-Maen Vicarage (1898) and a house built for Mrs. Eleanor Frost (*c.* 1898), the donor of both church and vicarage, are both unusual for Douglas in being symmetrical. The vicarage has variant versions of the Hoghton bay, and both are faced with pebble-dash rendering and stone. Douglas's earliest known use of pebble-dash is in the asymmetrical pair of cottages at Eccleston (at west end of village, 1881–3), where white-painted moulded window frames project beyond the surface of the wall. Like pebble-dash these reappear in his later work, for instance at St. Paul's Vicarage, Colwyn Bay (1895), a building which can confidently be attributed to him. With these windows and with timber barge-boards its character is vernacular rather than Elizabethan, though its gabled frontage, symmetrical in mass but not in detail, renders it conveniently classifiable with the other Colwyn Bay houses of the '90s.

The Cottage Hospital, Droitwich, Worcestershire (*c.* 1898), a Dyson Perrins benefaction, is of diapered brick and terra-cotta and has coped gables with ball finials. More remarkable instances of the

Right: Friars School Bangor, Caernarfonshire, built 1898–1900, to competition design of 1888. (*Builder*, 87, 1904, 467. Drawing by E. Hodkinson, 1898)

152

Douglas & Fordham: Secular Buildings

Elizabethan manner being applied to the design of public buildings are provided by two schools. The Friars School, Bangor, Caernarfonshire, was built 1898–1900 with Douglas & Minshull as architects, though a competition for it was won in 1888 by Douglas & Fordham. As with Abbeystead, the building as executed displays a long spreading frontage successfully resolved in terms of Douglas's Elizabethan elements. Vertical punctuations take the form not of canted bay windows (though there is one of these) but of tall mullioned and transomed windows rising through the eaves. As used in the 1870s, this feature frequently terminated in a hipped dormer. Here coped gables with ball finials are used. The horizontal dominance of the ridge is challenged only by a tower, set into the frontage and forming the focal point of the elevation, but sufficiently low and bulky as not to disturb the repose and harmony of the whole. With a low pyramid roof recessed behind a parapet and terminating in a vane, the tower seems an eminently confident and characteristic Douglas touch, and unmistakably Late Victorian in its squareness and its studied artistry. Yet it is identical in form to the astonishingly prophetic pyramid-roofed tower which Douglas placed in the façade of the Boteler Grammar School, Warrington (1862–4). It is not clear if the Friars School was executed to the original 1888 design, though this would seem likely in view of the fact that Ruthin Grammar School, Denbighshire, which is of 1891–3, is similar in style and method of composition.

That the Elizabethan manner has roots traceable in Douglas's earlier buildings, that it became readily integrated within the recognisable canon of his work and that it happily assimilated detailed such as the elliptical doorways and varyingly shaped heads of window lights, provides further reason for reluctance in crediting D. P. Fordham with its evolution. However, also approximately

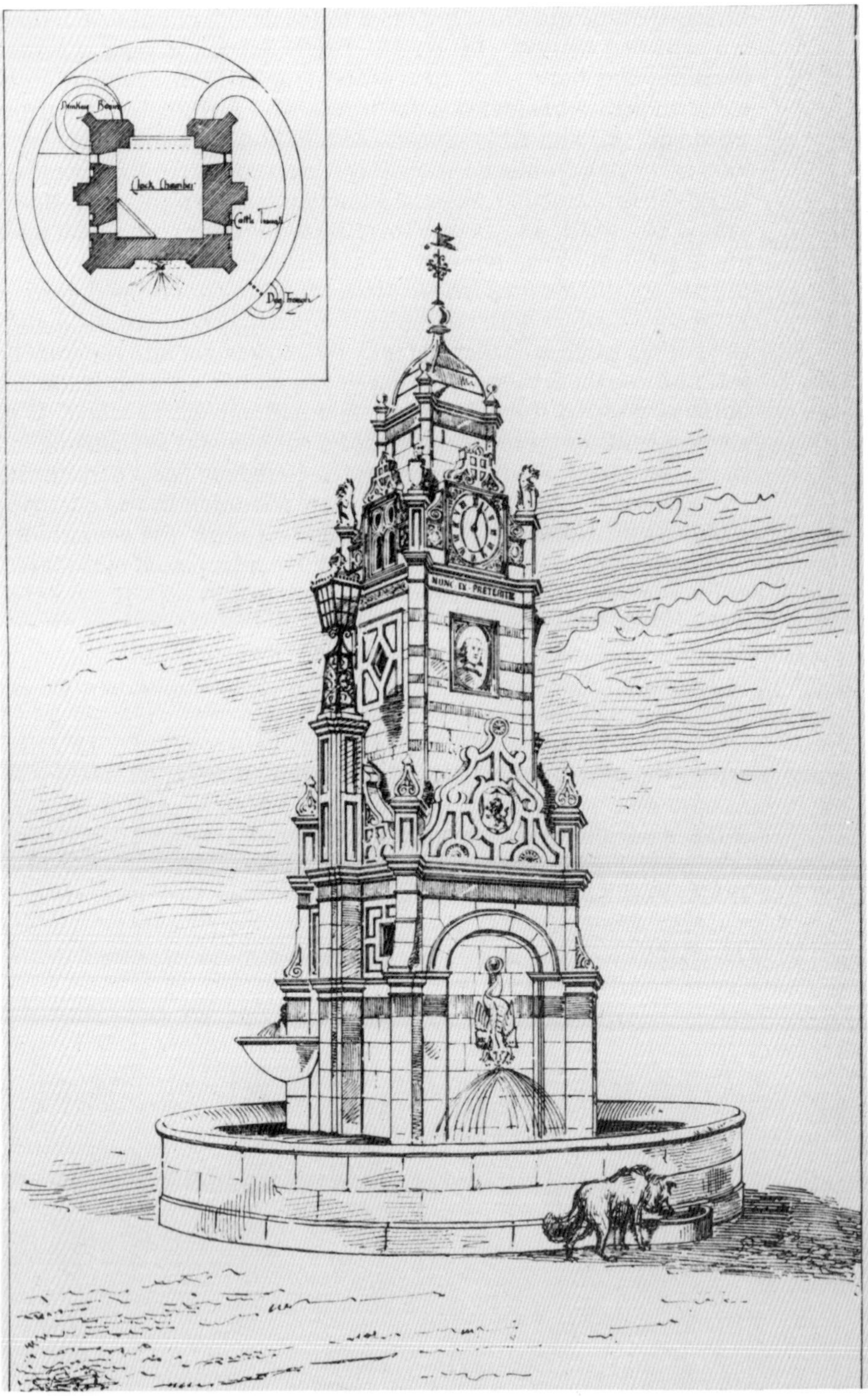
Drinking Basin
Clock Chamber
Cattle Trough
Dog Trough

Douglas & Fordham: Secular Buildings

coinciding with the formation of the partnership a new decorative element in the form of Jacobean motifs, particularly strapwork, made its appearance. Though used in a number of Douglas & Fordham buildings, this inclines to heaviness and does not possess either the refinement or the feeling of inevitability otherwise associated with Douglas detailing and ornament. A guess may thus be hazarded as to whether at any rate this was a Fordham innovation or speciality.

A porch and oriel which Douglas added to Vale Royal for Lord Delamere (1877) has delicate ornament carved in relief, including two vertical panels of floriated trails rising from pots. Although an 'artistic' device closely related to sunflowers and pies, this possesses enough specifically Renaissance character to suggest the subsequent use of Jacobean detail. Douglas's liking for posts and shafts is evident in semi-octagonal piers flanking the doorway. Diagonally-placed corner shafts occurred on the original design for the Peers Memorial Fountain and Clocktower, Ruthin (c. 1883, not as executed) as well as elliptical arches and bands of contrasting stone. There was, moreover, a full complement of strapwork.

The remodelling of the Castle Hotel, Conwy, Caernarfonshire (1885) dates, unlike the Vale Royal addition and the Peers Memorial, from after the formation of the Douglas & Fordham partnership. An unusual feature is the use of small broken pieces of limestone as a facing material, producing a flint-like appearance, and this occurs also at St. Paul's Vicarage, Colwyn Bay. Dressings at Conway are of brick and terra-cotta, and along with the familiar depressed ogee window lights are panels of strapwork, crude fleurs-de-lis as ornaments over windows, and Corinthian columns, also of Jacobean character, flanking the entrance. Only within this 'incorrect' English late sixteenth or early seventeenth century context did Douglas make rare use of the orders. Roman Doric of similar flavour was used together with strapwork and an ogee roof (like one which crowned the Peers Memorial design) in a scheme for a clock tower on the Eastgate, Chester (different from that which eventually materialised) when this idea was revived in 1897 as a Diamond Jubilee memorial.

Some fleurs-de-lis over windows and some strapwork occurred in the remodelling, in the Elizabethan manner, with Hoghton-type bays, of Bolehall Manor House, Tamworth, Staffordshire (c. 1892) for the Revd. W. MacGregor, vicar of Tamworth. Jacobean detail appears with greater force in the remodelling of the larger house of The Wern, Tremadoc, Caernarfonshire (1892), particularly with the porch and the bay window of the added great hall or 'saloon.' Strapwork appears over windows at Brocksford Hall, Derbyshire (1893), which is a major country house in Elizabethan manner, and the last house which Douglas designed on so large a scale. The plan is a very free adaptation of the Hinderton-Oakmere type, but since the

Peers Memorial Fountain and Clocktower, Ruthin, Denbighshire, c. 1883. (Not as executed) (*British Architect*, 20, 1883, p. 244)

155

The Work of John Douglas

Brocksford Hall, Derbyshire, 1893. (*Building News*, 64, 1893, p. 867. Drawing by E. Hodkinson, 1893)

staircase is relegated to an outer corner it can perhaps no longer be properly considered as such, and the service quarters are again largely in the main block. The materials are diapered brick with stone dressings, and there is an oriel over the entrance and a pyramid roof at the service end. The entrance court is yet again enclosed by a projecting range, through which access to the stable yard is gained by a gatehouse. This has clock turret, pyramid roof merging into a smaller turret-like roof, and a window rising through the eaves and flanked by wall shafts and ending in a coped gable with ball finials.[4]

For the most part, designs which include Jacobean detailing are not of outstanding quality in comparison with Douglas's work in general. Brocksford, however, is an exception, and any shortcomings which the elevations of the Castle Hotel, Conwy, Bolehall Manor or The Wern may have can perhaps largely be attributed to the restrictions imposed by the retention of earlier structures. Certainly the temptation must be resisted of necessarily attributing to Fordham anything in which strapwork occurs and which may not be up to Douglas's highest standards. Sandiway Manor is the result of a remodelling (date unknown) of the farmhouse which John Douglas senior entered into agreement to buy in 1845. Though unmistakably Douglas-like in its Elizabethan elements (including a Hoghton bay) and window detailing, the massing and proportions are not entirely happy. There are also hints of Jacobean detailing. With its personal associations, and with it in any case almost certainly being his own property, it is unlikely that Douglas would have completely delegated responsibility for the scheme. Buildings with Jacobean detail and a degree of dullness must thus not all be blamed on Fordham.

With the advent of the Elizabethan manner and (of lesser importance) Jacobean detailing, by the mid-1880s all the styles and elements peculiar to Douglas's work had matured. After the mighty crescendo of the late 1870s and early '80s, Germanic played a comparatively minor part, though among secular buildings it is seen

Douglas & Fordham: Secular Buildings

in a conical-roofed turret for the design of a house at Largs, Ayrshire (c. 1886), which is otherwise largely Elizabethan. It appears also in an octagonal strongroom with pointed roof added to Hawarden Castle, Flintshire, for W. E. Gladstone (1887–8, where a porch was also added to the main entrance, 1890), or in the Brocksford gatehouse. Nevertheless, its presence was still felt, not least in churches, and the themes of vernacular, Germanic, Late Victorian Gothic and Elizabethan, and the ground bass of idiosyncratic detailing intermingled with fugal complexity.

Among vernacular buildings, the lozenge brick patterns of the 1870s appear at the Parsonage, Cotebrook, Cheshire (1888), and simple half-timber, though scarcely of the 'light' sort, at Tallarn Green with Kenyon Cottages (1892) and the Lodge at The Gelli (1893) for the Misses Kenyon. The largest house in which half-timber ever appeared on an extensive scale is Glangwna, Caernarvon (1892–3), which is entirely black-and-white above a stone ground storey, but despite quite elaborate woodwork, there is little of Douglas's individuality. When exhibited at the Royal Academy, it was considered by *The Builder* to be, 'all very satisfactorily carried out,' while noting that it, 'does not present any very marked character to distinguish it from other houses of the same style and of the same scale.'[5] More characteristic of the half-timber of the Douglas & Fordham era is that which appeared at the Young Men's Institute and Baths, Tamworth (1885–6, demolished). This was a benefaction

Institute and Baths, Tamworth, Staffordshire, 1885. (Demolished) (Photograph 1891)

Black and White Cottages, Pulford Approach, Eaton Hall, Cheshire, 1885–6.

of the Revd. Mr. MacGregor, and provided a swimming bath, fives court, billiard room and reading room. The timberwork had something of the elaboration and the proliferation of Gothic detail apparent at Rowden Abbey (1881). The enrichment included carved bressumers, with cusping, and cusped and traceried window heads, and the somewhat mechanical nature suggests that a degree of the spontaneity of the Little Nag's Head Cocoa House (1877) (see page 106) must have been lost. Roofing tiles and brick supplied by J. C. Edwards must further have contributed to the hardness and crispness.

Most of the vernacular buildings of the Douglas & Fordham years, indeed the majority of all the fruits of the partnership, are on the Eaton estate, and so numerous are they that only a few outstanding or representative ones can be mentioned. Exceptional as being one of Douglas's rare uses of half-timber as sole walling material is the asymmetrical pair on the Pulford Approach of Eaton Hall known as Black and White Cottages (1885–6). The roof is tiled, though not in bright red, and there is no local precedent for the twisted brick chimneystacks, but the form of the timberwork is within the Cheshire tradition, and although the carved ornament, as distinct from the black-and-white patterns, is more lavish than would have been the case in so small a building, it is just sufficient to provide a sense of richness and craftmanship without becoming mechanical or stereotyped. Though this charming little building is unusual in its degree of historical authenticity, its timberwork is typical of much of that of the 1880s and '90s on the estate in so far as being neither the 'light' variety of the '70s on the one hand nor in having an extreme measure of ornamentation on the other.

With 'light' half-timber there disappeared also the Germanic roof

Saighton Lane Farm, Saighton, Cheshire, 1888–9.

forms, but in Eccleston Hill Lodge, Eccleston Hill and The Paddocks (1882–3) (see page xix), the estate possesses three of the buildings in which the culmination of the Germanic manner met up with the extensive use of red pressed brick. Although this material continued to be used thenceforth by Douglas, and by the 1890s was almost ubiquitously employed for Eaton estate brickwork, there are many buildings of the '80s in which no hint of it appears. The result is a group of buildings in a condition of equipoise, with neither the striking roof forms of Douglas's early maturity nor the assertive colouring of his later work. Even when diapering was used, and used it frequently was, the bricks have the subtle colours or softer textures familiar from the '70s. Among these quiet and unassuming but exceedingly alluring works are farm buildings at Mount Farm, Saighton (1886–8), with half-timbering, and Gorstella Farm, Gorstella (1885–6), a complete farmstead, picturesquely contrived, and carried out in brick, with sparing use of stone for mullions and other dressings. Brookside Farm, Pulford (1885–6), a version of the Gorstella house with large shaped gables, is doubtless that referred to in, and resulting from, a letter of instruction in which Cecil Parker wrote, 'We are building a Farm House on the Gorstella Plan but the Duke wishes the elevations to be rather prettier. He likes the Wrexham Road Farm design. . . .'[6] Very simple, like Gorstella, and reminiscent of the cottages near the Cuckoo's Nest at Pulford (c. 1872–6), are some at Aldford (c. 1883–4) including two blocks of three originally known as Primrose Hill Cottages.

Also belonging to this series is Brookdale Farm, Waverton (1887–9), though perhaps the most notable is Saighton Lane Farm,

Saighton (1888–9). Another complete farmstead, all of one build, it is one with which Douglas must have been pleased, for he chose this and Wrexham Road (1877–84) for exhibition at the Royal Academy in 1888. An informal group of farmhouse and buildings, it has walling of gently-textured diapered brick, much half-timbering, and gabled and tiled roofs. The brick chimneys are of the twisted sort already seen at Black and White Cottages, and represent one of several stacks of similar south-eastern (rather than local) Tudor type designed by Douglas & Fordham for mass production in purpose-made brick by J. C. Edwards. *The British Architect*, with its usual approbation of things appertaining to Douglas commented that, 'For those who want ready-made things of the kind these excellent designs will be invaluable,'[7] and he himself used them so extensively for Eaton commissions that red twisted chimneys, like diapered brick, have become a familiar feature of the estate.

Saighton Lane Far_ Saighton, Cheshire 1888–9. (Drawing Eaton Estate Offic as engraved for *Building News*, 54, 1888, p. 838)

With their somewhat mechanical nature, such chimneys, together with the general use of red pressed brick, form component parts in the hard and smooth character typical of Eaton estate work of the 1890s. Yet the Douglas command of media is apparent in the avoidance of excessive redness by the tempering effect of other materials – stone dressings, half-timber, or green slates as an alternative to red tile for roofs. Or again walling might be in common brick, with bright red restricted to limited quantities of Ruabon, or to terra-cotta which was in any case extensively used for dressings, including depressed ogee window details, copings for shaped gables, or ball finials. Buildings of this character, largely classifiable as vernacular but with some evidence of the Elizabethan manner, include Hope's Place (1890–92) and Bretton Hall Farms, Bretton, where the estate spills over into Flintshire, Dodleston Lane Farm,

Douglas & Fordham: Secular Buildings

Dodleston (1890–92), Churton Stud, Churton (1893–5), Iron Bridge Lodge, Eaton Hall (1894–5), a gamekeeper's house at Belgrave (1894–6), the remodelling of the Grosvenor Arms, Aldford (1891–3, interior altered) and that at Pulford (1897, interior altered) and Manor Farmhouse, Pulford (1896–8), a Ruabon brick gabled and finialed house in the Elizabethan manner.

Among the most sumptuous of these buildings are two of 1893–4 at Eaton Hall – the Gardeners' Bothy (see page 70) and the Eccleston Lodge. The former is of diapered Ruabon brick with stone bands and dressings and much half-timbering. The more elaborate of Edwards's standard chimneys are used, and there are shaped and traceried heads of panels in stone and of window lights in stone and

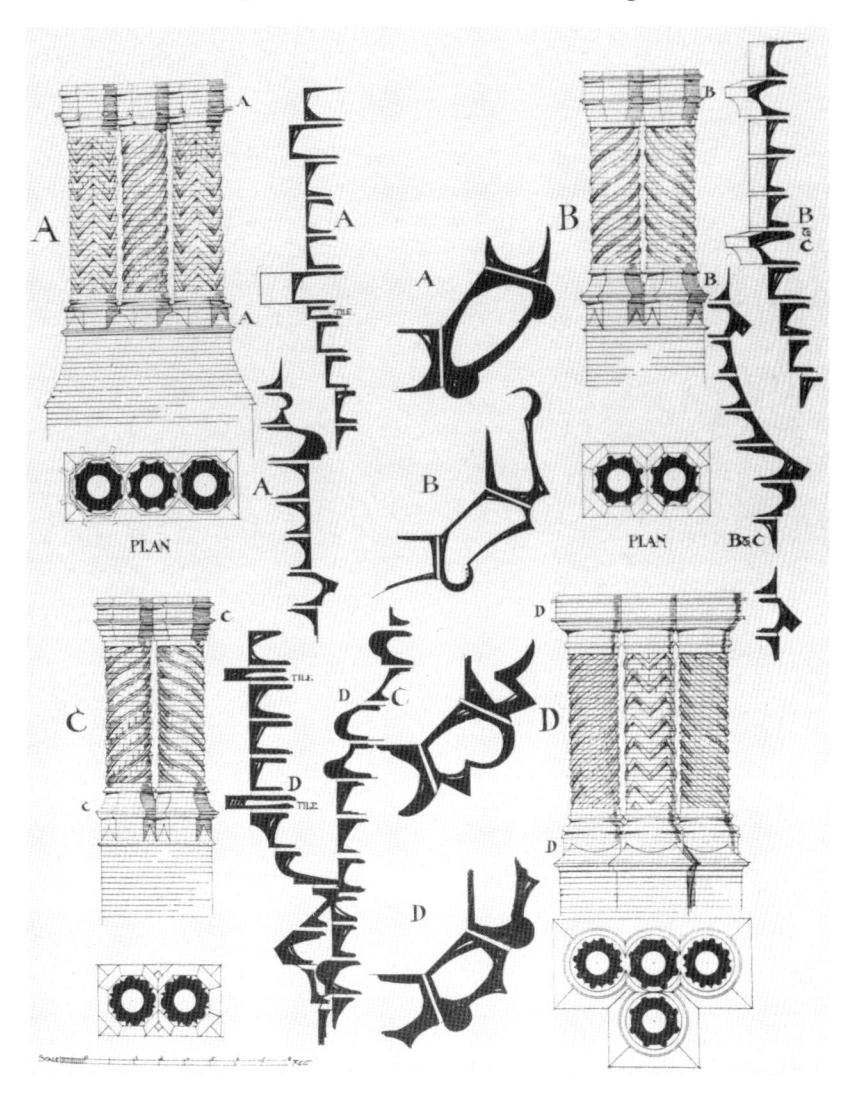

Designs for terracotta chimneystacks, made by J. C. Edwards of Ruabon. (*British Architect*, 43, 1895, p. 96).

Top left: Eccleston Lodge, Eaton Hall, Cheshire, 1893–4.

Right: Pair of cottages, Eaton Estate. (Undated drawing at Eaton Estate Office, with names of Douglas Minshull and Josh Smith, Clerk of Works)

Bottom left: Group four cottages and shop, Eccleston, Cheshire, c. 1889. (*Builder*, 56, 1889, p. 68)

timber. An octagonal Germanic turret makes a surprise reappearance at Eccleston Lodge, and there is a greater concentration of effort, with stone, diapered brick and heavily-carved half-timber arranged in quite free sculptural massing (including canted corners turning rectangular) under a green slate roof. The cusped and traceried Gothic ornament of barge-boards, bressumers and timber-framed window lights recalls Rowden Abbey or the Tamworth Institute in appearing more intricate in its carving than that at the Little Nag's Head, particularly as a result of the cusped and traceried windows. When the smooth and hard style of the 1890s is

162

Douglas & Fordham: Secular Buildings

found at the Gardeners' Bothy and Eccleston Lodge, there is a combined with detailing of such meticulously crisp precision as is danger that some liveliness or spontaneity will be lost. The lodge also has something of the excessive neatness which can render model estate building cloying and oppressive, but what is nevertheless a little masterpiece is saved by its inventiveness of form, the clear and joyous expression of natural colours and, when all is said and done, by the quality and originality of the detailing.

At Eccleston, a group of four cottages and a former shop (*c.* 1889), with twisted chimneys, is grouped round three sides of an open court. It is thus a departure from the more usual pairs or occasional single cottages or blocks of three on the estate, and the prolific outburst of cottage building in the 1890s was of a more stereotyped nature, with few 'one off' jobs in evidence. Some repeated designs had earlier been built, but the movement for standardisation can be seen as beginning with three almost identical pairs, of brick, with terra-cotta dressings, curved window lights and two small gables on

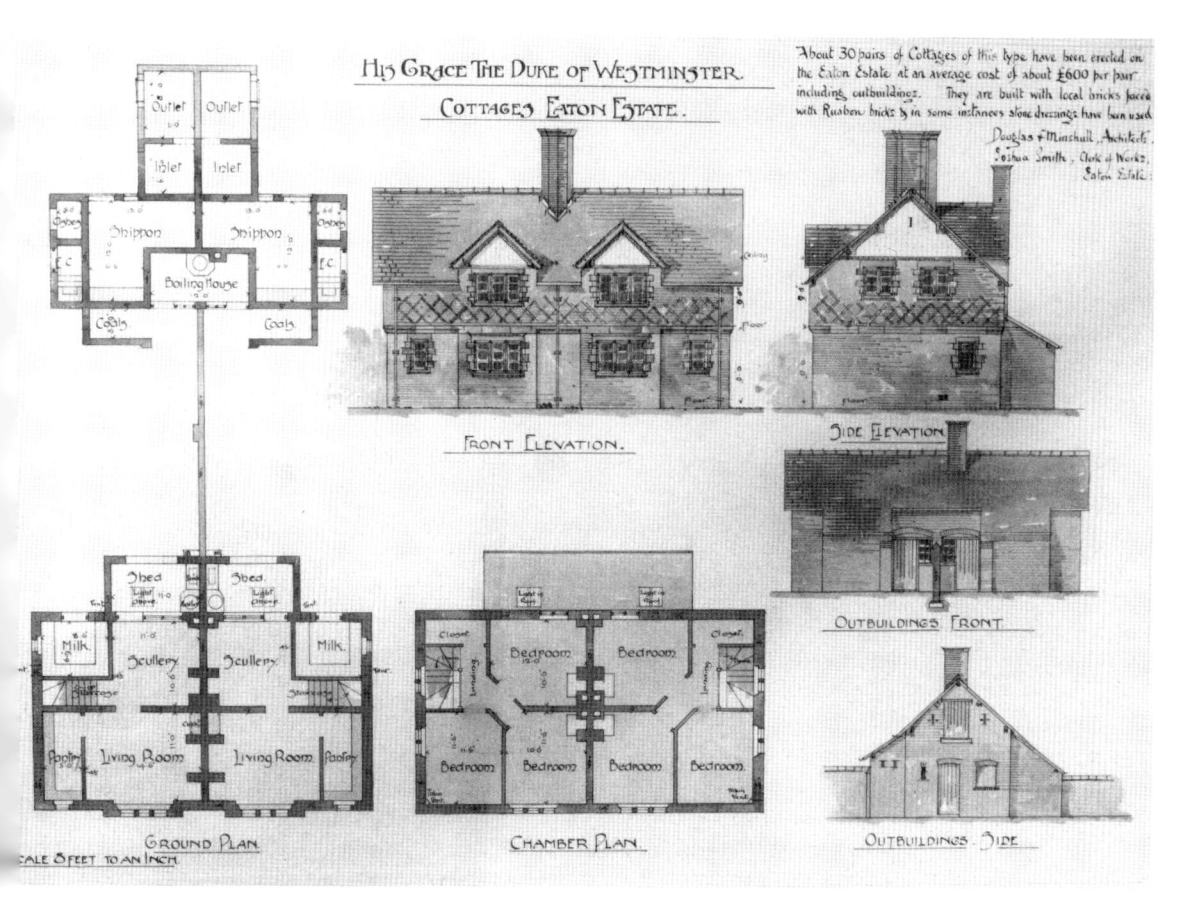

The Work of John Douglas

Left: Pair of cottage[s?]
Church Lane,
Aldford, Cheshire.

each front elevation, built (1887–8) at Balderton (immediately south of Cheese Factory), Belgrave (quarter mile north of Belgrave Lodge on west side of Wrexham Road) and Eccleston (Wrexham Road Cottages). There followed (1889–91) the more elaborate near-identical set of three, with some half-timbering and with large gables, as well as with diapering and twisted chimneys, at Aldford (south of Grosvenor Arms), Pulford (at north end of village on east side of Wrexham Road) and Waverton (southernmost of two blocks north of church on east side of village street). It was this latter design which was plagiarised in the estate office to form the simplified adaptation (retaining the twisted chimneys) which may be called the standard large gable type and which, with at least sixteen pairs having been built, led to the dispute over fees between Douglas and Parker.

Of pairs carried out in the normal way with Douglas & Fordham as architects, a considerable measure of uniformity and repetition was also established, with the earlier small gable design serving as a prototype for a more mechanical version of this with stone dressings, and for a design with curved terra-cotta gables surmounted by ball finials. Examples of the former, all of 1895–6, are at Aldford (three blocks in north road in village west of cottage opposite Aldford Lodge) and Saighton (south of Yew Tree Farm) and of the latter at Balderton (east of railway) and Saighton (north of Yew Tree Farm) built 1895–6, and Dodleston (east of school) and Waverton (north-east of Church Farm) built 1897. It was apparently these two types of elevation, rather than any variation of internal arrangement, which

Opposite: Eaton
Estate cottages,
Cheshire. Similar
pairs built at Aldf[ord]
Pulford, and
Waverton. (*Moder[n]
Cottage Architectur[e]*
ed. Maurice B.
Adams, 1904, pla[te]

164

Douglas & Fordham: Secular Buildings

Parker referred to as 'Plans A. & B.'[8] Some simpler cottages with white-painted casemate windows as the dominant feature also appeared, including three pairs at Saighton (one in Millfield Lane and two north of Millfield Lane on east side of main road, 1893–5). Extreme simplicity and white-painted woodwork characterise a few buildings which include a smallholding at Balderton (1897, now Balderton Lodge) and Yew Tree Bank Farmhouse, Lower Kinnerton (1893–5), with ambition and distinctiveness being restricted to diapered brick and the datestones with incised ornament which adorn most of the Douglas & Fordham estate buildings.

In addition to the lodges, farms and cottages which give such special character and quality to the park at Eaton and to the villages and hamlets and to miles of countryside south and east of Chester, buildings for which Douglas was responsible include the brick and half-timber Eccleston Ferry House (1887–8), picturesquely sited on the bank of the Dee, and also former wheelwrights' shops, smithies and smithy houses and – evidence of the Duke's serious-minded benevolence – reading rooms. Smithy groups which received a greater degree of architectural embellishment than most cottages but less than most farmhouses are at Eccleston (1896–8), Gorstella (1887–8), Saighton (1891) and Waverton (1895–6). Reading rooms of Ruabon brick with stone dressings and Gothic detail are at

The Work of John Douglas

Aldford (1896–7, Dodleston (1896–8, with a pair of Elizabethan manner cottages) and Waverton (1898–9). The coach house and stable near the church at Eccleston (1870) was converted to a reading room in 1892.

A departure from routine building types is provided by the obelisk (1890–91) which punctuates the Belgrave Avenue and made so strong a contribution to the drama and monumentality of the long axial approach to Eaton Hall. Record of an impromptu appointment in Chester in connection with this survives in a letter from the estate office which requests, 'Please meet the Duke outside the Grosvenor Hotel today at 1 o'clock with any plans or designs you may have for shields on the obelisk,' adding, 'His Grace is passing there about that time on his way to the 1.30 train.'[9]

In Chester itself, distinctive details and materials associated with Douglas and with Westminster commissions are seen at the Sexton's Cottage at the church of St. Mary-without-the-Walls, Handbridge (1887–8), of diapered Ruabon brick with stone dressings and having a stepped gable, chunky unmoulded corbels, depressed ogee window lights and twisted chimneys. Similarly, the former House of Shelter, Vicar's Lane (1889–90), a further welfare scheme on the part of the Duke, is of diapered Ruabon brick with twisted chimneys, and in addition has elliptical arches and something of the wiry blank tracery first noted at the Grosvenor Club (1881–3). Of commercial buildings for the Duke, No. 38 (Row No.) Bridge Street (1897) seems, surprisingly, to be the only true Row building which Douglas contributed to Chester. It is also one of his most heavily decorated half-timber works, with carved barge-boards and Gothic cusping and tracery applied not only to bressumers and window lights but to some of the upright members and to the coved framing below a pair of oriels. Favourite Douglas shapes appear in curved brackets, attached octagonal shafts and, most prominently, in sturdy octagonal posts, themselves with cusped Gothic ornament, carrying the structure at Row level. Although some stonework occurs, it is subservient to the wood, and the facade reads as almost completely timber-framed. It may be this concentration upon the properties and potentialities of one material which frees the building from the more mechanical quality apparent when similar carving occurs in combination with masonry of equally precise detailing or with red brick.

At Handbridge in Chester are terraces of urban cottages in Overleigh Road, and Hugh Street (1896–7), in which familiar materials and details appear, but yet more notable is a block of tenements in Foregate Street known as Parker's Buildings (1888–9), the alleged poor materials and workmanship of which led him after whom they were named to wax so exceeding wroth. In the initial stages Parker consulted the secretary of the Improved Industrial Dwellings

No. 38 Bridge Street Chester, 1897. (Drawing at Eaton Estate Office, as engraved for *Building News*, 73, 1897, p. 471)

Company, and it was arranged that Douglas, when on a visit to London, should study the company's Stalbridge Buildings.[10] The result was a three-storey block containing 30 flatted dwellings, with stairways enclosed within the building but open to the air, as familiar from Bethnal Green prototypes. Although too late in date to have pioneering historical significance in terms of a privately-owned urban housing scheme, and with Douglas and the estate following where others had led, it nevertheless provides a rare departure from his usual building types. With walls of common brick and terracotta dressings, minimal Douglas detailing is displayed by segmental heads of window lights. The tenements are set back from the street, and were originally to have been reached through a screen block, fronting onto the street, and containing shops. In the event, two separate blocks, each containing one shop, flank the approach. That to the left (No. 113 Foregate Street, 1890–91) represents a remodelling. The other (No. 117, 1889–90) is an exceptionally rewarding example of the materials and detailing of Douglas & Fordham Grosvenor work of these years – classifiable as Elizabethan as much as vernacular – with diapered Ruabon brick, stone dressings, shaped and coped gables, cusping and twisted chimneys.

The Work of John Douglas

Though the quantity of buildings designed for any other single client or family, such as the Kenyons, the Gladstones or the vicar of Tamworth, pales into insignificance in comparison with the Duke of Westminster's commissions, it may be noted that there are several further buildings in the neighbourhood of Vale Royal and Whitegate which may be attributed to Douglas and the patronage of Lord Delamere, and that further work for Lord Sefton included the well cover at St. Helen's Well, Sefton, Lancashire (1891, demolished). A more surprising Douglas & Fordham aristocratic scheme was for estate cottages (unexecuted) at Holkham, Norfolk, while nearer home a farm (unidentified) was provided in Cheshire on the Cholmondeley estate of the Marquess of Cholmondeley, who also paid for Bickley church (1892). Work was in addition done for the Earl of Ellesmere (or the Bridgewater Trustees) at Worsley, Lancashire, including the conversion of a mill to form the Lady Ellesmere Coffee Tavern (1895, now the estate office) and the stone and half-timber Bridgewater Hotel. Of 1902, this is thus a Douglas & Minshull job, and with there being some of the Jacobean strapwork, it provides additional reason for hesitancy in ascribing this feature to Fordham. In this quarter Wardley Hall, near Worsley, is one of Douglas's most extensive restorations (1894) and that it can be ascribed to him personally is suggested by his name and not that of the firm appearing on the published illustrations in 1898.[11] A courtyard house, originally all timber-framed and probably early sixteenth century, the restoration was again selectively conservative, with early parts of the house being carefully recovered, repaired or re-instated, but with even the quite extensive new designing (including half-timbering and refenestration in later brick walls) being quite tactfully done.

Hardly to be considered as an aristocratic client, as his first step in the peerage came only after Douglas's death, but an exceptionally interesting one, was William Hesketh Lever, later Viscount Leverhulme (1851–1925). A fascinating and dynamic character, Lever was a compound of connoisseurship, humanitarianism and the megalomania and astute business sense on which his vast soap manufacturing empire was built. A passionate concern for architecture and civic and landscape design was reflected in private building activity, in public benefactions, and in his activities as an enlightened (albeit paternalistic) employer, with the factory village of Port Sunlight his chief exercise in 'prosperity sharing.' Bringing together for the first time the social traditions of improved housing and enlightened employment and the visual tradition of the sylvan suburb and spacious verdant layout, Port Sunlight occupies a unique place in the history of town planning. Between Birkenhead and Bromborough, Cheshire, it was founded in 1888, nominally by the firm of Lever Bros., but with W. H. Lever himself, as senior partner, the originator and controlling force. An interesting comparison may be drawn

School (now Lyceum), Port Sunlight, Cheshire, 1894–6. (*Builder*, 67, 1894, p. 83. Drawing by E. Hodkinson, 1894)

between Lever and the Duke of Westminster – self-made industrialist and hereditary landed magnate, but both acting as discerning patrons of architecture in the furtherance of social welfare.[12]

Of the numerous architects who, over the years, worked at Port Sunlight, the first was William Owen of Warrington, who was responsible for the earliest cottages; the first public building (the Gladstone Hall) came in 1891 with the firm of William & Segar Owen as architects, and the same year saw the advent of Grayson & Ould with the village shop (now Post Office) and with Douglas's former pupil Edward Ould doubtless being the designer. Douglas & Fordham appeared in the team the following year, contributing blocks of cottages in Wood Street (Nos. 17–23) and Park Road (Nos. 19–23). The latter is largely of half-timber, above a brick ground floor having stone dressings and elliptical entrance arches, and there are twisted chimneys. The block includes Bridge Cottage (No. 23) which has the broken limestone facing of the Castle Hotel, Conwy and St. Paul's Vicarage, Colwyn Bay, and also a fanciful corner bay window with shaped gable. These cottages overlook The Dell, a landscaped hollow formed from one of the tidal inlets which formerly traversed the site of the village, and which is spanned by the Dell Bridge (1894). This sandstone arch, carrying a pedestrian walkway is also a Douglas & Fordham contribution and has some of the Jacobean ornament, and originally there were ball finials.

Adjoining is the former school (1894–6, now Lyceum) which, until the church was built, served also as a place of worship. In 1902, that is, before the public buildings and village institutions had multiplied, Lever said, '. . . the buildings of which we are most proud at Port Sunlight, both architecturally and otherwise, are the School buildings . . . all the social work of the Village centres round these buildings.'[13] Like the Park Road cottages, the Lyceum is well endowed with recognisable Douglas characteristics. The walling is of diapered Ruabon brick with stone dressings; there are shaped gables, elliptical window lights and heads, and some swirling wiry tracery, as well as hints of Jacobean detailing. A short octagonal spire is recessed behind the parapet of a tower with ball finials, and the joinery has unmitred mouldings. Yet something is lacking. There is nothing wrong with the building. Indeed there is much which is very right and very attractive, but along with the usual detailing there is, over the doorway, carved ornament which can only be described as rococo and does not belong to the usual repertoire, and the tower and spire are indeterminate, belonging neither to the low and spreading nor to the slender and vertical among Douglas's tower and turret forms. Like certain of the other buildings with Jacobean ornament and certain of the independent works of former pupils and assistants, there is something (perhaps in the general proportions and in the outline of the tower and spire) which falls short of the indefinable sense of happy inevitability of the master at his best.

The same probably applied to the typically Lever-sounding Employees' Provident Stores and Collegium (*c.* 1898, demolished) and apparently also to work (*c.* 1896) at Thornton Manor, Lever's own house at Thornton Hough, Cheshire. This formed part of a long series of alterations and additions by many architects, reflecting the owner's sustained enthusiasm for building. Though largely destroyed or overlaid by later work, the Douglas & Fordham portion at one time constituted the main block of the house, and was in the Elizabethan manner, with shaped gables and bay windows. Douglas detailing was apparent in elliptical and depressed ogee window lights, but the garden front, though dignified and carefully detailed, was unusual for Douglas in being symmetrical, and seems moreover to have been very staid and stolid.

The admittedly tenuous evidence of the spirit of the Lever commissions may thus be adduced in suggesting some responsibility on the part of Fordham, and reference exists to his having been the designer of the Dell Bridge.[14] Moreover, the Wood Street cottages and seven other blocks at Port Sunlight show few signs of Douglas authorship other than raised and moulded timber window frames (as at Nos. 284-286 New Chester Road, 1896) and brick lozenge patterns (at Nos. 128-132 New Chester Road with Nos. 10-16 Boundary Road, 1897). On the other hand a row of cottages on Lever's rural estate at Thornton Hough (Nos. 1-7 Neston Road, 1893) is a riot of well-tried elements and details, with diapered brick at one end, half-timber at the other, and every house between expressed in contrasting styles and materials, lavishly ornamented. The panache with which this is accomplished does nothing to suggest a hand other than Douglas's own, and the fragmentation would seem an ingenious way of solving the problem of a long frontage. Yet the sacrifice of any attempt at architectural unity in what appears a self-conscious exercise in being frivolously rural is inconsistent with the

Detail of cottages, Neston Road, Thornton Hough, Cheshire, 1893.

greater seriousness, which pervaded the output of Douglas's practice throughout his career, and in which enjoyment would avoid descent into playfulness.[15]

The possibility of Fordham having been the partner with whom W. H. Lever dealt is further suggested by only two complete Douglas & Minshull commissions for him being recorded, in the form of further blocks of cottages at Port Sunlight (Nos. 268-274 New Chester Road with Nos. 71-75 Bolton Road, 1898, and Nos. 55-67 Pool Bank, 1899). Yet Sandiway Manor and the strapwork at Worsley enjoin caution in attempts to discriminate responsibility, and as Douglas's architectural personality indisputably saturates the vast majority of the products of his office, the buildings of the later 1880s and the 1890s must be appraised as a whole and in terms of his own developments and achievements. This applies equally to secular and ecclesiastical buildings, and the churches indeed present so steady a picture of quality and evolution as to provide no possible stylistic evidence for the sharing or delegation of design.

St Deiniols Ch Criccieth : N Wales.

x Douglas & Fordham: Churches

By the mid-1880s, the stylistic strands which make up the texture of Douglas's mature work had all come into existence, with the years which led up to the formation of the Douglas & Fordham partnership having seen the emergence of the Elizabethan manner coinciding with the maturing of Late Victorian Gothic. The Neo-Perpendicular of Warburton New Church (1882–5) (see page 138), the wider eclecticism (embracing Germanic elements) of Pulford (1881–4) (see page 72) and also the Early English lancet forms to which quite a steady loyalty had been shown in the 1870s (as at St. John's, Mold, 1878–9) had set the ecclesiastical scene, and provided the material for the churches which were to come.

The chapel of the Good Shepherd, added to the mansion of Carlett Park, Eastham (1884–5), has lancet windows within the quiet and refined context of mature Late Victorian Gothic. Its character as such derives not least from the red sandstone masonry with (as at Pulford) an interior of beautiful even ashlar, and which, in the north-west, is so closely associated with the highly finished Late Victorian Gothic of Paley & Austin. The integrity of the masonry is, however, here further emphasised by Douglas's device (again as at Pulford) of occasional courses of lighter stone, flush with the rest of the wall surface, externally. There are, moreover, Perpendicular touches in the detailing, including that of a spired bell turret, which has cusping as well as, in its lower stages, distinctive detailing of shafts and corbels, here in connection with a canopied niche (such as occurs in the porch at Warburton). That of the internal woodwork which remains displays unmitred mouldings, conventionalised tracery and sunflower pies. The client was the Revd. W. E. Torr, squarson of Eastham, at whose church Douglas seems several times to have worked, and although the house itself (1859–60 by T. H. Wyatt) has been demolished, the chapel remains.

St. Deiniol's church, Criccieth, Caernarfonshire (1884–7) for which a limited competition was held, also has lancets. There is plate tracery as well, and Douglas's stylistic freedom is shown in the design for the west tower (not built). This had a short spire, with low broad broaches, like that of the Warburton Old Church remodelling scheme, and which, with its Germanic suggestions, illustrated a further development of the fascination with distinctive roof forms and skylines.

Design for spire (unexecuted), St Deiniol's Church, Criccieth, Caernarfonshire, 1884–7. (Drawing at St Catherine's Church, Criccieth)

Closely related in style to Warburton New Church is Christ Church, Rossett (1886–92). With a pinnacled tower, sturdily buttressed, over the choir, and with a north aisle having an arcade with octagonal piers, it was described by Goodhart-Rendel as, 'A very

The Work of John Douglas

Christ Church, Rossett, Denbighshire, 1886–92. (*Building News*, 50 1886, p. 822. Drawing by E. Hodkinson)

pretty and perfect little church of that squat rather military looking Perpendicular. . . .' He referred to the 'sandstone – *excellent* not red,' and to woodwork, 'rather rich and well designed,' and considered that, 'Inside and out this building has real charm and is beautifully thorough in detail.'[1] In the design of buttresses, Douglas succeeded in imposing quite an advanced feeling of basic form and simplicity, either by means of battered shapes without offsets, as at Hartford (1873–5) and St. John's, Mold, or by placing them flush with a wall plane as with the porch at Warburton New Church. This occurs also at Rossett, where the tower has buttresses on the north and south sides only, and in line with the east and west faces. The Douglas *cognoscente* will also observe depressed ogee lights, sculptural use made of the lower stages of the vice, and the porch with coped gable, canopied niche, and further spreading side buttresses. The distinctive version of Perpendicular tracery, with divisions into 'key-hole' motifs above cusped lights and contained within straight heads also occurs. In the aisle the internal openings for these windows have segmental heads, a significant detail already noted at Tattenhall (1869–70) and Hartford, and the Late Victorian simplicity inherent in this is strongly present in the tower arches which define the choir. These are chamfered only, with no mouldings or capitals. Among the woodwork are unmitred mouldings, curved and panelled bench-ends, blank and pierced traceried panels and conventionalised poppyheads.

If criticism were to be made of Rossett church, it would be on the grounds of scale. Though described by Goodhart-Rendel as 'little' and although its plan is simple, it is in fact quite broad and lofty –

Douglas & Fordham: Churches

more so perhaps than even the dominating tower and high east gable suggest. Comparison of the porch with the nave windows indicates something of this discrepancy between real and implied size.

Some similar discrepancy exists at St. Paul's, Colwyn Bay, the external appearance of which fails adequately to express the enormous volume of this church. Its nave is of 1887–8, the chancel of 1895, though apparently to the original 1887 design. The north-west tower on the other hand was to have had a spire – quite a straightforward one recessed behind the parapet and reminiscent of Paley & Austin – but it was added only in 1911 and to a revised design with no spire. St. Paul's is an extraordinary building, and may join St. Ann's, Warrington (1868–9) and St. Paul's, Boughton (1876), as the prodigy church of its decade. Like them it owes much of its special nature to bold and unconventional planning, and, in addition to the chancel, it includes transepts and an exceptionally broad and spacious nave with narrow passage aisles. Stylistically it is closer to Early Decorated than to anything else, though there is considerable inventiveness and eclecticism in the tracery. Goodhart-Rendel wrote of 'An excellent church of the passage aisle type, but with transepts that seem to me a mistake inside – tho' looking well outside. The outside is really admirable, limestone with Runcorn dressings,'[2] and it may be added that the red Runcorn also includes occasional contrasting horizontal bands. Internally the distinctive features include, as well as the usual furnishings, some wall shafts and inverted semi-cone corbels and also chunky curved unmoulded corbels. The sedilia, with an ogee corbel or bracket and central shaft,

St Paul's Church, Colwyn Bay, Denbighshire, 1887–8, chancel added 1894–5. Interior.

The Work of John Douglas

St Paul's Church, Colwyn Bay, Denbighshire, 1887–8. Detail of passage-aisle.

may be cited as an example of the many instances of Douglas lavishing idiosyncratic details upon this particular feature. The piers of the nave arcade are rectangular, with chamfers carried up into the arches, the inner mouldings of which die into the piers. The basic sort of nature of this accords strangely with the more historicist window tracery or the highly personal corbelling, and the overall effect of the interior of the nave is of quirky detailing set within a context of spaciousness, light and simplicity of a degree almost ahead of its time.

St. Andrew's, West Kirby, Cheshire, represents a return to

St Andrew's Church, West Kirby, Cheshire, nave 1889–91, east end 1907. Interior.

Douglas & Fordham: Churches

Church of St John the Divine, Barmouth, Merioneth, 1889–95.

greater orthodoxy and to the use of red sandstone outside and, smoothly, within. The east end was added later (1907) to a new design, but the nave is of 1889–91. Clerestoreyed, and with octagonal arcade piers and another of the coped gable porches, it is a particularly lucid and harmonious example of the Neo-Perpendicular *genre*. Similar in character is the church of St. John the Divine, Barmouth (1889–95), which is one of the largest, most consistent and most supremely confident of all Douglas's churches. Its grandeur is emphasised by the site, set as it is against a steep hillside and with its great bulk riding proudly above the roofs of the little seaside town. There is a central tower over the choir, as at Rossett, but here the nave has a generous clerestorey of windows with four-centred heads and the tower has (as well as a frieze of quatrefoils in lozenges) a pyramid roof recessed behind the parapet. This helps the church successfully to assert itself in mass and outline against the hillside. There is again characteristic tracery, a porch with canopied niche (though due to the peculiarities of the site the entrance is at the side) and the occasional horizontal bands of contrasting material, the external use of red sandstone being in this case confined to these courses and to dressings.

The background history of the building of Barmouth church

Christ Church, Bry y-Maen, Denbighshire, 1897–9. Exterior.

would deserve detailed investigation. It is known that in 1888 a competition was held, but it is not clear whether Douglas & Fordham were the winners or whether the competition was abortive and they were called in subsequently. In any event, the building was made larger and more elaborate than originally intended, thanks to the generosity of Mrs. F. S. Perrins, who met the cost of the eastern parts, that is, the chancel, tower, north-east chapel, organ chamber and vestries. This was as a memorial to her late husband, James Dyson Perrins, one of the original partners in the firm of Lea & Perrins, makers of Worcester sauce. Mrs. Perrins, who at that time lived at Plas Mynach (though Douglas's client for whom it was built in 1883 was one W. H. Jones) was again widowed in 1899 when, as Mrs. Williams, she was the recipient of Douglas's already-quoted letter of condolence.

What Douglas referred to as 'the Calamity'[3] occurred on the night of 11th September 1891, when the tower of Barmouth church, within a few feet of completion, collapsed, bringing down with it most of the chancel and east end and a considerable portion of the nave. With construction having reached so advanced a state, the fall cannot be attributed to failure of centreing or an accident of the moment, and some sort of faulty construction must have been perpetrated. In issuing an appeal for funds for reconstruction, the parish reported that 'We have failed from various causes to have this great loss repaired by the parties supposed to be liable under the contracts.'[4] Mrs. Perrins seems to have met the cost of rebuilding the memorial east end, and Douglas agreed to contribute £1,550 towards the cost of the remainder, thus implying the acceptance of some responsibility. Under the superintendence of another architect who was called in (a move which Douglas considered unnecessary)[5] the church was completed, apparently to the same design, though the tower as existing is slightly shorter and less ornate than that shown in the original published scheme.[6] Without further knowledge of the circumstances, no judgement can be passed on Douglas's professional rôle in the affair, either as designer or site supervisor, though his financial vagaries came to the fore when, several years later, he re-opened the subject with Mrs. Williams (as she had by then become) and received such short shrift from her Worcestershire solicitor. As has been noted, Douglas was in error in considering him to have stated that 'it is preposterous for me to receive payment for my services as Architect,'[7] though he did succeed in reducing Douglas's claim on Mrs. Williams from over £2,400 to one pound thirteen shillings.[8]

Also built at the expense of a widow in memory of her husband is Christ Church, Bryn-y-Maen, Colwyn Bay (1897–9), where her commission also included the vicarage (1898) and the house for herself (*c.* 1898). The donor was Eleanor Frost, whose life began in humble circumstances and who, when a poor servant girl, so the story romantically runs, vowed that if ever she became rich she would build a church. Be that as it may, the church of this little hamlet in the hills behind Colwyn Bay is a gratifyingly thorough and complete item in Douglas's Neo-Perpendicular canon. It is not

Christ Church, Bryn-y-Maen, Denbighshire, 1897–9. Interior.

The Work of John Douglas

large, and there is but one aisle (with octagonal arcade piers) but is expensively fitted up and has a red ashlar interior. Externally sandstone is confined to dressings, the walling being of light local limestone. Again there is a central tower above the choir, carried on transverse arches. These are of extreme simplicity in their mouldings, and are almost semicircular, and the tower itself is low and squat, with prominent vice turret but with neither pinnacles nor any form of pitched roof. As such it is reminiscent of some of the earlier domestic towers, but as used in this ecclesiastical context, it indicates that, although Douglas continued to pitch the roofs at a goodly angle, he was influenced by current tendencies towards squareness and horizontality. Of the internal woodwork, Gothic ornament of the sort used in furnishings and for the enriching of half-timbering is here applied to structural carpentry as embellishment to the roof timbers – something which does indeed occur in other churches of this period. Spandrels and collar beams of the nave roof have complicated wiry tracery. The furnishings themselves form a particularly good set, with the usual unmitred mouldings, conventionalised poppyheads and pierced and solid traceried panels. Although the font is not of Douglas's central and clustered shaft variety, the font cover is of a kind he frequently used, encircled with miniature flying buttresses. So thorough and complete is the church that even an umbrella stand and an almsbox bear the stamp of Douglas's detailing.

All Saints', Deganwy, Caernarfonshire (1897–9), on a magnificent site overlooking the Conwy estuary, was also built as a memorial church, the client in this case being Lady Augusta Mostyn. Fashionable horizontality is here apparent in low straight-headed windows in aisles and clerestorey (with depressed ogee lights in the aisles) and the roofs are of quite moderate pitch. Emphasis is given to the roofs, however, by that of the chancel being higher than that of the nave. This is also the case at Rossett and Barmouth, but in those churches the transitions are disguised by the towers, whereas here an abrupt junction results. The Deganwy tower is at the west end, and a remarkable one it is. Low and broad, it has a short spire with miniature hipped dormers and broaches which are themselves low and broad; buttresses terminate in their own hipped roofs against the broaches, and a vice wraps round the lower stages of one of the buttresses. There is nothing new in the elements, but the extreme originality and wilfulness of their arrangement (particularly in the giving of roofs to the buttresses) is in accordance with contemporary exploring of new modes of expression. In having over the years perpetrated High Victorian sculpturesque qualities in his Germanic manner, Douglas came into his own again in the age of the Arts & Crafts Movement. The authors of the North Wales *Shell Guide* are wrong to detect in the tower the influence of Lethaby[9]: there is nothing there whose ancestry cannot readily be traced to Oakmere

All Saints' Church, Deganwy, Caernarfonshire, 1897–9. *British Architect*, 48, 1897, p. 423. Drawing by E. Hodkinson, 1897)

Hall (1867) (see page 50) or of which incipient indications cannot be seen even at the south wing of Vale Royal (1860–61). Extreme trickiness also occurs internally in the detailing of the nave arcade, where inverted semi-cone corbels are used in unconventional ways. Also unusual is the internal use of tooled rubble walling, though the chancel is lined in ashlar. Miniature turned balusters form an optional but comparatively rarely used extra in Douglas's armoury of joinery details, but appear here, together with the usual features, in the stalls. The altar rails, with balusters, segmental arches, and posts with ball finials, seem a logical and appropriate application of his joinery style, though these also are a rarity, with a simple rail on wrought iron supports being more usual.

A complicated and sad story accompanies the building of St. James's, Haydock, Lancashire. There existed a church of 1866–7 by the Hay brothers of Liverpool, and a scheme for enlarging this was prepared, *c*. 1885, by Douglas's former assistant George Smith, who seems to have set up in practice on his own not long before. This was abandoned in favour of the idea of an entirely new church, for which Smith also made designs, though nothing had been put in hand when, in 1885, he died. In 1887 it was intended that Smith's scheme would be executed by Douglas & Fordham,[10] though in fact there was carried out, at a later date (1891–2), a fresh design which did, after all, allow for the retention of the earlier building. The interest

The Work of John Douglas

of the new scheme lies in it being a reversion to half-timbered design, ten years after the series which began at Whitegate (1874–5) (see page 124) had ended with Hopwas (1881) (see page 127). Although Haydock was the last church on which vernacular elements were used on so considerable a scale, it marked the beginning of another period in which timber framing sometimes played a significant part, and in which it became assimilated into the context of Late Victorian Gothic.

St. Wenefrede's, Bickley, Cheshire (1892), built largely at the expense of the Marquess of Cholmondeley has, as usual, a fine open roof, but also timber posts and beams (a feature which Smith had proposed for dividing the old and new buildings in his first Haydock project) forming an arcade for a north passage aisle. Here again is a broad west tower (its arch so wide as to correspond with that of the chancel) with a slated spire with low broaches. A fairly similar spire, together with much internal structural woodwork, resulted from the remodelling (1896, lychgate built 1897) of the gloriously sited church at Maentwrog, Merioneth. This is the church which, under-

St Wenefrede's Church, Bickley, Cheshire, 1892. Detail of timber arcade.

Maentwrog Church, Merioneth, remodelled 1896. (*British Architect*, 48, 1898, p. 166. Drawing by R. Davison)

standably, contributed so greatly to the enjoyment of the day out in 1897 which, as has been noted, Raffles Davison took with Douglas himself as a travelling companion. The west spire with low broaches (though in stone) and also a north passage aisle with timber posts and beams occurs at the church of St. John the Evangelist, Weston, Runcorn, Cheshire (1897–8). There is also a raised chancel roof, similar to that at Deganwy. It was a church with low broached spire, raised chancel roof and half-timbered porch gable with which T. Alfred Williams embellished his caricature drawing, together with a house with brick lozenge patterns, ball finials and conical-roofed staircase turret.

At Weston Perpendicular motifs were forsaken for lancets and plate tracery. Lancets were also employed at the Methodist Chapel (1891–2) built for the Duke of Westminster at Aldford, though of Douglas's few Nonconformist churches the Congregational at Great Crosby, Lancashire (1897–8) has tracery.

A tower with broached spire and characteristic detail which was added to Holy Trinity, Capenhurst, Cheshire (c. 1889–90) may confidently be attributed to Douglas, and other churches on which he conspicuously left his mark include St. Peter's, Chester, where a pyramidal spire, with tiered articulation, dates from a restoration of 1886. Of the interior, a local writer commented that, 'It is one of the only restorations in England that has not quite destroyed the ancient character of the building, and great credit is due to Mr. Douglas, who has preserved the Hanoverian features, now so generally swept away by "restorers."'[11] Such restraint is hardly consistent with Douglas's work elsewhere, but whatever may have dictated his action (or lack of it) such gross negligence did not long remain unremedied, for new furnishings were introduced (whether or not by Douglas is not clear) in 1890 and 1899. When in 1881 the west tower of the church of St. John the Baptist, Chester, collapsed, it destroyed in its fall the Early English north porch. Douglas reproduced this (1881–2) and at the same time as adding the spire to St. Peter's gave to St. John's a bell tower (1886–7) yet more characteristic of him in the Germanic forms of its roof. There followed the

Church of St John the Baptist, Weston near Runcorn, Cheshire, 1897–8. (*Architect*, 64, 1900 p. 248)

Douglas & Fordham: Churches

rebuilding of the north aisle (1887) in Early English style at the expense of the Duke of Westminster. Also for the Duke was the restoration of St. Peter's, at the Eaton estate village of Waverton (1887-9), involving extensive reconstruction. The pyramid roof recessed behind the parapet of the tower must be an addition of this time, and the church in its new condition is shown in a drawing dated 1889 in the last volume of the *Abbey Square Sketch Book*.[12]

The Georgian church of 1733 at Over Wyresdale, Lancashire, in the neighbourhood of Abbeystead, was 'properly dealt with'[13] in a remodelling for Lord Sefton (1893-4) and quite extensive work was also done at St. Michael's, Marbury, Cheshire (1891-2). This involved the recasting of an early nineteenth century Gothic chancel in Neo-Perpendicular and the removal of a plaster ceiling from the genuinely Perpendicular nave, an open roof, with Gothic traceried carving as at Bryn-y-Maen, being substituted. A good set of the usual furnishings has conventionalised poppyheads, pierced and solid traceried panels in both chancel and nave seating, and shafts with castellated caps to the organ case.

Routine restorations in which Douglas left his mark in furnishings and details rather than in architectural form include those of St. Oswald's, Malpas, Cheshire (c. 1886, involving the removal of plaster and box pews), St. Mary's, Cilcain, Flintshire (1888-9), St. Michael's, Trelawnyd (or Newmarket), Flintshire (1895-7, where the telltale signs of authorship include distinctive tracery) and St. Boniface's, Bunbury, Cheshire (1894). It seems that in this case plans for new fittings, including a rood screen, were not all carried out, and a discouraging message from the Duke of Westminster was conveyed to Douglas & Fordham by Cecil Parker, who wrote, 'His Grace has seen the Screen Plan, Bunbury Church, which you forwarded yesterday, and desires me to say that he wishes his Subsn. to go the general works of the Church, and not be expended on the Screen.'[14]

Several restorations, embellishments and monuments at St. Deiniol's church, Hawarden, largely under Gladstone patronage, included a memorial tablet to W. H. Gladstone, son of the statesman (c. 1891) and the chancel porch (1896), also to his memory, with coped gable, buttresses and canopied niche. An ecclesiastical contribution to Ellesmere country came with a lectern at St. Mark's, Worsley (1894), and a further instance of individual church furniture jobs is provided by prayer desks (or clergy stalls) at the church of St. Mary and All Saints, Great Budworth (c. 1884). Though these have enormous disc-like terminations to the bench-ends instead of the usual poppyheads, the unmitred mouldings and traceried panels are more typical.

The churches of the Douglas & Fordham period present a picture of consistent quality and of steady consolidation of the Late

The Work of John Douglas

Victorian Gothic manner established at Pulford and Warburton. Vernacular elements were occasionally accommodated; the low-broached spire was added to the range of Germanic roof forms, and a slight process of evolution is seen in some response to tendencies towards horizontality of form and simplicity of moulding. A remarkable stability accompanies the design of joinery detail, with furnishings of the 1890s showing little change from those of Douglas's early maturity at the beginning of the 1870s, and remaining every bit as lively and enthusiastic. Unlike the secular buildings the churches provide no stylistic fodder for rumination on the subject of divided authorship, and evidence of Douglas's own involvement at Carlett Park chapel is provided by a commemorative plaque, set up by the Revd. Mr. Torr, naming John Douglas and not the firm as architect. Also, in connection with St. Paul's, Colwyn Bay, reference was made to 'when Mr. Douglas, the architect, gave his final certificate to'[15] the contractor; as far as is known the Barmouth affair involved only him and not Fordham, and at Bryn-y-Maen he donated a small stained glass window to Mrs. Frost's church.

To an even stronger and more consistent extent than do the secular buildings, the churches of this period continue to reflect the confidence and incisive power of a great creative artist.

Prayer desk, Church of St Mary and All Saints, Great Budworth, Cheshire, c. 1884. (*British Architect*, 22, 1884, p. 198. Drawing by R. Davison)

XI Douglas & Minshull

The retirement of Daniel Porter Fordham and his replacement as partner by Charles Howard Minshull took place in 1897, though apparently quite late in the year, with some degree of transition extending into 1898. At this time John Douglas was well advanced in his 60s, and in view of his increasing age it is reasonable to suppose that the 1900s might have seen some relinquishing of responsibility on his part; that the report of his becoming less active in the practice and assuming more of a consultative role is likely to be correct, and that some credit for designing thus definitely belongs to Minshull or other members of the staff.

In considering the Douglas & Fordham secular buildings, it was suggested that although design work may have devolved upon Fordham, he had acquired some facility for Douglas's styles and details, and was capable of producing buildings recognisable as having had their origins at 6 Abbey Square. This is less likely to have been the case with Minshull. There are certain Douglas & Minshull buildings which, like the Port Sunlight School (1894–6) (see page 169) or Thornton Manor (c. 1896), might be considered as having something of the substance of Douglas without the spirit. They do not, however, provide sufficient evidence for worth-while speculation, and of greater significance are the facts that there are other works which bear little Douglas-like appearance at all, and that after his death the firm of Douglas, Minshull & Muspratt is not known to have produced anything reminiscent of the master.

Compared with the prolific output of previous years, the 1900s seem to have seen a considerable slackening in the quantity of work handled by the practice. Even allowing for the cessation of Eaton estate commissions with the death of the Duke of Westminster in 1899, the number of works which has come to light is surprisingly small. Though there may be more buildings which, without the hallmark of Douglas's own designing ability, are of less interest and have remained unrecorded and undetected, so greatly reduced a volume of known work must mean that the office was less busy than once it had been.

Yet despite whatever decrease in activity there may have been on the part of the practice and of Douglas himself, there is ample evidence to show that his own work retained consistency and individuality. A splendid series of buildings, extending for a decade after the formation of the Douglas & Minshull partnership, and with a particularly fertile concentration in the early years, is of undiminished vigour. If any proof of Douglas's own participation in this series is required, other than the evidence of style and quality, it

The Work of John Douglas

is provided by the fact that a number of the buildings have personal associations, with Douglas acting as his own client.

Walmoor Hill is dated 1896 and is thus earlier than the creation of the second partnership. As the house which Douglas designed for himself in Dee Banks, Chester, it is, however, one of the most important of the group of buildings with personal associations, and should be considered along with the rest of them. With banks of mullioned and transomed windows and an oriel and coped gable above the porch, it might be classified as belonging to the Elizabethan manner. Typical of Douglas also are the service wing (which remained incomplete) extending at right angles to the entrance front, an elliptical entrance arch and some cusped window lights. His concern for materials is reflected in differing toolings and textures of the red sandstone masonry. Less familiar is the very free grouping of uncompromisingly blunt masses. To the left of the porch, with an octagonal staircase turret corbelled out in the angle between them is a flat-roofed tower. This is suggestive of the earlier domestic towers which reached their fulfilment at Abbeystead (1885–7) (see pages 149–50), or that of Bryn-y-Maen church (1896–9) (see pages 178–9), but on the opposite side of the house it figures in a most unusual composition. Its stark angular quality is emphasised by a corner bay window around the top of which the solid parapet is carried without a break, and it is linked by a lower range to another tower-like block. This also has a vice turret in an internal angle, and the roof is unmistakably Douglas-like, being hipped, with a miniature hipped dormer and big finial and vane, all recessed behind a castellated parapet. The steep fall of the ground towards the river produces an effect of extreme height, and although the elevation is a curiously restless one, Douglas doubtless knew what he was doing, and this craggy fortress-like eyrie for himself and his apparently unappreciative son is unique in his work. The principal rooms are planned on the side opposite the entrance, thus enjoying the view, and the interior is fitted up with Douglas joinery of excellent vintage, including the staircase with its landing arcade, and the woodwork of a little oratory or chapel which occurs above the porch.

In 1907 *The British Architect* published a 'Design for a Hillside House in Cheshire,'[1] ascribed not to Douglas & Minshull but to John Douglas, and the following year an 'Alternative Design for a Hillside House in Cheshire,' by the same.[2] Despite it being stated that the former was soon to be commenced, no such house is known to exist, and both have the character of hypothetical projects. They bristle with Germanic roof forms and there are French allusions, but although both are larger than Walmoor Hill, there are between them certain similarities of plan and accommodation. One has a chapel as its most important component, but the other what is called a 'prayer room' over the porch, as at Walmoor Hill. It may be wondered if

Design for a hillside house, Cheshire, c. 1907. (*British Architect*, 68, 1907, pp. 440, 444)

these schemes represent earlier pipe dreams by Douglas for a house for himself.

Again dating from the Douglas & Fordham period, but again something with which John Douglas was most closely associated as his own client, is the brilliant range of buildings in St. Werburgh Street, Chester (c. 1895–7), erected when the street, which runs from Eastgate Street to the cathedral, was widened. In this work, the city's half-timber revival reached its very apogee. The ground floor at the Eastgate Street corner is a stone-faced bank, and it was here that the Douglas commemorative tablet was placed in 1923. The remainder of the ground storey consists of shop fronts, and above is an unbroken expanse of gorgeously ornamented half-timber. That this is anything but pastiche is shown by the Germanic turret at the upper corner, and although the long elevation is further diversified by no less than eleven gables, it is broken down into five separate units, each a complete composition in itself and with its own individuality. This irregularity is well suited to the treatment of street architecture, with the range visible in its entirety only in oblique perspective while at the same time the one unifying material prevents fragmentation such as is seen at the Thornton Hough Cottages

The Work of John Douglas

(1893) (see page 171). Leaded glazing patterns contribute not a little to the all-pervading sense of richness and craftmanship, but it is the loving care lavished on the timber detailing which makes St. Werburgh Street as fine as anything of its kind within the entire Vernacular Revival movement. Though preceding No. 38 Bridge Street (1897), St. Werburgh Street exceeds it in liveliness and inventiveness of ornament, and extends beyond the confines of Douglas's normal range of styles and motifs. There are quatrefoils as well as cusped lozenge patterns, and stumpy Renaissance arches and pilasters as well as Gothic devices, and the sheer profusion and exuberance of the Gothic elements themselves – traceried and cusped bressumers and windows *et al*. – is such as completely to overwhelm any inherent mechanical tendencies.

In its obituary, the *Chester Chronicle* wrote, 'It was a bold and public spirited act on the part of Mr. Douglas to build this property. The Corporation having demolished the old row of shops for widening the street, the question arose how to deal with the vacant sites. It was proposed to offer them for sale in separate lots, but in order to save the street from becoming an incongruous jumble of haphazard styles, Mr. Douglas himself boldly bought the entire length of the street, and then proceeded to treat it architecturally in a unity of design. Nothing today is more admired than the carved woodwork of these gable-fronted shops in St. Werburgh Street, and a more picturesque street approach to the Cathedral would tax the imagination to conceive. Mr. Douglas had of course run the risk of having the big block of property left on his hands, but fortunately the Bank of Liverpool acquired the most important site, and in time he disposed of the other shops too.'[3]

The implementation of the scheme involved expenditure in excess of £17,000 – more than half Douglas's total capital at the time of his death.

Behind all this lies a complicated story, elucidation of which would result from further investigation in the minutes of the City Council and its Improvement Committee. It can, however, be said that the proposal for street widening seems to have been of long standing, and although Douglas may at an early stage have expressed interest and concern, it was a chance conversation with the mayor that made him aware of the intention to sell off the sites for piecemeal redevelopment and determined his purchasing of the entire length of the street. In view of the superbly successful achievement which resulted, it is disappointing to learn that half-timber was adopted only at the special request of the Duke of Westminster, and that Douglas's original design was Gothic, with some stepped Flemish gables and much wiry tracery, to be executed in stone and diapered brick. Despite undoubted merit, this would not have possessed the aesthetic and popular appeal of the scheme as built (see endpaper).

East side of St Werburgh Street, Chester, *c*. 1895–7 (*British Architect*, 1898, p. 364. Drawing by R. Davison)

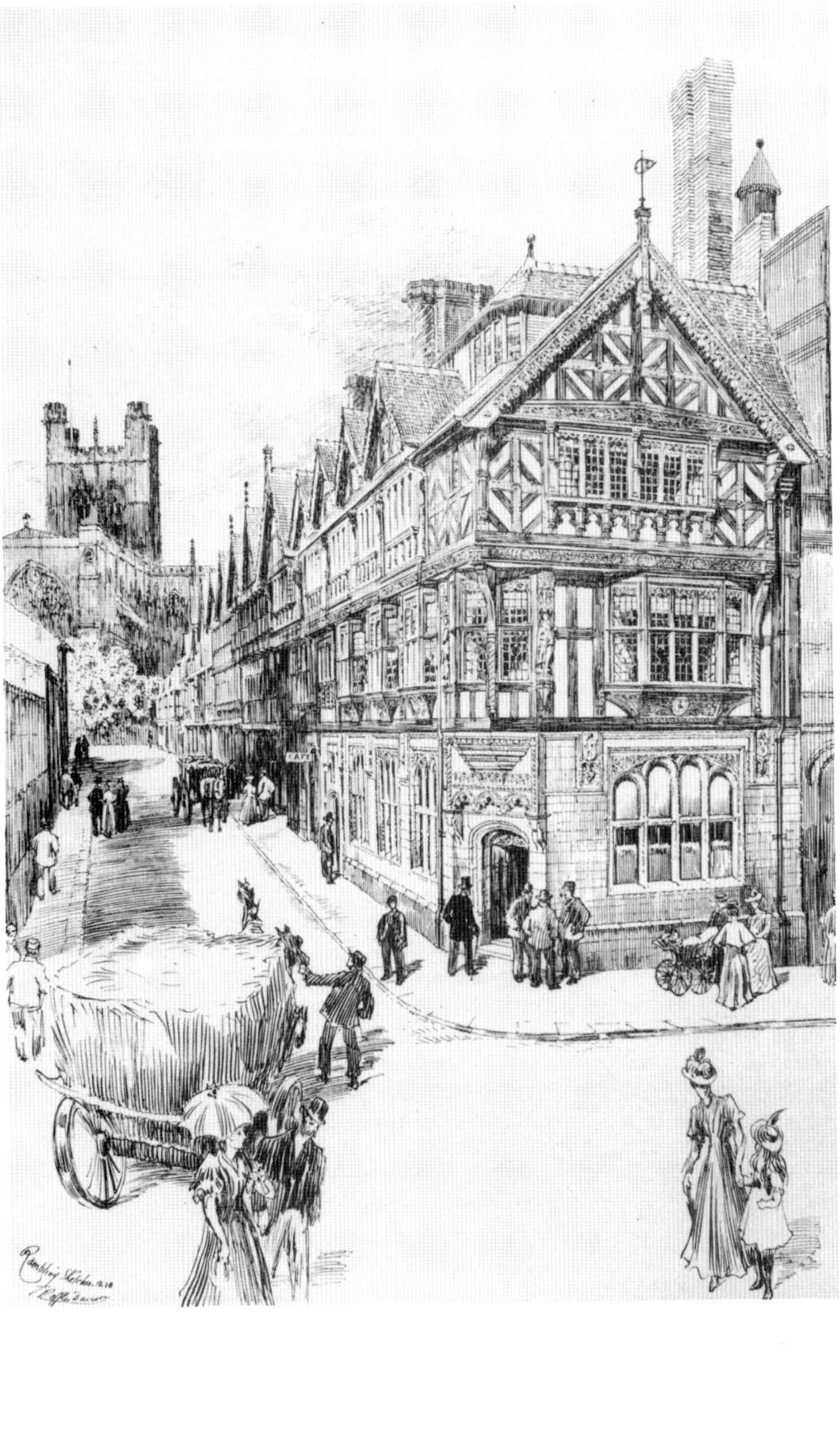
Rambling Sketches

The Work of John Douglas

The greatest difficulty was encountered in connection with the site of St. Oswald's Chambers (1898) at the top of the street. This is a two-storey office block of stone and half-timber, with a Germanic turret, standing between the range of shops and the cathedral graveyard. The site seems not to have been included in the Corporation's widening scheme and Douglas, who purchased it, formulated a plan whereby the buildings which occupied it would be demolished and the land partly given over to road improvement and the remainder left open and unbuilt upon. The Corporation agreed to fall in with the proposal only if £500 could be raised by subscription towards the costs involved. Consequently Douglas opened the 'Cathedral Approach Improvement Fund,' with the manager of the Bank of Liverpool branch, already installed in its new premises at the foot of the street, as treasurer. Despite contributions of £100 each from the Duke of Westminster and H. Lyle Smith (the grain merchant for whom Barrowmore Hall was built and who was also a director of the Bank of Liverpool), only £300 was raised, and Douglas was obliged to make up the difference himself. Moreover, trouble was encountered from the firm of Dicksons Ltd., seed merchants and nurserymen, whose premises extended behind and parallel with St. Werburgh Street, between Eastgate Street and the cathedral graveyard. Part of Douglas's scheme for his open site was that any future building on the adjoining portion of this firm's land should be restricted to one storey in height. Far from entering into any such agreement, Mr. Dickson informed Douglas that he could build as high as the Tower of Babel if he liked, and, though refraining from anything quite so ambitious, he did set about to erect some unsightly sheds. This prompted the Duke to suggest that a building be put up to act as a screen to hide the Dickson aberrations; the other subscribers to the Improvement Fund agreed, and the result was St. Oswald's Chambers, which was kept low and in line with the range of shops so as not to obstruct the newly-formed view of the cathedral from Eastgate Street. The Dean and Chapter, through the agency of the Ecclesiastical Commissioners, had agreed to contribute £100 to the fund, but withdrew because the condition that the site remain open and unbuilt upon was not being complied with. As late as 1906 Douglas re-opened the question with the Chapter Clerk, and pointed to the enormous improvements which, with the buildings in St. Werburgh Street, he had made to the city and the setting of the cathedral, but he never received his £100.[4]

The purchasers of the St. Werburgh Street shops were bound by restrictions concerning maintenance, alterations, advertising signs and usage. These included prohibition of any co-operative store and the opening of any business run on co-operative principles,[5] though disapproval of such for St. Werburgh Street did not prevent Douglas from designing premises for the Chester Co-operative Society,

Detail of Nos. 1-11
Bath Street, Chester,
1903.

together with a Sub-Post Office, on land belonging to him at Boughton Cross (1898–1901). Though executed less elaborately than at first intended, this is a picturesque building, with much half-timber, providing an excellent townscape feature at the fork of the Tarvin and Christleton Roads. What must have been the last of his ventures in building on his own land in Chester is a terrace of houses in Bath Street (Nos. 1-11, 1903). The scale is modest – they are no more than two-storey cottages – but they are executed in sandstone of high quality, have intriguing detail, and are dominated by a series of bulging conical-roofed turrets, with which miniature hipped dormers are combined. It all presents another instance of street architecture of controlled irregularity, and groups with the former Prudential Assurance Building (1903) on the Foregate Street corner. Of similar material and also quite small in scale, this has Jacobean detail (post-Fordham be it noted) and the liking for octagonal posts

193

The Work of John Douglas

Church of St John the Evangelist, Sandiway, Cheshire 1902–3.

is interpreted in terms of window mullions. At the opposite end of the Bath Street terrace is a house (No. 13, 1903) in similar style to the others, but different in its materials. This was to have formed part of the projected street which would have linked up with Grosvenor Park Road. Though apparently about to be put in hand in 1906, nothing more ever materialised.

Of similar date is the church of St. John the Evangelist, Sandiway (1902–3) for which Douglas not only gave the land, but also met the cost of the chancel and the lych-gate. The lych-gate is a substantial stone structure, with attached octagonal shafts and inverted semi-cone corbels, and the church itself is a highly personal statement which provides a veritable treasure house for the student of Douglas's skill and individuality. Neo-Perpendicular style is combined with idiosyncratic detailing, and although the church is small and aisleless, it has an ashlar interior and is marvellously thorough and complete. The west tower (completed posthumously to Douglas's design) is in scale with the small nave, giving the whole building a diminutive character, and Goodhart-Rendel wrote of, 'A dear little toy church in the better than Caröe manner one expected from *happy* Douglas.'[6]

The chancel roof is higher than that of the nave; most of the windows are straight-headed, with simple tracery consisting of paired subdivisions above curved-headed lights; the lower stages of the vice and also the vestries are given free sculptural treatment, and Douglas's hand is also apparent in blank wall panelling, enlarged to considerable scale, on the west face of the tower. There is some carved work, including a figure of St. John in a canopied niche, though for the most part the sense of richness and care results not so much from ornamentation but from the high quality of the masonry and from the manipulation of shape and form. This is particularly true of the structure internally, where generally simple stone walling is enlivened by unconventional treatment largely involving corbels, particularly at the west end. Here the tower arch is on inverted semi-cone corbels and is flanked by window lights placed asymmetrically in arched recesses, and a heavy corbel table is also worked in. The sedilia are equally curious and quirky; the nave roof principals rise from versions of semi-cone corbels and there are more of these flanking the nave window openings. Particularly interesting are free-standing octagonal shafts dividing the window openings. These are closely related to the motif as used at the same time at the Prudential Building, Chester, but as well as providing a further example of the guises in which octagonal posts appeared, they are direct descendants of the shafts in the clerestoreys at St. John's, Over (1860–63, externally) (see page 42), and Aldford (1865–6, internally) (see page 48). A feature which began within the High Victorian phase thus survived to be translated into a Late Victorian – even to some extent an Arts & Crafts – context. A yet greater tenacity of purpose is seen in the furnishings at Sandiway, for they repeat details which had been continually used for some thirty years previously. Sun-flowers and pies were no longer used and baluster motifs (included in the Sandiway choir stalls) had become more habitual, but there remained the unmitred mouldings, conventionalised poppyheads and solid and pierced traceried panels. Despite the style having matured so long before, the Sandiway fittings show not the slightest diminution of excellence.

The use in the 1900s of the style of joinery design which emerged in the 1870s was the result of unswervingly faithful use of well-tried vocabulary of detailing which remained constant over the years. In contrast, a reversion to, rather than a steady continuation of, features of the 1870s is provided by the former parsonage (now Croft House, and enlarged) west of the church at Sandiway. It is of 1905–6, but brick lozenge patterns and mullions and curved-headed lights of moulded brick imply an earlier date. Equally exceptional in this respect is a nearby pair of cottages (1906) – the pair which bears the initials of both John and Sholto Theodore Douglas. This not only has some similar window lights (though some unusual terra-cotta baluster mullions also) but even a suggestion of 'light' half-timbering in the black-and-white upper storey. The brick and terra-cotta for these buildings was supplied not by J. C. Edwards, but by Jabez Thompson of Northwich, for whom a house had been designed not far away in the Douglas & Fordham days (Abbotsford, 1890) and who was also a benefactor of Sandiway church. Thompson doubtless also supplied the terra-cotta dressings used at The Homestead, Sandiway (c. 1906–7, now Redwalls Children's Home) standing on

The Work of John Douglas

land which had belonged to Douglas and attributable to him. There is pebble-dash rendering, consistent with the Edwardian date, but the house perpetuates a version (all within one block) of the Hinderton-Oakmere plan form, and there again appears an entrance court enclosed on two sides with a covered gateway giving access to the stables.

Work in Shoemakers Row, Northgate Street, Chester, belongs to this series of buildings of the decade following the formation of the Douglas & Minshull partnership. It too belongs to the group with personal associations, for Douglas had at least a partial proprietary interest in this street improvement scheme in half-timber (with walkways at street level and thus not built as a true Row). He was not, however, responsible for the whole design. The earliest parts (Nos. 21-23, and No. 3) were built in 1897 and 1898-9 respectively to the designs of H. W. Beswick. Douglas's contributions include Nos. 5-9 (1900), of which he himself was the owner, and which have much characteristic Gothic detail, Nos. 11-13 (1900), probably No. 19 (*c.* 1900), and Nos. 27-31 (1902), forming a prominent feature on the corner of the market square. This is less intricate than Nos. 5-9, but has a slender spirelet and a figure of Edward VII, just as there are canopied statues of Queen Victoria at Walmoor Hill and St. Werburgh Street. He probably also to some extent rebuilt No.25 in 1903, but it was substantially altered *c.* 1914 to a design made in 1909 by James Strong, who was also responsible in 1909 for Nos. 15-17[7].

After several abortive schemes over the years in connection with the Eastgate, a Diamond Jubilee Memorial Clock was finally erected over the arch in 1899. It has the ogee roof of the 1897 scheme, but is otherwise a complete departure from it, being an open wrought iron structure, executed by James Swindley, and safer and more logical for erection over the apex of the arch than the heavy masonry structure previously proposed. It is a popular feature in the Chester scene, though of greater interest within the context of Douglas's work is the Public Baths, Union Street (1898-1901). The interest lies not so much in Douglas's previous ownership of the site, mention of which has already been made, but on account of the job being so notable a departure in terms of building type, involving technical complexity and specialist engineering work. It was rare occasion which led the firm of Douglas & Minshull to write to the Town Clerk in such terms as, 'In consequence of several cases which have come to our knowledge quite recently of fractures occurring in the tanks of swimming baths, and consequent leaking through the cement lining, we strongly recommend your Committee to sanction the substitution of a bituminous lining for the cement contracted for; the additional cost of this will be £150. . . .'[8]

The amendment was agreed to, and the Boating and Baths Committee of the City Council had already displayed a model

Douglas & Minshull

Public Baths, Union Street, Chester, 1898–1901.

approach on the part of clients to architect when, in first commissioning Douglas, it had supplied information, 'to give him the idea of the accommodation the Committee consider is required, but in no way to limit the exercise of his judgment.'[9] Douglas himself seems to have remained involved with the job, though on one occasion he was represented at a meeting of the committee by Minshull and one Mr. Muspratt – doubtless Minshull's future partner, who is thus shown to have been a member of the office staff. On another date Muspratt alone attended.

The aesthetic implications of the unfamiliar building type were not logically pursued, for the structure is for the most part utilitarian, but with a frontage of Ruabon brick, stone dressings, half-timber with Gothic detail and having twisted chimneys, all in the smooth and crisp manner of Eaton estate work of the '90s. Some justification for so domestic an elevation may be found in the fact that it houses a caretaker's flat, but, pleasing as it is, it bears little relation in plan or character to what lies behind.

Mention was made of Deganwy spire (1897–9 (see page 181) standing in line of descent from Oakmere Hall (1867) (see page 50), and Germanic was carried unabated into the twentieth century with Bank Buildings, Charing Cross, Birkenhead, Cheshire (1901) for the Bank of Liverpool – a commission which probably stemmed from the contact established in Chester with St. Werburgh Street. The former branch bank with steep hipped roof, miniature hipped dormers, two hexagonal turrets and a conical-roofed staircase turret, is the focal point of a curving frontage. On either side there are shop premises – those to the right having roofs recessed behind parapets and with miniature dormers, and those to the left with gabled ends of diapered brick. The shop fronts were uniformly designed within elliptical arches, and the upper windows are elaborately Gothic. Also Germanic is the extension (1908) to the Grosvenor Club and North and South Wales Bank, Chester, but in being so was designed to accord with the turret of the earlier building of 1881–3.

Unabated proficiency in half-timbered design was displayed by a scheme for almshouses in Chester (*c.* 1907) for the second Duke of Westminster, but like the Duke's commission for a children's home at Pulford (*c.* 1903) they remained unexecuted. With only occasional and minor jobs being carried out for Bend'Or, and the Eaton estate being of negligible importance in the work of Douglas & Minshull, there was little correspondence from the estate office. Such letters as were written, however, show that Cecil Parker had in no way grown conciliatory with the passage of time.

St. Deiniol's Library, Hawarden, is not only the most important secular building of the Douglas & Minshull period, but in view of the nature of the commission is something of a crowning achievement in Douglas's professional career. The Library was founded by W. E. Gladstone as a place for study and a centre of Christian learning under a trust established in 1895, and he transferred his own books from Hawarden Castle to the temporary buildings in which it was first housed. After his death in 1898 it was agreed between the trustees and the Gladstone National Memorial Committee, set up under the chairmanship of the Duke of Westminster, that as part of the National Memorial a worthy home should be provided for the Library. In 1899 the first sod was cut by Mrs. Gladstone and the foundation stone laid by the Duke, so shortly before his own death, and the library accommodation and wardens'

Bank Buildings, Charing Cross, Birkenhead, Cheshire, 1901. (*Building News*, 8 1901, p. 139)

rooms were completed in 1902. This, however, comprised only about half of the building as planned. It was completed (1904–6) to a revised design and at the expense of the Gladstone family by the addition of a hostel to provide residential facilities for students, visitors and staff.

The main library itself is a splendid apartment, rising through two storeys and with an open timber roof. There are galleries and two tiers of octagonal timber posts carry the galleries and roof timbers respectively, and there is much characteristic detail.[10] This is partly in the form of cusping and swirling Gothic blank tracery, and includes cusping applied to the octagonal shafts, as at No. 38 Bridge Street, Chester.

The building is of E-plan, symmetrical in its general massing but completely irregular in the detailed disposition of elements. The left hand portion, up to and including the central porch, represents the earlier build. The materials are red sandstone and green slate; the character is refined and harmonious, and the style is Douglas's Elizabethan manner, with coped gables and versions of the Hoghton bay. There are, however, also miniature hipped dormers and a considerable measure of Gothic infiltration. This is seen not only in oriels, pointed doorways and the detailing of cusped and other idiomatic window lights, but also in pinnacles and statues within canopied niches. The group is low and spreading, with horizontal roof lines predominating, though the weight of the projecting wings and the lesser emphasis of the porch control and co-ordinate. As at Abbeystead (1885–7) (see pages 149–50) the Elizabethan manner provides the solution for a long spreading frontage. In considering Abbeystead and its related houses of the 1880s, comparison was made with the isolated and immature attempt to resolve a similar design problem in Neo-Elizabethan terms at the south wing of Vale Royal (1860–61). There is, however, more than just a notional

Deiniol's Library, Hawarden, Flintshire, 1899–1902 and 1904–6.

The Work of John Douglas

stylistic resemblance between Vale Royal and St. Deiniol's, for both are asymmetrical, of E-plan and have a small central gable and differing projecting end wings. Though separated by forty years and the experience of a professional lifetime, striking comparison may be drawn between what were Douglas's first and last major commissions.

Douglas & Minshull ecclesiastical work includes the practice's only known London job. This, and Home Place (1894) (see page 152), are Douglas's furthest recorded penetrations southwards. It was a scheme (undated) for adding chancel, chapel, porch and tower with spire to St. Mary's, Edmonton, Middlesex, an incomplete church of 1883 by Butterfield. Of this project, which was not an altogether characteristic one stylistically, only the south-west porch seems to have been carried out, and the church has now been demolished.

Nearer home, the building of St. Ethelwold's, Shotton, Flintshire (1898–1902), was initiated by W. E. Gladstone. An intended tower and spire remained unbuilt, but it is a large church, with clerestorey and – a feature shared by other Douglas & Minshull churches and included in the Edmonton scheme – a three-sided apse. The interior is of red ashlar and the details and external massing have a characteristically Late Victorian combination of trickiness with broad simplicity of form. Despite the freedom and simplicity of the detailing, the general character is that of sober and careful Gothic. There is some tracery, but the windows are mostly lancets, and Goodhart-Rendel described the style as, 'Douglas Early Pointed, refreshing in those days of "Perp."'[11] The Neo-Perpendicular tradition in his Late Victorian Gothic manner was continued at the church of St. John the Baptist, Old Colwyn, near Colwyn Bay (1899–1903), though again with a considerable freeing-up apparent, and with the detailing of the nave arcade comparable with that at Deganwy in its unarchaeological modishness. Again the interior is red ashlar, but externally light local limestone is used, giving, with the straight-headed clerestorey windows, the feel of a fresh and breezy turn of the century seaside church. Its character would, however, have been very different, and the sense of simple massing lost, had the original design for a complicated octagonal west tower been carried out. It may have been at about this time that another freely detailed nave arcade was built, at Christ Church, Chester. Though the reconstruction of the building began in 1876, and the east end evolved in the 1890s, the completion of the nave dates from 1900.

St. Matthew's, Buckley, Flintshire, is perhaps the most surprising, and is certainly one of the most enjoyable, churches of this period. Like Christ Church it resulted from gradual rebuilding, though over a shorter period of time. The previous building was of

Douglas & Minshull

1821–2 by John Oates. Vestries were added in 1897–9; in 1900–2 a chancel and south-west porch were added, the tower remodelled and a timber-framed lych-gate built, and in 1904–5 the nave was rebuilt and aisles added. Again the style is Perpendicular, and there is a three-sided apse. In accordance with plentiful Douglas precedent the apse roof is hipped and recessed behind a parapet. There is, though, in the blockiness of this parapet and the squatness of the battlemented and pinnacled tower and in the simplified Gothic detailing of buttresses and pinnacles a suggestion of the extreme horizontality and conventionalised squaring off such as occurs in the work of Austin & Paley (as distinct from that of the Paley & Austin era). Yet Douglas continued to assert his individuality by giving a fair pitch to the roof and – a great surprise – by extensive use of timber-framing. Buckley was his last great fling in the use of vernacular elements for a church. The clerestorey is half-timbered, and inside there is a frieze of painted panels between the clerestorey and a timber nave arcade.[12] Painted decoration was also provided in the baptistery under the tower, and it may be supposed that stencilled patterning at St. Paul's Boughton (1876) dates from the time when, shortly before, Douglas added to this church the south aisle with its external brick nogging (1902) (see page 125).

Much of the work at Buckley was at the expense of the Gladstone

St Ethelwold's Church, Shotton, Flintshire, 1898–1902. Interior. *Architect*, 72, 1904, p. 264)

The Work of John Douglas

family, and a further instance of their patronage is the Gladstone Memorial Chapel added to St. Deiniol's church, Hawarden (*c.* 1901–3) to contain a monument to Mr. and Mrs. W. E. Gladstone. Formed at the east end of the north aisle, it is rib vaulted, and has inverted semi-cone corbels, and it received its monument, by William Richmond, in 1906.

The Congregational Church, Hoylake, Cheshire (1906), is another Neo-Perpendicular building with a three-sided apse. A sign of the Edwardian times is the use of soft-textured rustic brick, but there is characteristic Douglas detailing, and a fairly steep roof originally with a Germanic flèche. Not far away, St. Andrew's, West Kirby, was completed in 1907 by the addition of a cruciform east end to the nave of 1889–91 (see page 177), though not in accordance with the original design. It is in quite rich Perpendicular, with elaborate tracery and statues in canopied niches. Buttresses have set-offs, rather than being simple batters, but being in line with adjacent wall planes they nevertheless result in a strong feeling of rectangularity. Moreover, the conventionalised squaring off, typical of the period and noted at Buckley, is suggested by the side parapets of the sanctuary roof with low steps in their outlines and isolated rectangular traceried panels, and by the parapet motif being carried across the east gable. Internally the crossing arches differ in height and detail. Externally the roof of the chancel is higher than that of the nave, but the change is effected not by a central tower or an abrupt step, but by an ingenious system of gables and a slate-hung spire which rises from the crossing. One of the most striking of all Douglas's ecclesiastical Germanic skylines, the spire is octagonal, with a diagonally-placed square base and a cluster of four pinnacles. This second stage of work at St. Andrew's is typical of Douglas at his best in combining historical knowledge with unmistakable individuality and an awareness of contemporary thought and development.

With timberwork used in the separation of nave and aisles, but a building less sure in its touch than the Douglas & Minshull works so far mentioned, is the little church of the Resurrection and All Saints, Caldy, Cheshire (1906–7). It is however, merely a remodelling of an earlier school (of 1868 by Street) and the net result is something of a compromise. To a yet greater extent St. Matthew's, Saltney Ferry, Flintshire (*c.* 1905–11), has certain Douglas characteristics but is nevertheless not of special quality. The same applies to the earlier Douglas & Fordham church of All Saints, Higher Kinnerton, Flintshire (1893) and comparable with certain of the Douglas & Fordham secular buildings discussed is Clare Lodge, Abbots Park, Chester (*c.* 1904). Quite an impressive house, it is its general character rather than any lack of quality which calls for mention, with its materials and elements suggesting, as at the Port Sunlight School, the work of Douglas's followers and imitators rather than his own.

In so far as it is possible to draw conclusions from a single gable-ended elevation, the same general comment might apply to the Church House, St. Asaph (1908).

More significant as far as speculation over authorship is concerned, may be Colshaw Hall, Lower Peover, Cheshire (1903) which although a house in the Elizabethan manner has certain alien details mixed with others from the long-established vocabulary. As for Lonnin Garth, Portinscale, Cumberland (undated), it is a pleasant cottagey house with some rendering and some local stone facing, but so devoid of recognisable features to make it difficult to believe that Douglas himself made any contribution to it. A hand other than his must also have had, at the very least, much to do with The Sundial, Hawarden (1907), built for Helen Gladstone, a daughter of the statesman. It uses brick and half-timber as well as having some pebble-dash rendering, but there is nothing (except for vague hints in window detailing) to indicate its authorship and to distinguish it from innumerable prosperous suburban houses of similar date and style. The joinery detailing is similarly anonymous, with unmitred mouldings forsaken for the more routine classically-derived forms of the period, with bolection mouldings, lugs to the architraves of fireplace surrounds and segmental pediments over doorways. An elaborate Gothic screen inserted in the Boteler Chapel at St. Elphin's church, Warrington (1903) has a limited degree of Douglas-like authenticity about it, though very little of the kind can be discerned in the sanctuary fittings designed for St. Mary's Roman Catholic church, Latchford, Warrington (*c.* 1907, and the practice's only known Roman Catholic commission incidentally), where the tendency for curves in The Sundial doorcases is worked into a Gothic context.[13]

The evidence of decreased activity and a degree of delegation on Douglas's part makes the dissolving of the Douglas & Minshull partnership in 1909 all the more strange and inexplicable. The addition of a south aisle to his earlier (1868–70) church of St. Paul, Helsby is of 1909, but is still a Douglas & Minshull work, whereas the chancel at Holy Trinity, Greenfield, Flintshire (1910, added to a Ewan Christian church of 1870–71) belongs to the final period in which, during the last year or so of his life, he remained in practice alone.

In 1912 the reconstituted firm of Douglas, Minshull & Muspratt added a west tower to the church at Old Colwyn – a simple battlemented structure, with a vice turret, and having quite strong rectangular emphasis. It is related to, though less squat than, the Bryn-y-Maen tower, and is very different from the octagon which was first intended. It is not known if this was a new design of 1912 or a posthumous execution of one made in Douglas's lifetime. Also carried out in 1912, after his death, is the south aisle added to All

The Work of John Douglas

Saints', Hoole, Chester (1867 by S. W. Dawkes). This is credited to him and to one J. Walley, suggesting that, in the absence of a partner, he entered into collaboration with others. This was certainly the case with schools in Chester at Egerton Street (1909–10) and Cherry Grove, Boughton (1910–11) which were done jointly with W. T. Lockwood, one of the two sons of T. M. Lockwood. Cherry Grove School is of brick and terra-cotta with Baroque touches, quite commonplace among schools of the period and typical of the younger Lockwood. Egerton Street, much smaller, is an extraordinary building, for the joint authorship is clearly obvious, with some of Douglas's old roof and window forms intermingled with Lockwood's more ordinary motifs.

Happily, Douglas's career ended on a less sad and unsatisfactory note, with his last work, which he longed in vain to live to see finished, being the tower at St. Paul's, Colwyn Bay. Praised by Goodhart-Rendel as, 'a great success,'[14] it is not dissimilar to that originally designed in 1887, but is raised to a greater height to compensate for the lack of the spire. The scale seems surer than that of the body of the church, with its great size indicated by a cavernous opening at the base, forming the church entrance, and by tiers of small windows (of differing design and very freely detailed) leading up to the belfry stage. The horizontal emphasis of shallow battlements places it within the category of Douglas's late towers, while at the same time boldly modelled buttresses complete a picture of craggy firmness. It is a vigorous and courageous tower, and is a not unworthy conclusion to John Douglas's full and fruitful life as an architect.

XII Conclusion

In assessing the career and achievements of John Douglas, account must be taken of the influence which he exerted on other architects – a subject which would provide adequate material for extended study – and some mention must particularly be made of persons who are either known to have passed through his office or may be deduced to have done so.

A special case was Douglas's cousin and assistant Walter Edwards, whose involvement is said to have been related particularly to constructional and technical matters.[1] The earliest reference to him is as clerk of works for Hartford church (1873–5)[2] and mention of him is found, when he was attached to the office, in connection with structural reports, site supervision, or costings.[3]

Best known among those who themselves emerged as architects are Edmund Kirby (1838–1920) and Edward A. L. Ould (1853–1909). Kirby, who is chiefly remembered for his Roman Catholic churches, was a pupil of E. W. Pugin and was with Douglas as an assistant during the High Victorian period, establishing his own practice in Liverpool in 1867.[4] Later, his work showed certain affinities with aspects of Douglas's, suggesting either some parallel development or else conscious awareness of what his former employer had been doing. The similarities may be seen in virtuosity in the use of bright red brick and an amorphous solidity (carried to greater and more logical lengths than Douglas himself ever did) in the design of large red houses, among which Redcourt, Claughton, Birkenhead (1876–9, now St. Anselm's Junior School)[5] may be cited.

The case of Ould is particularly illuminating, in showing how well versed a pupil and assistant could become in the characteristics of Douglas's style and manner. Between leaving the Abbey Square office and being in 1886 taken into partnership by the Liverpool architect G. E. Grayson, he was responsible for a number of buildings in and around Chester so Douglas-like as readily to invite misattribution. They include Uffington House, Dee Hills Park (1886),[6] a red brick structure with Germanic turrets and strongly vertical emphasis, and the Queen's School (1882–3)[7] with diapered brick, wall panelling, Germanic turret, cusped window lights and a hipped roof recessed behind a castellated parapet. That Grayson & Ould's firm is today perhaps more widely known than is Douglas probably results from their having worked at Cambridge (at Trinity Hall and Selwyn) and for their having been responsible for the carefully-cherished period piece of Wightwick Manor, Staffordshire (1887 and 1893), even though it is the Mander collection rather than the architecture for which Wightwick is celebrated. It may readily be

The Work of John Douglas

imagined that Douglas's tuition imparted to Ould the enthusiasm for half-timber which is reflected at Wightwick and in a book on timber-framed houses,[8] and which found its greatest expression at Bidston Court, Birkenhead (1891, now reconstructed as Hill Bark, Frankby). The Queen's School was a project with which the Duke of Westminster was associated, and work given to Ould directly by the Duke included the former rectory at Halkyn (1885).[9] It would seem likely that this resulted from agreement on the part of the Duke and Douglas (perhaps at the latter's suggestion) to give encouragement to the young man at the outset of his independent career.

This would also seem to have been the case with George Smith, who, like Ould,[10] was among the numerous contributors to the *Abbey Square Sketch Book*.[11] Mention has already been made of his having been an assistant in Douglas's office and to having been engaged, on his own account, on projects for Haydock church at the time of his premature death in 1885. As well as the Haydock schemes he was, in independent practice, responsible for a house in Claughton, Birkenhead (No. 59 Shrewsbury Road, *c.* 1884),[12] which is of brick and half-timber and is astonishingly Douglas-like in its windows and other detailing, and also for the Smithfield Cocoa House, Chester (*c.* 1885, demolished),[13] with a rather Germanic turret. This was for the Chester Cocoa House Co. Ltd., with which the Duke was closely associated, and also for the company Smith commenced alterations and restoration at the half-timbered Falcon, Lower Bridge Street, which, after his death, were continued by Grayson & Ould.[14]

The influence of Douglas may also be perceived in the work of Richard Thomas Beckett who, as has been noted, was the son of Douglas's brother-in-law by a second marriage. Influence is further traceable in a number of more obscure figures who contributed to *Abbey Square Sketch Book* and who may be assumed to have had connections with the office. They include Harold Hignett,[15] whose buildings include a half-timbered one at Northwich,[16] A. E. Powles,[17] who was responsible for the Brunner Guildhall, Winsford, Cheshire (1899),[18] of brick, with Douglas-like detail, and James Strong,[19] who did the heavily-decorated half-timbered former fire station in Chester (1911).[20]

One Heber Rimmer is known to have been employed in the office, and like T. W. Haigh signed some of the published perspectives of Douglas's buildings as well as contributing to *Abbey Square Sketch Book*.[21] The case of Edward Hodkinson was different, for although he also did much for *Abbey Square Sketch Book*,[22] and was responsible for numerous excellent perspectives for Douglas, including many of those shown at the Royal Academy,[23] he was himself an architect with his own practice in Chester. As he remodelled the Porden church at Eccleston (1853)[24] as well as rebuilding Saighton

Conclusion

Grange for the second Marquess of Westminster, he must have been of advanced age when he died in 1909.[25] His only other known independent design, however, is for a house (probably unexecuted) which showed considerable Douglas influence in its use of shaped gables, stone banding and diapered brick.[26] Extensively employed for Douglas's perspectives, he carried out similar work as a draughtsman for T. M. Lockwood.

Lockwood himself evolved a personal and recognisable style and distinctive manner of detailing, and was an able exponent of half-timbering. He too, though, was affected by Douglas, as is made clear by his cribbing of brick diapering and stone banding at the former rectories at Aldford (1897)[27] and Eccleston (c. 1896)[28] and at the block on the corner of Bridge and Watergate Streets, Chester (1892),[29] all for the Duke of Westminster. Lockwood set up on his own after having been with T. M. Penson,[30] and thus had no professional dealings with Douglas and his office. With both being exact contemporaries, and the two most successful Chester architects of their generation, and with one prepared to some extent to imitate the other, it would be interesting to know what personal or social relations existed between them, though all that can be said is that Douglas attended Lockwood's funeral.

Henry Beswick, the Cheshire County Architect, was a pupil of Lockwood, but some of his brick buildings show the influence of Douglas – Oakfield, for instance (largely 1892, at which Ould and Hignett had previously worked, now Chester Zoo)[31] with diapering, shaped gables and J. C. Edwards standard chimneys. Again, a restoration by W. M. Boden of St. Mary's church, Bruera, for the Duke of Westminster,[32] is strongly Douglas-like in its detailing.

Also in Cheshire Daresbury Lodge has characteristic brickwork, windows and chimneys, but there is sufficient clumsiness in the proportions to suggest the work of a pupil or imitator rather than that of Douglas himself. The brick and half-timber Royal Oak, Kelsall, has a Lockwood look about it, but whether or not it is his, it would never have taken the form it did without Douglas and his example. In Chester itself are many buildings of which, in their use of Ruabon brick or half-timber, the same could be said. Some are thoroughly sub-Douglas in quality. Others may be unidentified work of his, but in any case, together with the scores of authenticated buildings by him and his followers in the city and on the Eaton estate, they succeed in giving a distinctive flavour to much of the building of the Late Victorian era over a wide region. Maurice B. Adams rightly commented that, '. . . John Douglas . . . created quite a school of his pupils . . .'[33] and if his influence as well as his own architecture is considered, Muthesius was justfied in writing that 'his houses gave the newer parts of Chester its character'.[34]

With the combination of the half-timber revival, the patronage of

The Work of John Douglas

the Duke of Westminster and the work and influence of John Douglas, Chester makes a special contribution to the story of Late Victorian architecture, and this was recognised at the time, most notably by Muthesius and Raffles Davison.

In making a distinctive contribution to the region in which he worked while at the same time executing some commissions over a wider field, Douglas exemplified the rôle which could be played by an architect of stature practising away from London. In contributing as they did to the overall richness and quality of the whole national picture, leading architects in the provinces may be seen as being of special importance and significance by reason of their very provinciality. Appreciation of this seems to underlie Davison's appraisals of Douglas, and it was doubtless he who wrote in *The British Architect*, '... we can but hope that such firms as Douglas & Fordham, of Chester, and Austin & Paley, of Lancaster, will have, if possible, equally good successors to uphold the credit of English provincial architecture.'[35] It would, moreover, be difficult to challenge the *Chester Chronicle*'s evaluation of Douglas at the time of his death as 'the doyen of provincial architects.'[36]

The study and appraisal of Douglas's work involves not the discovery of a hitherto little-known architect, but the rediscovery of a major figure of national importance, who achieved widespread recognition within his lifetime. That he should, except within a restricted local field, have subsequently faded from remembrance is symptomatic of the twilight which enveloped the Victorian age and its artistic achievements. Kenneth Clark was able, in 1928, to write even of Pugin having been forgotten[37] and later to refer to having rescued him from oblivion.[38] It is now, however, more difficult to account for the fact that Douglas has continued to remain in obscurity. Although his buildings stare from the pages of the major architectural journals, and despite the perceptive praise of Muthesius and Goodhart-Rendel, the recent upsurge of interest, appreciation and scholarship concerning nineteenth century architecture has hitherto passed him by. The excessive emphasis which tends to be placed on metropolitan activity and the consequent underestimation of provincial architects must partly be to blame. Nevertheless the churches of Paley & Austin are known outside the region in which most of them are to be found, and the firm of Grayson & Ould seems to have been heard of by more people than are familiar with the name of Douglas, and it would be difficult to contend that either H. J. Austin or Edward Ould was a more accomplished architect than was he.

That Douglas and Paley & Austin should in neighbouring counties have simultaneously designed series of refined and highly finished Late Victorian Gothic churches invites (especially in view of Douglas's own early connection with the Lancaster office) comparison between the two practices. While retaining their individuality

Conclusion

and distinctiveness, the respective products do show certain similarities of form and detail. Austin had had no professional contact with Paley before being taken into partnership in 1867, so he and Douglas never worked together, and it is not known if they were personally acquainted. Each must surely, however, at the very least, have been aware of the work and development of the other, and although there can be no clear evidence to what extent (if at all) who may have influenced whom, the possibility of some cross-fertilisation may be propounded.

In any case, the churches of both practices were part of that movement which, in the form of sober and basically English-inspired Gothic, succeeded High Victorian ecclesiastical design, and of which Bodley may be seen to have been the leader. Similarly, the domestic architecture of Douglas's maturity equally stemmed from the example of Nesfield and Shaw – in the first instance, it would seem, particularly and directly from that of Nesfield. Like Shaw, with whose life-span his own almost exactly coincided, Douglas proved himself to be a master of creative eclecticism, though drawing on a more restricted range of stylistic sources. The Germanic element and the admixture of the mediaeval and the seventeenth century in detailing were special and distinctive features embodied within the corpus of his work, but except for occasional use in ornament and detail classical components are absent, and there are none of the audacious extremes to which Shaw's welding of disparate styles could reach.

Some comparison between the careers of Douglas and Shaw and also that of Waterhouse may be suggested by the circumstance of all three men being almost exact contemporaries. It may be noted that although one commenced practice in London from the start, another widened already broad horizons by forsaking Manchester for the capital, while the third chose always to seek fulfilment of his ideals and ambitions in his cathedral city and county town. Just as Douglas's earliest vernacular cottages and lodges at Eaton contrast so forcibly with the High Victorian histrionics being brought into being at the mansion itself, his mature work, like that of Shaw, is in its entirety significantly different from that of Waterhouse, for the latter's name was made early, and it is in Mid rather than Late Victorian terms that his reputation rests. Though with many houses to his credit, it was as a designer of public and commercial buildings that Waterhouse's abilities as an architect were most apparent; Shaw is remembered chiefly as a domestic architect who also turned his hand to public and commercial works and to churches, while Bodley or Paley & Austin were ecclesiastical architects who occasionally designed houses. Douglas is not primarily associated with any one single building type, and his reputation must depend equally upon churches and upon houses.

The Work of John Douglas

Although a leading provincial architect and one who exerted noticeable direct influence on others, Douglas was never a leader in the sense of being a pioneer of any significant new development or lasting school of design. He was, though, at times, a close follower of national stylistic trends while at the same time retaining his own individuality. Capable of remaining true to himself while keeping abreast of current thought, he evolved, within the context of the architecture of his time, highly personal interpretations of the Gothic, Vernacular and Domestic Revivals. Even when most closely following historical precedents, his buildings are of distinctly individual stamp. Consistent characteristics are sure proportions, imaginative massing and grouping (with tendencies to verticality and attenuated forms), immaculate detailing and a superb sense of craftmanship and feeling for materials. 'Born and resident in Cheshire, the home of true half-timbering', wrote Muthesius, 'he devoted himself most lovingly to the reintroduction of the style, mastered it down to the last detail, and produced buildings of great charm. Yet he also handled brick and stone with great skill. His buildings always reflect consummate mastery of form and are yet simple enough in feeling and natural-looking fitness for purpose to stand comparison with the old houses'.[39]

Operating largely within the framework of traditional building types and with technical innovations playing little part in his work,[40] Douglas produced no *magnum opus* or any single masterpiece to stand apart from the general corpus of his labours and, as *The British Architect* put it, the practice, 'not often had the stimulus of "great occasion," or glittering circumstance.'[41] Instead there appeared over the decades a steady stream of small and medium-sized buildings, ranging from estate cottages to large but not vast country houses, and remarkable for comprehensive quality and carefulness. The 'same level of thoroughness and high level of accomplishment' ran through all, and *The British Architect* may further be endorsed in its view that there had 'been no practice of the art of architecture in this country more consistent in its general excellence of aim and attainment than that carried on for many years by Mr. John Douglas of Chester.'[42]

The contemporary appraisals formulated by Muthesius and *The British Architect* remain valid and are admissible contributions to the assessment of Douglas's ability and achievements. The praises of the journal were lavish, but were nevertheless measured and rational. No more was ever claimed, either on grounds of originality or influence, than was warranted by the circumstances of an architect who, within the limits of a practice restricted in its scope and coverage, has left progeny of ubiquitous and outstanding merit. The work of John Douglas is, moreover, architecture which can be enjoyed as well as admired, and in the pleasure which is to be derived from it, and in its facility to delight the eye and stir the heart, there can be shared some of his own passionate enthusiasm for the art which he served so well.

References

Chapter I John Douglas's Life

1. (a) Cheshire County R.O. (EDB). Bishop's Transcripts of Weaverham Parish Registers. (b) Memorial tablet in south aisle of St. Paul's church, Boughton, Chester.
2. Cheshire County R.O. (EDT 416/1). Tithe Award, Parish of Weaverham, Apportionment. (EDT 416/2a). Tithe Award, Parish of Weaverham, Map No. 1, Township and Lordship of Weaverham, 1838.
3. (a) Cheshire County R.O. (EDB). Bishop's Transcripts, *op. cit.* (b) Douglas memorial window in south aisle of St. Mary's church, Weaverham.
4. C.R. Township of Weaverham-cum-Milton, 1851, 1861.
5. (a) Cheshire County R.O. (EDB). Bishop's Transcripts, *op. cit.*, and (b) Douglas memorial window in south aisle of St. Mary's church, Weaverham, state that he was 64 at the time of his death in 1862. On the other hand, (c) C.R. Township of Weaverham-cum-Milton give his age as 40 in 1841, 51 in 1851 and 61 in 1861. Also (d) the death certificate (General Register Office, Somerset House, London) states that he was 62 in 1862.
6. Probate Office, Somerset House, London, and Cheshire County R.O. Will of John Swindley the elder of Eccleston, 1852.
7. (a) Cheshire County R.O. (P/91/3/2). Aldford Parish Registers, Baptisms 1780–1812 and Burials 1781–1812. (b) C.R. Township of Weaverham-cum-Milton, 1861, name her birthplace as Eaton. (c) C.R. Township of Eccleston give Aldford as the birthplace of older and younger brothers and sisters.
8. (a) Slater's *Directory . . . of Cheshire*, 1848, 1855, 1888. (b) Bagshaw's *. . . Directory of the County Palatine of Chester*, 1850. (c) White's *. . . Directory of Cheshire*, 1860. (d) Morris's *. . . Directory . . . of Cheshire*, 1864, 1874. (e) *Post Office Directory of Cheshire* (Kelly's), 1864, 1878. (f) Kelly, 1896. (g) C.R. Township of Eccleston, 1841, 1851, 1871. (h) Probate Office, Somerset House, London, and Cheshire County R.O. Will of John Swindley the elder of Eccleston, 1852.
9. (a) Kelly, 1896 and subsequent editions. (b) Successive editions of Kelly's *Directory of Chester*.
10. E.g. Gates at Belgrave Lodge, Eaton Hall, Cheshire (1890–91); gates and railings at Eccleston Lodge, Eaton Hall (1893–4); garden gates (unidentified), Eaton Hall (1894–5); Diamond Jubilee Memorial Clock, the Eastgate, Chester (1899); gates, Mostyn Hall, Flintshire (1896).
11. Cheshire County R.O. (EDB). Bishop's Transcripts, *op. cit.*
12. (a) Slater's *Directory . . . of Cheshire*, 1848, 1855. (b) Bagshaw's *. . . Directory of the County Palatine of Chester*, 1850. (c) White's *. . . Directory of Cheshire*, 1860. (d) C.R. Township of Weaverham-cum-Milton, 1841, 1851, 1861.
13. *The Mansions of England and Wales*, Edward Twycross, 4 (*The County Palatine of Chester*, 1), London,. 1850, p. 149.
14. C.R. Township of Weaverham-cum-Milton, 1851.
15. Cheshire County R.O. (EDT 416/1 and EDT 416/2a). Tithe Award, *op. cit.*, indicates property which can be identified as Park Cottage as being a house, building yard and garden, owned by Lord Delamere and occupied by John Douglas.
16. C.R. Township of Weaverham-cum-Milton, 1841, 1851, 1861.
17. Probate Office, Somerset House, London, and Cheshire County R.O. Will of John Douglas of Sandiway, 1862.
    [Mr. Andrew Saint points out that sums in probate valuations tended to include only personalty, not landed property, so that Douglas may in fact have left much more than £800.]

The Work of John Douglas

18. Probate Office, Somerset House, London, and Cheshire County R.O. Will of John Edwards of Witton, late of Sandiway, 1846. Will signed 23rd May 1845 refers to articles of agreement entered into with John Douglas, builder, of Sandiway, 20th May 1845, covenanting to convey the property before 29th September.
19. Cheshire County R.O. (QDV 3/2). *A Return of Persons entitled to Vote . . . Southern division of the County of Chester*, 1832. Also subsequent issues. (Cuddington listed in township of Weaverham-cum-Milton.)

    [A pocket book kept by Henrietta, Lady Delamere, betweeen 1810 and 1849 (Cheshire County R.O. DBC/Acc. 2309) records under the year 1848: 'Land about Sandyway, 19 acres, purchased and exchanged with Douglas cost £1700'. The same source refers to building work done for Lord Delamere by Douglas (Church Lodge, 1830; Grenville Lodge, 1841; small farm in Petty Pool Park, 1844). Doubtless there was more.

    The rôle of John Douglas Senior in forwarding his son's career may well have been more significant than previously appeared to be the case. In 1834 he is described as 'architect' on a plaque recording the building of the Cheshire Hunt Kennels at Sandiway (*Cheshire Life*, July 1985, p.30). Work on the Arley Estate for R. E. Egerton-Warburton included repairs to 'John Lewis's house' in 1844; the building (and presumably designing) of Stockley Farm, Aston by Budworth, 1844 (now demolished), and possibly of the new front to Carter's House (now the Parsonage), Arley Green, 1845; and also estimating for the conversion of a barn at Boxhedge into two cottages, 1845 (information from Arley Estate Papers supplied to Edward Hubbard in 1980 by Mrs K. M. Harris of Appleton). Douglas Junior was to do much work on the Estate from at least 1868 onwards. Even more remarkable is the fact that one of William Burn's drawings for Eaton Hall, dated by his office '21 May 1846', is also signed '1847 Feby 24th John Douglas' (RIBA Wat. A [19]/a/1). The drawing (for the 'octagonal towers at angles of Drawing and Dining Rooms') hardly looks like a contract drawing, but Douglas Senior must presumably have been acting as builder.]
20. *B.A.* ob.
21. Cheshire County R.O. (EDT 416/1 and EDT 416/2a). Tithe Award, *op. cit.*, indicates that the present Sandiway Manor occupies the site of a farmhouse owned in 1838 by John Edwards, with whom the 1845 agreement was entered into by John Douglas senior.
22. Cheshire County R.O. (HDT 2469). Title Deeds of Redwalls Children's Home, Sandiway.
23. *B.A.*, 69, 1908, pp. 40, 42.
24. General Register Office, Somerset House, London.
25. (a) White's . . . *Directory of Cheshire*, 1860. (b) C.R. Township of Hartford, 1861, 1871.
26. (a) General Register Office, Somerset House, London. (b) Douglas memorial window in south aisle of St. Mary's church, Weaverham.
27. (a) General Register Office, Somerset House, London. (b) Douglas memorial window in south aisle of St. Mary's church, Weaverham. (c) Cheshire County R.O. (EDB). Bishop's Transcripts, *op. cit.*
28. Kelly.
29. C.R. Township of Hartford, 1861, 1871.
30. (a) C.R. Township of Eccleston, 1841, 1851, 1871. (b) Probate Office, Somerset House, London, and Cheshire County R.O. Will of John Swindley the elder of Eccleston, 1852, and Will of John Douglas of Sandiway, 1862.
31. Information from Mrs. A. D. Edwards.
32. E.g., all in Cheshire, church of St. John the Evangelist, Over (1860–63); restoration of St. Peter's church, Little Budworth (1870–71); St. John's church, Hartford (1873–5); agent's house, Ruloe, Norley (*c.* 1873); remodelling of St. Mary's church, Whitegate (1874–5); oriel window and porch, Vale Royal (1877); Whitegate Vicarage (1878); cottage, Sandiway (on Chester road, north-east of Blue Cap Hotel, *c.* 1879);

References

Barrowmore Hall, Great Barrow (c. 1881); cottage and shop, Saighton (1882–3).
33. (a) Inferred from C.R. Township of Hartford, 1861, 1871. (b) Confirmed by the Revd. David Hinge.
34. (a) *A.S.S.B.*, 3, pls. 56, 62. (b) Information from the Revd. David Hinge.
35. Information communicated to Mr. Peter Howell by the late Mr. S. Colwyn Foulkes.
36. (a) *B.N.* ob. (b) *B.A.*, 43, 1895, p. 55. Obituary of E. G. Paley. In addition, Douglas is mentioned as having been in the office of Sharpe & Paley in (c) *B.A.* ob., (d) *Cheshire Observer*, ob., (e) *Chester Chronicle* ob. and (f) *R.I.B.A.J.* ob.
37. *B.A.*, 43, 1895, p. 55. Obituary of E. G. Paley.
38. (a) Chester City R.O. (CED/22). Lists of Parliamentary Voters. *Lists of Freeman of, and Occupiers of Premises in the City and Borough of Chester*, 1860. This is the first issue which lists Douglas as an occupier in Abbey Square, and although the house number is not given, it may be assumed that he was at No. 6, as this is specifically mentioned as his address in (b) C.R. Chester Cathedral, 1861. (c) Chester City R.O. (CCB/54). Minutes of the Improvement Committee, 1878–1881, p. 36. Letter from John Douglas, 14th Feb. 1880 in which, writing on the subject of Abbey Square, he states, 'I have been here now 20 years. . . .'
39. Morris's . . . *Directory* . . . *of Cheshire*, 1864.
40. Implied in Chester City R.O. (CCB/54). Minutes of the Improvement Committee, 1878–1881, p. 36. Letter from John Douglas, 14th Feb. 1880.
41. General Register Office, Somerset House, London.
42. Evidence of the age of Douglas's wife is provided by (a) C.R. Chester Cathedral, 1861, 1871, (b) Records in office at Overleigh Cemetery, Chester, relating to burials in Grave No. 2829 in Old Cemetery, (c) Inscription on this gravestone and (d) General Register Office, Somerset House, London (death certificate of Elizabeth Douglas, 1878).
43. C.R. Chester Cathedral, 1861.
44. General Register Office, Somerset House, London.
45. (a) *Ibid.* (b) Records in office at Overleigh Cemetery, Chester, relating to burials in Grave No. 2829 in Old Cemetery. (c) Inscription on this gravestone.
46. C.R. Chester Cathedral, 1871.
47. (a) Morris's . . . *Directory of* . . . *Cheshire*, 1874. (b) General Register Office, Somerset House, London (death certificates of Jerome Douglas, 1869, and John Percy Douglas, 1873).
48. *Post Office Directory of Cheshire* (Kelly's), 1878.
49. (a) General Register Office, Somerset House, London. (b) Records in office at Overleigh Cemetery, Chester, relating to burials in Grave No. 2829 in Old Cemetery. (c) Inscription on this gravestone.
50. (a) Chester City R.O. (CCB/50). Minutes of the Improvement Committee, 1861–1866, pp. 799, 801, 810, 811, 814–5. (b) Chester City R.O. (DT/1). Town Clerk's Department. Letters and Papers. Letter from John Douglas to the Chairman of the Improvement Committee, 11th Dec. 1865.
51. Information from Mr. and Mrs. P. S. Dutton and Dr. and Mrs. K. A. Turner.
52. Chester City R.O. (CED/37). Lists of Parliamentary Voters. *List of Freeman of, and Occupiers of Premises in the City and Borough of Chester*, 1876.
53. (a) General Register Office, Somerset House, London (death certificates of Elizabeth Douglas, 1876, and Colin Edmunds Douglas, 1887). (b) Records in office at Overleigh Cemetery, Chester, relating to burials in Grave No. 2829 in Old Cemetery. (c) Inscription on this gravestone.
54. General Register Office, Somerset House, London (death certificate of Colin Edmunds Douglas, 1887).
55. E.E.O. Drawings. 'New Farm House, Pulford. No. 3.' Plans for Ironhouse Farmhouse, Pulford, Cheshire, Douglas & Fordham, 22nd Jan. 1884.
56. General Register Office, Somerset House, London (death certificate of Daniel Porter Fordham, 1899).

The Work of John Douglas

57. Inferred from *Ibid*.
58. (a) *A.S.S.B.*, 1, pl. 46; 2, pls. 46, 67; 3 pls. 2, 31. (b) *B.A.*, 23, 1885, pp. 54, 66, 114; 29, 1888, pp. 6. 15.
59. *Bldr.* ob.
60. *A.S.S.B.*, 1, pl. 46.
61. *Journal of the Chester Archaeological and Historic Society*, new series, 1, 1887, pp. 233, 234. Fordham's name appears among the list of members, corrected to 30th May 1887. He is not in the previous list, which was published in 1885.
62. (a) Slater's *Directory of Cheshire*, 1880. (b) Kelly, 1892. (c) Chester City R.O. (CEE/7). *Register of Persons Entitled to Vote . . . Chester*, 1885–6; (CEE/13). *Register of Persons Entitled to Vote . . . Chester*, 1891–2.
63. (a) *Bldr.* ob. (b) *B.N.* ob. (c) *Cheshire Observer* ob. (d) *Chester Chronicle* ob. (e) *Chester Courant* ob. (f) *Liverpool Daily Post* ob.
64. *B.A.*, 49, 1898, pp. 360–61.
65. *Ibid.*, 49, 1898, p. 363.
66. E.E.O., 700, p. 11. Letter from Cecil T. Parker to Douglas & Minshull, 25th Nov. 1897.
67. (a) General Register Office, Somerset House, London (death certificate of Daniel Porter Fordham, 1899). (b) Probate Office, Somerset House, London.
68. Chester City R.O. (DT/2). Town Clerk's Department. Improvement Committee. Letter from Douglas & Minshull, 1st May 1899.
69. Obituaries of C. H. Minshull in (a) *Cheshire Observer*, 22nd Sep. 1934, (b) *Chester Chronicle*, 26th Sep. 1934, (c) *Chester Courant*, 26th Sep. 1934 and (d) *Journal of the Chester and North Wales Architectural Archaeological and Historic Society*, new series, 31, part 1, 1935, pp. 81–3.
70. *Memorials of Old Cheshire*, ed. Edward Barber and P. H. Ditchfield, London, 1910, pp. 80–99, 'The Half-Timbered Architecture of Cheshire,' C. H. Minshull.
71. (a) Kelly, 1896 and subsequent editions. (b) Chester City R.O. (CEE/21). *Register of Persons Entitled to Vote . . . Chester*, 1899 and subsequent issues.
72. Information from Mrs. A. D. Edwards.
73. *B.A.* ob. refers, in May 1911, to the partnership having been dissolved about eighteen months previously.
    [In a letter of 7th December 1909 to W. Swire, C. H. Minshull wrote: 'In view of a change that the firm of Douglas and Minshull may shortly be undergoing, it would be a convenience to receive the balance of our account before the end of the year.' (Letter in the possession of Mrs. Anne Stevens of Longden Manor, Shropshire.)]
74. (a) Kelly, 1910. (b) Chester City R.O. (CEE/32). *Register of Persons Entitled to Vote . . . Chester*, 1910. (c) E.E.O., 706, pp. 42, 137, 184, 196. Letters from Cecil T. Parker to John Douglas, 11th June, 13th Aug., 1st Oct., 7th Oct. 1909.
75. (a) *R.I.B.A.J.* ob. (b) Kelly. (c) Chester City R.O. (CEE/33). *Register of Persons Entitled to Vote . . . Chester*, 1911; (CEE/34). *Register of Persons Entitled to Vote . . . Chester*, 1912.
76. (a) Information from Mrs. A. D. Edwards. (b) Information from Mr. H. Morgan.
77. Chester City R.O. (CEE/23). *Register of Persons Entitled to Vote . . . Chester*, 1901.
78. Chester City R.O. (DT/1). Town Clerk's Department. Letters and Papers. Letter from John Douglas to the Chairman of the Improvement Committee, 17th Mar. 1874.
79. (a) Kelly, 1892. (b) Chester City R.O. (CEE/16). *Register of Persons Entitled to Vote . . . Chester*, 1894.
80. Kelly, 1902, 1914.
81. Cheshire County R.O. (EC/1769/24). Correspondence and papers on improvements in St. Werburgh Street by John Douglas, architect, 1896–1906. Letters from John Douglas to C. Coppack, Chester Cathedral Chapter Clerk, 25th June, 29th June, 2nd July, 29th Nov. 1906.
82. (a) *B.A.* ob. (b) *B.N.* ob. (c) *Cheshire Observer* ob. (d) *Chester Chronicle* ob. (e) *Chester Courant* ob. (f) *Liverpool Daily Post* ob. (g) *R.I.B.A.J.* ob.

References

83. Probate Office, Somerset House, London, and Cheshire County R.O. Will of John Douglas, 1911.
84. (a) *B.A.* ob. (b) *Liverpool Daily Post* ob.
85. (a) Records in office at Overleigh Cemetery, Chester, relating to burials in Grave No. 2829 in Old Cemetery. (b) Inscription on this gravestone.
86. *Chester Chronicle*, 3rd June 1911.
87. Probate Office, Somerset House, London, and Cheshire County R.O. Will of John Douglas, 1911.
88. (a) Kelly, 1914, 1923. (b) Chester City R.O. (CEE/34). *Register of Persons Entitled to Vote . . . Chester*, 1912. Also subsequent issues including (CEE/39). *Register of Persons Entitled to Vote . . . Chester*, 1918.
89. (a) Probate Office, Somerset House, London. Will of Sholto Theodore Douglas, 1945. (b) Records in office at Overleigh Cemetery, Chester, relating to burials in Grave No. 2829 in Old Cemetery. (c) Inscription on this gravestone.
90. Information from Mr. Peter Howell and Mr. Malcolm Graham.
91. Probate Office, Somerset House, London. Will of Sholto Theodore Douglas, 1945.
92. *B.N.*, 58, 1890, p. 686.
93. (a) Information from Mrs. A. D. Edwards. (b) Information from Mr. H. Morgan.
94. Material in possession of Design Group Partnership, 9 Abbey Square, Chester.
95. Information from Mrs. T. A. Williams.
96. Information from Mr. H. Morgan.
97. *Ibid.*
98. Information communicated to the Revd. E. J. Basil Jones by the late Mr. Herbert Furber.
99. *Chester Chronicle* ob.
100. Chester City R.O. (DT/1). Town Clerk's Department. Letters and Papers. Letter from John Douglas, 29th Dec. 1869.
101. *Chester Chronicle* ob.
102. *Journal of the Chester and North Wales Architectural, Archaeological and Historic Society*, new series, 181, 1911, pp. 215, 217.
103. (a) *Ibid.* (b) *A.A.H.S.C.C.N.C.J.*, 2, 1864, pp. 405, 419, 423; 3, 1885, pp. 529, 532–3.
104. *A.S.S.B.*, 2, pls. 22, 65, 72; 3, pls. 43, 44, 63.
105. *Ibid.*, 3, pl. 67.
106. *Chester Chronicle*, 3rd June 1911.
107. Memorial tablet in south aisle of St. Paul's church, Boughton, Chester.
108. *R.I.B.A.J.*, ob.
109. *R.I.B.A.J.*, 3rd series, 19, 1911–12, p. 644, in 'Architects from George IV to George V,' Maurice B. Adams.
110. Chester City R.O. (DT/1). Town Clerk's Department. Letters and Papers. Letter from John Douglas, 15th Apr. 1868.
111. Material in possession of Design Group Partnership, 9 Abbey Square, Chester. Envelope of papers relating to church of St. John the Divine, Barmouth, Merioneth. Draft for letter from John Douglas to Mrs. Williams, Plas Mynach, Barmouth, 23rd Dec. 1899.
112. *Ibid.* Copy of letter from John Douglas to Mrs. Williams, 2nd Sep. 1899.
113. E.E.O. Box No. 2 of personal papers of first Duke of Westminster. Letter from John Douglas to David Scotland, 11th Dec. 1884, annotated by Scotland for forwarding to H. J. Boodle, the Grosvenor family solicitor in London.
114. E.E.O., 706, pp. 42, 137, 184, 196. Letters from Cecil T. Parker to John Douglas, 11th June, 13th Aug., 1st Oct., 7th Oct. 1909.
115. Material in possession of Design Group Partnership, 9 Abbey Square, Chester. Envelope of papers relating to church of St. John the Divine, Barmouth, Merioneth. Letter from Mrs. Williams, Plas Mynach, Barmouth, to John Douglas, 6th Sep. 1899.

The Work of John Douglas

116. *Ibid.* Letter from Edward Nevinson, of Nevinson & Barlow, Malvern, to John Douglas, 7th Oct. 1899.
117. *Ibid.* 'Notes on Mr. Douglas's Statements accompanying his letter to Mrs. Williams of the 2nd September 1899,' Edward Nevinson, 3rd Oct. 1899.
118. *Ibid.* Copy of 'St. John's Church Barmouth N. Wales, General Statement,' compiled by John Douglas.
119. Cheshire County R.O. (EC/1769/24). Correspondence and papers on improvements in St. Werburgh Street by John Douglas, architect, 1896–1906.
120. *Ibid.* Letter from John Douglas to C. Coppack, Chester Cathedral Chapter Clerk, 25th June 1906.
121. *Journal of the Chester and North Wales Archaeological and Historic Society*, new series, 27, part 1, 1926, p. 25.
122. Chester City R.O. (79C, Nos. 44, 45). Corporation Conveyances.
123. Chester City R.O. City and County Borough of Chester. Minutes of Proceedings, 1896–7, pp. 171, 176. City Council Meeting 18th Mar. 1897.
124. (a) Chester City R.O. (76C). Corporation Conveyances. (b) Chester City R.O. City and County Borough of Chester. Minutes of Proceedings, 1897–8, pp. 486–7, 499, 510, 562.
125. Chester City R.O. (85C). Corporation Conveyances.
126. The setting up of the plaque, by 'a few of those whom Mr. Douglas trained, or who were personally associated with him in his work', was marked by an appreciation published in *Builder*, 124, 1923, p. 923.

Chapter II Architectural background and training

1. *Edmund Sharpe (1809–77). A study of a Victorian Architect*, Robert Jolley, Thesis submitted for degree of Master of Arts in the School of Architecture, Faculty of Arts, University of Liverpool, 1966, pp. vi, 114, 115.
2. (a) *Archt.*, 53, 1895, p. 57. Obituary of E. G. Paley, pp. 82–6, 'E. G. Paley's Churches.' (b) Information from Mr. David McLaughlin.
3. For the Cambridge Camden Society and the early history of the Ecclesiological Society see *The Cambridge Movement*, James F. White, Cambridge, 1962.
4. Jolley, *op. cit.*, pp. 41, 45
5. *Report of the Cambridge Camden Society for MDCCCXLII*, Cambridge, 1842, p. 41.
6. He is listed as such in the Index in *The Ecclesiologist*, 3, 2nd edn., 1847. The notice in this volume of his steeple at Kirkham (pp. 23–4 in Nos. XXV, XXVI, Sep. 1843) is indeed approving, but that of the terra-cotta church at Lever Bridge (pp. 86–7 in Nos. XXIX, XXX, Feb. 1844) is decidedly to the contrary.
7. (a) *Archt.*, 53, 1895, p. 57, Obituary of E. G. Paley, pp. 82–6, 'E. G. Paley's Churches.' (b) Jolley, *op. cit.*, p. 114.
8. Jolley, *op. cit.* p. 114.
9. *Report of the Cambridge Camden Society for MDCCCXLI*, Cambridge, 1841, p. 51.
10. (a) *Ibid., for MDCCCXLII*, Cambridge, 1842, p. 31. (b) *Ibid., for MDCCCXLIII*, Cambridge, 1843, p. 33. (c) *Ibid., for MDCCCXLIV*, Cambridge, 1844, p. 35. (d) *A Manual of Gothic Mouldings*, F. A. Paley, 5th edn., ed. W. M. Fawcett, London, 1891, p. ix.
11. Paley, *op cit.*, p. xi.
12. *Ibid.*, pp. xi, xii.
13. *Ibid.*, p. x.
14. (a) *The Ecclesiologist*, 3, 2nd edn., 1847, pp. 86–7. (b) Jolley, *op. cit.*, pp. 188, 207–29. (c) *Architectural Review*, 146, 1969, pp. 426–31, 'Edmund Sharpe and the Pot Churches,' Robert Jolley.
15. Jolley, *op. cit.*, pp. vi, 115, 203, etc.
    [Sharpe did design at least one building after 1851 – St Paul's Church, Scotforth, Lancaster, designed in 1874.]

References

16. Information from Mr. David McLaughlin.
17. *Archt.*, 53, 1895, pp. 82–6, 'E. G. Paley's Churches.'
18. Kelly.
19. (a) Jolley, *op. cit.*, p. 115. (b) G.R. Index. (c) *The Buildings of England. North Lancashire*, Nikolaus Pevsner, Harmondsworth, 1969.
20. (a) Jolley, *op. cit.*, p. 115. (b) G.R. Index.
21. (a) G.R. Index. (b) Pevsner, *op. cit.*

Chapter III Chester in the nineteenth century

1. *A.A.H.S.C.C.N.C.J.*, 1, 1857, pp. 463–4, Appendix, 'Street Architecture in Chester.'
2. *Ibid.*, 1. 1857, pp. 463–4, Appendix, 'Street Architecture in Chester.'
3. *Ibid.*, 1, 1857, pp. 463–4, Appendix, 'Street Architecture in Chester.'
4. *Ibid.*, 1, 1857, p. 184.
5. *Ibid.*, 1, 1857, p. 337.
6. *The Stranger's Handbook to Chester*, Thomas Hughes, Chester, 1856, pp. 46–7.
7. *The Seven Lamps of Architecture*, John Ruskin, London, 1849, pp. 162–82, 'The Lamp of Memory.'
8. *Bldr.*, 14, 1856, p. 471.
9. *B.N.*, 6, 1860, pp. 400, 401.
10. (a) *A.A.H.S.C.C.N.C.J.*, 2, 1864, pp. 398–9. (b) *B.N.*, 7, 1861, p. 952.
11. *A.A.H.S.C.C.N.C.J.*, 2, 1864, pp. 399, 405.
    [On James Harrison see *Journal of the Chester Archaeological Society*, 63, 1980, pp. 85 – 94, 'The Other Harrison of Chester', Peter Howell.]
12. (a) *Chester Record*, 11th June 1864. Obituary of T. M. Penson. (b) *B.N.*, 5, 1860, pp. 400, 401.
13. (a) *Chester Record*, 11th June 1864. Obituary of T. M. Penson. (b) *Bldr.*, 24, 1866, pp. 629–31.
14. (a) *Chester Courant*, 18th July 1900. (b) *Bldr.*, 76, 1899, p.422.
15. *Country Life*, 133, 1963, pp. 68–71, 'An English Carcassonne', David Lloyd.
    [Peter de Figueiredo and Julian Treuherz, *Cheshire Country Houses*, Chichester, 1988, p. 5 claim that the half-timber revival in Cheshire 'was anticipated by the antiquarian-trained architect Edward Blore, not in his Cheshire houses, but on estate buildings at Worsley in Lancashire in the 1840s'. However, it appears that the only half-timber work likely to be by Blore at Worsley is at the Old Hall, where he added to a basically half-timber house (drawings at the RIBA). The architect of the remarkably effective Court House (1849), Packet House (*c.* 1850), and Bank Cottage (1851) is unfortunately unknown. Blore seems not to have worked for the Earl of Ellesmere after 1846 (information from Mr Hugh Meller). The plan for a Court House by H. L. Elmes, dated 1846 (at the RIBA) does not correspond to the executed building. Two other Elmes drawings at the RIBA are for a Smithy: they show one half-timbered gable. They are dated 1847, the year of Elmes's death.]

Chapter IV Architectural practice

1. (a) Ormerod, 2, p. 158. (b) Burke's *Peerage*.
2. (a) *Chester Chronicle* ob. (b) *R.I.B.A.J.* ob.
3. *B.A.*, 49, 1898, pp. 360–61.

The Work of John Douglas

4. *Chester Chronicle* ob.
5. *Liverpool Daily Post* ob.
6. *B.N.*, 58, 1890, p. 706.
7. *Lady Elizabeth and the Grosvenors*, Gervas Huxley, London, 1965, pp. 19–20.
   [The earliest reference to Douglas in the Second Marquess's diaries occurs on 18th August 1863: 'Mr Douglas with Lady Westminster at Aldford Church from 11 to 2'. They contain further references to him in connection with this church up to February 1866, and also in connection with a school at Flookersbrook (identifiable with 'Bishopsfield School' – see p. 239) between October 1865 and January 1866, and in connection with Grosvenor Park in December 1866. (Information from Mr. Andrew Saint.) Douglas's work for the family may also be explained by his father's connection with Eaton Hall (see p. 212).]
8. Cheshire County R.O. (SL/300/5/5). Witton Grammar School. Correspondence with John Douglas re Building of Master's House. 1874–8.
9. *Ibid.* Letter from John Douglas to Black & Trafford, 7th Oct. 1875.
10. *Ibid.* Letter from John Douglas to Black & Trafford, 11th Dec. 1875.
11. *Ibid.* Letter from John Douglas to Black & Trafford, 26th July 1876.
12. *Ibid.* Letter from John Douglas to Black & Trafford, 17th Jan. 1877.
13. (a) Cheshire County R.O. (SL/300/5/10). Witton Grammar School. School and Master's House. Plans Elevations and Sections. 1870–1888. This includes the ground floor and drainage plan of the master's house, dated Nov. 1878. (b) Cheshire County R.O. (SL/300/5/4). Witton Grammar School Master's House. Correspondence relating to Leasing of the Site, Tenders, Contract and Accounts. Some of the facts given in the text are derived from this source as well as from the letters.
14. Cheshire County R.O. (SL/300/5/5). Witton Grammar School. Correspondence with John Douglas re Building of Master's House. 1874–8. Telegram from George Smith to Black & Trafford, 9th Dec. 1875.
15. Chester City R.O. (DT/1). Town Clerk's Department. Letters and Papers. Letter from George Smith, 14th Mar. 1877.
16. *Ibid.* Letter from John Douglas, 13th Feb. 1872.
17. Chester City R.O. (CCB/52). Minutes of the Improvement Committee. 1870–74, p. 512.
18. *Architect and Patron*, Frank Jenkins, London, 1961.
19. (a) *The Times*, 3rd Mar. 1891. (b) *Memoirs of an Architect*, Reginald Blomfield, London, 1932, pp. 61–4, 67–8. (c) *Recollections of Thomas Graham Jackson*, ed. Basil H. Jackson, London, 1950, pp. 224–7. (d) Jenkins, *op. cit.* p. 224.
20. (a) *B.N.* ob. (b) Douglas's name does not appear in card index of members, 1834–86, at R.I.B.A. Library, or in (c) subsequent issues of R.I.B.A. Kalendar.
21. *B.N.*, 11, 1864, pp. 168, 169.
22. *Ibid.*, 58, 1890, p. 706.
23. *B.A.*, 8, 1877, p. 180.
24. *Ibid.*, 25, 1886, p. 489.
25. *Ibid.*, 21, 1884, p. 218.
26. *Ibid.*, 21, 1884, p. 219.
27. *Ibid.*, 21, 1884, p. 253.
28. *Ibid.*, 40, 1893, pp. 182–3.
29. *Ibid.*, 48, 1897, p. 161.
30. *Ibid.*, 49, 1898, pp. 360–61.
31. *B.A.* ob.
32. *Chester Chronicle* ob.
33. Mr. Peter Howell drew my attention to (a) the passage in *Gazette des Beaux Arts*, 35, 1887, p. 273, *et seq.*, accompanied by two illustrations, and (b) one illustration in *Ibid.*, 33, 1886, p. 195.
34. *L'Architecture Moderne en Angleterre*, Paul Sédille, Paris, 1890, pp. 86–9.
35. *Ibid.*, p. 86. I am indebted to Mr. Stephen Wilcockson for the translation.

References

36. *Die Englische Baukunst der Gegenwart*, Hermann Muthesius, Leipzig and Berlin, 1900, pp. 67, 91–3, 131–4, 157–8, 160, pls. 26, 44, 45, 78, 80, 97, 100.
37. *Die Neuere Kirchliche Baukunst in England*, Hermann Muthesius, Berlin, 1901, p. 48.
38. *Das Englische Haus*, Hermann Muthesius, Berlin, 1, 1904, p. 136; 2, 1904, p. 43. (Translated as *The English House*, London, 1979, pp. 32, 33, 87.)
39. *Ibid.*, 1, 1904, pp. 137–40. (Translation by Janet Seligman from *The English House*, London, 1979, p. 32.)
40. (a) *Cheshire Observer* ob. (b) *Chester Chronicle* ob.
41. *B.A.* ob.
42. *R.I.B.A.J.*, 3rd series, 19, 1911–12, p. 644, in 'Architects from George IV to George V,' Maurice B. Adams.

Chapter V High Victorianism

1. Ormerod, 2, pp. 153, 155, illustration of 1775 opposite p. 159.
2. (a) *The Mansions of England and Wales*, Edward Twycross, 4 (*The County Palatine of Cheshire*, 1), 1850, p. 102. (b) *Cheshire Country Houses*, Peter de Figueiredo and Julian Treuherz, Chichester, 1988, pp. 189–96. (c) *Journal of the Chester Archaeological Society*, 70, 1987–8, pp. 51–79, 'An Architectural and Topographical Survey of Vale Royal Abbey', R. McNeil and R. C. Turner.
3. *The Parish of Eastham*, Isabel Tobin, Liverpool, 1920, pp. 22, 51.
4. *A.A.H.S.C.C.N.C.J.*, 2, 1864, pp. 405, 419, 423.
5. General Register Office, Somerset House, London (death certificate of Elizabeth Douglas, 1878).
6. *Remarks on Secular & Domestic Architecture, Present & Future*, George Gilbert Scott, London, 1857, p. 170.
7. *Ibid.*, pp. 174–5.
8. *Ibid.*, p. 195.
9. *Ibid.*, pp. 195–6.
10. *Ibid.*, pp. 275–85.
11. E.E.O. Estate Papers: Eaton Estate: Chester: Miscellaneous Papers 15th to 20th Century. Nos. 13–19 (Box 59). No. 15. Grosvenor Park. Miscellaneous Accounts & Papers 1864–8. Letter from Benjamin Owens, Shipgate Street, Chester, 3rd Feb. 1866.
12. *Ibid.* Letter from Benjamin Owens, 28th July 1866.
13. *Ibid.* Letter from Benjamin Owens, 22nd Sep. 1866.
14. *Ibid.* Annotation of letter from Benjamin Owens, 28th July 1866; receipt from Benjamin Owens, 22nd Sep. 1866.
15. *Ibid.* Letter from William Bakewell, 28th Nov. 1866.
16. Chester City R.O. (CCF/8). New Park Committee. Letters and Papers.
17. *Bldr.*, 19, 1861, p. 96.
18. G.R. Index.
19. Scott, *op. cit.*, p. 145.
20. *The True Principles of Pointed or Christian Architecture*, A. Welby Pugin, London, 1841, p. 52.
21. Scott, *op. cit.*, p. 145.
22. *Bldr.*, 17, 1859, pp. 42–3.
23. *The Gentleman's House*, Robert Kerr, 3rd edn., London, 1871, p. 443.
24. *Ibid.*, p. 94.
25. *Ibid.*, p. 107.
26. *Warrington Church Notes*, William Beamont, Warrington, 1878, p. 199.
27. *Church Design for Congregations*, James Cubitt, London, 1870, p. 55 n.
    [The author considered that more needed to be said on church planning. 'For the

The Work of John Douglas

most part', he wrote, 'Douglas's ecclesiastical work follows conventional Gothic Revival lines, serving the Anglican requirements of the period. Occasionally, however, an exceptional "prodigy" church appeared, usually marked by exceptionally wide planning of the nave, perhaps with narrow passage-aisles'. St Ann's, Warrington, is a particularly striking example, and it may well have been based on the Cathedral of Gerona, described and illustrated by G. E. Street in his *Gothic Architecture in Spain*, London, 1865, for there too not only the apsidal vaulted chancel, but also the arches to the flanking choir aisles (vestry and organ-chamber at Warrington) open directly into the nave. At Gerona the width of the nave is 73 feet, at Warrington 40. 'Passage-aisles' first appeared in Prichard and Seddon's design of 1859 for St Andrew's, Cardiff, and were combined with an ingenious version of the Gerona arrangement in Street's design for All Saints', Clifton (1863).

In his subsequent churches Douglas liked to keep his naves broad, even when there were 'normal' aisles. At St Paul's, Colwyn Bay (1887–8), he used very narrow passage-aisles to flank an extraordinarily wide nave (p. 175). However, another feature of which he was fond, the crossing-tower, was difficult to reconcile with breadth and openness, and it is a tribute to his skill that he succeeded in doing so at such churches as Bryn-y-Maen, Rossett, and especially Barmouth (though the problems which arose in that case are eloquent testimony to the difficulties involved).]

Chapter VI Principal patron

1. *The Buildings of England, Cheshire*, Nikolaus Pevsner and Edward Hubbard, Harmondsworth, 1971, p. 208.
    [For John Douglas Senior's involvement with Burn's work at Eaton, see p. 212 n. 19. The pair of lodges at Pulford are attributed to Burn by Tim Mowl and Brian Earnshaw, *Trumpet at a Distant Gate*, London, 1985, pp. 194–5, but there is no documentary evidence.]
2. For the second Marquess of Westminster and the first Duke of Westminster see: (a) *Lady Elizabeth and the Grosvenors*, Gervas Huxley, London, 1965. (b) *Victorian Duke*, Gervas Huxley, London, 1967. (c) Article on Hugh Lupus Grosvenor, first Duke of Westminster, in *Dictionary of National Biography, First Supplement*, 1901.
3. (a) *Journal of the Architectural, Archaeological and Historic Society for . . . Chester*, new series, 15, 1909, p. 134. (b) *Country Life*, 23, 1908, p. 738.
4. (a) *Bldr.*, 11, 1853, p. 773; 12, 1854, p. 9. (b) Ormerod, 2, p. 827.
5. *The Times*, 23rd Dec. 1899.
6. *The Victorian Country House*, Mark Girouard, revised edition, New Haven and London, 1979, p. 4.
7. Pevsner and Hubbard, *op. cit.*, p. 208.
    [Tim Mowl and Brian Earnshaw, *Trumpet at a Distant Gate*, London, 1985, p. 197, state that Douglas 'had hoped to design the new hall', but there is no evidence to this effect, and it would surely have been a most unrealistic hope.]
8. In addition to the following references, most of the buildings here mentioned are well documented at E.E.O.
    [For the Duke as patron of architecture see *Survey of London*, 39, 1977, especially pp. 47f. and 140f.]
9. (a) *B.N.*, 20th July 1883. (b) *Lectures on the History of S. John Baptist Church and Parish . . . Chester*, S. Cooper Scott, Chester, 1892.
10. (a) G.R. Index. (b) Kelly.
11. (a) *A.A.* 1893, p. 30. (b) *Bldr.*, 65, 1893, p. 453.
12. (a) R.I.B.A. Drawings Collection. (b) Information from Mr. Nicholas Taylor.
13. (a) G.R. Index. (b) *Architectural Review*, 11, 1902; 23, 1908.

References

14. E.E.O., 477, loose sheet inserted at p. 31.
15. Huxley, *Victorian Duke, op. cit.*, p. 114.
16. *Ibid.*, p. 146.
    [On Cheshire farming in this period, see *Squire and Tenant: Life in Rural Cheshire, 1760–1900*, Geoffrey Scard, Chester, 1981.]
17. [However, according to *Survey of London*, 39, 1977, p. 48, between 1874 and 1899 £650,000 was received from lease renewals etc in Mayfair, of which £200,000 was spent on improving the London and Cheshire 'settled estates'.]
18. Huxley, *Victorian Duke, op. cit.*, p. 145.
19. *Journal of the Royal Agricultural Society of England*, second series, 7, 1871, pp. 42–60; 11, 1875, pp. 261–300.
20. (a) *B.A.*, 43, 1895, p. 283. (b) *The Duffield Bank and Eaton Railways*, Howard Clayton, 1968.
21. *B.A.*, 16, 1881, p. 635.
22. *Ibid.*, 53, 1900, pp. 3–4.
23. Letter from John Douglas to the Duke of Westminster, Oct. 1878. Transcription in report accompanying measured drawings of 'Hilliards Farm' (Wrexham Road Farm) prepared in the Liverpool School of Architecture by P. L. Ford and K. J. McKay, 1960, and now in the collection of the University of Liverpool Archivist. The original of the letter is not in E.E.O. and was presumably among papers dispersed when Wrexham Road Farm and other portions of the estate were sold following the First World War.
24. *The Farm Homesteads of England*, J. B. Denton, London, 1863.
25. *Country Architecture*, John Birch, Edinburgh and London, 1874, p. 30, pls. 30, 30A.
26. E.E.O. Drawings
27. *Ibid.*, 690, p. 68. Letter from Cecil T. Parker to John Douglas, 7th Mar. 1882.
28. *Ibid.*, 690, p. 159. Letter from Cecil T. Parker to John Douglas, 11th May 1882.
29. *Ibid.*, 691, p. 52. Letter from Cecil T. Parker to John Douglas, 12th Oct. 1883.
30. *Ibid.*, 699, p. 410. Letter from Cecil T. Parker to Douglas & Fordham, 21st Nov. 1896.
31. *Ibid.*, 700, p. 96. Letter from Cecil T. Parker to Douglas & Minshull, 25th Jan. 1898.
32. (a) *Burke's Peerage.* (b) *Cheshire at the Opening of the Twentieth Century. Contemporary Biographies*, Robert Head, Brighton, 1904, p. 152. (c) *Who Was Who. 1929–1940*, London, 1941.
33. Huxley, *Victorian Duke, op. cit.*, p. 146.
34. Information from Mrs. N. Wild.
35. E.E.O., 699, p. 382. Letter from Cecil T. Parker to Douglas & Fordham, 10th Nov. 1896.
36. *Ibid.*, 695, p. 184. Letter from Cecil T. Parker to Douglas & Fordham, 18th May 1891.
37. *Ibid.*, 695, p. 572. Letter from Cecil T. Parker to Douglas & Fordham, 21st Jan. 1892.
38. *Ibid.*, 695, p. 675. Letter from Cecil T. Parker to Douglas & Fordham, 14th Mar. 1892.
39. *Ibid.*, 695, p. 633. Letter from Cecil T. Parker to Douglas & Fordham, 26th Feb. 1892.
40. *Ibid.*, 696, p. 434. Letter from Cecil T. Parker to Douglas & Fordham, 27th June 1893.
41. *Ibid.*, 695, p. 504. Letter from Cecil T. Parker to Douglas & Fordham, 3rd Dec. 1891.
42. *Ibid.*, 699, p. 565. Letter from Cecil T. Parker (sgnd. E.G.) to Douglas & Fordham, 17th Feb. 1897.
43. *Ibid.*, 697, p. 621. Letter from Cecil T. Parker to Douglas & Fordham, 29th Oct. 1894.

The Work of John Douglas

44. *Ibid.*, 697, p. 725. Letter from Cecil T. Parker to Douglas & Fordham, 12th Jan. 1895.
45. *Ibid.*, 697, p. 227. Letter from Cecil T. Parker to Douglas & Fordham, 22nd Jan. 1894.
46. *Ibid.*, 701, p. 288. Letter from Cecil T. Parker (sgnd. E.W.) to John Douglas, 11th May 1900.
47. *Ibid.*, 701, p. 305. Letter from Cecil T. Parker to John Douglas, 25th May 1900.
48. *Ibid.*, 701, p. 121.
49. *Ibid.*, 701, p. 122.
50. *Ibid.*, 690, pp. 190, 406, 523-4. Letters from Cecil T. Parker to John Douglas, 24th May, 17th Oct. 1882, 8th Jan. 1883.
51. Information from Mrs. N. Wild.
52. (a) E.E.O., 479, pp. 14, 15, 16; 695, pp. 913, 927; 696, pp. 47, 180.
    (b). Identification of cottages referred to on site.
53. E.E.O., 696, p. 47. Letter from Cecil T. Parker to Douglas & Fordham, 25th Oct. 1892.
54. *Ibid.*, 479, pp. 14, 15, 16, 24; 696, pp. 180, 189.
55. *Ibid.*, 696, p. 189. Letter from Cecil T. Parker to Douglas & Fordham, 7th Feb. 1893.
56. (a) *Ibid.*, 479, pp. 31, 61, 82. (b) Identification of cottages referred to on site.
57. E.E.O., 706, pp. 42, 137, 196.
58. *Ibid.*, 706, p. 196. Letter from Cecil T. Parker to John Douglas, 7th Oct. 1909.
59. *Ibid.*, 477. Letter from Samuel Beckett to John Douglas, 20th Dec. 1878. Loose sheet inserted at p. 31.
60. *Das Englische Haus*, Hermann Muthesius, Berlin, 1, 1904, p. 140. (Translation by Janet Seligman from *The English House*, London 1979, p. 32.)
61. Huxley, *Victorian Duke, op. cit.*, p. 134.
62. *Memorials of Old Cheshire*, ed. Edward Barber and P. H. Ditchfield, London, 1910, p. 99, in 'The Half-Timbered Architecture of Cheshire,' C. H. Minshull.
63. Shown, e.g. in framed plan and elevation on top landing at E.E.O.

Chapter VII Early maturity: secular buildings

1. *The Swinburne Letters*, ed. Cecil Y. Lang, 2, 1959, p. 32.
2. *A History of the Gothic Revival*, Charles L. Eastlake, London, 1872. The list of works given by Eastlake, known to have been based on information supplied by architects in answer to questionnaire, applies the term 'Old English' to several Nesfield and Shaw buildings, pp. 404, 418, 420, 422. Nesfield's cottages at Hampton-in-Arden are so described, though the stylistically similar ones at Crewe Hall are given as 'English XVII century,' p. 404. See also *Richard Norman Shaw*, Andrew Saint, New Haven and London, 1976.
3. *A.S.S.B.*, 1, pl. 17.
4. *B.A.*, 22, 1884, pp. 282-4. 'The Village of Great Budworth', T. Raffles Davison.
5. [Information about the Croxteth buildings was derived by the author partly from drawings now (1990) at Croxteth Hall, and partly from correspondence with Mr Andrew Saint. The Cheshire connections between Anthony Salvin, his brother-in-law William Andrews Nesfield, the latter's son William Eden Nesfield, and also William Burn, in whose office the younger Nesfield began his training, need to be further investigated. Both Salvin and W. A. Nesfield worked at Arley. It is known that W. A. Nesfield worked at Croxteth in 1855-9, and he and his son both worked on the Crewe Hall estate. In fact, W. E. Nesfield is said to have received the commission for the Crewe tomb at Barthomley (executed 1856) and the Memorial Cross at West Derby (executed 1860, not for Lord Sefton, although close to the gates of Croxteth,

References

but for J. Pemberton Heywood) while still in Salvin's office (i.e. before 1857). Salvin's first work in Cheshire was the chapel at Arley (1841–5), and subsequently he did much more, including the restoration of the Douglas family's parish church at Weaverham (1853–5), and that of Great Budworth church (1856–7). W. A. Nesfield also worked at Dorfold Hall, and at Eaton Hall, together with Burn. Finally, it may be worth noting that both W. E. Nesfield and Douglas made designs for cottages at Holkham in Norfolk, that Nesfield made unexecuted proposals in 1876 for rebuilding Wigfair, Denbighshire, which Douglas rebuilt in 1882–4, that the west wing of Gloddaeth, Caernarfonshire, was built in 1889, not to Nesfield's design of 1875, but to a new design by Douglas, and (although the dates do not suggest any link) that W. A. Nesfield designed the gardens at Worsley Hall, Lancashire, where Douglas worked from 1894.]

6. *Archt.*, 5, 1871, p. 10.
7. *A.S.S.B.*, 1, pl. 67.
8. *B.A.*, 23, 1885, pp. 54, 66, 114.
9. *Chester Chronicle*, 22nd Sep. 1934. Obituary of C. H. Minshull.
10. *Bldr.*, 24, 1866, pp. 155, 232, 542, 543, 686, 850; 25, 1867, p. 113.
11. *Ibid.*, 28, 1870, pp. 386, 387; 30, 1872, pp. 806–7; 31, 1873, pp. 326–7, 386.
12. *Archt.*, 14, 1875, p. 256; 17, 1877, p. 8.
13. *Architectural Sketches from the Continent*, Richard Norman Shaw, London, 1858, pl. 91.
14. My attention was drawn to this by Dr. Paul Crossley, to whom I am grateful for many helpful comments and suggestions concerning the German influence on Douglas's work.
15. *A.S.S.B.*, 1, pl. 23.
16. *Ibid.*, 2, pl. 58.
17. *Ibid.*, 1, pls. 5, 9, 16, 21, 36, 39, 72; 2, pls. 28–35, 48, 57, 60, 61, 72; 3, pls. 18, 29, 33, 34, 47, 54, 58.
18. *Specimens of Mediaeval Architecture . . . in France and Italy*, W. Eden Nesfield, London, 1862, pls. 51, 52.
19. *Hints on Household Taste*, Charles L. Eastlake, London, 3rd edn., 1872; 4th edn., 1878. In the respective editions cf. pls. XXI and XX, XXVI and XXV, pp. 208 and 205, 217 and 213. In the 4th edn. see also pl. XXIV and pp. 165, 217.
20. *A.S.S.B.*, 1, pls. 11, 29; 3, pls. 49, 50, 55.
21. *Ibid.*, 1, pl. 31.
    [Lozenge patterns in polychrome brick occur at Crewe Hall (1615–39) and Dorfold Hall (begun 1616), both in Cheshire, and both influential models for Arley Hall, designed for Rowland Egerton-Warburton by George Latham of Nantwich and built in 1832–45 (*Country Life*, 184, 1990, pp. 140–5). Egerton-Warburton was obviously fond of local brickwork patterning; for example, raised headers are used on the stables at Arley (dated 1845), and a group of cottages north of the crossroads at the approach to the Hall has diaper brickwork, as well as a pargetted half-timbered gable (a drawing for these cottages at Arley Hall, not by Douglas, is dated 1866).]
22. *Ibid.*, 1, pl. 24.
23. *E.E.O.*, 691, p. 954. Letter from Cecil T. Parker to John Douglas, 14th or 15th Apr. 1885.
    [Wrexham Road Farm is now sadly stranded in the Chester Business Park.]
24. *L'Architecture Moderne en Angleterre*, Paul Sédille, Paris, 1890, p. 86. I am indebted to Mr. Stephen Wilcockson for the translation.
25. *A.S.S.B.*, 1, pl. 7.
26. *B.A.*, 8, 1877, p. 255.
27. *A.S.S.B.*, 2, pl. 19.
    [There were similar chimneystacks (of the nineteenth century?) at Carden Park, the ancestral home of Florence Leche, whom Kenyon had married in 1875 (*Cheshire Country Houses*, Peter de Figueiredo and Julian Treuherz, Chichester, 1988, p. 223).

The Work of John Douglas

Legend had it that Llannerch Panna was based on Carden (Clwyd R. O. FC/LA/2/62. Sale Particulars, 1929).]
28. *Ibid.*, 1, pl. 3.
29. [In view of the apparent importance of Rowland Egerton-Warburton's Arley estate buildings for Douglas, it may be worth noting that he had strong opinions about sham half-timbering. In *A Looking-Glass for Landlords* (Chester, 1875; republished in *Poems, Epigrams and Sonnets*, London, 1877, p. 30), he wrote, on the subject of building cottages:

> Some interlap, plain brickwork to conceal,
> Sliced planks of sawn attenuated deal;
> Such lime and lath some think the eye will cheat –
> A timber building in their own conceit!
> Panel and plank, alternate black and white,
> The painted gew-gaw then perfection quite!]

30. *A.S.S.B.*, 3, pl. 28.
31. Information from the Society's Archivist, Miss Cecily Greenhill.
    [In fairness to Douglas, it should be mentioned that it is probable that the front (east) elevation of Bent Farmhouse had been Georgianised, and R. E. Egerton-Warburton would no doubt have insisted on something more in keeping with the rear elevation. Douglas retained some Georgian features inside.]
32. These buildings were brought to my notice by Dr. Crossley.
33. (a) *B.A.*, 15, 1881, p. 159; 16, 1881, p. 632. (b) *B.N.*, 58, 1890, p. 533; 62, 1892, p. 622. (c) *Victorian Ceramic Tiles*, Julian Barnard, London, 1972, pp. 41, 43, 82, 160. (d) *Victorian Society Annual* 1982–3, pp. 9–31, 'The Terracotta Revival', Michael Stratton. (e) *Dictionary of Business Biography*, London, 1984, pp. 234–6, article 'Edwards, James Coster (1828–96)'.
34. (a) Chester City R.O. (DT/2). Town Clerk's Department. Improvement Committee. Letter from John Douglas, 16th Apr. 1889. (b) Chester City R.O. (32D). Corporation Leases, Agreements, etc.
35. Chester City R.O. (DT/2). Town Clerk's Department. Improvement Committee. Letter from John Douglas, 16th Apr. 1889.
36. *Ibid.*
37. *B.A.*, 16, 1881, pp. 632–5.
38. *The Stones of Venice*, John Ruskin, 1, London, 1851, pp. 286–7.
39. Sédille, *op. cit.*, p. 88.
40. *Archt.*, 30, 1883, p. 209.
41. *Ibid.*, 32, 1884, p. 281.
42. *B.A.*, 15, 1881, p. 158.

Chapter VIII Early maturity: churches

1. *B.A.*, 19, 1883, p. 53.
2. *A.S.S.B.*, 2, pl. 24.
3. *Ibid.*, 1, pl. 4.
4. *Bldr.*, 28, 1870, p. 692.
5. *A.S.S.B.*, 1, pl. 30.
6. *Ibid.*, 3, pl. 29.
7. *Ibid.*, 1, pls. 56, 57, 60, 62, 64–6.
8. *Ibid.*, 1, pl. 36.
9. *Ibid.*, 3, pl. 24.
10. E.g., at Eaton Hall itself, St. Mary's church, Handbridge, Chester, and Douglas's church of St. Mary, Pulford (1881–4).
    [In a letter of 4th October 1883 (Cheshire R. O. P 68/6/68) Douglas wrote to the

References

Revd G. Egerton-Warburton, Rector of Warburton: 'The beautiful window at Halkyn was drawn by a Mr Frampton for Heaton Butler and Bayne – he has also painted the subjects on the Reredos in the same Church: – & is a very clever man. He has lately set up on his own account. I am sure the window would be excellent if he did it.' The reference is to the east window at Warburton (which Frampton did not do). On Edward Reginald Frampton (1845–1928) see *Victorian Stained Glass*, Martin Harrison, London, 1980, p. 61. Frampton supplied glass for several churches at which Douglas worked (St Paul's, Boughton; Carlett Park Chapel; St John's, Chester; St Mary's, Eastham; Hawarden; Shotton), and wall-paintings for Backford, Hawarden, and Maentwrog. Since the Duke of Westminster paid for the west window of St John's, Chester, and Frampton also did glass for St Mary-without-the-Walls, Chester, the Duke seems to have shared Douglas's admiration for him.]

11. E.g., at St. John's church, Over (1860–3).

    [In a letter of 22nd February 1892 (Cheshire R.O. P/68/6/138) to the Revd G. Egerton-Warburton, concerning estimates for the altar rails for Warburton, Douglas wrote, 'Harts are good people'. The rails were, however, executed by James Swindley, for a lower sum than Hart's estimate.]

12. *Bldr.*, 29, 1871, p. 132.

13. [In 1986 the bell-turret, which had begun to lean, was taken down. It is hoped that it will eventually be replaced.]

14. [Street had added an aisle to Salvin's chapel at Arley Hall for R. E. Egerton-Warburton in 1856–7. The latter explained why he decided 'to retain the dear old church' at Warburton in a letter to his nephew, the Revd Geoffrey Egerton-Warburton (Rector of Warburton) of 7th April 1883: 'I at first proposed to restore and enlarge the old church, but, after a careful examination by Mr. Douglas, I was assured that, if I ventured to meddle with the old building, it would certainly tumble to pieces, but if untouched might last for centuries' (Cheshire R.O. P 68/6/64). He was in any case opposed to over-restoration (*A Looking-Glass for Landlords*, Chester, 1875, pp. 14–15). The repair of the church by Douglas is recorded by an inscription in the north aisle.]

Chapter IX Douglas & Fordham: secular buildings

1. E.E.O., 694, p. 760. Letter from Cecil T. Parker to Douglas & Fordham, 12th Aug. 1890.
2. *A.S.S.B.*, 1, pls. 49–54.
3. *Modern Homes*, T. Raffles Davison, London, 1909, p. 136.
4. [The house was not executed exactly in accordance with the published design, the main difference being that the stable gatehouse was done in half-timber.]
5. *Bldr.*, 64, 1893, p. 403.
6. E.E.O., 691, p. 954. Letter from Cecil T. Parker to John Douglas, 14th or 15th April 1885.
7. *B.A.*, 43, 1895, p. 94.
8. E.E.O., 698, p. 52. Letter from Cecil T. Parker to Douglas & Fordham, 21st Feb. 1895.
9. *Ibid.*, 694, p. 618. Letter from Cecil T. Parker (sgnd. J.E.G.) to Douglas & Fordham, 23rd May 1890.
10. [On Stalbridge Buildings, built in 1888, see *Survey of London*, 40, 1980, pp. 96–8.]
11. *B.N.*, 74, 1898, p. 161.
12. For W. H. Lever see (a) *Viscount Leverhulme*, by his son, London, 1927; (b) *Lord Leverhulme*, Catalogue of an exhibition at the Royal Academy of Arts, 1980. For Port Sunlight see (a) *The Buildings Erected at Port Sunlight and Thornton Hough*, Paper read by W. H. Lever, at a meeting of the Architectural Association, London, March 21st,

The Work of John Douglas

1902; (b) *Port Sunlight*, T. Raffles Davison, London, 1916; (c) *A Guide to Port Sunlight Village*, Edward Hubbard and Michael Shippobottom, Liverpool, 1988.
13. Lever, *op. cit.*, p. 14.
14. *Civic Art*, Thomas H. Mawson, London, 1911, p. 196.
15. [Mr Michael Shippobottom points out that a drawing at the Port Sunlight Heritage Centre 'shows blocks of cottages in a corner of the village with the names of their architects written alongside in a sort of shorthand: thus, "Owen", "Fordham".' He also suggests that 'being older than Lever by some twenty years and having already achieved fame (a fame not derived from Lever work), Douglas would have proved less amenable to Lever than Fordham. Certainly the work of well-known architects whom Lever knew and employed – Lutyens, Ernest George, Ernest Newton, and Vincent Harris – is slight in comparison with that of his favoured group of northwestern practitioners.']

Chapter X Douglas & Fordham: churches

1. G.R. Index.
2. *Ibid.*
3. Material in possession of Design Group Partnership, 9 Abbey Square, Chester. Envelope of papers relating to church of St. John the Divine, Barmouth, Merioneth. Copy of letter from John Douglas to Mrs. Williams, 2nd Sep. 1899.
4. Communicated to me by Mr. Peter Howell from *The Fall of Barmouth Church*, pamphlet in John Johnson Collection (box marked 'Church Restorations'), Bodleian Library, Oxford.
   [The Revd P. Flavell reports that papers in the possession of the church suggest that the collapse was due to poor workmanship on the part of the builders (Winnard of Wigan). The author was informed by Mr. N. H. Davies that (according to William Matson) the tower was rebuilt by 'daywork'. That Mrs. Williams did not hold Douglas to blame is shown by the fact that in 1898 she and her husband employed him to restore St Michael's Church, Manafon, Montgomeryshire, and probably to rebuild their house, Henllys Hall.]
5. (a) *Ibid.* (b) Material in possession of Design Group Partnership, 9 Abbey Square, Chester. Envelope of papers relating to church of St. John the Divine, Barmouth, Merioneth. Letter from Edward Nevinson, of Nevinson & Barlow, Malvern, to John Douglas, 7th Oct. 1899. Also 'Notes on Mr. Douglas's Statements accompanying his letter to Mrs. Williams of the 2nd September 1899,' Edward Nevinson, 3rd Oct. 1899, and John Douglas's annotations thereon.
6. (a) *A.A.*, 1889, p. 36. (b) *Bldr.*, 56, 1889, p. 430.
7. Material in possession of Design Group Partnership, 9 Abbey Square, Chester. Envelope of papers relating to church of St. John the Divine, Barmouth, Merioneth. Letter from Edward Nevinson to John Douglas, 7th Oct. 1899, and John Douglas's annotations thereon.
8. *Ibid.* Letter from Edward Nevinson to John Douglas, 7th Oct. 1899. 'Notes on Mr. Douglas's Statements accompanying his letter to Mrs. Williams of the 2nd September 1899,' Edward Nevinson, 3rd Oct. 1899. Copy of 'St. John's Church Barmouth N. Wales, General Statement,' compiled by John Douglas.
9. *A Shell Guide, North Wales*, Elisabeth Beazley and Lionel Brett, London, 1971, p. 33.
10. (a) *Archt.*, 33, 1885, p. 279. (b) *B.N.*, 50, 1886, p. 700; 53, 1887, p. 487.
11. *The Visitors' Chester Guide*, Alfred Rimmer, Chester, n.d. (c. 1888), p. 83.
12. *A.S.S.B.*, 3, pl. 63.
13. *V.C.H. Lancashire*, 8, 1914, p. 78.
14. *E.E.O.*, 697, p. 648. Letter from Cecil T. Parker to Douglas & Fordham, 15th Nov. 1894.

References

15. Letter from the Revd. W. Venables Williams, vicar of Llandrillo, to parishioners, 15th May 1893, quoted in guide book: *The Story of the Parish Church of Colwyn Bay*, W. Hugh Rees, Gloucester, 1970.

Chapter XI Douglas & Minshull

1. *B.A.*, 68, 1907, pp. 440, 444.
2. *Ibid.*, 69, 1908, pp. 3, 6.
3. *Chester Chronicle* ob.
4. (a) Cheshire County R.O. (EC/1769/24). Correspondence and papers on improvements in St. Werburgh Street by John Douglas, architect, 1896–1906.
   (b) Chester City R.O. (CCB/58). Minutes of the Improvement Committee. 1890–4.
   (c) Chester City R.O. (CCB/59). Minutes of the Improvement Committee. 1894–8.
   (d) *Chester Chronicle* ob. (e) *B.A.*, 49, 1898, p. 162; 72, 1909, pp. 182, 186. (f) *B.N.*, 83, 1902, p. 185.
5. Chester City R.O. (62C). Corporation Conveyances.
6. G.R. Index.
7. [Information about the rebuilding of Shoemakers Row was provided, from the Minutes of the Chester City Council Improvement Committee, by Mr. Oliver Bott.]
8. Chester City R.O. City and County Borough of Chester. Minutes of Proceedings, 1900–01, p. 246.
9. *Ibid.*, 1897–8, p. 562.
10. [The octagonal timber posts are 'not in themselves load-bearing, but with steel or iron cores' (*The Buildings of Wales, Clwyd*, Edward Hubbard, Harmondsworth, 1986, p. 368).]
11. G.R. Index.
12. [The timber posts of the nave arcade enclose steel columns (*The Buildings of Wales, Clwyd*, Edward Hubbard, Harmondsworth, 1986, p. 333). The use of half-timber for the clerestorey may well have been for practical reasons, because of its comparative lightness.]
13. [A particularly surprising and uncharacteristic work is the former premises of the Chester Cooperative Society in Foregate Street, Chester, the shop-fronts of which are framed by half-columns supporting a cornice. In 1904 the Improvement Committee of the City Council recorded its dissatisfaction at the lack of vernacular character in the elevations: as a result, it was agreed that partly leaded glazing would be put in the upper windows. (Minutes of 11th and 25th May 1904 – information from Mr. Oliver Bott.)]
14. G.R. Index.

Chapter XII Conclusion

1. Information from Mrs. A. D. Edwards.
2. *Bldr.*, 31, 1873, p. 935.
3. E.g. (a) Chester City R.O. (CCB/58). Minutes of the Improvement Committee, 1890–4, p. 592. (b) E.E.O., 701, p. 305.
4. *Edmund Kirby & Sons, 1868–1968*. Centenary booklet produced by the firm.
   [This gives the date 1867 for his setting up in practice at 24 Fenwick Street, Liverpool, but an unexecuted scheme for a Steward's House at Arley (at Arley Hall) is dated 'Derby Buildings, Fenwick St, Liverpool, 1865', and a drawing for the Toll House at Warburton Bridge (at Warburton New Church) is dated 1866. It is interesting to note that Kirby was apparently working for R. E. Egerton-Warburton before Douglas.]
5. *B.N.*, 49, 1885, p. 326.

The Work of John Douglas

6. (a) *B.A.*, 36, 1891, pp. 451, 453, 491–8. (b) *Bldr.*, 49, 1885, pp. 456–7. (c) *B.N.*, 49, 1885, p. 286.
    [On the work of Grayson and Ould see *Builders' Journal and Architectural Record*, 11th Jan. 1899, pp. 355–9. Ould's father was Rector of Tattenhall, Cheshire, where Douglas rebuilt the church in 1869–70. (*Edwardian Architecture, A Biographical Dictionary*, A. Stuart Gray, London, 1985, p. 275).]
7. (a) *B.N.*, 42, 1882, p. 760. (b) Kelly.
8. *Old Cottages, Farm Houses, and other Half-Timber Buildings in Shropshire, Herefordshire and Cheshire*, James Parkinson and E. A. Ould, London, 1904.
9. *B.N.*, 48, 1885, p. 646.
10. *A.S.S.B.*, 2, pls. 22, 23, 36, 48, 50, 54, 56, 57, 58, 61, 66, 68, 72; 3, pls. 7–9, 12, 13, 15, 16, 18.
11. *Ibid.*, 1, pls. 4, 15, 36; 3, pls. 64–7.
12. *B.N.*, 47, 1884, p. 344.
13. *Ibid.*, 48, 1885, p. 208.
14. *Ibid.*, 50, 1886, p. 700.
15. *A.S.S.B.*, 1, pls. 7, 26, 27, 30; 2, pl. 24.
    [A plan for alterations to the stables at Soughton Hall, dated 1868 (Clwyd R.O. D/SH/858) bears the monogram 'H.H.', as does a drawing for houses and shops at Great Budworth, dated October 1870 (at Arley Hall).]
16. *Archt.*, 18, 1877, p. 15.
17. *A.S.S.B.*, 3, pls. 11, 12, 16, 17, 29, 49.
18. (a) *B.N.*, 81, 1901, p. 349. (b) Kelly.
19. *A.S.S.B.*, 3, pls. 6, 7, 28, 35–7, 39–42.
20. Chester City R.O. City and County Borough of Chester. Minutes of Proceedings.
21. [Heber Rimmer (1869–95), the son of the Liverpool architect and author Alfred Rimmer, was a pupil of Douglas & Fordham, and subsequently worked in their office between 1892 and 1894: see *Heber Rimmer Memorial*, London, 1896, with text signed 'E. H.' (presumably Edward Hodkinson).]
22. *A.S.S.B.*, 1, pls. 5, 18, 24, 42, 48, 69, 71; 2, pls. 20, 21, 26, 30, 31, 33–5, 42–5, 51, 53, 55, 58–60, 62-5, 69; 3, pls. 1, 2, 23, 31.
23. E.g. (a) Abbeystead, *B.N.*, 51, 1886, p. 54, (b) Barmouth church, *A.A.*, 1889, p. 36, (c) Glangwna, *Bldr.*, 64, 1893, p. 194, and (d) Port Sunlight School, *Bldr.*, 67, 1894, p. 83.
24. *Bldr.*, 11, 1853, p. 773; 12, 1854, p. 9.
25. *Journal of the Architectural, Archaeological & Historic Society for . . . Chester*, new series, 15, 1909, p. 134.
26. *A.A.*, 1891, p. 39.
    [Hodkinson is mentioned in the diaries of the second Marquess of Westminster as early as 1848, in connection with alterations to Halkyn Castle, which continued until 1851; in 1851, with reference to Eccleston Church; and in 1863 ('saw architects Messrs. Penson and Hodkinson') (information from Mr. Andrew Saint). He was the nephew and pupil of the Chester architect Thomas Jones (c. 1794–1859), who had built the Grosvenor Lodge at Eaton Hall for the first Marquess in 1835, and assisted him with the Vicarage at Gresford, Denbighshire (1850), later claiming the design as his own. For the second Marquess, he also built schools at Handbridge and Saighton (*Architects', Engineers', and Building Trades Directory*, London, 1868, p. 118, listing other works also).]
27. *A.A.*, 12, 1897.
28. *Ibid.*, 9, 1896.
29. (a) Date on building. (b) E.E.O. Drawings. (c) *A.A.*, 1891, p. 21.
30. *Chester Courant*, 18th July 1900.
31. *Bldr.*, 82, 1902, p. 346.
    [Information about Beswick's pupilage was given to the author by his son, Mr. William Beswick.]

References

32. (a) *Bldr.*, 71, 1896, p. 103. (b) *B.N.*, 71, 1896, p. 62. There is also documentation at (c) E.E.O.

    [He must presumably be the same W. M. Boden who appears in *Architects', Engineers', and Building Trades Directory*, London, 1868, as a pupil of T. M. Penson. The only works listed are model cottages (perhaps the ones for whose design he won a prize at the Royal Agricultural Society Leeds Meeting in 1861), and Bishop Graham's Memorial School, Chester. There are drawings for cottages at Saighton by him at E.E.O. (02056-8).]
33. *R.I.B.A.J.*, 3rd series, 19, 1911–12, p. 644, in 'Architects from George IV to George V,' Maurice B. Adams.
34. *Das Englische Haus*, Hermann Muthesius, Berlin, 1, 1904, p. 140. (Translation by Janet Seligman from *The English House*, London, 1979, p. 32.)
35. *B.A.*, 49, 1898, pp. 360–1.
36. *Chester Chronicle* ob.
37. *The Gothic Revival*, Kenneth Clark, 2nd edn., London, 1950, p. 195. (First edn. was 1928.)
38. *Ibid.*, p. 1.
39. Muthesius, *op. cit.*, p. 140. (English translation p. 32.)
40. The Public Baths, Chester (1898–1901) are exceptional in having presented specialised technical requirements. The engineering work was by Saunders & Taylor of Manchester, and, within the field of the servicing of traditional building types, the same firm was responsible for heating and ventilating at St. Deiniol's Library (1899–1902) and Colshaw Hall (1903). This not particularly large house may thus have been quite lavish in its equipment. Electricity was installed. Company electricity was presumably not available in Chester as far out as Dee Banks when Walmoor Hill was built (1896). The installation of a generator would have been a mark of modernity, but Douglas chose to light his house with gas. (Information from Mr. H. Morgan.)

    [The Wern (1892) incorporated various technical innovations, but these were presumably due more to the owner, R. M. Greaves, who was fascinated by such things, than to Douglas. (Information from the late Sir Clough Williams-Ellis.)

    In a letter to the Revd G. Egerton-Warburton of 13th January 1897 (Cheshire R.O. P 68/6/153), Douglas writes, 'There are very few professed heaters of churches who know much about it', and goes on to recommend the services of S. Saunders of Manchester, who had put right the defective heating of Bunbury Church, which Douglas had let to a firm who did work for Paley and Austin, and heated Frodsham Church for Bodley. Douglas mentions that Saunders is heating the new offices at Worsley for the Bridgewater Estate, and ends, 'owing to his success we are giving him considerable work'.]
41. *B.A.*, 49, 1898, pp. 360–1.
42. *Ibid.*, 49, 1898, pp. 360–1.

Appendix I

Correspondence from the Honourable Cecil Thomas Parker relating to the building of the Paddocks, Eccleston.

All letters (some of them dealing primarily with other subjects) which contain references to the house are given. The E.E.O. reference is given at the foot of each.

Feb. 21 1882

Dear Sir
    His Grace wishes Messrs George Smith & Co. to be invited to tender for the Building of my house, as well as the other four Builders whose names I gave you.
Yours Faithfully
Cecil T. Parker

John Douglas Esq.
(690, p. 52)

Feb. 22 1882

Dear Sir
    The Duke will be glad if you will get out plans etc. for a new Farm Dwelling House at Waverton to be erected close to the Church, partly on the site of the house at present occupied by Mr. Salmon. I find that many plans, elevations etc. made by you for Bldgs. on his Grace's property have not been sent to this office. I will send you shortly a list of the Bldgs. of which we require the plans.
    I hope that the specifications for my house are nearly completed & that we may have the Tenders in shortly. I am anxious for a start to be made.
Yours Faithfully
Cecil T. Parker

John Douglas Esq.
6 Abbey Square, Chester
(690, p. 53)

March 25 1882

My dear Sir
    His Grace has accepted Mr. Hughes's tender to build my House. I return his Tender and the others. I have carefully looked thro' the specifications and have made a few remarks.
    I daresay you will make arrangements for Mr. Hughes to begin forth with.
Salmon's Waverton
The Duke approves of the plans having made a few alterations – you can now get out an elevation.
Yours Faithfully
Cecil T. Parker

John Douglas Esq.
(690, p. 93)

Appendix I Correspondence

April 22 1882

Dear Sir

I agree to the floor level being as you propose, i.e, being level with the floor of boxes and will tell Stead.

Please note the school room can be divided as I suggested making [? them to be] similar to the two below. The fire place in the man's bed room on the ground floor is *unnecessary* and may be taken out.

Shall you be able to work any of the big Mahogany doors in, by cutting them down & taking off the tracery?

Yours Faithfully
Cecil T. Parker

John Douglas Esq.
(690, p. 32)

Enclosure   *May 22 1882*
Dear Sir

Enclosed is a copy of an authority given to Mr. Hughes to add soil to the East front of the house.

Aldford Hall Bldgs.

When will you go with me to look at the old materials?

Yours Faithfully
Cecil T. Parker

John Douglas Esq.
(690, p. 182)

May 30 1882

Dear Sir

Aldford Hall

I cannot make up my mind if it is advisable to have a loft over the covered yards, and therefore when the specifications and quantities are offered to the Builders I should wish them to tender for the Bldgs *with* and also *without* the loft over the covered yards.

My House

I mentioned once to you that I shd. like the school room made into two rooms same as those underneath – but I have changed my mind and do not wish the school room divided but to remain as originally planned.

Yours Faithfully
Cecil T. Parker

John Douglas Esq.
6 Abbey Square
(690, p. 196)

Enclosure   *Oct. 17 1882*
Dear Mr. Douglas

Pulford Church

His Grace accepts Mr. Joyce's estimate *No. 2* for six bells £285.12.3. *One* face to the Clock will be sufficient, and this is to be on the North side of the Tower over the entrance door.

I mentioned to Mr. Smith that the Tiles for my house are to be the same as those used on Pulford Church.

Yours Very Truly
Cecil T. Parker

The Work of John Douglas

John Douglas Esq.
His Grace also approves of the plans for the outbuildings for the cottage at Saighton. The next question is, *Who is to carry out the work?* Mr. Beckett has been so extraordinarily dilatory both in the cottage work and at the Broxton addition.
(690, p. 406)

Oct. 23 1882

Dear Sir
Can you conveniently come here tomorrow morning at 10 am? The Duke wishes me to see you respecting the stables for my new House. He wishes the present loose boxes to be utilised and I think that this is quite possible.
    Yours Faithfully
    Cecil T. Parker

John Douglas Esq
Architect
6 Abbey Square
Chester
(690, p. 427)

Dec. 14 1882

Dear Sir
There are several marble columns at Eaton 2' 3" by 6". They are very handsome. They are not required at Eaton and might I think be used in my new house with advantage. Will you have a look at them sometime when you are passing and see if you can work them in.
    Yours Faithfully
    Cecil T. Parker

John Douglas Esq..
(690, p. 495)

2 Enclosures   *Jan. 8 1883*
Dear Mr. Douglas
I find the large bookcases from *Eaton*, are oak, with glass fronts & cupboards below. (These are besides the Grosvenor House Mahogany book cases.) The oak book cases are at the *Cuckoos Nest* and I should much like you to see them, this you might do on your way to Pulford Church. I think I prefer the *oak* bookcases in the *Library* as they will be much more useful to me than the mahogany ones. In this case will it not be better to panel the Library with *oak* and not Honduras, & panelling the Drawing room with Honduras, and putting some of the mahogany Bookcases in this room. His Grace approves the plans of cottages for Eccleston. You will see his remarks which kindly make notes of. Old material to be used as much as possible, mullions which were cut for the Stud and now lying in the Eccleston quarry. The cost of Building should not exceed £1100 allowing £100 for contingencies. Total *£1200*.
 George Parker to be asked to build.
 I enclose Lady Middleton's letter re Parsonage.
    Yours Truly
    Cecil T. Parker

John Douglas Esq.
 P.S. Is not the shop at Saighton finished *yet*?!!!
Can you let me have the specifications of the buildings of Aldford & Balderton when *first* built about the year 1875. I only want them to look over.
    CTP
(690, pp. 523–4)

Appendix I Correspondence

Feb. 19 1883

Dear Sir

Please do not forget to send the plans & specifications of the two Eccleston Cottages asked for in my letter of 16th. Please make a note that the W.C. seats in my new house shall be on hinges & the [?——] to be made to [?——] up so that in case of accidents the whole of the closet may be got at without the trouble of sending for a Carpenter.

       Yours Faithfully
       Cecil T. Parker

John Douglas Esq.
(690, p. 594)

Feb. 20 1883

Dear Sir

I find that there are very few masons working at my house, Stead tells me that they are waiting for details of Gables, and they have not received any details for inside work. Is this the case? He also tells me that the tiles for the corner pinnacles will not be ready for a fortnight. I am afraid if more progress is not made, the house will not be habitable by the time I want it.

       Yours Faithfully
       Cecil T. Parker

John Douglas Esq.
(690, p. 602)

Mar. 7 1883

Dear Sir

    Waverton, Salmon's House

I must ask for a tracing of *one* Elevation and the ground plan of this house to send to London they can be on one sheet of tracing cloth. I send the plans of ground near my house, I was unaware that I had these.

       Yours Faithfully
       Cecil T. Parker

John Douglas Esq.
(690, p. 631)

Mar. 9 1883

Dear Sir

His Grace has decided this morning that there is to be *no* sunk fence to my house. I have told Stead.

His Grace approves of the Feeding shed as sketched this sketch I return I will see you as to details.

       Yours Faithfully
       Cecil T. Parker

John Douglas Esq.
(690, p. 640)

The Work of John Douglas

July 9 1883

Salmon's Waverton.

Dear Sir
  You can have a cellar put into this house cost not to exceed £25. The Cellar can be placed under the parlor.
                              Yours Faithfully
                              Cecil T. Parker

John Douglas Esq.
Architect
Chester
  You can get out a plan for the Shippon etc for my house as pointed out to Mr. Smith this day.

(690, p. 868)

July 27 1883

Dear Sir
  I asked Mr. Hughes yesterday to show me the details for the lower rooms of my House. & I was surprised to find that he had not yet received any from you. I trust that you will get them out at once, so that there may not be a great rush at the last moment.
                              Yours Faithfully
                              Cecil T. Parker

John Douglas Esq.
(690, p. 909)

Augt. 3 1883

Dear Sir
  I find a 'Fields' trap has been put in for the scullery, if you remember I distinctly told you I wished for a *Deans* fat trap & scullery trap combined. I cannot see any advantages in 'Fields' on the contrary many *disadvantages & faults*. Please do not order anything of that sort without first letting me know.
                              Yours faithfully
                              Cecil T. Parker

John Douglas Esq.
(690, p. 924)

Augt. 21 1883

Dear Sir
  I should like that the lower part of the mahogany bookcase in the *Library* be closed in – i.e. made into cupboards. I understand that all the bookcases have gone to Mr. Hughes's yard, Chester. I should like to know the sizes of those that will not be required in the Library & Drawing room.
  I can settle the plan for drains at Aldford Hall on Friday next if Mr. Smith has them ready.
                              Yours Faithfully
                              Cecil T. Parker

John Douglas Esq.
Architect
(690, p. 696)

Appendix I Correspondence

Augt. 29 1883

Dear Sir

Mr. Parker has been given to understand that his new house appears in the Building News of last week, & he desires me to write you to send him three copies, if possible?

I remain
Yours Faithfully
Ed: Wells

John Douglas Esqre.
Abbey Square
Chester
(690, p. 978)

Enclosure   *Oct. 15 1883*
Dear Sir

I return the tracing of the lift machinery. It appears to me elaborate for lifting goods to one floor. Perhaps you will ascertain if it is the simplest & best.

I think a mistake has been made in covering up the flushing tank in the scullery *entirely*. At the end of the flushing tank, there is a small cover [sketch follows] for lifting off in case any stoppage occurs, and this has now been built in, and no chance of getting to it without breaking up the pavement.

Yours Faithfully
Cecil T. Parker

John Douglas Esq.
(691, p. 56)

Oct. 20 1883

Dear Sir

I return the Office plan and have made a few remarks in pencil.

£24 is absurd for the Gates. If he cannot make them for less I will have them made at the *Cuckoo's Nest*.

I will see His Grace as to hassocks and seats. Have you done anything about Umbrella Stands? [Presumably relates to Pulford church.]

Yours Faithfully
Cecil T. Parker

John Douglas Esq.
(691, p. 73)

The Grate (Boyds [H ?———]) sent for the Day Nursery will not do, as it is not possible to get cold air in. So it will have to be changed.

We have an old oak mantel in our *present* dining room. I wish this utilized. If there is no where else, it can go in my *Office*.

Stead has had no orders about preparing for the lift yet!

(691, p. 74)

The Work of John Douglas

Oct. 9 1884

Dear Sir
  Glad to hear you have disposed of the grates. You had better dispose of the gates as you suggest.
                    Yours Faithfully
                    Cecil T. Parker

Messrs. Douglas & Fordham
(691, p. 647)

Jan. 5 1885

Dear Sir
  I shall be glad if you will let Mr. Edwards come out here tomorrow morning at 10 am. I am writing Mr. Hughes to be here at the same time there is something wrong with the sink on the back stairs and also with the Lavatory, which Mr. Hughes should I think put right.
                    Yours Faithfully
                    Cecil T. Parker

Messrs. Douglas & Fordham
(691, p. 766)

Enclosures   *Dec. 29 1886*
Dear Sir
                    Heating Office
  This can be proceeded with at once as shown on the plan enclosed. Could not however the present furnace & or boiler in my house be utilized for the Office, & a larger one put in my house? This should considerably reduce the cost as only one new boiler instead of two would be necessary. It would be well if you could come here with Mr. Gibbs on Friday morning early to see me say 10 oClock.
                    St. Johns Church repair
  His Grace wishes the repair marked A. to be done – and tenders to be invited from Messrs. Hughes, Parker & Parrott.
                    Yours Faithfully
                    Cecil T. Parker

Messrs. Douglas & Fordham
(692, p. 909)

                                                  April 1 1887
Dear Sirs
                    Heating Apparatus these Offices
  12.45. Therm. 47. Farh.!!!
  Miserable failure! A capital advertisement for Messrs. Gibbs.
                    Yours Faithfully
                    Cecil T. Parker

Messrs. Douglas & Fordham
(693, p. 46)

Appendix I Correspondence

Oct. 10 1887

Dear Sir
   I shall be much obliged if you will give me the receipt of the preparation used for staining the oak in my house.
                    Yours Faithfully
                      Cecil T. Parker

John Douglas Esq.
(693, p. 323)

Nov. 17 1887

Dear Sirs
   The attempt to heat these offices by Mr. Renton Gibbs is a complete failure. The clerks are shivering & I am barely warm, even with a fire. Something must be done, as it impossible [sic] to work here this winter if it is severe.
                    Yours Faithfully
                      Cecil T. Parker

Messrs. Douglas & Fordham
(693, p. 368)

Appendix II. Catalogue of Works

John Douglas was in practice in Chester from 1855 or 1860 until 1911, in partnership with D. P. Fordham c. 1884–97 and with C. H. Minshull c. 1897–1909.

Although most of the buildings listed below have been traced and visited, it may be that some of those not fully investigated no longer exist. All known instances of demolition or major alteration have, however, been noted.

Mention is made of a date appearing on a building only in instances where no other evidence of such dating exists. Works are not listed in date order within each year. Dates given may not in all cases represent the complete building-period of the work.

References to counties represent them as in Douglas's liftetime, and ignore the changes resulting from local government reorganisation in 1974.

* Indicates Grosvenor patronage. The client was the first Duke of Westminster (third Marquess of Westminster until 1874) unless otherwise stated.

Attributions (indicated as ATTRIB.) are on stylistic grounds coupled with the evidence of known local association.

Editor's Note

The Catalogue of Works has been much revised and amplified, chiefly on the basis of the author's own notes. Editorial interventions have only rarely been identified as such (by means of square brackets). No purely stylistic attributions are included other than those made by the author himself. Reference is not generally made to the relevant volumes of *Buildings of England, Wales*, or *Scotland*.

1856	**Garden Ornament** (flower vase and sundial), **Abbots Moss, Oakmere, Cheshire.** For the Honourable Mrs. Cholmondeley. (No longer extant). *B.A.*, 43, 1895, pp. 146, 148.
1860–61	**South Wing, Vale Royal, Cheshire.** For second Lord Delamere. (a) Dates on building. (b) *B.N.*, 58, 1890, p. 706. (c) Reference to Douglas exhibiting "Restored Vale Royal Abbey," in *A.A.H.S.C.C.N.C.J.*, 3, 1885, pp. 532–3. References to work at Vale Royal in (d) *B.A.* ob., (e) *Cheshire Observer* ob., and (f) *Chester Chronicle* ob.
1860–63	**Church of St. John the Evangelist, Over, Cheshire.** For second Lord Delamere. (a) *Bldr.*, 18, 1860, p. 222; 21, 1863, p. 484. (b) *B.N.*, 6, 1860, p. 256; 11, 1864, pp. 168, 169; 58, 1890, p. 706. (c) *A.A.H.S.C.C.N.C.J.*, 2, 1864, p. 274. (d) *B.A.* ob. (e) *B.N.* ob. (f) *Liverpool Daily Post* ob. (g) G.R. Index. (h) Kelly. (i) Ormerod, 2, p. 185. (j) Cheshire R.O. (P 222/5/1). Ground plan.
1862–3	**Restoration of Chancel, St. Mary's Church, Eastham, Cheshire.** For Miss White. *The Parish of Eastham*, Isabel Tobin, Liverpool, 1920, pp. 22–3, 51.
1862–4	**Boteler Grammar School, School Brow, Warrington, Lancashire.** (Now Corporation Highways Department). (a) *A.A.H.S.C.C.N.C.J.*, 2, 1864, pp. 405, 419, 423. (b) Kelly's *Directory of Lancashire*, 1913. (c). V.C.H. *Lancashire*, 2, 1908, pp. 601–3.
1864	**Shop Premises, Nos. 19 & 21 Sankey Street, Warrington, Lancashire.** For Robert Garnett & Sons. (Shopfront and interior now reconstructed). (a) Date on building. (b) *Works*.
1865	**House, No. 21 Upper Northgate Street, Chester.** For W. Denson. (Demolished) (a) Chester City R.O. (CCB/50). Minutes of the Improvement Committee 1861–

Appendix II Catalogue of Works

1866, pp. 553, 562, 692, 757, 759–60. (b) Chester City R.O. (DT/1). Town Clerk's Department. Letters and Papers. Letters from John Douglas 4th and 21st Aug. 1865. (c) Chester City R.O. (1283C, 1235C). Corporation Conveyances. (d) Chester City Library. Photographic Survey. Neg. No. WR.8/24.

Congregational Chapel, Over, Cheshire. (Now United Reformed Church). *Bldr.*, 23, 1865, p. 510.

1865–6 * **Church of St. John the Baptist, Aldford, Cheshire.** For second Marquess of Westminster.
(a) E.E.O. Drawings, 01899, 01900, 01900(A). (b) D.G.P. Photographs. (c) *Bldr.*, 24, 1866, p. 414. (d) Kelly. (e) Ormerod, 2, p. 758.

House, No. 23 Upper Northgate Street, Chester. For Dr. W. M. Dobie. (Demolished)
(a) Chester City R.O. (CCB/50). Minutes of the Improvement Committee 1861–1866, pp. 575, 579–60, 832. (b) Chester City R.O. (CCB/53). Minutes of the Improvement Committee 1874–1878, pp. 500, 509. (c) Chester City R.O. (DT/1). Town Clerk's Department. Letters and Papers. Letters from John Douglas 4th and 21st Aug. 1865 and 16th Feb. 1877. (d) Chester City R.O. (1283C, 1235C). Corporation Conveyances. (e) Chester City Library. Photographic Survey. Neg. No. WR.8/24.

1865–7 * **Entrance Lodge, Gates, Well Cover, etc., Grosvenor Park, Chester.** For second Marquess of Westminster.
(a) E.E.O., 1105. (b) E.E.O. Estate Papers: Eaton Estate: Chester: Miscellaneous Papers 15th to 20th Century. No. 15. (Box 59). Grosvenor Park. Miscellaneous Accounts and Papers 1864–8. No. 16 (Box 59). Disbursements on account of The New Park at Chester. (c) Chester City R.O. (CCF/8). New Park Committee. Letters and Papers. (d) Chester City R.O. (CCB/50). Minutes of the Improvement Committee 1861–1866, p. 736. (e) Chester City R.O. (CCB/51). Minutes of the Improvement Committee 1866–1870, pp. 30, 36, 84. (f) Chester City R.O. (DT/1). Town Clerk's Department. Letters and Papers. Letters from John Douglas 13th July and 13th Oct. 1866, 15th Apr. 1868, 4th May 1869. (g) *Bldr.*, 25, 1867, pp. 260, 772, 828. (h) Kelly. (i) Ormerod, 1, p. 372. (j) *A History of . . . Chester*, George Lee Fenwick, Chester, 1896, p. 520. (k) *Gresty's Chester Guide*, revised John Hicklin, Chester, n.d. (1873), pp. 59–61. (l) *The Visitor's Chester Guide*, Alfred Rimmer, Chester, n.d. (c. 1888), pp. 45–6.

St. Bartholomew's Church, Sealand, Flintshire.
(a) G.R. Index. (b) *Bldr.*, 23, 1865, p. 666; 25, 1867, p. 809. (c) Thomas, 1, 1911, p. 375. (d) *A History of the Parish of Hawarden*, W. Bell Jones, typescript at Clwyd R.O., 2, 1945, p. 374.

c. 1865 **Work at No. 7 Abbey Square, Chester.** For J. N. Bennett. (a) E.E.O. Estate Papers: Eaton Estate: Chester: Miscellaneous Papers 15th to 20th Century. No. 15 (Box 59). Grosvenor Park. Miscellaneous Accounts and Papers, 1864–8. Letter from Benjamin Owens, 3rd Feb. 1866 referring to Douglas and to completed work "at Mr. Bennetts' Abbey Square." Address ascertained from (b) Kelly (*Post Office Directory*) 1864 and (c) Morris's *. . . Directory . . . of Cheshire*, 1864, 1874.

c. 1865–7 * **Bishopsfield (or Flookersbrook) Girls' and Infants' School, Westminster Road (formerly Peploe Street), Hoole, Chester.** For second Marquess of Westminster. (Enlarged 1893.)
(a) E.E.O. Estate Papers: Eaton Estate: Chester: Miscellaneous Papers 15th to 20th Century. No. 15 (Box 59). Grosvenor Park. Miscellaneous Accounts and Papers, 1864–8. Letters from John Douglas, 25th June 1866, 20th July 1867. (b) Diaries of second Marquess of Westminster, 3rd October and 20th Nov. 1865, 8th Jan. 1866. (Information from Mr Andrew Saint.) (c) Chester City R.O. (DES/26).

1866 **Structural Report, House, St. John Street, Chester.** (With R. Davies). Chester City R.O. (CCB/50). Minutes of the Improvement Committee 1861–1866, pp. 888, 889.

The Work of John Douglas

1866 **Burford Lane Farm, Heatley, Oughtrington, Cheshire.** For George C. Dewhurst.
(a) Reference to Douglas exhibiting 'farm buildings on the estate of Mr. Dewhurst of Lymm', in *A.A.H.S.C.C.N.C.J.*, 3, 1885, pp. 532–3. (b) *B.N.*, 17, 1869, pp. 288, 290. (c) Date on building.

1867 **Shop Premises, Eastgate Street/St. Werburgh Street, Chester.** For F. & A. Dickson. (Demolished).
(a) Chester City R.O. (CCB/51). Minutes of the Improvement Committee 1866–1870, pp. 201–2. (b) Chester City R.O. (DT/1). Town Clerk's Department. Letters and Papers. Letters from John Douglas, 13th and 25th June 1867.
Oakmere Hall, Cheshire. For John Higson. (Interior altered).
(a) Date on building. (b) *Works*. (c) *Archt.*, 79, 1908, p. 257. (d) *B.N.*, 58, 1890, p. 706. (e) *A.A.H.S.C.C.N.C.J.*, 3, 1885, pp. 532–3. (f) *B.A.* ob. (g) *Bldr.* ob. (h) *B.N.* ob. (i) *Cheshire Observer* ob. Identity of client confirmed from (j) Morris's *. . . Directory . . . of Cheshire*, 1874, and (k) Kelly (*Post Office Directory*), 1878.

1867–8 **Dene Cottages, Warrington Road, Great Budworth, Cheshire.** For R.E. Egerton-Warburton.
(a) *B.A.*, 22, 1884, pp. 282–4. (b) Account Book at Arley Hall.

1867–9 **Remodelling of Soughton (Sychden) Hall, Northop, Flintshire.** For John Scott Bankes. ATTRIB.
(a) *Annals and Antiquities of the Counties and County Families of Wales*, T. Nicholas, London, 1872, 2, p. 444. (b) Clwyd R.O. Soughton Hall MSS, D/SH. Introduction to List. (c) Ibid. (D/SH/695). Accounts.

1868 **Restoration of chancel, St. Dunawd's Church, Bangor Is-coed, Flintshire.**
Thomas, 1, 1911, p. 432.
Rectory, Bangor Is-coed, Flintshire. (Partially demolished.)
Thomas, 1, 1911, p. 431.
Lower Lodge and alterations to stables, Soughton (Sychden) Hall, Northop, Flintshire. For John Scott Bankes.
Clwyd R.O. (D/SH/858-9). Plans and elevation.

1868–9 **St. Ann's Church, Warrington, Lancashire.**
(a) G.R. Index. (b) *Bldr.*, 27, 1869, p. 212. (c) *B.N.*, 17, 1869, pp. 26, 28, 29. (c) *A.A.H.S.C.C.N.C.J.*, 3, 1885, pp. 532–3. (d) Kelly's *Directory of Lancashire*, 1913. (e) V.C.H. *Lancashire*, 3, 1907, p. 324. (f) *History of Lancashire*, Edward Baines, 3rd edn., ed. James Croston, 4, 1891, p. 427. (g) *Warrington Church Notes*, William Beamont, Warrington, 1878, p. 199. (h) *Church Design for Congregations*, James Cubitt, London, 1870, p. 55n.

1868–70 **St. Paul's Church, Helsby, Cheshire.**
(a) G.R. Index. (b) *Works*. (c) *B.N.*, 25, 1873, p. 194. (d) *B.A.* ob. (e) *B.N.* ob. (f) *Liverpool Daily Post* ob. (g) Kelly. (h) Ormerod, 2, p. 71.

1869 **Triumphal Arch, City Road, Chester,** in connection with visit of Prince of Wales. (Temporary structure. Demolished).
(a) Chester City R.O. (DT/1). Town Clerk's Department. Letters and Papers. Letter from John Douglas, 3rd Nov. 1869. (b) Illustration at Grosvenor Museum, Chester. (c) *Cheshire Observer*, 16th Oct. 1869. (d) *Chester Chronicle*, 16th Oct. 1869. (e) *Chester Courant*, 20th Oct., 1869. (f) *Illustrated London News*, 55, 1869, pp. 414, 416. (g) *Wrexham Advertiser*, 16th Oct. 1869.
Pair of Houses, Nos. 31 & 33 Dee Banks, Chester. For himself.
(a) Date and inscription on building. (b) Information from Dr. and Mrs. K. A. Turner and Mrs. P. S. Dutton.
Restoration of Barnston Chapel, St. Chad's Church, Farndon, Cheshire.
Bldr., 27, 1869, p. 551.
Witton Grammar School, Northwich, Cheshire. (Altered. Now local authority offices).

Appendix II Catalogue of Works

(a) Cheshire County R.O. (SL/300/5/3). Witton Grammar School. Rebuilding of the School 1866–71. Includes Correspondence, Tenders, Contract and Account. (b) Cheshire County R.O. (SL/300/5/6). Witton Grammar School. School Buildings. Mainly enlargement of School 1883–5. Contract, Tenders, Correspondence. (c) Cheshire Country R.O. (SL/300/5/7). Witton Grammar School. School Extension 1888–9. Enlargement of School. Correspondence, Tenders, Vouchers. (d) Cheshire County R.O. (SL/300/5/10). Witton Grammar School. School and Master's House. Plans, Elevations and Sections 1870–88. (e) *Chester Chronicle* ob.

1869–70 **★ St. Mary's Church, Dodleston, Cheshire.** (Retaining portions of earlier church). Lychgate and boundary wall only for third Marquess of Westminster.
(a) E.E.O. Notebook. (b) E.E.O., 477, p. 31. (c) D.G.P. Photographs. (d) G.R. Index. (e) *Works*. (f) *A.A.H.S.C.C.N.C.J.*, 3, 1885, pp. 532–3. (g) *Bldr.*, 27, 1869, p. 592; 28, 1870, p. 692. (h) *B.N.*, 19, 1870, p. 123; 58, 1890, p. 706. (i) *B.N.* ob. (j) Kelly. (k) Ormerod, 2, pp. 850–51. (l) *Notes on the Churches of Cheshire*, Stephen R. Glynne, ed. T. A. Atkinson, Chetham Society, 32, 1894, p. 123.
St. Alban's Church, Tattenhall, Cheshire. (Retaining portions of earlier church).
(a) *A.A.H.S.C.C.N.C.J.*, 3, 1885, pp. 532–3. (b) *Bldr.*, 28, 1870, p. 972. (c) *B.N.*, 19, 1870, p. 374; 20, 1871, p. 83; 58, 1890, p. 706. (d) *B.N.* ob. (e) Kelly. (f) Ormerod, 2, p. 718. (g) *Notes on the Churches of Cheshire*, Stephen R. Glynne, ed. J. A. Atkinson, Chetham Society, 32, 1894, p. 42.

c. 1869 **Weaver Bank Farm, Minshull Vernon, Cheshire.** For Lewis Lloyd.
B.N., 17, 1869, pp. 209. 211.

1870 **★ Farmhouse, Green Lake Farm, Aldford, Cheshire.**
(a) Date on building. (b) E.E.O., 477, p. 31. (Referred to in E.E.O. records as "Parsonage's Farm." Identified through Estate Rentals). (c) D.G.P. Photographs.
★ School, Dodleston, Cheshire. (Altered).
(a) E.E.O. Notebook. (b) E.E.O. Photographs. (c) E.E.O. Drawings. 02869. (d) E.E.O., 477, p. 31. (e) D.G.P. Photographs. (f) *Works*. (g) *Archt.*, 10, 1873, p. 6. (h) Kelly.
★ Eaton Stud and Stud Groom's House, Eaton Hall, Cheshire. (Unexecuted scheme).
(a) E.E.O. Drawings. (b) E.E.O., 477, pp. 31, 43.
Church Cottage, Eccleston, Cheshire.
(a) Date on building. (b) E.E.O. Drawings. 02237. (c) E.E.O. Photographs. (d) E.E.O., 477, p. 31. (Referred to in E.E.O. records as "Cottage at Eccleston"). (e) *Works*. (f) *B.N.*, 38, 1875, p. 64.
★ Coach-House, Eccleston, Cheshire. (Now offices). (a) Date on building. (b) E.E.O. Notebook. (c) E.E.O., 477, pp. 31, 39. (d) *Works*. (e) *B.N.*, 38, 1875, p. 64.
School-Chapel, Eyton, Denbighshire. (Demolished.)
Thomas, 1, 1911, p. 433.
Shippon, Budworth Heath Farm, Great Budworth, Cheshire. For R. E. Egerton-Warburton.
(a) Drawings at Arley Hall. (b) Date on building.
Restoration, St. Garmon's Church. Llanarmon-yn-Ial, Denbighshire.
(a) *B.N.*, 58, 1890, p. 706. (b) Thomas, 2, 1911, p. 81.

1870–71 **★ Gamekeeper's Cottage and Kennels, Eaton Hall, Cheshire.** (Now Eaton Lodge).
(a) E.E.O. Notebook. (b) E.E.O. Photographs. (c) E.E.O. Drawings. 02263. (d) E.E.O., 477, pp. 31, 39. (e) *Works*. (f) *Archt.*, 10, 1873, p. 120.

The Work of John Douglas

Restoration, St Peter's Church, Little Budworth, Cheshire.
(a) *Bldr.*, 29, 1871, p. 132. (b) Ormerod, 2, p. 223.
* **Farm Buildings, William Parker's Farm, Lower Kinnerton, Cheshire.** (Probably Shippon, Moor End Farm; now converted into a house.)
E.E.O., 477, pp. 31, 34.

1870–72   * **Park Keeper's Cottage, Eaton Hall, Cheshire.** (West of Eccleston Lodge; now Deer Park Cottage.)
(a) E.E.O. Notebook. (b) E.E.O. Photographs. (c) E.E.O. 477, pp. 31, 39. (d) *Works*. (e) *Archt.*, 10, 1873, p. 120.
Alterations and Additions, St Mary's Church, Lymm, Cheshire.
(a) *Archt.*, 3, 1870, p. 108. (b) Kelly.

c. 1870   **Nos. 54–57 High Street, Great Budworth, Cheshire.** For R.E. Egerton-Warburton.
(a) *B.A.*, 22, 1884, pp. 282–4. (b) Drawings at Arley Hall.
Vicarage, Polesworth, Warwickshire. (Incorporating earlier parts.)
(a) *Works*, (b) *B.N.*, 41, 1881, p. 880. (c) *V.C.H. Warwickshire*, 4, 1947, p. 186.

c. 1870–72   * **Belgrave Kennels, Eaton Hall, Cheshire.**
(a) E.E.O. Notebook. (b) E.E.O., 477, p. 31.
* **Work at Saighton Grange, Cheshire.**
E.E.O., 477, p. 31.
* **Cottage, Saighton, Cheshire.** (¾ m. north of Hatton Heath Lodge on west side of Whitchurch Road),
(a) E.E.O. Notebook. (b) E.E.O., 477, p. 31. (Referred to in E.E.O. records as "Rodens." Identified through Estate Rentals).

1871   * **Boys' School, Aldford, Cheshire.** (Altered).
(a) E.E.O. Notebook. (b) E.E.O., 477, p. 31. (c) D.G.P. Photographs. (d) *Works*. (e) *Archt.*, 10, 1873, p. 6. (f) Kelly.
* **Girls' School, Aldford, Cheshire.** (Altered. Now a house).
(a) E.E.O. Notebook. (b) E.E.O., 477, p. 31. (c) Kelly.
Hield House Farm, Aston-by-Budworth, Cheshire. For second Lord de Tabley. (Incorporating earlier parts.)
(a) *B.A.*, 22, 1884, pp. 282–4. (b) Date on building. (c) Information from Mrs. K. M. Harris.
* **Pair of Cottages, Belgrave, Cheshire.** (West of Belgrave Lodge on west side of Wrexham Road).
(a) E.E.O. Notebook. (b). E.E.O. Photographs. (c) E.E.O. Drawings. 02315. (d) E.E.O., 477, p. 31. (e) D.G.P. Photographs.
Restoration, St. John's Church, Burwardsley, Cheshire.
Bldr., 29, 1871, pp. 812–3.
* **Eccleston Lodge (or Weighing Machine Lodge), Eaton Hall, Cheshire.** (Unexecuted scheme).
E.E.O. Drawings.
* **Loose Boxes in Paddocks, Eccleston, Cheshire.** (In connection with the Eaton Stud).
(a) E.E.O. Notebook. (b) E.E.O. Photographs. (c) E.E.O. Drawings. 02708. (d) E.E.O., 477, p. 31.
Restoration, St Bartholomew's Church, Great Barrow, Cheshire.
Bldr., 29, 1871, p. 812.
* **Remodelling, The Elms, Pulford, Cheshire.**
(a) E.E.O. Notebook. (b) E.E.O. Photographs. (c) E.E.O., 477, pp. 31, 34. (Referred to in E.E.O. records as "Captain Scotlands". Identified through Estate Rentals).
* **Farm Buildings, Manor Farm, Pulford, Cheshire.**
E.E.O., 477, pp. 31, 34. (Referred to as "Woolscoft Farm." Identified through Estate Rentals).

Appendix II Catalogue of Works

1871–2 **Organ Chamber, Reredos, etc., St Mary's Church, Lymm, Cheshire.**
(a) *Archt.*, 3, 1870, p. 108. (b) Kelly.
School, Warburton, Cheshire. For R. E. Egerton-Warburton. (Converted into a house).
(a) Drawings and specification at Warburton New Church. (b) Cheshire R.O. (P 68/17/4–6). Plan and elevations. (c) Kelly. (d) *B.A.*, 15, 1881.

1871–3 **Cottage in the Gardens (The Bothy), Arley Hall, Cheshire.** For R.E. Egerton-Warburton.
Drawings at Arley Hall.
Restoration (excluding that of Chancel), St. Chad's Church, Holt, Denbighshire.
(a) *Bldr.*, 25, 1867, p. 250; 31, 1873, p. 814. (b) *B.N.*, 58, 1890, p. 706. (c) Thomas, 3, 1913, p. 260.

1872 *** Alterations to the Eastgate, Chester.** (Unexecuted scheme).
Chester City R.O. (CCB/52). Minutes of the Improvement Committee 1870–1874, pp. 288, 291–2.
Terrace of Houses, east side of Grosvenor Park Road, Chester. (Unexecuted scheme).
(a) Chester City R.O. (CCB/52). Minutes of the Improvement Committee 1870–1874, pp. 274–5. (b) Chester City R.O. (DT/1). Town Clerk's Department. Letters and Papers. Letter from John Douglas 13th Feb. 1872. (c) *A.A.H.S.C.C.N.C.J.*, 3, 1885, pp. 529, 532–3.
*** Dutch Tea House, Eaton Hall, Cheshire.**
(a) Date on building. (b) E.E.O., 477, pp. 31, 39. (c) D.G.P. Photographs. (d) *B.A.*, 11, 1879, p. 194. (e) *The Visitors' Chester Guide*, Alfred Rimmer, Chester, n.d. (*c.* 1888), pp. 195–6.
Additions to Plas Tan-y-Bwlch, Maentwrog, Merioneth. For W. E. Oakeley.
(a) *B.N.*, 58, 1890, p. 706. (b) *Annals and Antiquities of the Counties and County Families of Wales*, T. Nicholas, London, 1872, 2, p. 706. (c) Datable photographs at the house.
*** The Limes Farmhouse, Pulford, Cheshire. (Now Green Paddocks.)**
(a) Date on building. (b) E.E.O. Photographs. (c) E.E.O., 477, p. 31. (Referred to in E.E.O. records as 'Saladine' and 'Alcock'. Identified through Estate Rentals.) (d) D.G.P. Photographs. (e) *Works*. (f) *Archt.*, 11, 1874, p. 212.
Shotwick Park, Great Saughall, Cheshire. For H. D. Trelawny.
(a) Date on building. (b) *B.A.*, 11, 1879, pp. 36, 46. (c) Ormerod, 2, p. 573. (d) Kelly. (e) *B.A.* ob. (f) *B.N.* ob.
Game Larder, Soughton (Sychden) Hall, Northop, Flintshire. For John Scott Bankes.
Clwyd R.O. (D/SH/864). Plan and elevation.
Remodelling, Mill, Warburton, Cheshire. For R. E. Egerton-Warburton. (Unexecuted scheme).
Drawings at Warburton New Church.

1872–3 **St. Werburgh Chambers, St. Werburgh Street, Chester.** For G. Hodgkinson. (Offices. Now shop premises, Nos. 29–33 St. Werburgh Street).
(a) Chester City R.O. (CCB/52). Minutes of the Improvement Committee 1870–1874, pp. 274–5, 296, 299, 300–301, 304, 333–4, 452–4, 551–2, 554–5. (b) Chester City R.O. (DT/1). Town Clerk's Department. Letters and Papers. Letters from John Douglas, 13th Feb. 1872, 8th July 1873.

c. 1872 **Colwyn Bay Hotel, Colwyn Bay, Denbighshire.** (Demolished).
(a) *Bldr.*, 30, 1872, p. 593. (b) *Seventy-Two Views of North Wales*, London, N.D. (two illustrations, dated 1877 and 1878.)

The Work of John Douglas

* **Cottages, Saighton, Cheshire.** (Block of three on west side of village street north of Post Office, and block of four on east side of village street at south end).
(a) E.E.O. Notebook. (b) E.E.O., 477, p. 31. (c) *Works*, (d) *B.N.*, 38, 1875, p. 8.

c.1872–6 * **Addition of Spire, new Reredos, etc., Church of St. John the Baptist, Aldford, Cheshire.**
(a) E.E.O. Notebook. (b) E.E.O., 477, p. 31. (c) D.G.P. Photographs.
* **Pair of Cottages, Eccleston, Cheshire.** (Probably Church Villas, south-west of church).
(a) E.E.O. Photographs. (b) E.E.O., 477, p. 31.
* **Pairs of Cottages, Pulford, Cheshire.** (West of The Cuckoo's Nest on road to Oldfield's Farm).
(a) E.E.O. Notebook. (b) E.E.O. Photographs. (c) E.E.O., 477, p. 31. (d) D.G.P. Photographs.
* **Cottage, Waverton, Cheshire.** (East of entrance of lane to Cotton Farm).
(a) E.E.O. Notebook. (b) E.E.O., 477, p. 31.

1873 * **Pumphouse, Aldford, Cheshire.** (Unexecuted scheme).
E.E.O. Drawings.
* **Farmhouse, Lea Hall Farm, Aldford, Cheshire.**
(a) E.E.O. Notebook. (b) E.E.O., 477, p. 31; 478, p. 4. (c) D.G.P. Photographs. (d) *Works*. (e) *B.A.*, 8, 1877, p. 180.
Cottage, Arley Green, Cheshire. For R. E. Egerton-Warburton. (West of The Old Parsonage.)
Drawing at Arley Hall.
* **Pumphouse, Dodleston, Cheshire.** (Unexecuted scheme.)
E.E.O. Drawings.
Harp and Crown Inn, No. 30 Bridge Street, Chester. (Unexecuted scheme.)
(a) Chester City R.O. (D/JWW/582). Drawings. (b) *B.A.*, 17, 1882, p. 147.
Additions to The Manor House, Great Barrow, Cheshire. For George Okell. ATTRIB.
Cheshire Life, Nov. 1984, p. 30.
* **Farmhouse, Cotton Abbots Farm, Waverton, Cheshire.**
(a) Date on building. (b) E.E.O. Notebook. (c) E.E.O. 477, p. 31; 693, p. 911. (d) D.G.P. Photographs. (e) *Works*. (f) *B.A.*, 8, 1877, p. 44.

1873–4 **St. Werburgh's Mount, St. Werburgh Street, Chester.** For G. Hodgkinson. (Shop premises. Nos. 15–27 St. Werburgh Street).
(a) Chester City R.O. (CCB/52). Minutes of the Improvement Committee 1870-1874, pp. 345, 347, 349, 400, 403–4, 411, 432, 434, 439, 441, 448, 450–55, 457, 512, 524–5, 538, 540, 542–4, 551–2, 596, 598–600, 617–8, 678–82, 686, 689–90, 737, 739, 744, 747. (b) Chester City R.O. (CCB/53). Minutes of the Improvement Committee 1874–1878, pp. 38, 40–42, 76, 79. (c) Chester City R.O. (DT/1). Town Clerk's Department. Letters and Papers. Letters from John Douglas, 8th July 1873, 19th May 1874.

1873–5 **St John's Church, Hartford, Cheshire.**
(a) G.R. Index. (b) *Works*. (c) *B.A*, 2, 1874, p. 104. (d) *Bldr.*, 31, 1873, p. 935. (e) *B.N.*, 58, 1890, p. 706. (f) *B.A.* ob. (g) *B.N.* ob. (h) Kelly. (i) Ormerod, 2, p. 199. (j) *Hartford Parish Church, 1875–1975*, Ian Newton, 1975.

c. 1873 * **Farmhouse, Lea Newbold Farm, Bruera, Cheshire.**
(a) E.E.O. Notebook. (b) E.E.O. Drawings. 02818. (c) E.E.O., 477, p. 31. (d) D.G.P. Photographs. (e) *Works*. (f) *B.A.*, 8, 1877, p.116.
Remodelling, Broxton Higher Hall, Cheshire. For Sir Philip de M. Grey Egerton. (Remodelled again 1961 (*Broxton Old Hall*, anon. [?J. D. McKechnie], and 1987–8 (*Building Refurbishment*, March 1988 and March 1989).)

Appendix II Catalogue of Works

(a) *B.N.*, 24, 1873, p. 558. (b) Ormerod, 2, pp. 671–3.
Agent's House, Ruloe, Norley, Cheshire. For George F. Wilbraham. (Now Ruloe House, Wood Lane.)
(a) *Works*. (b) *B.N.*, 25, 1873, p. 536. (c) Ormerod, 2, p. 136.

1874　★ **Block of Four Cottages, Aldford, Cheshire**. (Rushmere View, Rushmere Lane – west end of south road in village.)
(a) Date on building. (b) E.E.O. Notebook. (c) E.E.O., 477, p.31. Probably among "Ten New Cottages at Aldford," referred to in (d) E.E.O. 478, pp. 4, 24. (e) D.G.P. Photographs. (f) *B.A.*, 37, 1892, p. 208.
School, Bunbury Heath, Bunbury, Cheshire.
(a) *Works*. (b) *B.A.*, 19, 1883, pp. 70–71. (c) Kelly. (d) Ormerod, 2, p. 268.
St. Paul's Church, Marston, Cheshire. (Demolished).
(a) G.R. Index. (b) *Works*. (c) *B.A.*, 7, 1877, p. 354. (d) Kelly. (e) Ormerod, 1, p. 633.
Market Hall, Northwich, Cheshire. (Demolished).
(a) *Works*. (b) Morris's . . . *Directory . . . of Cheshire*, 1874.

1874–5　★ **Cheese Factory, Balderton, Cheshire.**
(a) E.E.O. Notebook. (b) E.E.O. Photographs. (c) E.E.O., 477, p. 31; 690, pp. 523–4. (d) *Journal of the Royal Agricultural Society of England*, 2nd series, II, 1875, p. 295.
★ **Cheese Factory, Bruera, Cheshire. (Aldford Cheese Factory).**
(a) Date on building. (b) E.E.O. Notebook. (c) E.E.O., 477, p. 31; 690, pp. 523–4. (d) D.G.P. Photographs. (e) *Works*. (f) *Journal of the Royal Agricultural Society of England*, 2nd series, 11, 1875, p. 295. (g) *B.A.*, 24, 1885, pp. 266–7. (h) *Das Englische Haus*, Hermann Muthesius, Berlin, 1. 1904, p. 136.
Restoration of Chancel, St. Mary's Church, Eastham, Cheshire. ATTRIB.
(a) *The Parish of Eastham*, Isabel Tobin, Liverpool, 1920, p. 24. (b) Kelly. (c) Ormerod, 2, p. 408.
Two entrance lodges, entrance gates, and railings, Bryn-y-Pys, Overton, Flintshire. For Edmund Peel.
Clwyd R.O. (A.N. 1767/61–2).
Station Lodge, Penbedw, Nannerch, Flintshire. For W. B. Buddicom.
Clwyd R.O. (D/B/209). Letter books of W. B. Buddicom, 1874–6, pp. 44, 165, 189, 200; 1877–82, p. 166.
Remodelling, St Mary's Church, Whitegate, Cheshire. For second Lord Delamere.
(a) G.R. Index. (b) *Works*. (c) *Archt.*, 14, 1875, p. 318. (d) *Bldr.*, 32, 1874, p. 715; 33, 1875, p. 473. (e) *B.N.*, 58, 1890, p. 706. (f) *Transactions of the Historic Society of Lancashire and Cheshire*, 92, 1941 (for 1940), pp. 210–13. (g) *B.A.*, ob. (h) Kelly. (i) Ormerod, 2, p. 145.

1874–8　**Master's House, Witton Grammar School, Northwich, Cheshire**. (Now local authority offices).
(a) Cheshire County R.O. (SL/300/5/4). Witton Grammar School. Schoolmaster's House. Correspondence relating to Leasing of the Site, Tenders, Contracts, and Accounts. (b) Cheshire County R.O. (SL/300/5/5). Witton Grammar School. Correspondence with John Douglas re Building of Master's House 1874–8. (c) Cheshire County R.O. (SL/300/5/10). Witton Grammar School. School and Master's House. Plans, Elevations and Sections 1870–1888.

1874–81　★ **School, Eccleston, Cheshire.**
(a) E.E.O. Notebook. (b) E.E.O. Photographs. (c) E.E.O., Drawings. 02370, 02371, 02372. (d) E.E.O., 477, loose sheet (letter from Samuel Beckett, 20th Dec. 1878) inserted at p. 31; 487, pp. 15, 19, 25, 45. (e) *Works*. (f) *B.A.*, 11, 1879, p. 26. (g) Kelly. (h) Ormerod, 2, p. 829.

The Work of John Douglas

c. 1874   *** Block of Four Cottages, Aldford, Cheshire.** (Probably Clements Cottages, at south end of centre road in village on west side).
(a) E.E.O. Notebook. (b) E.E.O., 477. Probably among "Ten New Cottages at Aldford," referred to in (c) E.E.O., 478, pp.4, 24.
* Pair of Cottages, Aldford, Cheshire. (South end of west road in village (School Lane), on east side.)
(a) E.E.O. Notebook. (b) E.E.O., 477, p. 31. Probably among "Ten New Cottages at Aldford," referred to in (c) E.E.O., 478, pp. 4, 24. (d) D.G.P. Photographs. (e) *Works*. (f) *B.A.*, 8, 1877, p. 180.
* Pumphouse, Eccleston, Cheshire.
(a) E.E.O. Notebook. (b) E.E.O. 477, p. 31. (c) *Works*. (d) *B.A*, 3, 1875, p. 344.

1875   **Overdale, Tarporley Road, Cuddington, Cheshire.** For G. F. Wilbraham. ATTRIB.
Information from Mr. Oliver Bott.
Hill Bark Farm, Frankby, Cheshire. For Septimus Ledward.
The Hundred of Wirral, Philip Sulley, Birkenhead, 1889, p. 51.
School, Overton, Frodsham, Cheshire.
(a) *Works*. (b) *B.A.*, 8, 1877, p. 166. (c) Kelly.
Remodelling, The George and Dragon, Great Budworth, Cheshire. For R. E. Egerton-Warburton.
(a) *Archt.*, 14, 1875, p. 318. (b) *B.A.*, 22, 1884, pp. 282–4.
Presbyterian Chapel, Rossett, Denbighshire.
(a) *Works*. (b) *B.A.*, 7, 1877, p. 354; 49, 1898, pp. 360–61. (c) *Bldr.*, 35, 1875, p. 782.
St Ethelwold's School, Shotton, Flintshire. (Enlarged, possibly c. 1900.)
(a) *A History of the Parish of Hawarden*, W. Bell Jones, typescript at Clwyd R.O. (b) Identified as by Douglas by William Matson. (Information from Mr. N. H. Davies.)
Sunday School, Warburton, Cheshire. For R. E. Egerton-Warburton.
Drawings at Warburton New Church.

1875–6   **Additions and alterations to British School, and Master's House, Glanrafon Road, Mold, Flintshire.**
Drawings at Clwyd R.O. (E/SBD/3/3-4).

1875–7   **Cilcain Hall, Flintshire.** For W. B. Buddicom.
(a) Date 1877 on building. (b) Clwyd R.O. (D/B/210). Letter books of W. B. Buddicom, 1874–6, pp. 2, 32, 52, 57; 1877–82, p. 166.
Entrance Lodge, Cilcain Hall, Flintshire. For W. B. Buddicom.
Clwyd R.O. (D/B/210). Letter books of W. B. Buddicom, 1874–6, p. 365; 1877–82, pp. 66, 166.

1875–8   *** Upper Servants' Houses, Eccleston, Cheshire.** (Now Morris Oak).
(a) E.E.O. Notebook. (b) E.E.O. Photographs. (c) E.E.O., 478, pp. 4, 24. (d) *Works*. (e) *Archt.*, 14, 1875, p. 366.
* Farm Buildings, Cheaveley Hall Farm, Huntington, Cheshire.
(a) E.E.O. Notebook. (b) E.E.O. Drawings. 02805, 02806, 02807, 02808. (c) E.E.O., 477, p. 31; 478, pp. 7, 17, 24. (d) D.G.P. Photographs, (e) *B.A.*, 16, 1881, p. 632.

1876   *** Aldford Hall Farm, Cheshire.** (Unexecuted scheme.)
E.E.O. Drawings.
Rebuilding of Christ Church, Chester. (Unexecuted scheme.)
[There is a report by Douglas on the condition of the church dated 1869 in Cheshire R.O. (P 17/6/1). It seems likely that the date 1876 (which comes from G.R. Index) is the date of the scheme shown in an engraving (apparently unpublished), in the author's collection. This is signed 'John Douglas Architect'.

Appendix II Catalogue of Works

The scheme bears no resemblance to that executed in stages between 1893 and 1900.]
* Wall, gate and railings to churchyard, Church of St John the Baptist, Chester.
(a) Cheshire R.O. (EDP 73/2 pt 1). Plans and elevations of railings. (b) E.E.O. Notebook.
Alterations to chancel seats, Church of St John the Baptist, Chester.
Cheshire R.O. (EDP 73/2/ pt 1). Plans and elevations.
St Paul's Church, Boughton, Chester. (Retaining portions of earlier church.)
(a) G.R. Index. (b) *B.A.* ob. (c) *B.N.* ob. (d) *Cheshire Observer* ob. (e) *Chester Courant* ob. (f) *Liverpool Daily Post* ob. (g) Kelly. (h) *St Paul's, The Finest Victorian Church in Chester*, anon., c. 1976.
Dunsdale, Frodsham, Cheshire. For Charles Broadbent.
(a) Date on building. (b) *Works.* (c) *B.A.*, 8, 1877, p. 166.
Structural Report, Gredington, Flintshire. For the Honourable George T. Kenyon.
Clwyd R.O. (D/KT/64).

1876–7 **Reredos, Church of St John the Baptist, Chester.**
Lectures on the History of S. John Baptist Church and Parish . . . Chester, S. Cooper Scott, Chester, 1892, pp. 245, 248, 251.
St Stephen's Church, Moulton, Cheshire.
(a) G.R. Index. (b) Kelly.
Restoration, St Peter's Church, Northop, Flintshire.
(a) Tablet in church. (b) *Works.* (c) *B.N.*, 58, 1890, p. 706. (d) Thomas, 2, 1911, pp. 431–2. (e) Clwyd R.O. (P/45/1/63, 269, 304). Papers relating to the restoration.

1876–8 *** Two Pairs of Cottages, Aldford, Cheshire.** (North of Lea Hall Farm.)
(a) E.E.O. Notebook. (b) E.E.O., 478, pp. 4, 24.
Alterations and Addition of Chancel, St Mark's Church, Connah's Quay, Flintshire.
(a) *Bldr.*, 36, 1878, p. 335. (b) Clwyd R.O. (P/15/1/48). Faculty papers, 1876. (c) Clwyd R.O. (NT/146). Copy of 'Record of Events connected with St Mark's Church, Connah's Quay, 1861–1909' (original at church). (d) G.R. Index. (e) Thomas, 2, 1911, p. 175.
* Block of Three Cottages, Waverton, Cheshire. (Nos. 50–54 Guy Lane.) ATTRIB.
(a) E.E.O. Notebook. (b) E.E.O., 478, p. 4.

1877 **Restoration, St Dunawd's Church, Bangor Is-coed, Flintshire.**
(a) *Bldr.*, 35, 1877, p. 645. (b) *B.N.*, 58, 1890, p. 706. (c) Thomas, 1, 1911, p. 432. (d) *Archaeologia Cambrensis*, 98, 1945, p. 186.
* Little Nag's Head Cocoa House, Foregate Street, Chester. (Remodelling of former inn. Demolished).
(a) E.E.O. Notebook. (b) E.E.O. Drawings. 01548, 01549, 01551. (c) *B.A.*, 8, 1877, p. 255. (d) *Bldr.*, 49, 1885, pp. 456–7. (e) *B.N.*, 33, 1877, p. 508. (f) *Die Englische Baukunst der Gegenwart*, Hermann Muthesius, Leipzig and Berlin, 1900, p. 67, pl. 26. (g) *The Visitors' Chester Guide*, Alfred Rimmer, Chester, n.d. (c. 1888), p. 47. (h) *Lectures on the History of S. John Baptist Church and Parish . . . Chester*, S. Cooper Scott, Chester, 1892, p. 252.
St Barnabas's Mission Church and Curate's House, Sibell Street, Chester. (Sold 1988.)
(a) Cheshire R.O. Account, 4th Feb. 1878, and plan. (b) Kelly. (c) Report on Inspection of Fabric by Stroud, Nullis and Partners, 1985.
* Luncheon Room, Eaton Hall, Cheshire. (Unexecuted scheme.)
E.E.O. Drawings.

The Work of John Douglas

Gateway, St Deiniol's Church, Hawarden, Flintshire. In memory of Sir S. R. Glynne.
B.A., 17, 1882, pp. 187–8.
Sessions House, Northop, Flintshire. For John Scott Bankes.
(a) Date on building. (b) *B.A.*, 19, 1883, pp. 70–71. (c) *Bldr.*, 35, 1877, p. 1041.
The Gelli, Tallarn Green, Flintshire. For the Honourables Georgina and Henrietta Kenyon.
(a) Date on building. (b) *Works*. (c) *B.A.*, 17, 1882, p. 30. (d) *B.N.*, 58, 1890, p. 706. (e) Photographs *c.* 1880 at Arley Hall.
Oriel Window and Porch, Vale Royal, Cheshire. For second Lord Delamere.
(a) Date on building.(b) *B.A.*, 11, 1879, p. 194. References to work by Douglas at Vale Royal in (c) *B.A.*, ob., (d) *Cheshire Observer* ob., and (e) *Chester Chronicle* ob.
Remodelling of Library, Vale Royal, Cheshire. For second Lord Delamere. ATTRIB.
Cheshire Country Houses, Peter de Figueiredo and Julian Treuherz, Chichester, 1988, pp. 193–6.
Restoration (excluding that of Chancel), St. Mary's Church, Weaverham, Cheshire.
(a) *B.A.*, 8, 1877, p. 290. (b) *Bldr.*, 35, 1877, p. 1209. (c) *B.N.*, 58, 1890, p. 706. (d) *Journal of the Chester and North Wales Architectural, Archaeological and Historic Society*, new series, 34, part 2, 1940, p. 146. (e) Kelly. (f) *Notes on the Churches of Cheshire*, Stephen R. Glynne, ed. J. A. Atkinson, Chetham Society, 32, 1894, p. 57.

1877–8   * **Church of St. Mary the Virgin, Halkyn, Flintshire.**
(a) Date on building. (b) Drawing at church. (c) *Works*. (d) G.R. Index. (e) *Bldr.*, 36, 1878, p. 1211. (f) *B.N.*, 42, 1882, p. 760. (g) *B.A.* ob. (h) *Bldr.* ob. (i) *Cheshire Observer* ob. (j) *Chester Chronicle* ob. (k) *Chester Courant* ob. (l) *R.I.B.A.J.* ob. (m) *The Royal Academy of Arts. A Complete Dictionary of Contributors and their Work from its foundation in 1769 to 1904*, Algernon Graves, 1, 1905, p. 358. (m) Thomas, 2, 1911, pp. 185–6.
* **Remodelling, Farmhouse, Cheavely Hall Farm, Huntington, Cheshire.** (Unexecuted scheme).
E.E.O. Drawings.
Cottage Hospital, Gwernaffield Road, Mold, Flintshire.
(a) *Bldr.*, 36, 1878, p. 1207. (b) Clwyd R.O. (D/B/209–10). Letter Books of W.B. Buddicom, 1874–6, p. 293; 1877–82, p. 205. (c) Photograph *c.* 1880 at Arley Hall.
Tai Cochion, Nannerch, Flintshire. For W.B. Buddicom.
Clwyd R.O. (D/B/210). Letter Book of W.B. Buddicom, 1877–82, pp. 134, 166.
* **School, Waverton, Cheshire.**
(a) E.E.O. Notebook. (b) E.E.O. Drawings. 02558. (c) E.E.O. 478, pp. 5, 25. (d) Photograph *c.* 1880 at Arley Hall. (e) *B.A.*, 19, 1883, pp. 70–71. (f) Kelly. (d) Ormerod, 2, p. 791.

1877–9   * **Aldford Lodge, Eaton Hall, Cheshire.**
(a) E.E.O. Notebook. (b) E.E.O., 478, pp. 5, 39. (c) *Works*. (d) *Archt.*, 17, 1877, p. 76.
* **Upper Belgrave Lodge, Eaton Hall, Cheshire.**
(a) Date on building. (b) E.E.O. Notebook. (c) E.E.O. Photographs. (d) E.E.O. Drawings. (e) E.E.O., 478, p. 5.
Restoration, St. Mary's Church, Tilston, Cheshire.
(a) *B.N.*, 58, 1890, p. 706. (b) *Journal of the Chester and North Wales Architectural, Archaeological and Historic Society*, new series, 31, part 2., 1936, p. 100; 34, part 2, 1940, p. 143. (c) Kelly. (d) Ormerod, 2. p. 695. (e) *Notes on the Churches of Cheshire*, Stephen R. Glynne, ed. J. A. Atkinson, Chetham Society, 32, 1894, p. 44. (f) Cheshire R.O. (P 18/7/20). Plan of graves in churchyard dated 1879.

Appendix II Catalogue of Works

1877–84 * **Wrexham Road Farm, Eccleston, Cheshire.**
(a) E.E.O. Notebook. (b) E.E.O. Photographs. (c) E.E.O. Drawings. (d) E.E.O., 478, pp. 10, 25, 73. (Referred to in E.E.O. records as "Hilliards" and "Morris." Identified through Estate Rentals). (e) Letter from John Douglas to the Duke of Westminster, Oct. 1878. Transcription in report accompanying measured drawings of "Hilliards Farm" (Wrexham Road Farm) prepared in the Liverpool School of Architecture by P. L. Ford and K. J. McKay, 1960, and now in the collection of the University of Liverpool Archivist. The original of the letter is not in E.E.O. and was presumably among papers dispersed when Wrexham Road Farm and other portions of the estate were sold following the First World War. (f) *Bldr.*, 54, 1888, p. 427. (g) *B.N.*, 54, 1888, p. 838. (h) *The Royal Academy of Arts. A Complete Dictionary of Contributors and their Work from its foundation in 1769 to 1904*, Algernon Graves, 1, 1905, p. 358.

c. **1877** * **Gas Works Cottages, Eaton, Cheshire.** (Now Eaton Boat).
(a) E.E.O. Notebook. (b) E.E.O. Photographs. (c) E.E.O. Box No. 2 of Personal Papers of first Duke of Westminster. Letters to David Scotland from John Douglas, 27th and 30th Apr. 1877, and from Samuel Beckett 30th Apr. 1877, and from Thomas M. Rickman, 19th May and 19th June 1877. (d) D.G.P. Photographs.

1878 **House, St. John Street, Chester.** (Unexecuted scheme or Demolished). Chester City R.O. (CCB/53). Minutes of the Improvement Committee 1874–1878, pp. 865, 869–70.
Reredos, St. Mary's Church, Mold, Flintshire.
Bldr., 36, 1878, p. 733.
Vicarage, Whitegate, Cheshire. For second Lord Delamere.
(a) *Works*. (b) *B.A.*, 11, 1879, p. 114. (c) Kelly. (d) Ormerod, 2, p. 145.

1878–9 **St Michael's Church, Altcar, Lancashire.** For fourth Earl of Sefton.
(a) G.R. Index. (b) *B.A.*, 19, 1883, pp. 632–5. (c) *B.N.*, 58, 1890, p. 706. (d) *B.A.* ob. (e) *B.N.* ob. (f) *Liverpool Daily Post* ob. (g) *History of Lancashire*, Edward Baines, 3rd edn., ed. James Croston, 5, 1893, p. 247. (h) Kelly's *Directory of Lancashire*, 1913. (i) V.C.H. *Lancashire*, 3, 1907, p. 221. (j) Molyneux Muniments (at Croxteth Hall, 1990), Estate Accounts, 1878–9; also letters and accounts (57/2).
Welsh Church of St John the Evangelist, Mold, Flintshire.
(a) G.R. Index. (b) *Works*. (c) *Bldr.*, 36, 1878, p. 1211. (d) *B.N.*, 36, 1879, p. 412. (e) Thomas, 2, 1911, p. 414. (f) Clwyd R.O. (P/40/1/32). Drawings dated 1876.
Llannerch Panna, Penley, Flintshire. For the Honourable George T. Kenyon. (Not completed. Now Tudor Court.)
(a) Date on building. (b) *Works*. (c) *B.N.*, 36, 1879, p. 198; 58, 1890, p. 706. (d) *B.A.* ob.

c. **1878** **Restoration and Addition of Chancel, St John's Church, Burwardsley, Cheshire.** ATTRIB.
(a) Kelly. (b) Ormerod, 2, p. 176.
* **Remodelling, Farmhouse, Rake Farm, Eccleston, Cheshire.**
E.E.O., 477, loose sheet (letter from Samuel Beckett, 20th Dec. 1878) inserted at p. 31.

1879 **Reredos, All Saints' Church, Gresford, Denbighshire.**
Vicars' Books, Gresford Vicarage.
Enrichment of Altar Table, St Peter's Church, Northop, Flintshire.
Clwyd R.O. (P/45/1/55). Drawing.

1879–80 **Grosvenor Park Baptist Chapel, Grosvenor Park Road, Chester.**
(Flèche demolished).
(a) Date on building. (b) *B.A.*, 16, 1881, pp. 632–5. (b) *Bldr.*, 49, 1885, pp. 456–

The Work of John Douglas

7. (d) *R.I.B.A.J.* ob. (e) *Chester Chronicle* ob. (f) Kelly. (g) *The Visitors' Chester Guide*, Alfred Rimmer, Chester, n.d. (*c.* 1888). p. 45.

c. 1879
* **Alterations, The Falcon Cocoa House, Lower Bridge Street, Chester.**
E.E.O., 478, p. 39.
* **Boundary Wall and Railings, Maypole, Handbridge, Chester.** (Unidentified).
E.E.O., 478, p. 39.
* **Additions, School, Pulford, Cheshire.**
(a) E.E.O. Notebook. (b) E.E.O., 478, p. 39.
* **Wheelwright's Shop, Saighton, Cheshire.** (South of Dairy Farm,)
(a) E.E.O. Notebook. (b) E.E.O., 478, p. 39.
Model Cottage, Sandiway, Cheshire. Probably built on his own land. (On Chester Road, north-east of Blue Cap Hotel.)
(a) *Works.* (b) *B.A.*, 11, 1879, p. 204.

c. 1879–80 **Terrace of Houses, Grosvenor Park Road, Chester.** Built on his own land. (Nos. 6–11).
(a) Chester City R.O. (DT/2). Town Clerk's Department. Improvement Committee. Letter from John Douglas, 16th Apr. 1889. (b) Chester City R.O. (32D). Corporation Leases, Agreements, etc. (c) *Archt.*, 79, 1908, p. 257. (d) *B.A.*, 16, 1881, pp. 632–5. (e) *Cheshire Observer* ob. (f) *Chester Chronicle* ob. (g) *R.I.B.A.J.* ob. (h) *Die Englische Baukunst der Gegenwart*, Hermann Muthesius, Leipzig and Berlin, 1900, pp. 133–4, pl. 80. (i) *The Visitors' Chester Guide*, Alfred Rimmer, Chester, n.d. (*c.* 1888), p. 45.

1880
Competition Design, Town Hall, Bootle, Lancashire.
B.N., 38, 1880, p. 40.
St Oswald's Vicarage, Parkgate Road, Chester.
(a) Date on building. (b) Drawings formerly at Vicarage (missing 1990).
Restoration of upper part of tower, St Peter's Church, Northop, Flintshire.
Clwyd R.O. (P/45/1/63). Notes on Douglas's work.
Restoration, Bent Farm, Warburton, Cheshire. For R. E. Egerton-Warburton.
(a) *B.A.*, 58, 1902, pp. 437, 442. (b) Drawings at the house.

1880–81 **Remodelling, Bryn-y-Pys, Overton, Flintshire.** For Edmund Peel. (Unexecuted scheme.)
Clwyd R.O. (A.N. 1767/63–68).
Churchyard wall, St Mary's Church, Weaverham, Cheshire.
Cheshire R.O. (P 35/2/54–66). Correspondence.

c. 1880 **Extension to Tobacco Factory, Lord Nelson Street/St Vincent Street, Liverpool.** For Cope Bros. & Co. (Demolished.)
(a) *B.A.*, 26, 1886, pp. 104, 117. (b) *B.N.*, 39, 1880, p. 528.
Repair of St Werburgh's (Old) Church, Warburton, Cheshire. For R. E. Egerton-Warburton.
Tablet in north aisle.

1881
West Lodge, Abberley, Worcestershire. For John Joseph Jones. ATTRIB.
(a) Date on building. (b) Information from Mr Alan Crawford.
* **Aldford Hall Farm, Aldford, Cheshire.** (Unexecuted scheme.)
(a) E.E.O. Drawings. (b) E.E.O., 689, pp. 441, 506. (c) E.E.O. Box No. 2 of Personal Papers of first Duke of Westminster. Letters to David Scotland from John Douglas, 11th Dec. 1884, and from H. J. Boodle, 13th Dec. 1884.
* **Eccleston Hill Lodge, Eaton Hall, Cheshire.**
(a) E.E.O. Notebook. (b) E.E.O. Photographs. (c) E.E.O., 691, p. 334. (d) *B.N.*, 44, 1883, p. 908. (e) *Bldr.* ob. (Referred to as "Flemish Gateway"). (f) *Chester Chronicle* ob. (g) *R.I.B.A.J.* ob. (h) *The Royal Academy of Arts. A Complete Dictionary of Contributors and their Work from its foundation in 1769 to 1904*, Algernon Graves, 1, 1905, p. 358. (i) Date on building.

Appendix II Catalogue of Works

St. Chad's Church, Hopwas, Staffordshire.
(a) *Works*. (b) G.R. Index. (c) *B.N.*, 41, 1881, p. 12. (d) *B.A.*, ob. (e) Kelly's *Directory of Staffordshire*, 1916.
Competition Design, Exchange Station, Liverpool. (With C. F. Findlay). *B.A.*, 16, 1881, pp. 427–8.
* **House for Estate Clerk of Works, The Cuckoo's Nest, Pulford, Cheshire.** Remodelling of earlier house.
(a) E.E.O. Notebook. (b) E.E.O. Photographs. (c) E.E.O., 689, p. 307. (Referred to as "Mrs. Brough's House." Identified through Estate Rentals).
Coffee House, Rossett, Denbighshire. For Alexander Balfour. (Now National Westminster Bank).
(a) Date on building. (b) *B.A.*, 16, 1881, pp. 560, 562.
Rowden Abbey, Bromyard, Herefordshire. For H. J. Bailey.
(a) *Works*. (b) *B.N.*, 40, 1881, p. 8; 58, 1890, p. 706. (c) *B.A.* ob. (d) *The Royal Academy of Arts. A Complete Dictionary of Contributors and their Work from its foundation in 1769 to 1904*, Algernon Graves, 1, 1905, p. 358. (e) Kelly's *Directory of Hereford and Shropshire*, 1917.

1881–2
* **Aldford Hall Farm, Aldford, Cheshire.**
(a) E.E.O. Notebook. (b) E.E.O. Drawings. (c) E.E.O., 690, pp. 14, 106, 159, 182, 190, 196, 696; 691, pp. 94, 334, 882; 692, p. 209.
Remodelling, St. Mary's Church, Betws Gwerfil Goch, Merioneth.
(a) G.R. Index. (b) *Works*. (c) *B.A.*, 16, 1881, pp. 416–17. (d) *B.N.*, 58, 1890, p. 706. (e) Thomas, 2, 1911, pp. 136–8. (f) Dolgellau Area R.O. (Z/PE/24). Drawings and papers relating to restoration *c.* 1878–82. (g) Drawings at church.
Rebuilding of North Porch after collapse of tower, Church of St. John the Baptist, Chester.
(a) E.E.O., 689, p. 441. (b) *B.A.*, 15, 1881, p. 202. (c) *B.N.*, 40, 1881, p. 516; 58, 1890, p. 706, referring to portion of church restored by Douglas. (d) *The Strangers' Handbook to Chester . . .*, George Ashdown Audsley, Chester, 1891, p. 143. (e) *A History of . . . Chester*, George Lee Fenwick, Chester, 1896, pp. 304, 521. (f) *Notes on the Churches of Cheshire*, Stephen R. Glynne, ed. J. A. Atkinson, Chetham Society, 32, 1894, p. 143. (g) Kelly. (h) *The Visitors' Chester Guide*, Alfred Rimmer, Chester, n.d. (*c.* 1888), pp. 152–5. (i) *Lectures on the History of S. John Baptist Church and Parish . . . Chester*, S. Cooper Scott, Chester, 1892, pp. 238–41, 255–8, 267–9.
South-east Vestry and Organ Chamber, St. Mary's Church, Eastham, Cheshire. ATTRIB.
(a) Date in building. (b) *The Parish of Eastham*, Isabel Tobin, Liverpool, 1920, p. 59.
* **Stud Lodge, Eaton Hall, Cheshire.**
(a) E.E.O. Notebook. (b) E.E.O. Photographs. (c) E.E.O. Drawings. 02363. (d) E.E.O., 478, p. 72; 689, p. 506.
* **Eccleston Hill, Eccleston, Cheshire.** (House, Stables and Cottage). (Altered)
(a) Dates on and in building. (b) E.E.O. Notebook. (c) E.E.O. Photographs. (d) E.E.O. Drawings. 02277. (e) E.E.O., 690, pp. 391, 409. (f) E.E.O. Box No. 2 of Personal Papers of first Duke of Westminster. Letters to David Scotland from John Douglas, 11th Dec. 1884, and from H. J. Boodle, 13th Dec. 1884.

1881–3
Grosvenor Club and North and South Wales Bank, Eastgate Street, Chester. (Now Midland Bank. Interior altered).
(a) E.E.O., 697, pp. 363, 603. (b) Chester City R.O. Minutes of the Improvement Committee. (c) *B.A.*, 16, 1881, pp. 632–5; 32, 1889, p. 272. (d) *Bldr.*, 49, 1885, pp. 456–7. (e) *B.N.*, 42, 1882, p. 696. (f) *B.N.*, 58, 1890, p. 706. (g) *Chester Chronicle* ob. (h) *R.I.B.A.J.* ob. (i) Kelly. (j) *The Visitors' Chester Guide*, Alfred Rimmer, n.d. (*c.* 1888), pp. 71–2.

The Work of John Douglas

*Pair of Cottages, Eccleston, Cheshire. (Asymmetrical block at west end of village).
(a) E.E.O. Photographs. (b) E.E.O. Drawings. 02205. (c) E.E.O., 478, p. 49; 689, pp. 307, 407, 506, 537, 547; 690, pp. 585, 594. (d) *Works*. (e) *B.A.*, 31, 1889, p. 158.

1881–4 *St. Mary's Church, Pulford, Cheshire.
(a) E.E.O. Notebook. (b) E.E.O. Photographs. (c) E.E.O. Drawings. 02200. (d) E.E.O., 478, p. 78; 689, pp. 351, 367, 459, 463, 470; 690, pp. 351, 368, 406, 494, 755; 691; pp. 73, 94, 286, 334; 697, p. 236. (e) G.R. Index. (f) *Works*. (g) *Archt.*, 29, 1883, p. 706. (h) *Bldr.*, 40, 1881, p. 293; 41, 1881, p. 284. (i) *B.N.*, 58, 1890, p. 706. (j) *B.A.* ob. (k) *B.N.* ob. (l) *Cheshire Observer* ob. (m) *Chester Chronicle* ob. (n) *R.I.B.A.J.* ob. (o) *The Royal Academy of Arts. A Complete Dictionary of Contributors and their Work from its foundation in 1769 to 1904*, Algernon Graves, 1, 1905, p. 358. (p) *Notes on the Churches of Cheshire*, Stephen R. Glynne, ed. J. A. Atkinson, Chetham Society, 32, 1894, p. 126. (q) Kelly. (r) Ormerod, 2, p. 859. (s) Cheshire R.O. (P 101/8/4a; 6–7). Plans and letter.

c. 1881 *Clock Tower, The Eastgate, Chester. (In connection with Grosvenor Club and North and South Wales Bank. Unexecuted scheme)
(a) Chester City R.O. (CCB/52). Minutes of the Improvement Committee 1870–1874, pp. 288, 291–2. (b) *B.N.*, 42, 1882, p. 696.
Barrowmore Hall (or Barrow Court), Great Barrow, Cheshire. For H. Lyle Smith. (Demolished).
(a) *B.N.*, 41, 1881, p. 494; 58, 1890, p. 706. (b) *B.A.* ob. (c) *Chester Chronicle* ob. (d) *R.I.B.A.J.* ob. (e) *The Royal Academy of Arts. A Complete Dictionary of Contributors and their Work from its foundation in 1769 to 1904*, Algernon Graves, 1, 1905, p. 358. (f) *Das Englische Haus*, Hermann Muthesius, Berlin, 1, 1904, p. 43. (g) *Cheshire Life*, November 1984, p. 30.
Farm Bailiff's House and Cottage, Mount Alyn, Rossett, Denbighshire. For Alexander Balfour. (At Yew Tree Farm.)
(a) *Works*. (b) *B.A.*, 16, 1881, pp. 576, 579.
Remodelling, St Werburgh's (Old) Church, Warburton, Cheshire. For R. E. Egerton-Warburton. (Unexecuted scheme.)
(a) Survey drawings and perspective at Warburton New Church. (b) Cheshire R.O. P/68/6/62 and 64.

1882 **Cocoa House, Public Market, Chester.** For Chester Cocoa House Co. Ltd. (Unidentified. Probably in Market Hall, demolished.)
Chester City R.O. Minutes of the Improvement Committee.
Organ chamber and vestry, St Mary's Church, Eastham, Cheshire. ATTRIB.
The Parish of Eastham, Isabel Tobin, Liverpool, 1920, p. 59.
Stables, Cock Inn, Great Budworth, Cheshire. For R. E. Egerton-Warburton. (Demolished.)
Drawing at Arley Hall.
Remodelling, Forest Hey, Sandiway, Cheshire. (House, Stables and Cottage). ATTRIB.
Date on building.
Parsonage, Tallarn Green, Flintshire. For the Honourables Georgina and Henrietta Kenyon. (Now Vicarage).
(a) *Works*. (b) *B.A.*, 36, 1891, p. 456. (c) Thomas, 1 1908, p. 450.
Churton Memorial Fountain, Whitchurch, Shropshire. For John Churton.
(a) Date on structure. (b) *B.A.*, 20, 1883, pp. 242, 244. (c) *B.N.*, 58, 1890, p. 706.

1882–3 *Farm Buildings, Almere Farm, Allington, Denbighshire.
(a) E.E.O. Notebook. (b) E.E.O., 690, pp. 351, 702,. 736; 691, pp. 334, 441; 692, p. 808; 694, pp. 227, 875.

Appendix II Catalogue of Works

Remodelling, St. Martin's Welsh Church, St. Martin's Ash, Chester. (Demolished). For Robert Roberts.
(a) Chester City R.O. (CCB/55), Minutes of the Improvement Committee 1881–1884, pp. 217, 426–7, 429–30, 508–9. (b) Chester City Library Photographic Survey. Neg. No. G.M.3/16. (c) G.R. Index. (d) Kelly. (e) *The Visitors' Chester Guide*, Alfred Rimmer, n.d. (*c.* 1888), p. 93.

★ **The Paddocks, Eccleston, Cheshire.** (House, Estate Office and Stables.) (Partially demolished 1960.)
(a) E.E.O. Notebook. (b) E.E.O. Photographs. (c) E.E.O. Drawings. 02279, 02280. (d) E.E.O., 690, pp. 52–3, 93, 132, 182, 196, 427, 495, 523–4, 594, 602, 631, 640, 868, 909, 924, 966, 978; 691, pp. 56, 647, 766; 692, p. 909; 693, pp. 323, 368. (e) *Works*. (f) *B.N.*, 45, 1883, p. 288. (g) *B.A.* ob. (h) *Cheshire Observer* ob. (i) *Chester Chronicle* ob. (j) *Chester Courant* ob. (k) *R.I.B.A.J.* ob. (l) *The Royal Academy of Arts. A Complete Dictionary of Contributors and their Work from its foundation in 1769 to 1904*, Algernon Graves, 1, 1905, p. 358.

★ **Shop and Cottage, Saighton, Cheshire.** (Now Post Office).
(a) E.E.O. Notebook. (b) E.E.O., 478, p. 76; 690, pp. 8, 14, 68, 190, 406, 523–4, 952.

★ **Farmhouse, Church Farm, Waverton, Cheshire.**
(a) E.E.O. Notebook. (Referred to as "Salmon"). (b) E.E.O. 690, pp. 53, 61, 93, 631, 868; 691, pp. 26, 94, 130, 334; 692, p. 618.

1882–4 Rebuilding, Wigfair, Cefn Meiriadog, Denbighshire. For the Revd. R. H. Howard.
(a) *Works*. (b) *B.A.*, 24, 1885, p. 200. (c) *B.N.*, 58, 1890, p. 706. (d) *B.A.* ob. (e) *Buildings of Wales: Clwyd*, Edward Hubbard, Harmondsworth, 1986, p. 118.

1882–5 St. Werburgh's Church (New Church), Warburton, Cheshire. For R. E. Egerton-Warburton.
(a) Cheshire County R.O. (b) G.R. Index. (c) *Works*. (d) *B.A.*, 22, 1884, pp. 234, 237. (e) *B.N.*, 58, 1890, p. 706. (f) *B.A.* ob. (g) *B.N.* ob. (h) *Notes on the Churches of Cheshire*, Stephen R. Glynne, ed. J. A. Atkinson, Chetham Society, 32, 1894, p. 82. (i) Kelly. (j) Drawings at church.

1883 ★ **Green Bank Lodge, Eaton Road, Eccleston, Cheshire.** (Unexecuted scheme.)
(a) E.E.O. Drawings. (b) E.E.O., 691, p. 52.

★ **Plas-y-Mynydd (formerly Plas-yn-Balls), Northop Road, Flint.** ATTRIB.
Restoration, St. Bartholomew's Church, Great Barrow, Cheshire.
(a) *Bldr.*, 45, 1883, p. 905. (b) *Journal of the Chester and North Wales Architectural, Archaeological and Historic Society*, new series, 35, part 1, 1942, pp. 23–4. (c) *Transactions of the Lancashire and Cheshire Antiquarian Society*, 52, 1937, pp. 145–6. (d) *Notes on the Churches of Cheshire*, Stephen R. Glynne, ed. J. A. Atkinson, Chetham Society, 32, 1894, p. 120. (e) Kelly.

Restoration, St. Garmon's Church, Llanfechain, Montgomeryshire.
(a) *B.N.*, 58, 1890, p. 706. (b) Thomas, 2, 1911, p. 222.

Plas Mynach, Barmouth, Merioneth. For W. H. Jones.
(a) *B.A.*, 21, 1884, pp. 218–9, 228, 230, 242, 253–4. (b) *B.N.*, 58, 1890, p. 706.

Peers Memorial Fountain and Clocktower, Ruthin, Denbighshire.
(a) *Works*. (b) *B.A.*, 20, 1883, pp. 242, 244. (c) *B.N*, 58, 1890, p. 706. (d) *Rhuddenfab's Handbook to Ruthin*, Ruthin, 1896, p. 19.

1883–4 Chapel and Vagrants' Wards, Holywell Workhouse, Flintshire.
(a) Clwyd R.O. (6/B/32/6). (b) *Bldr.*, 45, 1883, p. 402.

***c.* 1883** ★ **Alterations, Saighton House, Saighton, Cheshire.**
(a) E.E.O. Notebook. (b) E.E.O., 691, p. 338.

***c.* 1883–4** ★ **Cottages, Aldford, Cheshire.** (Two blocks of three on road to Saighton, i.e. Primrose Hill Cottages; block of three at north end of west road in village on west

The Work of John Douglas

side, and block of two with shop at north end of centre road in village on west side.)
(a) E.E.O. Notebook. (b) E.E.O., 690, pp. 944; 691, pp. 334, 347, 657, 882; 692, p. 757.
* **Cottages, Eccleston, Cheshire.** (Unidentified).
E.E.O., 690, pp. 523-4; 691, p. 334.

1884
Cheshire County Constabulary (former), Foregate Street, Chester. (No. 142).
(a) Date on building. (b) *Bldr.*, 49, 1885, pp. 456-7. (c) *B.N.*, 58, 1890, p. 706. (d) *Chester Chronicle* ob. (e) *R.I.B.A.J.* ob. (f) *The Visitors' Chester Guide*, Alfred Rimmer, Chester, n.d. (c. 1888), p. 45. (g) Cheshire R.O. (CJP 20/4/13). Drawing.
Ornamental railing and clock, The Eastgate, Chester. (Unexecuted scheme.)
Chester City R.O. Minutes of Improvement Committee, 1881-4, pp. 505, 507.
Remodelling or rebuilding, Cornist Hall, Flint. For Richard Muspratt. (Partially completed scheme.)
(a) *Works.* (b) Date on building. (c) *B.A.*, 24, 1885, p. 267. (d) *B.N.*, 58, 1890, p. 706. (e) *B.A* ob. (f) *B.N.* ob.
* **Work at the Eaton Stud, Eaton Hall, Cheshire.**
E.E.O. 691, p. 409.
Improvements to Whitley Chancel, St Deiniol's Church, Hawarden, Flintshire.
B.N., 47, 1884, p. 563.
* **Farmhouse, Ironhouse Farm, Pulford, Cheshire.**
(a) E.E.O. Notebook. (Referred to as "Bishop"). (b) E.E.O. Photographs. (c) E.E.O. Drawings. (d) E.E.O., 691, p. 276.
* **Farm Buildings, Dairy Farm, Saighton, Cheshire.**
(a) E.E.O. Notebook. (Referred to as "Dutton." Traced through Estate Rentals). (b) E.E.O., 478, p. 89; 694, p. 227.

1884-5
Chapel, Carlett Park, Eastham, Cheshire. For the Revd. W. E. Torr.
(a) *Works.* (b) Tablet in chapel. (c) *B.A.*, 27, 1887, p. 210.

1884-6
* **Farm Buildings, Cotton Abbots Farm, Waverton, Cheshire.**
(a) E.E.O. Notebook. (b) E.E.O., 478, pp. 89, 91, 105, 112; 691, pp. 372, 441; 692, pp. 618, 991; 700, p. 11. (c) *Journal of the Royal Agricultural Society of England*, 3rd ser., 4, 1893, pp. 605-7.

1884-7
St. Deiniol's Church, Criccieth, Caernarfonshire. (Closed 1988.)
(a) G.R. Index. (b) *Works.* (c) *Archt.* 33, 1885, p. 41. (d) *B.N.*, 58, 1890, p. 706. (e) *Caernarvonshire Historical Society Transactions*, 22, 1961, pp. 20-31. (f) *B.A.*, ob. (g) *B.N.* ob. (h) *Cheshire Observer* ob. (i) *Chester Chronicle* ob. (j) Drawing at St Catherine's Church, Criccieth.

c. 1884
* **Pair of Cottages, Aldford, Cheshire.** (Probably Glebe Cottages).
(a) E.E.O. Notebook. (b) E.E.O., 691, pp. 334, 882.
Bronwylfa, St Asaph, Flintshire. For T. B. Watts. (Reconstructed after a fire).
(a) Material in possession of Design Group Partnership, 9 Abbey Square, Chester. Plan. (b) *Works.* (c) *Archt.*, 37, 1887, p. 301. (d) *B.N.*, 46, 1884, p. 14; 58, 1890, p. 706. (e) *The Royal Academy of Arts. A Complete Dictionary of Contributors and their Work from its foundation in 1769 to 1904*, Algernon Graves, 1, 1905, p. 358.
Prayer Desks, Church of St. Mary and All Saints, Great Budworth, Cheshire.
For A. H. Smith-Barry.
(a) *Works.* (b) *B.A.*, 22, pp. 198, 282-4.(c). Drawing at Arley Hall dated 1883.

1885
Alterations, House, Greyfriars/Nuns Road, Chester.
(a) Date on building. (b) Chester City R.O. (DT/2). Town Clerk's Department. Letter from Douglas & Fordham, 25th Aug. 1885.
Remodelling, Castle Hotel, Conwy, Caernarfonshire.

Appendix II Catalogue of Works

(a) *Works.* (b) *B.A.*, 42, 1894, pp. 272–4; 48, 1897, pp. 182, 184. (d) Hotel brochure.
Additions, Jodrell Hall, Cheshire. (Now Terra Nova School.)
(a) Date on building. (b) *B.N.*, 58, 1890, p. 706. (c) *B.N.*, ob.
Smithy, Wheelwright's Shop, and two Cottages, Kirkby, Lancashire. For fourth Earl of Sefton.
Molyneux Muniments (at Croxteth Hall 1990). Estate Accounts 1885.
Six Labourers' Cottages, Netherton, Lancashire. For fourth Earl of Sefton.
Molyneux Muniments (at Croxteth Hall 1990). Estate Accounts 1885.
Smithy, Tarbock, Lancashire. For fourth Earl of Sefton.
Molyneux Muniments (at Croxteth Hall 1990). Estate Accounts 1885.

1885–6 * **Black and White Cottages, Pulford Approach, Eaton Hall, Cheshire.**
(a) E.E.O. Notebook. (b) E.E.O. Photographs. (c) E.E.O. Drawings. 02822. (d) E.E.O., 478, pp. 90, 112; 691, pp. 945, 968; 692, pp. 190, 220, 251, 367, 653, 703, 757. (e) *Works.* (f) *B.N.*, 51, 1886, p. 1020. (g) *Modern Cottage Architecture*, Maurice B. Adams, London, 1904, p. 26, pl. XXX.
* **Shelter Shed, Eccleston, Cheshire.** (North-east of Eccleston Lodge).
(a) E.E.O. Notebook. (b) E.E.O., 478, p. 112; 692, pp. 334, 350, 363, 398, 417.
* **Gorstella Farm, Gorstella, Cheshire.**
(a) E.E.O. Notebook. (b) E.E.O. Photographs. (c) E.E.O., 478, pp. 91, 99, 112; 691, pp. 276, 919; 692, pp. 228, 248; 693, pp. 119, 763.
* **Farm Buildings, Yew Tree Farm, Poulton, Cheshire.**
(a) E.E.O. Notebook. (b) E.E.O. Photographs. (c) E.E.O., 478, pp. 105, 112; 692, pp. 127, 144, 352, 491. (Referred to in E.E.O. records as "Jackson's" and "Cookson." Identified through Estate Rentals).
* **Brookside Farm, Pulford, Cheshire.**
(a) E.E.O. Notebook. (b) E.E.O. Photographs. (c) E.E.O., 478, pp. 85, 96–7, 104, 112; 691, p. 954. (Referred to in E.E.O. records as "Dyke's". Identified through Estate Rentals).

1885–7 **Tower, St John's Church, Hartford, Cheshire.**
(a) G.R. Index. (b) Kelly. (c) *Hartford Parish Church, 1875–1975*, Ian Newton, 1975, p. 14.
Mansion and two Lodges, Abbeystead, Wyresdale, Lancashire. For fourth Earl of Sefton.
(a) *Works.* (b) *Archt.*, 40, 1888, p. 195; 78, 1907, p. 377. (c) *B.A.*, 25, 1886, p. 489; 40, 1893, pp. 182–4. (d) *Bldr.*, 50, 1886, p. 846; 52, 1887, p. 759. (e) *B.N.*, 51, 1886, p. 54; 58, 1890, p. 706. (f) *B.A.* ob. (g) *Bldr.* ob. (h) *B.N.* ob. (i) *Cheshire Observer* ob. (j) *Chester Chronicle* ob. (k) *Chester Courant* ob. (l) *R.I.B.A.J.* ob. (m) *The Royal Academy of Arts. A Complete Dictionary of Contributors and their Work from its foundation in 1769 to 1904*, Algernon Graves, 1. 1905, p. 358. (n) *Kelly's Directory of Lancashire*, 1913. (o) *Das Englische Haus*, Hermann Muthesius, Berlin, 1, 1904, p. 136. (p) *History of Over Wyresdale*, D. Schofield, Lancaster, 1909, pp. 55–6, 89. (q) *V.C.H. Lancashire*, 8, 1914, pp. 77–8. (r) *Modern Homes*, T. Raffles Davison, London, 1909, p. 52. (s) *V.C.H. Lancashire*, 8, 1914, pp. 77–8. (t) Molyneux Muniments (at Croxteth Hall 1990). Estate Accounts 1884–9.

c. 1885–6 **Institute and Baths, Tamworth, Staffordshire.** For the Revd. William MacGregor. (Demolished).
(a) *Works.* (b) *Archt.*, 35, 1886, p.8. (b) *B.A.*, 37, 1892, p.282. (c) *The Royal Academy of Arts. A Complete Dictionary of Contributors and their Work from its foundation in 1769 to 1904*, 1, 1905, p. 358. (d) *Kelly's Directory of Staffordshire*, 1916. (e) Photograph at N.B.R.

1886 **Additions to Manager's House, Chester Boat Co., The Groves, Chester.** (Demolished).
Chester City R.O. (DT/2). Town Clerk's Department, Improvement Committee.

The Work of John Douglas

Letters from Douglas & Fordham, 2nd and 16th Feb. 1886.
Widening and improvement of Northgate Street, Chester. (Unexecuted scheme.)
(a) Chester City R.O. (YS/1/3–4). (b) Supplement to *Cheshire Observer*, 8th Jan. 1887.
Restoration, St. Peter's Church, The Cross, Chester.
(a) *B.N.*, 58, 1890. p. 706. (b) *A History of . . . Chester*, George Lee Fenwick, Chester, 1896, p. 308. (c) Kelly. (d) *The Visitors' Chester Guide*, Alfred Rimmer, Chester, n.d. (*c.* 1888), p. 83. (e) *A History of the Church of St. Peter in Chester*, Frank Simpson, Chester, 1909, pp. 44–5.
Lych-Gate, St. Mary's Church, Eastham, Cheshire. ATTRIB.
The Parish of Eastham, Isabel Tobin, Liverpool, 1920, p. 59.
* **Additions, Halkyn Castle, Flintshire.**
(a) Date on building. (b) *B.N.*, 58, 1890, p. 706. (c) *B.N.* ob.

1886–7 * **Farm Buildings, Bank Farm, Aldford, Cheshire.**
(a) E.E.O. Notebook. (b) E.E.O., 478, pp. 90, 112; 692, pp. 744, 808. (Referred to in E.E.O. records as "L. Thomas." Identified through Estate Rentals).
* **Smithy, Aldford, Cheshire.** (Between Bank Farm and Oak Farm).
(a) E.E.O., 478, pp. 90, 112; 692, p. 744.
Bell Tower, Church of St. John the Baptist, Chester.
(a) Cheshire County R.O. (b) *A History of . . . Chester*, George Lee Fenwick, Chester, 1896, p. 304. (b) *Notes on the Churches of Cheshire*, Stephen R. Glynne, ed. J. A. Atkinson, Chetham Society, 32, 1894, p. 143. (d) Kelly. (e) *The Visitors' Chester Guide*, Alfred Rimmer, Chester, n.d. (*c.* 1888), pp. 155–6. (f) *Lectures on the History of S. John Baptist Church and Parish . . . Chester*, S. Cooper Scott, Chester, 1892, pp. 273–4. Reference to work at the church by Douglas in (g) *Chester Chronicle* ob., and (h) *R.I.B.A.J.* ob. (i) Cheshire R.O. (P 51/7/147). Elevations. (j) Cheshire R.O. (EDP 73/2/pt 2). Plan of vestry dated 1886.
Baptist Church (now Union Church), Bridge Lane, Frodsham, Cheshire. (Much enlarged 1912–15.)
Church Committee Minute Books. (Information from Mr Oliver Bott.)
* **Farm Building and Remodelling of Farmhouse, Cotton Farm, Waverton, Cheshire.**
(a) E.E.O. Notebook. (b) E.E.O., 478, pp. 99, 112; 692, pp. 398, 491, 537, 566, 685, 774; 694, p. 227. (Referred to in E.E.O. records as "Toft." Identified from Estate Rentals).

1886–92 **Christ Church, Rossett, Denbighshire.**
(a) *Works.* (b) G.R. Index. (c) *Bldr.*, 51, 1886, pp. 482, 492–3. (d) *B.N.*, 50, 1886, p. 822. (e) *B.A.* ob. (f) *Bldr.* ob. (g) *The Royal Academy of Arts. A Complete Dictionary of Contributors and their Work from its foundation in 1769 to 1904*, Algernon Graves, 1, 1905, p. 358. (h) Thomas, 3, 1913, pp. 288–9.

*c.*1886 **House, Largs, Ayrshire.** For W. G. Crum.
(a) *B.A.*, 26, 1886, pp. 80, 82. (b) *Chester Chronicle* ob.
Restoration, St. Oswald's Church, Malpas, Cheshire.
(a) *B.A.*, 26, 1886, pp. 374, 387. (b) *Bldr.*, 22, 1864, p. 33. (c) *B.N.*, 58, 1890, p. 706. (d) *Journal of the Chester and North Wales Architectural, Archaeological and Historic Society*, new series, 37, part 2, 1949, pp. 208–11. (e) *Notes on the Churches of Cheshire*, Stephen R. Glynne, ed. J. A. Atkinson, Chetham Society, 32, 1894, p. 38. (f) Kelly.
Coetmor, Bryn Goodman, Ruthin, Denbighshire. For Col. Cornwallis West.
B.A., 31, 1889, pp. 426, 428.
Dedwyddfa, Bryn Goodman, Ruthin, Denbighshire. ATTRIB.
Date on building.

Appendix II Catalogue of Works

1887 * **Restoration, North Aisle, Church of St. John the Baptist, Chester.**
(a) E.E.O. Notebook. (Refers to work at church). (b) E.E.O., 478, pp. 112, 131; 692, pp. 909, 921, 947. (c) Reference to work at church by Douglas in *R.I.B.A.J.* ob. (d) *Notes on the Churches of Cheshire*, Stephen R. Glynne, ed. J. A. Atkinson, Chetham Society, 32, 1894, p. 143. (e) Kelly. (f) *The Visitors' Chester Guide*, Alfred Rimmer, Chester, n.d. (c. 1888), pp. 155–6. (g) *Lectures on the History of S. John Baptist Church and Parish . . . Chester*, S. Cooper Scott, Chester, 1892, p. 276.
* **Work after a Fire, Farm Buildings, Yew Tree Farm, Poulton, Cheshire.**
E.E.O., 478, pp. 105, 112. (Referred to as "Jackson." Identified through Estate Rentals).

1887–8 * **Farm Buildings, Oak Farm, Aldford, Cheshire.**
(a) E.E.O. Notebook. (b) E.E.O. Drawings. 02012. (c) E.E.O., 478, pp. 90, 112; 693, pp. 29, 32. (Referred to in E.E.O. records as "Wells").
* **Pair of Cottages and Wheelwright's Shop, Balderton, Cheshire.** (Immediately south of Cheese Factory).
(a) E.E.O. Notebook. (b) E.E.O. Photographs. (c) E.E.O., 478, pp. 105, 112; 692, p. 925; 693, p. 22; 704, p. 478.
* **Pair of Cottages, Belgrave, Cheshire.** (¼ m. north of Belgrave Lodge on west side of Wrexham Road).
(a) E.E.O. Notebook. (b) E.E.O. Photographs. (c) E.E.O. Drawings. (d) E.E.O., 478, pp. 105, 112; 693, p. 418.
* **Sexton's Cottage, Church of St. Mary-without-the-Walls, Handbridge, Chester.**
(a) E.E.O. Notebook. (b) E.E.O. Drawings. (c) E.E.O., 478, pp. 112, 131; 692, pp. 964, 969, 990; 694, p. 227. (d) *B.A.*, 42, 1894, pp. 273–4.
Nave, St. Paul's Church, Colwyn Bay, Denbighshire.
(a) G.R. Index. (b) *B.A.*, 27, 1887, p. 342. (c) *B.N.*, 52, 1887, p. 874; 58, 1890, p. 706. (d) *The Royal Academy of Arts. A Complete Dictionary of Contributors and their Work from its foundation in 1769 to 1904*, Algernon Graves, 1, 1905, p. 358. (e) Thomas, 3, 1913, pp. 202–3. (f) Guide book: *The Story of the Parish Church of Colwyn Bay*, W. Hugh Rees, Gloucester, 1970. References to the church being by Douglas in (g) *B.A.* ob. (h) *Bldr.* ob. (i) *B.N.* ob. (j) *Cheshire Observer* ob. (k) *Chester Chronicle* ob. (l) *Chester Courant* ob. (m) *Liverpool Daily Post* ob. (n) *R.I.B.A.J.* ob.
* **Ferry House, Eccleston, Cheshire.**
(a) E.E.O. Notebook. (b) E.E.O. Photographs. (c) E.E.O. Drawings. 02812, 02813. (d) E.E.O., 478, pp. 90, 112; 693, pp. 40, 418; 694, p. 227.
* **Wrexham Road Cottages, Eccleston, Cheshire.**
(a) E.E.O. Notebook. (b) E.E.O. Photographs. (c) E.E.O., 478, pp. 105, 112; 692, p. 925; 693, p. 418; 694, pp. 223, 227; 704, p. 478.
* **Smithy and Pair of Cottages, Gorstella, Cheshire.**
(a) E.E.O. Notebook. (b) E.E.O. Photographs. (c) E.E.O., 478, pp. 112, 131; 694, p. 227; 693, pp. 167, 418.
Strongroom, Hawarden Castle, Flintshire. For W. E. Gladstone.
(a) Clwyd R.O. (B/33/6). W. E. Gladstone. Cost of Building Strong Room at Hawarden. (b) *B.N.* ob. (c) *Chester Chronicle* ob. (d) *R.I.B.A.J.* ob. Reference to work at Hawarden Castle by Douglas in (e) *B.N.*, 58, 1890, p. 706.
* **Block of Three Cottages, Pulford, Cheshire.** (West side of Wrexham Road, opposite road to Poulton. Altered).
(a) E.E.O. Notebook. (b) E.E.O. Photographs. (c) E.E.O., 478, pp. 105, 112; 693, pp. 24, 32, 418

1887–9 * **Restoration, St. Peter's Church, Waverton, Cheshire.**
(a) E.E.O. Notebook. (b) E.E.O., 478, p. 132; 479, p. 18; 693, pp. 377, 418, 555,

The Work of John Douglas

671, 792; 694, p. 87. (c) E.E.O. Drawings. (d) *Transactions of the Lancashire and Cheshire Antiquarian Society*, 52, 1937, pp. 142–3. (e) *Notes on the Churches of Cheshire*, Stephen R. Glynne, ed. J. A. Atkinson, Chetham Society, 32, 1894, p. 132. (f) Kelly.
* **Brookdale Farm, Guy Lane, Waverton.**
(a) E.E.O. Notebook. (b) E.E.O. Drawings. 02544. (c) E.E.O., 478, p. 107; 479, p. 17; 693, p. 304; 694, pp. 219, 227, 875. (Referred to in E.E.O. records as "Chalton.")

1888 **Winning Competition Design. Friars School, Bangor, Caernarfonshire.**
Bldr., 56, 1888, p. 381.
* **Shop Premises, Foregate Street, Chester.** (In connection with Parker's Buildings. Unexecuted scheme).
B.N., 55, 1888, p. 41.
Parsonage, Cotebrook, Cheshire.
(a) *B.A.*, 38, 1892, p. 58. (b) Kelly.
* **Shelter Shed, Ferry House, Eccleston, Cheshire.**
E.E.O., 693, p. 462.

1888–9 * **Parker's Buildings, Foregate Street, Chester.** (Model tenements).
(a) E.E.O. Notebook. (b) E.E.O. Drawings. 01560. (c) E.E.O., 478, p. 132; 479, pp. 10, 12, 17, 19, 21; 693, pp. 429, 436, 496, 558, 671, 795; 694, pp. 227, 356, 371, 416; 695, pp. 75, 158, 490; 698, p. 48; 699, p. 96; 701, pp. 723, 735. (d) *B.N.*, 55, 1888, p. 41. (e) *B.A.* ob. (f) Notes compiled by S. J. Lomas for Northern Counties Housing Association Ltd., 1982.
Restoration, St Mary's Church, Cilcain, Flintshire.
(a) Clwyd R.O. Cilcain Vestry Book, 1829–95. (b) *B.N.*, 58, 1890, p. 706. (c) *Cilcain and its Parish Church*, Frank Simpson, Chester, 1912, pp. 8–9, 19, 32, 42. (d) Thomas, 2, 1911, pp. 368–9.
* **Hatton Heath Lodge, Eaton Hall, Cheshire.**
(a) E.E.O. Notebook. (b) E.E.O. Drawings. 02066. (c) E.E.O., 478, p. 107; 479, p. 18; 694, p. 227.
* **Saighton Lane Farm, Saighton, Cheshire.**
(a) E.E.O. Notebook. (b) E.E.O. Drawings. 02152, 02153. (Also unsorted). (c) E.E.O., 478, p. 132; 479, p. 17; 693, pp. 571, 792; 694, pp. 219, 875; 695, p. 807. (d) Works. (e) *Bldr.*, 54, 1888, p. 427. (f) *B.N.*, 54, 1888, p. 838. (g) *The Royal Academy of Arts. A Complete Dictionary of Contributors and their Work from its foundation in 1769 to 1904*, Algernon Graves, 1. 1905, p. 358. (Referred to in E.E.O. records as "Jones").
* **Cheese Room, Cotton Abbots Farm, Waverton, Cheshire.**
E.E.O., 478, p. 107; 479, p. 18; 693, p. 979.

c. 1888 **Home Farm, Abberley, Worcestershire.** For John Joseph Jones (died 1888). (Converted into housing.)
(a) Drainage plan dated 1889, at Home Farm. (b) Initials J.J.J. on building.

c. 1888–9 **Gravestone of Sir Richard Brooke, St. Mary's Churchyard, Halton, Cheshire.**
B.A., 31, 1889, p. 426.
Memorial Tablet to Sir Richard Brooke, St. Mary's Church, Halton, Cheshire.
B.A., 31, 1889, p. 245.

1889 * **Outbuildings, Ferry House, Eccleston, Cheshire.**
(a) E.E.O. Notebook. (b) E.E.O., 479, p. 18.
West Wing, Gloddaeth, Caernarfonshire. For Lady Augusta Mostyn. (Now St David's College.)
(a) Booklet of 1906 at the house. (b) *Country Life*, 7th Dec. 1978, p. 1969.
Porch, Hawarden Castle, Flintshire. For W. E. Gladstone.
(a) *Chester Chronicle* ob. (b) *R.I.B.A.J.* ob.
Church Hall, Warburton, Cheshire. For R. E. Egerton-Warburton. ATTRIB.

Appendix II Catalogue of Works

1889-90 * **Farm Buildings and Alterations and Additions to Farmhouse, Elms Farm, Bretton, Flintshire.**
(a) E.E.O. Notebook. (b) E.E.O. Photographs. (c) E.E.O., 479, pp. 14, 19; 694, p. 115. (Referred to in E.E.O. records as "Higgonson." Identified through Estate Rentals).
Tower, Holy Trinity Church, Capenhurst, Cheshire.
(a) G.R. Index. (b) Kelly.
* **Shop Premises, No. 117 Foregate Street, Chester.** (In connection with Parker's Buildings).
(a) E.E.O. Drawings. (b) E.E.O., 479, pp. 10, 19; 695, p. 922; 696, p. 234; 698, p. 48.
* **House of Shelter, Vicar's Lane, Chester.**
(a) E.E.O. Notebook. (b) E.E.O. Drawings. 01691. (c) E.E.O., 479, pp. 10, 18; 693, p. 941; 694, p. 470. (d) *B.A.*, 32, 1889, p. 254.
* **Belgrave Lodge, Eaton Hall, Cheshire.** (Including Gatehouse, executed or partially executed but immediately demolished).
(a) E.E.O. Notebook. (b) E.E.O. Photographs. (c) E.E.O. Drawings. (d) E.E.O., 479, pp. 10, 19, 23, 55; 480, p. 1; 692, p. 429; 694, p. 37; 695, p. 807.
* **Alterations and Additions, Farmhouse, Green Farm, Poulton, Cheshire.**
(a) E.E.O. Notebook. (b) E.E.O. Photographs. (c) E.E.O. 479, pp. 11, 20; 695, p. 807. (Referred to in E.E.O. records as "R. Pickering," and "Drewson." Identified through Estate Rentals).

1889-91 * **Pair of Cottages, Aldford, Cheshire.** (South of Grosvenor Arms).
(a) E.E.O. Notebook. (b) E.E.O. Drawings. 01867. (c) E.E.O., 478, p. 107; 479, p. 19; 695, p. 807.
* **Pair of Cottages, Pulford.** (Probably block at north end of village on east side of Wrexham Road).
(a) E.E.O. Notebook. (b) E.E.O. Photographs. (c) E.E.O., 478, p. 107; 479, p. 19.
Nag's Head Inn, Thornton, Lancashire. For fourth Earl of Sefton.
Molyneux Muniments (at Croxteth Hall 1990). Estate Accounts 1891; Contract 1889 (70/3).
* **Pair of Cottages, Waverton, Cheshire.** (Southernmost of two blocks north of church on east side of village street).
(a) E.E.O. Drawings. 02575. (b) E.E.O., 478, p. 107; 479, p. 19. (c) *Modern Cottage Architecture*, Maurice B. Adams, London, 1904, p. 23, pl. IX.
Nave, St. Andrew's Church, West Kirby, Cheshire.
(a) G.R. Index. (b) Kelly. References to the church being by Douglas in (c) *B.A.* ob. (d) B.N. ob. (e) *Cheshire Observer* ob. (f) *Chester Courant* ob. (g) *Liverpool Daily Post* ob.

1889-92 **Grammar School, Ruthin, Denbighshire.**
(a) *Chester Chronicle* ob. (b) Thomas, 2, 1911, pp. 126-9.

1889-95 **Church of St. John the Divine, Barmouth, Merioneth.**
(a) Envelope of papers relating to Barmouth Church in possession of Design Group Partnership, 9 Abbey Square, Chester. (b) Correspondence, accounts, and plan (1891-5) at church. (c) *The Fall of Barmouth Church*, pamphlet in John Johnson Collection, Bodleian Library, Oxford, Box marked "Church Restorations." (d) G.R. Index. (e) *A.A.*, 1899, p. 36. (f) *Bldr.*, 55, 1888, 27th Oct., p. ii; 56, 1889, pp. 430, 327, 444-5; 57, 1889, pp. 10-11. (f) *B.N.*, 58, 1890, p. 706. (g) *B.A.* ob. (h) *Bldr.* ob. (i) *B.N.* ob. (j) *Cheshire Observer* ob. (k) *Chester Chronicle* ob. (l) *R.I.B.A.J.* ob. (m) *The Royal Academy of Arts. A Complete Dictionary of Contributors and their Work from its foundation in 1769 to 1904*, Algernon Graves, 1, 1905, p. 358.
[In 1971 Mr A.C. Bennett informed the author that 'some years ago' he had

259

The Work of John Douglas

presented the Vicar with 'some detail drawings of the west end'. These are now missing.]

c. 1889
* **Group of Four Cottages, Eccleston, Cheshire.** (Nos. 1–4 Hill Road, on west corner of road to Chester.)
(a) E.E.O. Photographs. (b) *Works.* (c) *B.A.*, 34, 1890, p. 170. (d) *Bldr.*, 56, 1889, p. 68. (e) *Bldr.* ob.
* **Work at Old Smithy and Piggeries, Gorstella, Cheshire.** (Unidentified.)
E.E.O. 479, p. 18.

1890
* **Shop Sign, No. 32 Eastgate Row, Chester.**
E.E.O. 694, p. 760.
Abbotsford, Warrington Road, Cuddington, Cheshire. For Jabez Thompson.
(a) Date on building. (b) Drawings at house.
* **Cheese Room, Wrexham Road Farm, Eccleston, Cheshire.**
E.E.O. 479, p. 21; 694, pp. 412, 554.
* **Pair of Cottages, Eccleston, Cheshire.** (Unidentified).
E.E.O., 479, pp. 11, 20; 695, p. 807.
* **Extension to Dairy, Gorstella Farm. Gorstella, Cheshire.**
E.E.O., 479. p. 21.
* **Restoration and Addition of Vestry, St. Peter's Church, Hargrave, Cheshire.** ATTRIB.
(a) Inscription in church. (b) *Journal of the Chester and North Wales Architectural, Archaeological and Historic Society*, new series, 35, part 1, 1942, pp. 15–16. (c) Kelly.
Porch, Hawarden Castle, Flintshire. For Gladstone family.
(a) *Country Life*, 141, 1967, pp. 1676, 1679–80. (b) *Chester Chronicle* ob. (c) *R.I.B.A.J.* ob.
School, Stockton-on-Teme, Worcestershire. For William Jones. ATTRIB.
(a) Date on building. (b) Information from Mr Alan Crawford.

1890–91
* **Ford Lane, Aldford, Cheshire.**
(a) E.E.O. Drawings. 02005. (b) E.E.O., 479, pp. 20, 45; 694, pp. 402, 490, 562, 824, 875; 695, pp. 188, 490. (Referred to in E.E.O. records as "Clarke").
* **Methodist Chapel, Aldford, Cheshire.**
(a) E.E.O., 479, pp. 22, 45; 694, pp. 639, 710; 695, p. 490 (b) E.E.O. Drawing. (c) *Bldr.*, 61, 1891, p. 246. (d) *Bldr.* ob.
* **Remodelling, Shop Premises, No. 113 Foregate Street, Chester.** (In connection with Parker's Buildings).
E.E.O., 479, pp. 12, 21; 695, p. 490.
* **Remodelling, Bruera Lodge, Eaton Hall, Cheshire.**
(a) E.E.O. Drawings. 02815. (b) E.E.O., 479, pp. 12, 22; 694, p. 490; 695, p. 490.
* **Obelisk, Belgrave Avenue, Eaton Hall, Cheshire.**
(a) E.E.O. Estate Papers. Accounts and Miscellaneous Papers re Building. No. 7. (Two drawings). (b) E.E.O., 479, pp. 11, 20; 694, pp. 618, 834; 695, p. 490.

1890–92
* **Hope's Place Farm, Bretton, Flintshire.**
(a) E.E.O. Photographs. (b) E.E.O., 479, pp. 14, 21; 694, pp. 679, 875.
* **Dodleston Lane Farm, Dodleston, Cheshire.**
(a) E.E.O. Photographs. (b) E.E.O., 479, pp. 14, 20; 694, p. 622; 695, p. 490.

1891
* **Shop Sign, No. 67 Watergate Row, Chester.**
(a) E.E.O., 695, p. 55. (b) Address ascertained from Kelly, 1892.
Cottage Hospital, Droitwich, Worcestershire. For Dyson Perrins. (Now St John's Hospital for Rheumatic Diseases.)
(a) *B.A.*, 50, 1898, pp. 291–2. (b) Date on building.
Well Cover, St. Helen's Well, Sefton, Lancashire. For fourth Earl of Sefton. (Demolished).

Appendix II Catalogue of Works

The Ancient Crosses and Holy Wells of Lancashire, Henry Taylor, Manchester, 1906, p. 171.
* **Smithy, Smithy House, etc., Saighton, Cheshire**.
E.E.O., 479, pp.12, 21; 695, p. 490.

1891-2 **Stables and adjoining pair of cottages, Abbeystead, Wyresdale, Lancashire**. For fourth Earl of Sefton.
(a) *Works*. (b) *B.A.*, 42, 1894, pp. 289-90. (c) Molyneux Muniments (at Croxteth Hall 1990). Estate Accounts 1891-2.
* **Churton Heath Lodge, Bruera, Cheshire**.
(a) E.E.O. Drawings, 02070. (b) E.E.O., 479, pp. 15, 22; 695, pp. 184, 799.
* **Shelter Shed, Edgar's Field, Handbridge, Chester**. (Demolished.)
E.E.O., 479, pp. 13, 22; 695, pp. 116, 132.
Restoration, St Berres's Church, Llanferres, Denbighshire.
(a) *Archaeologia Cambrensis*, 5th series, 9, 1892, p. 163. (b) *Slater's Directory of North and Mid Wales*, 1895. (c) Thomas, 2, 1911, p. 401. (d) G.R. Index. (e) *Llanferres Parish Church*, T. W. Pritchard, c. 1979.
Restoration, St Michael's Church, Marbury, Cheshire.
(a) *B.N.*, 63, 1892, p. 95. (b) *Notes on the Churches of Cheshire*, Stephen R. Glynne, ed. J. A. Atkinson, Chetham Society, 32, 1894, p. 20. (c) Kelly.
Mrs Whitaker's Farmhouse, Barn and Shippons, Wyresdale, Lancashire. For fourth Earl of Sefton.
Molyneux Muniments (at Croxteth Hall 1990). Estate Accounts 1891-2.

1891-3 * **Remodelling, Grosvenor Arms, Aldford, Cheshire**.
(a) E.E.O. Drawings, 01907. (b) E.E.O., 479, pp. 23, 45; 695, pp. 440, 675; 696, pp. 12, 257; 697, pp. 157, 227.
* **Bretton Hall Farm, Bretton, Flintshire**.
(a) E.E.O. Photographs. (b) E.E.O., 479, pp. 15, 22; 695, pp. 119, 807.

c. 1891 **Remodelling, Bolehall Manor, Tamworth, Staffordshire**. For the Revd. William MacGregor.
(a) *B.A.*, 37, 1892, pp. 334, 336. (b) Photograph by Bedford Lemere at N.B.R. dated 1891.

c. 1891-2 **St. James's Church, Haydock, Lancashire**.
(a) G.R. Index. (b) *Bldr.*, 61, 1891, p. 90; 63, 1892, p. 38. (c) *Bldr*. ob. (d) *B.N.* ob. (e) Kelly's *Directory of Lancashire*, 1913.

c. 1891-3 **Memorial Tablet to W. H. Gladstone, St. Deiniol's Church, Hawarden, Flintshire**. For W. E. Gladstone.
(a) *B.A.*, 39, 1893, pp. 112, 114. (b) Thomas, 2, 1911, p. 380.

1892 **Reredos, St. Oswald's Church, Backford, Cheshire**.
(a) *B.A.*, 39, 1893, pp. 76, 78. (b) *Notes on the Churches of Cheshire*, Stephen R. Glynne, ed. J. A. Atkinson, Chetham Society, 32, 1894, p. 119.
St. Wenefrede's Church, Bickley, Cheshire. For the Marquess of Cholmondeley.
(a) *B.A.*, 46, 1896, pp. 254, 256. (b) *B.N.*, 63, 1892, p. 9. (c) *B.A.* ob. (d) Kelly.
South-west Vestry and formation of Baptistery, St. Mary's Church, Eastham, Cheshire. ATTRIB.
The Parish of Eastham, Isabel Tobin, Liverpool 1920, p. 60.
Cottages, Park Road, Port Sunlight, Cheshire. For Lever Bros. Ltd. (Nos. 19-23, including Bridge Cottage, No. 23).
(a) Date on building. (b) Records, Estate Department, Unilever Merseyside Ltd. (c) *Bldr*. ob. (d) *B.N.* ob. (e) *Port Sunlight*, T. Raffles Division, London, 1916, pp. 11, 23, pl. 12. (f) *The Buildings Erected at Port Sunlight and Thornton Hough*, Paper read by W. H. Lever, at meeting of the Architectural Association, London, March 21st, 1902.

The Work of John Douglas

Cottages, Wood Street, Port Sunlight, Cheshire. For Lever Bros. Ltd. (Nos. 17–23).
(a) Date on building. (b) Records, Estate Department, Unilever Merseyside Ltd. (c) *Port Sunlight*, T. Raffles Davison, London, 1916, p. xii, pl. 28.
Pair of Cottages, Sandiway, Cheshire. (On Chester road, north-east of Blue Cap Hotel). ATTRIB.
Date on building.
Kenyon Cottages, Tallarn Green, Flintshire. For the Honourable Henrietta Kenyon.
(a) *Works*. (b) *B.A.*, 42, 1894, pp. 289–90, 292.
Remodelling, The Wern, Tremadoc, Caernarfonshire. For R. M. Greaves.
(a) *A.A.*, 1892, p. 26. (b) *Bldr.*, 62, 1892, pp. 432–3. (c) *B.N.*, 62, 1892, p. 697. (d) *The Royal Academy of Arts. A Complete Dictionary of Contributors and their Work from its foundation in 1769 to 1904*, Algernon Graves, 1, 1905, p.359.
Altar Rails, St Werburgh's (New) Church, Warburton, Cheshire.
Cheshire R.O. (P 68/6/132–3; 135; 138; 141–2).
* **Inglenook, Cotton Hall Farm, Waverton, Cheshire**.
E.E.O., 479, p. 78; 695, p. 734.

1892–3
* **Re-Slating, Church of St. Mary-without-the-Walls, Handbridge, Chester**.
E.E.O., 479, pp. 24, 31.
* **Conversion of Coach-House into Reading Room, Eccleston, Cheshire**.
(a) E.E.O. Photographs. (b) E.E.O., 479, p. 22.
Glangwna, Caernarfon. For J. E. Greaves.
(a) *Works*. (b) *A.A.*, 1893, 34–5. (c) *Bldr.*, 64, 1893, pp. 194, 403. (d) *B.A.* ob. (e) *Bldr.* ob. (f) *The Royal Academy of Arts. A Complete Dictionary of Contributors and their Work from its foundation in 1769 to 1904*, Algernon Graves, 1, 1905, p. 359.
* **Broad Hey Farm, Lower Kinnerton, Cheshire**.
(a) E.E.O. Photographs. (b) E.E.O., 479, pp. 24, 31; 695, pp. 572, 636.
* **Wallet's Farm, Straight Mile, Poulton, Cheshire**.
(a) E.E.O. Photographs. (b) E.E.O., 479, pp. 23, 31; 695, pp. 568, 572. (Referred to in E.E.O. records as "Ellis Gillam").
St David's Welsh Church (Dewi Sant), Broad Street, Rhosllannerchrugog, Denbighshire.
(a) Plan dated 1892 at St Mary's Church, Johnstown. (b) *Wrexham Advertiser*, 29th Sep. 1892. (c) *Bldr.* ob. (d) Thomas, 3, 1913, p. 273. (e) G.R. Index. (f) Typescript notes at St John's Vicarage, Rhosllannerchrugog.

1892–4
* **Farm Buildings, Lea Hall Farm, Aldford, Cheshire**.
(a) E.E.O. Drawings, 01914, 01916. (b) E.E.O., 479, pp. 16, 24; 695, p. 740. (c) *Journal of the Royal Agricultural Society of England*, 3rd series, 4, 1893, pp. 593–5.
* **Alterations and Additions, Eccleston Hill, Cheshire**.
(a) E.E.O. Drawings, 02270, 02276. (b) E.E.O., 479, pp. 24, 45; 695, p. 882; 697, pp. 363, 737.
Remodelling, Church, Over Wyresdale, Lancashire. For fourth Earl of Sefton.
(a) Molyneux Muniments (at Croxteth Hall, 1990). Estate Accounts 1892–5. (b) Kelly's *Directory of Lancashire*, 1913. (c) *History of Over Wyresdale*, D. Schofield, Lancaster, 1909, pp. 89–90. (d) V.C.H. *Lancashire*, 8, 1914, p. 78.

c. 1892
* **Shop Signs, Chester**. (Unidentified).
E.E.O., 479, p. 23.
* **Deer Fence, Eaton Hall, Cheshire**.
E.E.O., 479, p. 23.

1893
Brocksford Hall, Derbyshire. For C. W. Jervis Smith.
(a) *Works*. (b) *A.A.*, 1893, p. 108. (c) *B.N.*, 64, 1893, pp. 867–8. (d) *B.A.* ob.
New Sanctuary, Christ Church, Chester.
(a) Inscription in church. References to the church being by Douglas in (b) G.R.

Appendix II Catalogue of Works

Index, (c) *B.A.* ob., (d) *B.N.* ob., (e) *Cheshire Observer* ob., (f) *Chester Courant* ob., and (g) *Liverpool Daily Post* ob.

Cottage and Stables, Nicholas Street, Chester. (Demolished).
(a) Chester City R.O. (CCB/58). Minutes of the Improvement Committee 1890-1894, p. 593. (b) Chester City Library. Photographic Survey. Neg. No. G.M.3/23.

Structural Report, No. 41 Northgate Street, Chester.
(a) Chester City R.O. (CCB/58). Minutes of the Improvement Committee 1890-1894, pp. 591-2. (b) Address ascertained from Kelly, 1892.

Llety Dryw Hall, Colwyn Bay, Denbighshire. (House and remodelling of earlier building to form stables. Stables now altered).
(a) Date on building. (b) *B.A.*, 42, 1894, pp. 419-20, 459. (c) *Modern Homes*, T. Raffles Davison, London, 1909, p. 52.

* **Work at Laundry, Eaton Hall, Cheshire.**
E.E.O., 697, p. 168.

* **Lamps and Gateway, North Lodge, Eaton Hall, Cheshire.**
E.E.O., 697, p. 192.

* **Work at the Eaton Stud, Eaton Hall, Cheshire.**
E.E.O., 697, p. 133.

All Saints' Church, Higher Kinnerton, Flintshire.
(a) Date on building. (b) G.R. Index.

The Lodge, The Gelli, Tallarn Green, Flintshire. For the Honourable Miss Henrietta Kenyon.
Works.

Cottages, Neston Road, Thornton Hough, Cheshire. For W. H. Lever, later Viscount Leverhulme. (Nos. 1-7.)
(a) Date on building. (b) *Works*. (c) *B.A.*, 42, 1894, pp. 289-90, 292. (d) *The Studio*, 31, 1904, pp. 30-38. (e) *The Buildings Erected at Port Sunlight and Thornton Hough*, Paper read by W. H. Lever, at a meeting of the Architectural Association, London, March, 21st, 1902, pp. 24, 28.

Post Office, Warburton, Cheshire. For R. E. Egerton-Warburton.
Drawings at Warburton New Church.

1893-4
* **Bridge, Eccleston Approach, Eaton Hall, Cheshire.**
E.E.O., 479, pp. 32, 79.

* **Eccleston Lodge (or Weighing Machine Lodge), Eaton Hall, Cheshire.**
(a) E.E.O. Photographs. (b) E.E.O. Drawings. 02365. (c) E.E.O., 479, pp. 32, 55, 79; 697, pp. 34, 157, 227, 568, 616, 621, 648, 653. (d) *Works*. (e) *A.A.*, 1894, p. 62. (f) *Bldr.*, 66, 1894, p. 441. (g) *B.N.*, 66, 1894, p. 745. (h) *Chester Chronicle* ob. (i) *R.I.B.A.J.* ob. (j) *Modern Cottage Architecture*, Maurice B. Adams, London, 1904, p. 26, pl. XXXIV. (k) *The Royal Academy of Arts. A Complete Dictionary of Contributors and their Work from its foundation in 1769 to 1904*, Algernon Graves, 1, 1905, p. 359.

* **Gardeners' Bothy, Eaton Hall, Cheshire.**
(a) E.E.O., 479, pp. 32, 78; 697, pp. 34, 227. (b) *Works*. (c) *B.A.*, 69, 1908, pp. 206, 208.

* **Alterations and Additions, Saighton House, Saighton, Cheshire.**
E.E.O., 479, pp. 33, 79; 702, pp. 926, 935.

1893-5
* **Cottage, Aldford, Cheshire.** (Opposite Aldford Lodge).
(a) E.E.O. Drawings. 01866. (b) E.E.O., 479, pp. 61, 78. (Referred to in E.E.O. records as "Mrs. Parsonage").

* **Pair of Cottages and Shop, Aldford, Cheshire.** (North of Grosvenor Arms).
(a) E.E.O. Drawings. 01866. (b) E.E.O., 479, pp. 61, 79; 698, p. 52.

* **Churton Stud, Churton, Cheshire.**
E.E.O., 479, pp. 16, 78.

The Work of John Douglas

1893–5 Cont.
* **Farmhouse, Yew Tree Bank Farm, Lower Kinnerton, Cheshire.**
(a) E.E.O. Photographs. (b) E.E.O., 479, pp. 33, 79; 698, p. 511. (Referred to in E.E.O. records as "Eliz. Jones").
* **Three Pairs of Cottages, Saighton, Cheshire.** (Pair in Millfield Lane and two pairs north of Millfield Lane on east side of main road).
(a) E.E.O. Drawings. 02054, 02055. (b) E.E.O., 479, pp. 61, 78.

1894
Gun and Billiard Rooms, Abbeystead, Wyresdale, Lancashire. For fourth Earl of Sefton.
Molyneux Muniments (at Croxteth Hall 1990). Estate Accounts 1894.
Restoration and unexecuted scheme for Rood Screen, St. Boniface's Church, Bunbury, Cheshire.
(a) E.E.O., 697, p. 648. (b) Works. (c) *B.A.*, 43, 1895, p. 428. (d) *Journal of the Chester and North Wales Architectural, Archaeological and Historic Society*, new series, 34, part 2, 1940, p. 95.
Shop Premises, Northgate Street, Chester. (Demolished.)
Chester City R.O. Minutes of the Improvement Committee.
* **Cricket Pavilion, Eaton Hall, Cheshire.**
E.E.O., 697, p. 653.
Nos. 1–9 Bridge Street and No. 26 Park Road, Port Sunlight, Cheshire. For Lever Bros. Ltd.
(a) Records, Estate Department, Unilever Merseyside Ltd. (b) *Archt.*, 79, 1908, p. 257.
Dell Bridge, Port Sunlight, Cheshire. For Lever Bros. Ltd.
(a) Date on structure. (b) *B.N.*, 76, 1899, p. 7. (c) *Chester Chronicle* ob. (d) *R.I.B.A.J.* ob. (e) *Port Sunlight*, T. Raffles Davison, London, 1916, p. 2. (f) *The Buildings Erected at Port Sunlight and Thornton Hough*, Paper read by W. H. Lever, at a meeting of the Architectural Association, London, March 21st, 1902. (g) *Civic Art*, Thomas H. Mawson, London, 1911, p. 196.
Restoration, Wardley Hall, Lancashire. For Earl of Ellesmere.
(a) *B.N.*, 74, 1898, pp. 158–9, 161. (b) *History of Wardley Hall, Lancashire*, Henry Vaughan Hart-Davis, in collaboration with Strachan Holme, Manchester and London, 1908, pp. 1–2, 4–6. (c) V.C.H. *Lancashire*, 4, 1911, pp. 385–8.
Lectern, St. Mark's Church, Worsley, Lancashire.
B.A., 42, 1894, p. 273.

1894–5
Chancel, St. Paul's Church, Colwyn Bay, Denbighshire.
(a) G.R. Index. (b) Thomas, 3, 1913, pp. 202–3. (c) Guide book: *The Story of the Parish Church of Colwyn Bay,*. W. Hugh Rees, Gloucester, 1970. References to the church being by Douglas in (d) *B.A.* ob. (e) *Bldr.* ob. (f) *B.N.* ob. (g) *Cheshire Observer* ob. (h) *Chester Chronicle* ob. (i) *Chester Courant* ob. (j) *Liverpool Daily Post* ob. (k) *R.I.B.A.J.* ob.
St. Paul's Church Room, Colwyn Bay, Denbighshire. ATTRIB.
Guide book: *The Story of the Parish Church of Colwyn Bay*, W. Hugh Rees, Gloucester, 1970.
St. Paul's Vicarage, Colwyn Bay, Denbighshire. ATTRIB.
Guide Book: *The Story of the Parish Church of Colwyn Bay*, W. Hugh Rees, Gloucester, 1970.
* **Garden Gates, Eaton Hall, Cheshire.** (Unidentified).
E.E.O., 479, p. 55; 697, pp. 528, 573.
* **Iron Bridge Lodge, Eaton Hall, Cheshire.**
(a) E.E.O. Drawings. 02824, 02825. (b) E.E.O., 479, pp. 80, 84.
Shops and Girls' Institute, Bridge Street/ Bolton Road, Port Sunlight, Cheshire. For Lever Bros. Ltd.
(a) Records, Estate Department, Unilever Merseyside Ltd. (b) *The Buildings*

Appendix II Catalogue of Works

Erected at Port Sunlight and Thornton Hough, Paper read by W. H. Lever, at a meeting of the Architectural Association, London, March 21st, 1902. (c) *Port Sunlight*, T. Raffles Davison, London, 1916, p. 9.
Nos. 49–55 Wood Street, Port Sunlight, Cheshire. For Lever Bros. Ltd.
Records, Estate Department, Unilever Merseyside Ltd.
West Lodge, Worsley Hall, Lancashire. For Earl of Ellesmere. (Leigh Road.)
Drawings in Bridgewater Collection, Peel Estates Ltd., Estate Offices, Worsley.
Lodge, Worsley Old Hall, Lancashire. For Earl of Ellesmere. (No. 208 Walkden Road.)
Drawings in Bridgewater Collection, Peel Estates Ltd., Estate Offices, Worsley.

1894–6
* **Gamekeeper's House, Aldford, Cheshire (The Kennels).**
(a) E.E.O. Drawings. 01888. (b) E.E.O., 479, pp. 81–2.
* **Gamekeeper's House, Belgrave, Cheshire.**
(a) E.E.O. Photographs. (b) E.E.O. Drawings. 02317. (c) E.E.O., 479, pp. 81–2; 697, p. 640.
* **Mill Hill Farmhouse, Rake Lane, Eccleston, Cheshire.**
(a) E.E.O. Photographs. (b) E.E.O., 479, pp. 80, 84; 697, p. 416.
* **Alterations and Additions, Rake Farm, Rake Lane, Eccleston, Cheshire.**
E.E.O., 479, pp. 81, 84.
* **Gell Farm, Lower Kinnerton, Cheshire.**
(a) E.E.O. Photographs. (b) E.E.O., 479, pp. 62, 80; 697, p. 350. (Referred to in E.E.O. records as "James Roberts").
School, Port Sunlight, Cheshire. For Lever Bros. Ltd. (Now Lyceum).
(a) Records, Estate Department, Unilever Merseyside Ltd. (b) *Works*. (c) *Archt.* 60, 1898, p. 242. (d) *Bldr.*, 66, 1894, p. 441; 67, 1894, pp. 82–3. (e) *B.N.*, 75, 1898, p. 641; 76, 1899, p. 7. (f) *B.A.* ob. (g) *Bldr.* ob. (h) *Cheshire Observer* ob. (i) *Chester Chronicle* ob. (j) *R.I.B.A.J.* ob. (k) *Port Sunlight*, T. Raffles Davison, London, 1916. p. 1. (l) *The Royal Academy of Arts. A Complete Dictionary of Contributors and their Work from its foundation in 1769 to 1904*, Algernon Graves, 1, 1905, p. 359. (m) *The Buildings Erected at Port Sunlight and Thornton Hough*, Paper read by W. H. Lever, at a meeting of the Architectural Association, London, March 21st, 1902, p. 14, pl. IX. (n) *Die Englische Baukunst der Gegenwart*, Hermann Muthesius, Leipzig and Berlin, 1900, pp. 91–3, pls. 44–5.
* **Alterations and Additions, Stables, Saighton Grange, Saighton, Cheshire.**
E.E.O., 479, pp. 80, 85; 697, p. 564.

c. 1894
* **Pair of Cottages, Eccleston, Cheshire.** (East of back gate of The Paddocks).
E.E.O. Drawings. 02297.
* **Farm Buildings, The Limes Farm, Pulford, Cheshire.** (Now Green Paddocks).
E.E.O., 479, p. 80. (Referred to in E.E.O. records as "W. Edwards").

1895
* **Pair of Cottages, Aldford, Cheshire.** (Probably block in north road in village west of cottages opposite Aldford Lodge).
(a) Date on building. (b) E.E.O., 479, p. 81.
* **Pair of Cottages, Balderton, Cheshire.** (Block east of railway).
(a) Date on building. (b) E.E.O., 479, p. 81.
* **Conversion of House of Shelter, Vicar's Lane, Chester, to Private Residence.** (Unexecuted scheme. Now offices).
E.E.O., 698, pp. 225, 276.
Side Wings to Reredos, All Saints' Church, Gresford, Denbighshire.
Vicars' Books, Gresford Vicarage.
* **Two Pairs of Cottages, Saighton, Cheshire.** (Probably blocks north and south of Yew Tree Farm).
(a) Date on buildings. (b) E.E.O., 479, p. 81; 698, p. 52.

The Work of John Douglas

              Lady Ellesmere Coffee Tavern, Worsley, Lancashire. Conversion of former mill. For Earl of Ellesmere. (Now Estate Offices).
(a) Drawings in Bridgewater Collection, Peel Estates Ltd., Estate Offices, Worsley. (b) *B.A.*, 49, 1898, p. 397.

1895–6   * Smithy, Smithy House and Cottage, Waverton, Cheshire.
(a) E.E.O. Drawings. 02527, 02529. (b) E.E.O., 479, pp. 83, 101; 698, p. 319.
* Wheelwright's House and Shop, Waverton, Cheshire. (Now Fir Tree Farm).
(a) E.E.O. Drawings. 02555. (b) E.E.O., 479, pp. 82, 101; 698, pp. 52, 210.

1895–7   Restoration, St. Michael's Church, Trelawnyd (Newmarket), Flintshire.
Thomas, 1, 1911, p. 409.

1895–8   * Stannage Farm, Churton, Cheshire.
(a) E.E.O. Drawings. 02429, 02430, 02431, 02432. (b) E.E.O., 479, pp. 81, 86; 698, p. 52.

c. 1895   * Schoolmaster's House, Pulford, Cheshire.
(a) E.E.O. Photographs. (b) E.E.O. Drawings. 02381. (c) E.E.O., 700, pp. 328, 869.

c. 1895–7   East Side of St. Werburgh Street, Chester. For himself, built on his own land. (Shop premises, Nos. 2–18 St. Werburgh Street and Bank of Liverpool, now Barclays Bank, Eastgate Street).
(a) Dates on building. (b) Cheshire County R.O. (EC/1769/24). Correspondence and papers on improvements in St. Werburgh Street by John Douglas, architect, 1896–1906. (c) Chester City R.O. Minutes of the Improvement Committee. (d) Chester City R.O. (62C). Corporation Conveyances. (e) *Archt.* 64, 1900, p. 248; 79, 1908, p. 257. (f) *B.A.*, 49, 1898, p. 162; 50, 1898, p. 364; 72, 1909, pp. 182, 186. (g) *Bldr.*, 78, 1900, p. 544. (h) *B.N.*, 81, 1901, p. 520; 83, 1902, p. 185. (i) *Bldr.* ob. (j) *B.N.* ob. (k) *Cheshire Observer* ob. (l) *Chester Chronicle* ob. (m) *Chester Courant* ob. (n) *Liverpool Daily Post* ob. (o) *R.I.B.A.J.* ob. (p) *Die Englische Baukunst der Gegenwart*, Hermann Muthesius, Leipzig and Berlin, 1900, pp. 157–9, pl. 97.

1896   * Cottages, Aldford, Cheshire. (Probably two pairs in north road in village, opposite former Rectory).
(a) Date on buildings. (b) E.E.O., 479, p. 102.
* Shippons, Dodleston, Cheshire. (Unidentified).
E.E.O., 699, p. 460.
Walmoor Hill, Dee Banks, Chester. For himself.
(a) Date on building. (b) *B.A.*, 58, 1902, p. 442. (c) *B.A.* ob. (d) *Bldr.* ob. (e) *Cheshire Observer* ob. (f) *Chester Chronicle* ob. (g) *R.I.B.A.J.* ob. (h) *Walmoor House*, compiled by K. Dickinson for Cheshire Fire Brigade, 1981.
Chancel Porch, St Deiniol's Church, Hawarden, Flintshire. For Gladstone family.
(a) *B.A.*, 47, 1897, pp. 41–2. (b) *B.N.*, 70, 1896, p. 548. (c) Thomas, 2, 1911, p. 383.
Canopied Niche of South Porch, St Deiniol's Church, Hawarden, Flintshire. ATTRIB.
A History of the Parish of Hawarden, W. Bell Jones, typescript at Clwyd R.O., 1, 1943, p. 118.
Remodelling, Church, Maentwrog, Merioneth.
(a) Inscription in church. (b) *Works*. (c) *B.A.*, 48, 1897, pp. 161–2, 166; 49, 1898, pp. 360–61.
Entrance Gates, Mostyn Hall, Flintshire. For Lord Mostyn.
(a) Date on gates. (b) *Works*. (c) *Archt.*, 64, 1900, p. 200.

Appendix II Catalogue of Works

Cottages, New Chester Road, Port Sunlight, Cheshire. For Lever Bros. Ltd. (Nos. 284 and 286.)
Records, Estate Department, Unilever Merseyside Ltd.
Gatekeeper's Lodge, Stud Farm, Worsley Old Hall, Lancashire. For Earl of Ellesmere.
Drawings in Bridgewater Collection, Peel Estates Ltd., Estate Offices, Worsley. [Re-erected at the Boat Steps, 1989. Two identical lodges (date unknown) at Hilton Land and Ellenbrook Road now demolished. (Information from Mr Peter Nears.)]

1896–7 * **Reading Room, Aldford, Cheshire.**
(a) E.E.O. Drawings. 01853. (b) E.E.O., 699, pp. 410, 413, 598; 700, pp. 327–8, 869.
* **Cottages, Handbridge, Chester.** (Nos. 26–30 and Nos. 32–40 Overleigh Road, and Nos. 1–7 and Nos. 2–10 Hugh Street).
(a) Chester City R.O. (DT/2). Town Clerk's Department. Improvement Committee. Letter from Douglas & Minshull, 1st May 1899. (b) E.E.O., 479, p. 101; 698, p. 595; 699, p. 41; 700, pp. 327–8, 869; 707, pp. 847, 926, 946.

1896–8 * **Additions to Farm Buildings, Lea Newbold Farm, Bruera, Cheshire.**
E.E.O., 479, p. 102; 700, p. 328.
* **Reading Room and Two Cottages, Dodleston, Cheshire.**
(a) E.E.O. Photographs. (b) E.E.O. Drawings. 02866, 02867. (c) E.E.O., 479, p. 102; 698, p. 603.
* **Smithy, Pair of Cottages and Remodelling of Smithy House, Eccleston, Cheshire.**
(a) E.E.O. Photographs. (b) E.E.O. Drawings. 02302. (c) E.E.O., 479, p. 102; 699, p. 382; 700, p. 328.
* **Pair of Cottages, Gorstella, Cheshire**. (South-east of Gorstella Farm).
(a) E.E.O. Photographs. (b) E.E.O., 479, p. 102.
* **Farmhouse, Pear Tree Farm, Poulton, Cheshire.** (Now Grange Farm).
(a) E.E.O., 479, p. 103. (Referred to in E.E.O. records as "Wm. Jones," Identified through Estate Rentals).
* **Farmhouse, Manor Farm, Pulford, Cheshire.**
(a) E.E.O. Photographs. (b) E.E.O., 479, pp. 83, 101; 698, p. 675.

1896–9 **Christ Church, Bryn-y-Maen, Colwyn Bay, Denbighshire.** For Mrs. Eleanor Frost.
(a) G.R. Index. (b) *Works*. (c) *Archt.*, 65, 1901, p. 384. (d) *B.N.*, 73, 1897, p. 365. (e) *B.A.* ob. (f) *Bldr.* ob. (g) *Chester Chronicle* ob. (h) *R.I.B.A.J.* ob. (i) Guide book: *Christ Church, Brynymaen, Colwyn Bay*, Philip M. Robinson, n.d. (j) Thomas, 3, 1913, pp. 197–9.

c. 1896 **Additions, Thornton Manor, Thornton Hough, Cheshire.** For W. H. Lever, later Viscount Leverhulme. (Partly obscured and demolished in later alterations).
(a) Information from Mr. J. Lomax-Simpson. (b) National Buildings Record photographs.

c. 1896–7 **Cottages, New Chester Road, Port Sunlight, Cheshire.** For Lever Bros. Ltd. (Nos. 244–248).
Records, Estate Department, Unilever Merseyside Ltd.
Cottages, New Chester Road, Port Sunlight, Cheshire. For Lever Bros. Ltd. (Nos. 294 & 296).
(a) Records, Estate Department, Unilever Merseyside Ltd. (b) *Die Englische Baukunst der Gegenwart*, Hermann Muthesius, Leipzig and Berlin, 1900, p. 160, pl. 100.

1897 * **Smallholding, Aldford, Cheshire.** (Barrowcroft).
(a) E.E.O. Drawings. 01860. (b) E.E.O., 699, p. 682.

The Work of John Douglas

* **Smallholding, Balderton, Cheshire.** (Balderton Lodge).
(a) Date on building. (b) E.E.O., 699, p. 682.
* **Entrance Lodge, Rectory, Bangor Is-coed, Flintshire.**
E.E.O., 699, pp. 646, 663.
Diamond Jubilee Memorial Clock, The Eastgate, Chester. (Unexecuted scheme).
(a) Chester City R.O. Minutes of the Improvement Committee. (b) *B.A.*, 48, 1897, pp. 251, 253, 256.
* **Shop Premises, No. 38 Bridge Street (Row No.), Chester.**
(a) E.E.O. Framed perspective. (b) E.E.O. Drawings. 01539. (c) E.E.O., 700, p. 575. (d) *B.N.*, 73, 1897, p. 471.
Nos. 9 and 11 Dee Banks, Chester.
(a) Date on building. (b) Chester City R.O. Minutes of the Improvement Committee, 3rd Feb. 1897.
Porch, pulpit, and south-east Chapel in connection with Rebuilding of Christ Church, Chester.
(a) Inscription in church. (b) *Bldr.* 73, 1897, pp. 15–16. References to the church being by Douglas in (c) *B.A.* ob., (d) *B.N.* ob., (e) *Cheshire Observer* ob., (f) *Chester Chronicle* ob., and (g) *Liverpool Daily Post* ob.
* **Gas Works Cottage, Eccleston, Cheshire.**
(a) E.E.O. Drawings. 02253. (b) E.E.O., 699, p. 682; 700, p. 328.
* **Stables, Eccleston, Cheshire.** (Now incorporated in Village Hall).
(a) Date on building. (b) E.E.O. Drawings. 02243.
Lych-Gate, Church, Maentwrog, Merioneth.
(a) Date on structure. (b) *B.A.*, 48, 1897, pp. 161–2, 166.
Cottages, Corniche Road, Port Sunlight, Cheshire. For Lever Bros. Ltd. (Nos. 7–15).
Records, Estate Department, Unilever Merseyside Ltd.
Cottages, New Chester Road and Boundary Road, Port Sunlight, Cheshire. For Lever Bros. Ltd. (Nos. 128–132 New Chester Road, with Nos. 10–16 Boundary Road).
Records, Estate Department, Unilever Merseyside Ltd.
* **Remodelling, The Grosvenor Arms, Pulford, Cheshire.**
(a) E.E.O., 699, p. 579; 700, p. 869; 703, p. 301. (b) E.E.O. Drawings.
Restoration, Village Cross, Weston, Runcorn, Cheshire.
(a) *B.A.* 49, 1898, p. 6. (b) Kelly.

1897–8 **Congregational Church, Great Crosby, Lancashire.**
(a) Information from the Revd. W. Brown. (b) *Bldr.* ob.
Church of St. John the Evangelist, Weston, Runcorn, Cheshire.
(a) *Archt.*, 64, 1900, p. 248. (b) *B.A.*, 49, 1898, pp. 6. 21, 24. (c) G.R. Index. (d) *B.A.*, ob. (e) *Bldr.* ob. (f) Kelly. (g) Cheshire R.O. (P 68/6/148–9). Letters from J. Douglas to Revd. G. Egerton-Warburton.
St. John the Evangelist School, Weston, Runcorn, Cheshire.
B.A., 49, 1898, p. 6.

1897–9 **Vestries, St. Matthew's Church, Buckley, Flintshire.**
(a) *B.N.*, 91, 1906, p. 100. (b) Thomas, 2, 1911, pp. 361–4. References to the church being by Douglas in (c) G.R. Index, (d) *Bldr.*, 89, 1905, p. 368, (e) *B.A.*, ob., (f) *Bldr.* ob., (g) *B.N.* ob., (h) *Cheshire Observer* ob., (i) *Chester Chronicle* ob., (j) *Chester Courant* ob., and (k) *Liverpool Daily Post* ob., and (l) *R.I.B.A.J.* ob. (m) *Buckley Parish Church, 1822–1972*, J. Clifford Jones, 1974.
All Saints' Church, Deganwy, Caernarfonshire. For Lady Augusta Mostyn.
(a) G.R. Index. (b) *Works.* (c) *Archt.*, 79, 1908, p. 257. (d) *B.A.*, 48, 1897, pp. 423–4. (e) *Caernarvonshire Historical Society Transactions*, 22, 1961, pp. 20–31. (f) *B.A.* ob. (g) *Bldr.* ob. (h) *B.N.* ob. (i) *Cheshire Observer* ob. (j) *Chester Chronicle*

Appendix II Catalogue of Works

ob. (k) *Chester Courant* ob. (l) *Liverpool Daily Post* ob. (m) *R.I.B.A.J.* ob. (n) Thomas, 2, 1911, p. 330.

c. 1897
* Pair of Cottages, Dodleston, Cheshire. (Probably block east of School).
E.E.O., 700, pp. 327–8.
* Pair of Cottages, Waverton, Cheshire. (Probably block north-east of Church Farm).
E.E.O., 700, pp. 327–8.

1898
* Pair of Cottages, Bretton, Flintshire. (Bretton Lodge).
E.E.O., 700, p. 482.
* Stables at Shop Premises, No. 38 Bridge Street (Row No.), Chester.
E.E.O. 699, p. 669; 700, pp. 18, 236, 312.
Rebuilding, Shop Premises, No. 67 Brook Street, Chester. (Much altered.)
Chester City R.O. Minutes of the Improvement Committee, 6th Jul. 1898.
* Nurses' Home, Grosvenor Street, Chester.
(a) E.E.O. Drawings. (b) E.E.O., 700, pp. 202, 394.
Vestry, Organ Chamber and work on Chancel in connection with Rebuilding of Christ Church, Chester.
(a) Inscription in church. References to the church being by Douglas in (b) *B.A.* ob., (c) *B.N.* ob., (d) *Cheshire Observer* ob., (e) *Chester Chronicle* ob., and (f) *Liverpool Daily Post* ob.
* Pinfold Lane Farm, Handbridge, Chester.
(a) E.E.O. Drawings. 02882. (b) E.E.O., 700, p. 266.
East Side of St. Werburgh Street, Chester. St. Oswald's Chambers. (No. 22). Built on his own land. For S. J. R. Dickson.
(a) Date on building. (b) Cheshire County R.O. (EC/1769/24). Correspondence and papers on improvements in St. Werburgh Street by John Douglas, architect, 1896–1906. (c) Chester City R.O. Minutes of the Improvement Committee. (d) Chester City R.O. (62C). Corporation Conveyances. (e) Chester City R.O. (78C). Corporation Conveyances. (f) *Archt.*, 64, 1900, p. 248; 79, 1908, p. 257. (g) *B.A.*, 49, 1898, p. 162; 50, 1898, p. 364; 72, 1909, pp. 182, 186. (h) *Bldr.*, 78, 1900, p. 544. (i) *Bldr.* ob. (j) *B.N.* ob. (k) *Cheshire Observer* ob. (l) *Chester Chronicle* ob. (m) *Chester Courant* ob. (n) *Liverpool Daily Post* ob. (o) *R.I.B.A.J.* ob.
Vicarage, Bryn-y-Maen, Colwyn Bay, Denbighshire. For Mrs. Eleanor Frost.
(a) Date on building. (b) *Archt.*, 65, 1901, p. 384. (c) *Bldr.* ob. (d) *R.I.B.A.J.* ob. (e) Guide book: *Christ Church, Brynymaen, Colwyn Bay*, Philip M. Robinson, n.d. (f) Thomas, 3, 1913, p. 197.
* Farmhouse, Dodleston Farm, Dodleston, Cheshire.
E.E.O., 700, p. 482.
* Eaton Estate Farm (Wrexham Road), Cheshire. (Apparently unexecuted scheme).
E.E.O., 700, p. 349.
* Cottages, Eccleston, Cheshire. (Unidentified. Possibly unexecuted scheme).
E.E.O., 700, p. 536.
Restoration, St Michael's Church, Manafon, Montgomeryshire, for the Revd. and Mrs. T. J. Williams.
(a) Material on church restorations collected by the late Canon B.F.L. Clarke (at Council for the Care of Churches). (b) Thomas, 1, 1911, p. 489. (c) *The Best. A History of H. H. Martyn & Co.*, John Whitaker, Southam, 1985, pp. 66–67.
Henllys Hall, Manafon, Montgomeryshire. For the Revd. and Mrs. T. J. Williams. ATTRIB.
Information from Mr Richard Haslam.
Employees' Provident Stores and Collegium, Port Sunlight, Cheshire. For Lever Bros. Ltd. (Demolished),

The Work of John Douglas

(a) Records, Estate Department, Unilever Merseyside Ltd. (b) *Port Sunlight*, T. Raffles Davison, London, 1916, p. 9. (c) *The Buildings Erected at Port Sunlight and Thornton Hough*, Paper read by W. H. Lever, at a meeting of the Architectural Association, London, March 21st, 1902, pp. 13, 17, pls. VI, VII. (d) *Die Englische Baukunst der Gegenwart*, Hermann Muthesius, Leipzig and Berlin, 1900, pp. 131–2, pl. 78.

Cottages, New Chester Road and Bolton Road, Port Sunlight, Cheshire. For Lever Bros. Ltd. (Nos. 268–274 New Chester Road, with Nos. 71–75 Bolton Road).
Records, Estate Department, Unilever Merseyside Ltd.
Additions to Schools, Port Sunlight, Cheshire. For Lever Bros. Ltd.
(a) Records, Estate Department, Unilever Merseyside Ltd. (b) *B.N.*, 76, 1899, p. 7.

1898–9 *** Inn, Bretton, Flintshire.** (Unexecuted scheme).
E.E.O., 700, pp. 536, 717.
Litany Desk, Holy Trinity Church, Chester.
Cheshire County R.O.
* Reading Room, Waverton, Cheshire.
E.E.O., 700, p. 536.

1898–1900 **Friars School, Bangor, Caernarfonshire.** (Probably execution of 1888 competition design).
(a) *Works*. (b) *Bldr.*, 55, 1888, p. 381; 87, 1904, p. 467. (c) *Bldr.* ob. (d) *Chester Chronicle* ob. (e) *The History of Friars School, Bangor*, Henry Barber, Henry Lewis, Bangor, 1901, pp. 92–3, 94, 96, 99.

1898–1901 **Public Baths, Union Street, Chester.**
(a) Chester City R.O. City and County Borough of Chester. Minutes of Proceedings, 1896–7, pp. 171, 176; 1897–8, pp. 43, 59–60, 310, 486–7, 499, 510, 562, 611–13, 619, 623, 634; 1898–9, pp. 117–8, 291–2, 418–9, 551; 1900, pp. 277–8, 330–32, 394–5, 511; 1900–1901, pp. 246, 251, 261, 487–9, 544–5, 545–6, 549, 555–6, 607–9, 609–15, 671. (b) *B.A.*, 56, 1901, p. 248. (c) *B.N.*, 82, 1902, pp. 917–8. (d) *B.A.* ob. (e) *Bldr.* ob. (f) *Cheshire Observer* ob. (g) *Chester Courant* ob. (h) Kelly.
Shop Premises, Boughton Cross (Christleton Road/Tarvin Road), Chester.
Built on his own land.
(a) Date on building. (b) Chester City R.O. (81C). Corporation Conveyance. (c) *B.A.* 50, 1898, p. 364.

1898–1902 **St. Ethelwold's Church, Shotton, Flintshire.**
(a) G.R. Index. (b) *Works*. (c) *Archt.*, 60, 1898, p. 185; 65, 1901, p. 128; 72, 1904, p. 264; 79, 1908, p. 288. (d) *B.A*, ob. (e) *Bldr.* ob. (f) *B.N.* ob. (g) *Cheshire Observer* ob. (h) *Chester Chronicle* ob. (i) *Chester Courant* ob. (j) *Liverpool Daily Post* ob. (k) *R.I.B.A.J.* ob. (l) Thomas, 2, 1911, pp. 375, 391. (m) *A History of the Parish of Hawarden*, W. Bell Jones, typescript at Clwyd R.O., 2, 1945, pp. 375–6. (n) Engraving in vestry showing tower and spire.

c. 1898 **House, Bryn-y-Maen, Colwyn Bay, Denbighshire.** For Mrs. Eleanor Frost.
(a) *Archt.*, 65, 1901, p. 384. (b) *Bldr.* ob. (c) Guide book: *Christ Church, Brynymaen, Colwyn Bay*, Philip M. Robinson, n.d.
* Conversion of Farmhouse into Cottages, Churton, Cheshire. (Unidentified).
E.E.O., 700, pp. 327–8, 869.

1899 *** Smallholding, Bretton, Flintshire.** (Unidentified).
E.E.O., 700, p. 792.
Diamond Jubilee Memorial Clock, The Eastgate, Chester.
(a) Chester City R.O. Minutes of the Improvement Committee. (b) *Bldr.*, 76, 1899, p. 231. (c) *Bldr.* ob.
Chancel Screen, Holy Trinity Church, Chester. (Removed.)

Appendix II Catalogue of Works

Marston Memorial Chancel Screen, Parish of the Holy and Undivided Trinity, Chester, L. M. Farrall, Chester, 1899.

Gates, Hop Pole Paddock, Frodsham Street, Chester. For Chester Corporation. (Demolished.)
(a) Chester City R.O. (DT/2). Town Clerk's Department. Improvement Committee. Letter from Douglas & Minshull, 10th Apr. 1899. (b) *Bldr.* ob. (Hop Pole Paddock referred to as Bowling Green).

* **Pair of Houses, Handbridge, Chester.** (Nos. 65 & 67 Handbridge).
E.E.O., 700, pp. 877, 914; 701, pp. 248, 943; 702, p. 68.

* **Schoolmaster's House, Hargrave, Cheshire.**
E.E.O., 700, p. 760; 701, pp. 3, 41.

Restoration of St Beuno's Church, Penmorfa (Dolbenmaen), Caernarfonshire. For R.M. Greaves.
(a) Cheshire R.O. (P 68/6/168–9). Letters from J. Douglas to Revd G. Egerton-Warburton. (b) Drawing in Wern Collection (at Carreg Felen, Tremadoc).

Nos. 55–67 Pool Bank, Port Sunlight, Cheshire. For Lever Bros. Ltd.
(a) Records, Estate Department, Unilever Merseyside Ltd. (b) *Port Sunlight*, T. Raffles Davison, London, 1916, p. 19.

Nos. 6–14 Primrose Hill, Port Sunlight, Cheshire. For Lever Bros. Ltd.
Records, Estate Department, Unilever Merseyside Ltd.

Alterations and Addition of Vestry and Organ Chamber, St John's Church, Trofarth, Denbighshire.
G.R. Index.

Chancel Stalls, St Werburgh's (New) Church, Warburton, Cheshire.
Cheshire R.O. (P 68/6). Correspondence.
[Existing ones sold to St Michael's Church, Ffestiniog, Merioneth.]

* **Pair of Cottages, Greenlooms, Waverton, Cheshire.**
E.E.O. Drawings. 02560.

1899–1902 **St. Deiniol's Library, Hawarden, Flintshire. First stage** (including library accommodation and wardens' rooms) as part of Gladstone National Memorial.
(a) Clwyd County R.O. (A/24/1). Documents relating to St. Deiniol's Library. (b) *Works.* (c) *A.A.*, 22, 1902, pp. 108, 114. (d) *Archt.*, 71, 1904, p. 400. (e) *B.A.* 67, 1907, pp. 74, 76. (f) *Bldr.* 95, 1908, p. 530. (g) *B.N.*, 82, 1902, p. 809. (h) *B.A.* ob. (i) *Bldr.* ob. (j) *Chester Chronicle* ob. (k) *R.I.B.A.J.* ob. (l) *The Exhibition of the Royal Academy of Arts, 1906*, No. 1577. (m) Thomas, 2, 1911, pp. 385–6.

1899–1903 **Church of St. John the Baptist, Old Colwyn, Denbighshire.**
(a) G.R. Index. (b) *A.A.*, 43, 1913, p. 101. (c) *Archt.* 65, 1901, p. 160. (d) *B.A.* ob. (e) *Bldr.* ob. (f) Thomas, 3, 1913, pp. 200–202.

c. 1899 * **Cottages, Dodleston, Cheshire.** (Probably two pairs opposite Dodleston Farm).
E.E.O., 701, pp. 288, 305.

* **Post Office.** (Probably that at Eccleston).
E.E.O., 700, p. 869.

* **Pair of Cottages, Eccleston, Cheshire.** (South of School).
E.E.O. Drawings. 02206.

* **Cottages, Eccleston, Cheshire.** (Unidentified, possibly unexecuted scheme).
E.E.O., 701, p. 80.

1900 **Alterations to chancel and addition of vestry, Church of St. John the Evangelist, Ashton, Cheshire.**
G.R. Index.

Completion of Nave in connection with Rebuilding of Christ Church, Chester.
(a) Inscription in church. (b) References to the church being by Douglas in (b)

271

The Work of John Douglas

B.A. ob., (c) *B.N.* ob., (d) *Cheshire Observer* ob. (e) *Chester Chronicle* ob., and (f) *Liverpool Daily Post* ob.

Former Grotto Public House (previously Harp and Crown), No. 30 Bridge Street, Chester. ATTRIB.

Chester City R.O. Minutes of the Improvement Committee, 4th Jan. and 27th Sep. 1899. (Information from Mr Oliver Bott.)

Technical School, Talbot Street, Glossop, Derbyshire.

(a) *Bldr.* ob. (b) Kelly's *Directory of Derbyshire*, 1916.

Shop Premises, Nos. 5–9 Northgate Street, Chester. (Part of rebuilding of Shoemakers' Row.)

(a) Date on building. (b) Chester City R.O. Minutes of the Improvement Committee. (c) *Archt.*, 64, 1900, p. 200; 79, 1908, p. 288. References to work by Douglas in Shoemakers' Row or Northgate Street in (d) *B.N.* ob., (e) *Cheshire Observer* ob., (f) *Chester Chronicle* ob. (g) *Chester Courant* ob., and (h) *Liverpool Daily Post* ob.

Shop Premises, Nos. 11–13 Northgate Street, Chester. (Part of rebuilding of Shoemakers' Row).

(a) Date on building. (b) Chester City R.O. Minutes of the Improvement Committee. References to work by Douglas in Shoemakers' Row or Northgate Street in (c) *B.N.* ob., (d) *Cheshire Observer* ob., (e) *Chester Chronicle* ob., (f) *Chester Courant* ob., and (g) *Liverpool Daily Post* ob.

Joseph Richardson's Grocery Shop, Packet House, Worsley, Lancashire. For Earl of Ellesmere.

Drawings in Bridgewater Collection, Peel Estates Ltd., Estate Offices, Worsley.

c. 1900   **Shop Premises, No. 19 Northgate Street, Chester.** (Part of rebuilding of Shoemakers' Row). ATTRIB.

Information from Mr Oliver Bott.

1901   **Bank Buildings, Charing Cross, Birkenhead, Cheshire.** (Shop Premises and former Bank of Liverpool.)

(a) *Works*. (b) *B.N.*, 81, 1901, p. 139. (c) *Bldr.* ob.

South African War Memorial Cross, sculptural panel under east window outside, canopied niche over north door, St Deiniol's Church, Hawarden, Flintshire. ATTRIB.

Clwyd R.O. Hawarden Vestry Book 1654–1961. Vestry Meeting, 10th June 1901.

1901–2   * **Butler's Cottage, Combermere Abbey, Cheshire.** For Duchess of Westminster.

E.E.O., 701, pp. 537, 624, 647; 702, pp. 68, 73, 446.

c. 1901–2   **Chancel, in connection with Rebuilding of St. Matthew's Church, Buckley, Flintshire.**

(a) *B.N.*, 91, 1906, p. 100. (b) Thomas, 2, 1911, pp. 361–4. References to the church being by Douglas in (c) G.R. Index, (d) *A.A.*, 30, 1906, p. 140, (e) *Bldr.*, 89, 1905, p. 368, (f) *B.A.* ob., (g) *Bldr.* ob., (h) *B.N.* ob., (i) *Cheshire Observer* ob., (j) *Chester Chronicle* ob., (k) *Chester Courant* ob., (l) *Liverpool Daily Post* ob., and (m) *R.I.B.A.J.* ob. (n) *Buckley Parish Church, 1822–1972*, J. Clifford Jones, 1974.

c. 1901–3   **Gladstone Memorial Chapel, St. Deiniol's Church, Hawarden, Flintshire.** For Gladstone family.

(a) Clwyd R.O. Hawarden Parish Vestry Book, 1654–1961. Vestry Meetings, Easter Tuesday 1901, 10th June 1901, Easter Tuesday 1902. (b) Clwyd R.O. (FL 11). Hawarden Parish Magazine, Apr. 1906. (c) *Works*. (d) Thomas, 2, 1911, p. 381.

c. 1901–5   **Restoration, St. Deiniol's Church, Hawarden, Flintshire.**

(a) Clwyd R.O. Hawarden Parish Vestry Book, 1654–1961. Vestry Meetings,

Appendix II Catalogue of Works

Easter Tuesday 1902, Easter Tuesday 1904. (b) Clwyd R.O. (D/BJ/318). Payments for church repairs in Hawarden Churchwardens Accounts, *c.* 1900–1904. (c) Clwyd R.O. (FL/11). Hawarden Parish Magazine, Jan. 1906, Mar. 1906. (d) *B.A.* ob. (e) *B.N.* ob. (f) *Chester Courant* ob. (g) *Liverpool Daily Post* ob.

1902 * **Conversion of south-east Vestry to Chapel and Addition of north-west Vestry, Church of St. John the Baptist, Aldford, Cheshire.** For second Duke of Westminster.
(a) Cheshire County R.O. (P91/5/3). Faculty, 26th Feb. 1902. (b) Cheshire County R.O. (P91/8/2). Aldford Vestry Book 1798–1923. Vestry Meeting 6th Feb. 1902. (c) E.E.O., 702, p. 96.
West Porch, Remodelling of Tower and formation of Baptistery, in connection with Rebuilding of St. Matthew's Church, Buckley, Flintshire.
(a) *A.A.*, 27, 1905, p. 7. (b) *Bldr.*, 88, 1905, pp. 563–4. (c) *B.N.*, 91, 1906, p. 100. (d) *The Exhibition of the Royal Academy of Arts, 1905*, No. 1621. (e) Thomas, 2, 1911, pp. 361–4. References to the church being by Douglas in (f) G.R. Index, (g) *A.A.*, 30, 1906, p. 140. (h) *Bldr.*, 89, 1905, p. 368, (i) *B.A.* ob., (j) *Bldr.* ob., (k) *B.N.* ob., (l) *Cheshire Observer* ob., (m) *Chester Chronicle* ob., (n) *Chester Courant* ob., (o) *Liverpool Daily Post* ob., and (p) *R.I.B.A.J.* ob. (q) *Buckley Parish Church, 1822–1972*, J. Clifford Jones, 1974.
Shop Premises, Nos. 29–31 Northgate Street, Chester. (Part of Rebuilding of Shoemakers' Row).
(a) Date on building. (b) *Archt.*, 79, 1908, p. 288. (c) *R.I.B.A.J.* ob. References to work by Douglas in Shoemakers' Row or Northgate Street in (d) *B.N.* ob., (e) *Cheshire Observer* ob., (f) *Chester Chronicle* ob., (g) *Chester Courant* ob. and (h) *Liverpool Daily Post* ob.
* **Additions, Nurses' Home, Grosvenor Street, Chester.** For second Duke of Westminster.
E.E.O., 702, pp. 398, 425, 438, 499.
Addition of South Aisle, St. Paul's Church, Boughton, Chester.
(a) G.R. Index. (b) Kelly.
Rayner Memorial Clock Tower, Llangefni, Anglesey.
(a) Date on structure. (b) *Bldr.* ob.
Bridgewater Hotel, Worsley, Lancashire. For Earl of Ellesmere.
Drawings in Bridgewater Collection, Peel Estates Ltd., Estate Office, Worsley. Information communicated by the Revd. David Hinge and Mr. Harold Milliken.

1902–3 **St. David's Welsh Church, Colwyn Bay, Denbighshire.**
(a) G.R. Index. (b) *Bldr.* ob. (c) Thomas, 3, 1913, pp. 202, 204.
Church of St. John the Evangelist, Sandiway, Cheshire. Partly at his own expense.
(a) Information from the Revd. E. J. Basil Jones. (b) G.R. Index. (c) *Journal of the Architectural, Archaeological and Historic Society for the County and City of Chester, and North Wales*, new series, 181, 1911, p. 227. (d) *B.A.* ob. (e) *Bldr.* ob. (f) *B.N.* ob. (g) *Cheshire Observer* ob. (h) *Chester Chronicle* ob. (i) *Chester Courant* ob. (j) *Liverpool Daily Post* ob.

1903 **Houses, Bath Street, Chester.** Built on his own land. (Nos. 1–11 and No. 13).
(a) Date on buildings. (b) Chester City R.O. (93C). Corporation Conveyances. (c) Chester City R.O. (32D). Corporation Leases, Agreements etc. (d) *Archt.*, 79, 1908, p. 288. (e) *Cheshire Observer* ob. (f) *Chester Chronicle* ob. (g) *R.I.B.A.J.* ob.
Former Prudential Assurance Building, Foregate Street/Bath Street, Chester.
(a) Date on building. (b) *Chester Chronicle* ob. (c) *R.I.B.A.J.* ob.
Shop Premises, No. 25 Northgate Street, Chester.
[Formerly the Woolpack Inn; probably to some extent rebuilt by Douglas in 1903, but altered, probably substantially, *c.* 1914, to the design of 1909 by James Strong. (Information from Mr Oliver Bott.)]

The Work of John Douglas

Episcopal Church, Lockerbie, Dumfriesshire.
(a) *Bldr.*, 84, 1903, p. 440. (b) *Bldr.* ob. (c) *Chester Chronicle* ob.
Colshaw Hall, Over Peover, Cheshire.
(a) *A.A.*, 28, 1905, pp. 35, 45. (b) *Bldr.*, 88, 1905, p. 673. (c) *Bldr.* ob. (d) *The Exhibition of the Royal Academy of Arts, 1905*, No. 1586. (e) Peter de Figueiredo and Julian Treuherz, *Cheshire Country Houses*, Chichester, 1988, p. 226.
Screen, Boteler (north-east) Chapel, St. Elphin's Church, Warrington, Lancashire.
(a) *Works*. (b) *Archt.* 71, 1904, p. 400; 79, 1908, p. 288. (c) *Bldr.* ob.

1903–4 **Restoration, The Bear's Paw, Frodsham, Cheshire.**
(a) *Works*. (b) *Archt.*, 72, 1904, p. 264.

c. 1903 * **Children's Home, Pulford, Cheshire.** For second Duke of Westminster. (Unexecuted scheme).
E.E.O., 480, p. 11; 703, pp. 231, 247; 706, pp. 42, 137, 184. 196, 202.

1904 **Rebuilding of Nave, St. Matthew's Church, Buckley, Flintshire.**
(a) *B.N.*, 91, 1906, p. 100. (b) Thomas, 2, 1911, pp. 361–4. References to the church being by Douglas in (c) *A.A.*, 30, 1906, p. 140, (d) *Bldr.*, 89, 1905, p. 368, (e) *B.A.* ob., (f) *Bldr.* ob., (g) *B.N.* ob., (h) *Cheshire Observer* ob., (i) *Chester Chronicle* ob., (j) *Chester Courant* ob., (k) *Liverpool Daily Post* ob., and (l) *R.I.B.A.J.* ob. (m) *Buckley Parish Church, 1822–1972*, J. Clifford Jones, 1974.
Shop Premises for Chester Cooperative Society, Foregate Street, Chester.
Chester City R.O. Minutes of Improvement Committee, 11th and 25th May 1904. (Information from Mr Oliver Bott.)
Lodge and Public Conveniences, Hop Pole Paddock, Frodsham Street, Chester.
Chester City R.O. Minutes of Improvement Committee, 26th March 1904. (Information from Mr Oliver Bott.)
Widening of North Aisle, St Chad's Church, Over, Cheshire.
(a) Kelly. (b) *Old Cheshire Churches*, Raymond Richards, London, 1947, p. 264. (c) *Buildings of England: Cheshire*, N. Pevsner and E. Hubbard, Harmondsworth, 1971, p. 389.

1904–6 **St Deiniol's Library, Hawarden, Flintshire.** Completion. For Gladstone family.
(a) Clwyd R.O. (A/24/1). Documents relating to St Deiniol's Library. (b) Drawings at the Library, including a perspective of 1902, and seven drawings of 1901–4 showing alternative schemes for completing the building. (c) *Archt.*, 71, 1904, p. 400. (d) *B.A.*, 67, 1907, pp. 74, 76. (e) *Bldr.*, 95, 1908, p. 530. (f) *B.A.* ob. (g) *Bldr.* ob. (h) *Chester Chronicle* ob. (i) *R.I.B.A.J.* ob. (j) *The Exhibition of the Royal Academy of Arts, 1906*, No. 1577. (k) Thomas, 2, 1911, pp. 385–6.

c. 1904 **Clare Lodge, Abbots Park, Chester.**
Archt., 79, 1908, pp. 96, 145.

1905 * **Additions, Grosvenor Arms, Aldford, Cheshire.** For second Duke of Westminster.
E.E.O., 480, pp. 1, 11; 704, pp. 337, 343.
Clock Turret, St. Paul's Church, Boughton, Chester. ATTRIB.
Date on structure.
Competition design for Public Library, Wrexham, Denbighshire. (Unexecuted scheme.)
Drawings etc in possession of Design Group Partnership, 9 Abbey Square, Chester.

1905–6 **Minor alterations and additions, St Deiniol's Church, Hawarden, Flintshire.**
Clwyd R.O. (FL/11). Hawarden Parish Magazine, Jan. and Mar. 1906.
Congregational Church, Hoylake, Cheshire. (Flêche removed.)
(a) *B.A.* ob. (b) *Bldr.* ob. (c) *B.N.* ob. (d) *Cheshire Observer* ob. (e) *Chester Courant*

Appendix II Catalogue of Works

ob. (f) *Liverpool Daily Post* ob. (g) Kelly. (h) *The United Reformed Church, Hoylake, Wirral*. J. T. O'Neil, 1982. (h) *Victorian Society News*, Summer 1990, p. 3, 'A Forgotten Church', John Hawke-Genn.
Alterations and additions to Longden Manor, Shropshire. For William Swire. (Demolished.)
(a) *A.A.H.S.C.C.N.C.J.*, new series, 31, part 1, 1935, pp. 81–3. Obituary of C. H. Minshull. (b) Drawings, letters from C. H. Minshull, and accounts in the possession of Mrs Anne Stevens, Longden Manor.
Pair of cottages, Longden Manor, Shropshire. For William Swire.
(a) Date on building. (b) Drawing in the possession of Mrs Anne Stevens, Longden Manor.
Parsonage, Sandiway, Cheshire. Built on his own land. (Now Croft House, No. 82 Weaverham Road. Enlarged.)
(a) Date on building. (b) Cheshire County R.O. (HDT 2469). Title Deeds of Red Walls Children's Home, Sandiway. (c) *Works*. (d) *B.A.*, 69, 1908, pp. 40, 42.

c. 1905–7   **Stables, Longden Manor, Shropshire.** For William Swire.
Drawing and accounts in the possession of Mrs Anne Stevens, Longden Manor.

1906   * **Alterations and additions, Cottage, Eccleston, Cheshire.** For second Duke of Westminster. (Unidentified.)
E.E.O., 480, pp. 2, 11; 704, pp. 58, 208.
Croft Cottages (No. 84 Weaverham Road and No. 45 Norley Road), Sandiway, Cheshire. Built on his own land. (West of church.)
(a) Cheshire R.O. (HDT 2469). Title Deeds of Red Walls Children's Home, Sandiway. (b) *Works*. (c) *B.A.*, 69, 1908, pp. 40, 42.

1906–7   **Church of the Resurrection and All Saints, Caldy, Cheshire.** (Remodelling of former School of 1868 by G.E. Street.)
(a) Cheshire R.O. (P 46/20/2). Plan and sentence of consecration. (b) *West Kirby Parish Magazine*, Apr., Nov., Dec., 1907; Jan. 1908. (c) *Bldr.*, 120, 1921, p. 147. (d) *West Kirby and Hilbre*, John Brownbill, Liverpool, 1928, pp. 310–11.
The Homestead, Sandiway, Cheshire. For B. J. Sanby, to whom Douglas sold the land. (House and Stables, now Red Walls Children's Home). ATTRIB.
Cheshire R.O. (HDT 2469). Title Deeds of Red Walls Children's Home, Sandiway.

1907   * **Additions and Re-Instatement after Fire, Laundry, Eaton Hall, Cheshire.** For second Duke of Westminster. (Now Eaton Estate Office).
E.E.O., 704, p. 617.
The Sundial, Hawarden, Flintshire. For Miss Helen Gladstone.
(a) Date on building. (b) *A.A.*, 33, 1908, pp. 159–60. (c) *B.N.*, 102, 1912, pp. 415–6. (d) *Chester Chronicle* ob. (e) *R.I.B.A.J.* ob.
Baptistery, St Chad's Church, Over, Cheshire.
Cheshire R.O. (P 46/7/7).
All Saints' Church, St Andrews, Fifeshire. Chancel and belltower. (Nave 1920–23 by Paul Waterhouse).
(a) *St Andrews*, The Handbook of the St Andrews Preservation Trust to the City and its Buildings, revised ed., St Andrews, 1971, pp. 42–3. (b) Reference to work at St Andrews by Douglas in *Chester Chronicle* ob. (c) *All Saints' Church, St Andrews. A Handbook*, Judith W. George, 1975.
Rebuilding after fire and enlargement, Shotwick Park, Great Saughall, Cheshire. For Thorneycroft Vernon.
(a) Date on building. (b) Kelly's *Directory of Cheshire*, 1939.
St. Andrew's Church, West Kirby, Cheshire. Completion. (East end).
(a) G.R. Index. (b) *A.A.*, 35, 1909, p. 6. (c) *B.A.*, 72, 1909, pp. 164, 168. (d) *Bldr.*, 96, 1909, p. 546. (e) *The Exhibition of the Royal Academy of Arts*, 1909, No.

275

The Work of John Douglas

1562. References to the church being by Douglas in (f) *B.A.* ob., (g) *B.N.* ob., (h) *Cheshire Observer* ob., (i) *Chester Courant* ob., and (j) *Liverpool Daily Post* ob.

c. 1907 **Design for a Hillside House, Cheshire.** (Unidentified. Probably a hypothetical scheme).
(a) *Works.* (b) *B.A.*, 68, 1907, pp. 440, 444.
* **Almhouses, Chester.** For second Duke of Westminster. ('Group of cottages west of Cathedral'. Unexecuted.)
(a) E.E.O., 704, p. 502. (b) *B.A.*, 69, 1908, pp. 295, 298.
Sanctuary Screens and Fittings, St Mary's Roman Catholic Church, Latchford, Warrington, Lancashire.
(a) *A.A.*, 31, 1907, p. 9. (b) *Bldr.*, 92, 1907, p. 629; 94, 1908, p. 370. (c) *B.N.*, 92, 1907, pp. 685–6. (d) *Bldr.* ob. (e) *The Exhibition of the Royal Academy of Arts, 1907*, No. 1587.

1908 **Additions, Grosvenor Club and North and South Wales Bank, Eastgate Street, Chester.** (Now Midland Bank.)
(a) *A.A.*, 33, 1908, p. 154. (b) *B.N.*, 95, 1908, pp. 365–6. (c) Kelly.
Reconstruction and Extension of Cooperative Society Shop Premises, Garden Lane/Orchard Street, Chester.
Chester City R.O. Minutes of the Improvement Committee, 3rd June 1908. (Information from Mr Oliver Bott.)
Church House, St Asaph, Flintshire.
(a) Date on building. (b) *Bldr.* ob.

1908–9 **Vestries, St Deiniol's Church, Hawarden, Flintshire.**
(a) Clwyd R.O. Hawarden Parish Vestry Book, 1654–1961. Vestry Meetings, Tuesday in Easter Week 1906, 21st Apr. 1908, 13th Apr. 1909. (b) Clwyd R.O. (D/BJ/318). Hawarden Churchwardens' Accounts. (c) Clwyd R.O. St Deiniol's Library. Gladstone Estate and Household Papers. Leaflet concerning new Vestries, Hawarden Church, 1908. (d) Thomas, 2, 1911, p. 381.

1908–10 **Vestry, All Saints' Church, Gresford, Denbighshire.** (Execution of scheme initiated by Richard Creed.)
(a) Vicars' Books, Gresford Vicarage. (b) Thomas, 3, 1913, p. 253.

c. 1908 **Alternative Design for a Hillside House, Cheshire.** (Unidentified, Probably a hypothetical scheme.)
(a) *Works.* (b) *B.A.*, 69, 1908, pp. 3, 6.

1909 **Addition of South Aisle, St. Paul's Church, Helsby, Cheshire.**
G.R. Index.

1909–10 **Egerton Street School, Chester.** (With W. T. Lockwood).
(a) Date on building. (b) *Bldr.* ob. (c) Kelly.

1910 **Addition of Chancel, Holy Trinity Church, Greenfield, Flintshire.**
G.R. Index.

1910–11 **Cherry Grove School, Boughton, Chester.** (With W. T. Lockwood).
(a) *Chester Chronicle*, 8th Mar. 1911. (b) *Bldr.* ob. (c) Kelly.
Tower, St. Paul's Church, Colwyn Bay, Denbighshire. Completed posthumously.
(a) G.R. Index. (b) *B.A.* ob. (c) *Cheshire Observer* ob. (d) *Chester Chronicle* ob. (e) *R.I.B.A.J.* ob. (f) *B.A.*, 74, 1910, p. 251. (g) Thomas, 3, 1913, p. 202. (h) Guide book: *The Story of the Parish Church of Colwyn Bay*, W. Hugh Rees, Gloucester, 1970. References to the church being by Douglas in (i) *Bldr.* ob., (j) *B.N.* ob., (k) *Chester Courant* ob., and (l) *Liverpool Daily Post* ob.
St Matthew's Church, Saltney Ferry, Flintshire. (Possibly to a Douglas & Minshull design of 1905.)
(a) G.R. Index. (b) Date on building.

Appendix II Catalogue of Works

1911–12 **Organ Case, All Saints' Church, Gresford, Denbighshire.**
(a) Vicars' Books, Gresford. (b) Thomas, 3, 1913, p. 253.

1912 **Addition of South Aisle, All Saints' Church, Hoole, Chester.** (With F. Walley). Posthumous execution of a design made in Douglas's lifetime?
G.R. Index.
Tower. Church of St. John the Baptist, Old Colwyn, Denbighshire. By the firm of Douglas, Minshull & Muspratt, but possibly a posthumous execution of a design made in Douglas's lifetime.
(a) Drawings at church. (b) *A.A.*, 43, 1913, p. 101. (c) Thomas, 3, 1913, p. 202.

Undated **Estate Buildings, Abberley, Worcestershire.** For John Joseph Jones and William Jones. (Including The Corner House, North Lodge, and a pair of cottages.) ATTRIB.
(a) *Abberley Manor*, J. L. Moilliet, p. 70. (b) Information from Mr Alan Crawford.
* **Glebe Farm, Aldford, Cheshire.**
E.E.O., 700, p. 869; 703, p. 301.
* **Farm Buildings, Woodhouse Farm, Aldford, Cheshire.** ATTRIB.
E.E.O. Notebook.
Remodelling of Appleton Hall, Cheshire. For Thomas Henry Lyon. (Demolished.) [House built, in Italianate style, *c.* 1830. Remodelling possibly c.1860 – date on ruined Gothic lodge.]
(a) *The Mansions of England and Wales. The County Palatine of Chester*, E. Twycross, 1850, 2, pp. 81–2; (b) *Architects', Engineers' and Building Trades Directory*, London, 1868, p. 109. (c) Ormerod, 1, p. 616. (d) *B.N.*, 50. 1890, p. 706. (e) *B.N.* ob. (f) *Cheshire Country Houses*, Peter de Figueiredo and Julian Treuherz, Chichester, 1988, p. 211. (g) Information from Mrs. K. M. Harris.
Stalls and Prayer Desks, Christ Church, Bala, Merioneth.
Cheshire R.O. (P 68/6/148). Letter from J. Douglas to Revd. G. Egerton-Warburton, 25th Mar. 1896.
Bench-End in a Country Church. (Unidentified.)
B.A., 42, 1894, p. 252.
Competition Design for Church, Bramhall, Cheshire. (Unexecuted scheme.)
Drawings in possession of Design Group Partnership, 9 Abbey Square, Chester.
A Cheshire Farm for Thirty Acres. (Unidentified. Probably a hypothetical scheme.)
(a) *Works*. (b) *B.A.*, 70, 1908, pp. 347, 350.
Suburban House, Cheshire. For W. J. Wallington. Built in two stages. (Unidentified.)
B.A., 36, 1891, pp. 456, 497.
* **Row of Seven Cottages, Lumley Place, Chester.** ATTRIB.
E.E.O. Notebook.
Designs for brick chimneys, for manufacture by J. C. Edwards, Ruabon.
B.A., 43, 1895, pp. 94, 96.
Farm on the Cholmondeley Estate, Cheshire. (Unidentified.)
E.E.O., 700, p. 447.
Design for a Church. (Unidentified.)
Works.
* **Pair of Cottages, Churton, Cheshire.** (North of village on west side of road.)
E.E.O. Notebook.
Houses, Colwyn Bay, Denbighshire. (Unidentified.)
B.A., 48, 1897, p. 143.
House on a Corner Site (near Wrexham?). (Unidentified.)
B.A., 17, 1882, p. 30.
Gravestone, Christ Church, Churchyard, Crowton, Cheshire.
B.A., 31, 1889, pp. 320, 329.
Kennels, Croxteth Hall, Lancashire. For fourth Earl of Sefton.

The Work of John Douglas

Undated (a) *Chester Chronicle* ob. (b) *R.I.B.A.J.* ob.
Screen, North-East Chapel, St. Mary's Church, Eastham, Cheshire. ATTRIB.
* **Buerton Kennels, Eaton Hall, Cheshire.** ATTRIB.
E.E.O. Notebook.
* **Stallion Boxes, The Eaton Stud, Eaton Hall, Cheshire.**
(a) E.E.O. Notebook. (b) E.E.O. Photographs. (c) D.G.P. Photographs.
* **Police House, Eaton Road, Eccleston, Cheshire.** ATTRIB.
Addition of Chancel, North-East Chapel and North-West Tower and Spire, St. Mary's Church, Edmonton, Middlesex.
(Unexecuted scheme)
Works.
Addition of South-West Porch, St. Mary's Church, Edmonton, Middlesex. (Demolished). ATTRIB.
G.R. Index.
Elford House. (Unidentified).
B.N., 58, 1890, p. 706.
Additions to Glossop Hall, Derbyshire.
B.N. ob.
* **Pair of Cottages, Gorstella, Cheshire.** (Easternmost block on south side of road to Balderton). ATTRIB.
(a) E.E.O. Notebook. (b) E.E.O. Photographs.
Goldmine House, No. 26 Southbank, Great Budworth, Cheshire. For R. E. Egerton-Warburton.
B.A., 22, 1884, pp. 282–4.
* **Alterations, Halkyn Castle, Flintshire.** ATTRIB. (Probably contemporary with additions by Douglas, 1885.)
Reredos, St Peter's Church, Hargrave, Cheshire.
A.A.H.S.C.C.N.C.J., 15, 1909, p. 139.
Monument to Sir Stephen Glynne (died 1874), St Deiniol's Church, Hawarden, Flintshire.
B.A., 17, 1882, pp. 187–8.
Restoration, Dairy Farmhouse, High Legh, Cheshire. (Possibly Dairy Farm, Halliwell's Brow.)
B.A., 58, 1902, pp. 431, 442. (Referred to as 'Old Hall'.)
Estate Cottages, Holkham, Norfolk. (Unexecuted scheme.)
Drawing at Holkham. (Information from Dr. J. M. Robinson.)
A Hymn Board. (Unidentified.)
B.A., 50, 1898, p. 238.
Restoration, Cottage, Lymm, Cheshire. (Unidentified.)
B.A., 15, 1881, pp. 183, 185.
Farm(s), Lymm, Cheshire. For George C. Dewhurst. (In addition to Burford Lane Farm, Heatley, Oughtrington, c. 1866. Unidentified).
A.A.H.S.C.C.N.C.J., 3, 1885, pp. 529, 532–3.
Cottage and Two Entrance Lodges, Oakmere Hall, Cheshire. ATTRIB. (Probably contemporary with house by Douglas, 1867. Lodges much enlarged.)
Billiard Room etc, Oakmere Hall, Cheshire. (Probably later than rest of house.)
Lonnin Garth, Portinscale, Cumberland.
Country Cottages and Week-End Homes. J. H. Elder-Duncan, London, 1906, pp. 80, 84–5.
* **Farm Buildings, Meadow House Farm, Pulford, Cheshire.** ATTRIB.
(a) E.E.O. Notebook. (b) E.E.O. Photographs.
* **Pair of Cottages, Pulford, Cheshire.** (East of Manor Farm). ATTRIB.
(a) E.E.O. Notebook. (b) E.E.O. Photographs.
Outbuildings at Farmhouse and Cottage, Mount Alyn, Rossett, Denbighshire. ATTRIB. (Probably contemporary with the Farmhouse and Cottage, c. 1881).

Appendix II Catalogue of Works

Undated **Tower, Church of St. John the Evangelist, Sandiway, Cheshire.** Posthumous execution of Douglas's design.
(a) Information from the Revd. E. J. Basil Jones. (b) *Cheshire Observer* ob. (c) *Chester Chronicle* ob.
Forest Hey, Sandiway, Cheshire. (Original house, prior to later remodelling). ATTRIB.
Cottage, Forest Hey, Sandiway, Cheshire. (North-west of house). ATTRIB.
Manor House, Sandiway, Cheshire. (Remodelling of earlier farmhouse).
(a) *Archt.*, 72, 1904, p.264. (Referred to as 'Delamere Cottage'). (b) *B.A.*, 50, 1898, pp. 165–6.
Restoration, St Edith's Church, Shocklach, Cheshire. (Unexecuted scheme.)
Engraving at Arley Hall.
Stratton Park. (Unidentified.)
(a) *B.N.*, 58, 1890, p. 706. (b) *B.N.* ob.
Cottages, Twemlow Green, Cheshire.
(a) *Works.* (b) *B.A.*, 42, 1894, p. 292.
St Paul's School-Chapel, Utkinton, Cheshire.
Kelly.
Cottages (east of house) and Entrance Lodge, Vale Royal, Cheshire. For second Lord Delamere. ATTRIB.
* **Farmhouse and part of Farm Buildings, Avenue Farm, Waverton, Cheshire.** ATTRIB.
E.E.O. Notebook. (Referred to as 'Wright'. Identified through Estate Rentals).
* **Farm Buildings, Common Farm, Waverton, Cheshire.** ATTRIB.
E.E.O. Notebook. (Referred to as 'Gregory.' Identified through Estate Rentals).
* **Guy Lane Farm, Waverton, Cheshire.** ATTRIB.
E.E.O. Notebook. (Referred to as 'Mullock.' Identified through Estate Rentals).
* **Farm Buildings, Oak Farm, Waverton, Cheshire.** ATTRIB.
E.E.O. Notebook. (Referred to as 'Lee.' Identified through Estate Rentals).
Public Hall and Market, Whitchurch, Shropshire. (Unexecuted scheme).
Works.
Additions, Cassia Lodge, Whitegate, Cheshire. For second Lord Delamere. ATTRIB.
Cae-li-Cae Farmhouse, Willington, Malpas, Cheshire.
For the Gredington Estate. ATTRIB.
Stables, Youlgreave, Derbyshire.
B.A., 43, 1895, pp. 111–12.

The Work of John Douglas

ADDENDA

(i) Arley Hall Estate, Cheshire

The collection at Arley Hall includes many drawings made by Douglas for unexecuted projects, for Rowland Egerton-Warburton. They include a chair (1868); remodelling the Vicarage, Great Budworth (1872–3); pump near the Smithy, Great Budworth (1873); re-erecting the Hall screen in the Dining Room at Arley Hall (1873); cottages (1873); alterations to Birch Brook, Arley (1874); alterations to Dr. Willetts' house, Great Budworth (1874); Club Room, Great Budworth (first scheme, 1875); porch for Burgess' Cottage, Old Saracen's Head, Great Budworth (1875); two schemes for cottages (1875); cottages at Great Budworth (1875); remodelling the approach to the church, Great Budworth (first scheme, 1876); labourers' cottages and widow's cottage (1876); remodelling the approach to the church (second scheme) and lych-gate, Great Budworth (1877); Club Room, Great Budworth (second scheme, 1881); farmhouse (1882); pair of cottages (1882); Agent's House, Westage Lane, Great Budworth (1888).

Attribution of Douglas-like buildings on the estate to him is best avoided, since so many of the buildings erected by Rowland Egerton-Warburton have characteristics associated with Douglas, and drawings for buildings by other architects (especially Edmund Kirby) also show these characteristics. Furthermore, it seems probable that the Estate Office often adapted designs by Douglas and others. Later in the century, Piers Egerton-Warburton (Rowland's son and heir) played a part in this (*Arley Hall, Cheshire*, Charles Foster, 1982, p. 30).

The date of the cottage by Nesfield at Great Budworth (p. 80) can be settled by reference to two drawings at Arley Hall. One is dated 3rd Sep. 1866, the other (signed 'Nesfield and Shaw') 11th Oct. 1866. The latter, however, although showing the date 1866 in the pargetting, bears the note 'Draw 1866, perhaps 1865 would be preferred'.

(ii) Croxteth Hall, Lancashire.

The Kennels designed by Douglas were identified by the author as being the High Victorian ones ¾ mile east of Croxteth Hall (SE of Ewens Park), whereas he attributed the 'Vernacular' style Kennels ½ mile north of the Hall (near Coalpit Hey) to Nesfield. The Gamekeepers' Cottages next to these Kennels are probably also by Nesfield.

The Estate Account Book for 1854–1860 states that in 1860 W. A. Nesfield was paid £196 'for visits and plans for forming Park &c at Croxteth from 1855 to 1859', and also that W. E. Nesfield was paid £114 in 1859 for designs for four lodges, and also 'gates, posts, doorways &c'.

As the Douglas Kennels are High Victorian in style, they presumably date from before *c.* 1870, but the accounts for 1861–71 do not survive. In the 1870s, little building was done on the estate, partly because T. H. Wyatt's new Nursery Wing and the associated 'thorough renovation and alteration of the whole of the old Mansion' cost between £50 and £60,000. So the first work by Douglas recorded in the accounts is Altcar Church (1878–9). In 1885, the year in which Abbeystead was begun, the Agent explained to Lord Sefton that the greater expenditure on new buildings on his estates in that year was 'on account of the more expensive buildings which your Lordship allowed me to undertake from Mr Douglas's plans'.

Index

Numbers in **bold** type indicate illustrations

Abberley (Worcs) estate buildings 258, 277
   West Lodge 250
Abbey Square Sketch Book 11–3, **12**, 78, 79, 81, **83**, 83, **84, 85**, 86, 87–8, **88**, 89, **93**, 93, 95, 107, 108, 109, 130, 132, **133**, 133, 149, 185, 206
Abbeystead *see* Over Wyresdale
Adams, Maurice B., quoted 14, 36, 207
Aldford, Aldford Hall Farm 65, **66**, 93, 231, 246, 250
   Bank Farm 256
   cottages at, 90, **91**, 97, **164**, 245, 246, 247, 253–4, 259, 263, 265, 266, 267
   Ford Lane 260
   Gamekeeper's House 265
   Glebe Farm 277
   Green Lake Farmhouse 88, 241
   Grosvenor Arms 60, 161, 261, 274
   Lea Hall Farmhouse 33, **99**, 244, 262
   Lodge to Eaton Hall 90, 248
   Methodist New Connexion Chapel 184, 260
   Oak Farm 257
   Pumphouse 244
   Reading Room 267
   St John the Baptist 48, **49**, 56, 130, 195, 239, 244, 273
   schools 242
   smithy 256
   Woodhouse Farm 277
Allington, Almere Farm 252
Altcar (Lancs), St Michael's **126**, 126–7, 249, 280
Appleton Hall (Cheshire) 277
Arley estate buildings 212 n19, 222 n5, 223 n21, 224 n29, 227 n4, 243, 244, 280
Arley Hall 79, 233 n21, 280
   The Bothy 243
   chapel 225 n14
Ashton (Cheshire), St John the Evangelist 271
Astbury, St. Mary's, Stall-ends **133**
Aston-by-Budworth, Hield House Farm 242
Austin, H.J., architect 19, 21, 209

Backford, St Oswald's, reredos 261
Bailey, H.J. 251
Bakewell, William, clerk 48
Bala, Christ Church 277
Balderton Cheese Factory 245
   cottages at, 257, 265
   smallholding 268
Balfour, Alexander 251, 252
Bangor, The Friars School **153**, 153, 258, 270
Bangor Is-coed, St Dunawd's 141, 240, 247
   Rectory Lodge 268
Bankes, John Scott 240, 243, 248
Barmouth, Plas Mynach 33, 109, **110, 111**, 253
Barmouth, St John the Divine, 15–6, **177**, 177–9, 220 n27, 226 n4, 259–60
Beckett, Richard, builder 3, 71–2, 212–3 n32
Beckett, Richard Thomas, architect 3, 206
Beckett, Samuel, land agent 67, 74
Belgrave (Cheshire), Gamekeeper's House 265
   Wrexham Road cottages **18, 90**, 242, 257
Bennett, J.N. 239
Beswick, H.W., architect 196, 207
Betws Gwerfil Goch, St Mary's 141, 142, **143**, 251
Bickley, St Wenefrede's **182**, 182, 261
Birkenhead, Bidston Court (now Hill Bark) 206
   Charing Cross, Bank buildings 197–8, **198**, 272
   Redcourt, Claughton 205
Blore, Edward, architect 19, 40, 217 n15
Boden, W.M., architect 207, 229 n32
Bodley, George Frederick, architect 62, 71, 75, 77
Bootle Town Hall design 29, 116, 250
Borwick Hall (Lancs) 149
Bramhall (Cheshire) church design 277
Bretton (Flints), Bretton Hall Farm 261
   cottages at, 269

281

The Work of John Douglas

Elms Farm 259
Hope's Place Farm 260
Inn at, 270
smallholding at, 270
British Architect 2, 3–4, 6, 27, 33, 34, 36, 64, 80, 114, 188, 210
Broadbent, Charles 247
Brocksford Hall (Derbys) 155–6, **156**, 157, 262
Bromyard, Rowden Abbey 109, 132, 134, 251
Brooke, Sir Richard 258
Broxton, Higher Hall 105–7, 244
Bruera, Aldford Cheese Factory 36, 64, 99, 245
    Churton Heath Lodge 67, 261
    Lea Newbold Farmhouse **93**, 93, 244, 267
Bryn-y-Maen *see* Colwyn Bay
Bryn-y-Pys *see* Overton
Buckley, St Matthew's 200–1, 268, 272, 273, 274
Buddicom, W.B. 245, 246
Builder 23, 26, 33, 82, 130, 149, 157, 216 n126
Bunbury, Bunbury Heath School 245
    St Boniface's 185, 264
Burn, William, architect 59–60, 61, 220 n1
Burwardsley, St John's 139, 242, 249
Butterfield, William, architect 38, 39, 79, 200

Caldy, Church of the Resurrection 202, 274
Capenhurst, Holy Trinity 184, 259
Chester, Abbey Square 4
    No. 6   4, 5, 27, 31
    No. 7   239
    Abbots Park, Clare Lodge 202, 274
    All Saints, Hoole 204, 277
    Almshouses design 276
    Archaeological Society 11, 24–5, 26, 42
    Bath Street, Nos. 1–11 **193**, 193–4, 273
    Bishopsfield Girls' School, Hoole 239
    Boughton Cross shops 270
    Bridge Street, No. 30 244, 272
    No. 38 **166**, 166, **167**, 268, 269
    Brook Street, No. 67 269
    Cherry Grove School, Boughton 204, 276
    Christ Church 131, 200, 246–7, 262–3, 268, 269, 271

City Road Triumphal Arch 81, **82**, 82, 240
Dee Banks, Nos. 9 & 11 268
    Nos. 31 & 33 5, 5–6, 7, 56–8, 80, 240
    Walmoor Hill **8**, 8, 9, 11, 13, 188, 196, 229 n40, 266
Eastgate 243
    Jubilee clock tower **121**, 155, 196, 268, 270
    designs 252, 254
Eastgate Street, corner with St Werburgh Street 240
    Crypt Buildings 26
Edgar's Field, Shelter Shed 261
Egerton Street school 204, 276
Foregate Street, Co-operative stores 227 n13, 274
    Little Nag's Head Cocoa House **106**, 107, 141, 158, 162, 247
    No. 113 260
    No. 117 167, 258, 259
    No. 142 122, **123**, 254
    Parker's Buildings 69, 166–7, 258
    Police Station *see* No 142
Frodsham Street, Hop Pole Paddock 271, 274
Garden Lane, Co-operative stores 276
Greyfriars/Nuns Road, house 254
Grosvenor Club (now Midland Bank) 120–1, **121**, 132, 198, 251, 276
Grosvenor Park 28, 46–8
    Billy Hobby's Well 47, 50, 81
    entrance lodge **46**, 47, 56, 78, 88, 239
    irregular payments for, 47–8
    seats in, 14
    Baptist Church 114, 249–50
Grosvenor Park Road, Nos. 6–11 **112**, 113–4, 115, 117, 250, *see also* 243
Grosvenor Street, Nurses' Home 269, 273
The Groves, Manager's House 255–6
half-timber revival 24, 25, 26, 78
Handbridge, cottages at 267, 271
    Pinfold Lane farm 269
Harp & Crown Inn *see* Bridge Street No 30
Holy Trinity Church 270–1
in nineteenth century 23–6
Lower Bridge Street, Falcon Cocoa House 250
Lumley Place, cottages 277
Maypole, Handbridge 250
Nicholas Street, cottage 263

Index

Northgate Street, No. 19 272
  No. 21 238
  No. 23 239
  No. 25 273
Shoemaker's Row 196, 272, 273
  widening 256
Public Market, Cocoa House 252
Prudential Building 193–4, 195, 273
The Queen's School 205, 206
St Barnabas Mission Church 247
St John the Baptist 184–5, 247, 251, 256, 257
St John Street house 249
St Martin's Welsh Church 253
St Mary without the walls 262
  sexton's cottage 257
St Oswald's Vicarage 116, 250
St Paul's, Boughton 11, 13, **125**, 125–6, 128, 201, 247, 273, 274
St Peter's, restoration of, 184, 256
St Werburgh Street, east side
  endpapers, 15, 16–7, 31, 75, 79, 189–192, **191**, 266, 269
  St Werburgh Chambers 243 (now Nos. 29–33)
  St Werburgh's Mount 244 (now Nos. 15–27)
shop signs 260, 262
Uffington House, Dee Hills Park 205
Union Street Public Baths 16, 196–7, **197**, 229 n40, 270
Upper Northgate Street, Nos. 21 & 23 43, 47, 238–9, 239
Vicar's Lane, House of Shelter 166, 259, 265
Cholmondeley estate, farm at 277
Cholmondeley, Hugh, 2nd Baron Delamere 27, 40, 41, 238, 245, 248, 249, 279
Cholmondeley, the Hon. Mrs 27, 40, 238
Cholmondeley, Marquess of 261
Cholmondeley, Thomas, 1st Baron Delamere 1, 2, 212 n19
Churton, John 252
Churton, Churton Stud 263
  cottages at, 270
  Stannage Farm 266
Cilcain Hall (Flints) 246
Cilcain, St Mary's 258
Cloverley Hall (Salop) 77
Colwyn Bay, Bryn-y-Maen, Christ Church **178**, **179**, 179–80, 186, 188, 203, 267
  House 270
  Vicarage 152, 269

Colwyn Bay Hotel 110–11, 113, 117, 243
houses at, 277
Lletty Dryw Hall 152, 263
St David's Welsh Church 273
St John the Baptist *see* Old Colwyn
St Paul's 9, **175**, 175–6, **176**, 186, 204, 220 n27, 257, 264, 276
  Vicarage 152, 155, 169, 264
Combermere Abbey, Butler's cottage 272
Connah's Quay, St Mark's 247
Conwy, Castle Hotel 155, 156, 169, 254–5
Cotebrook (Cheshire) Parsonage 258
Crewe Hall, Stowford Cottages **78**
Criccieth, St Deiniol's **172**, 173, 254
Crowton, Christ Church, gravestone at 277
Croxteth Hall (Lancs) 80, 222–3, n5, 277, 280
Crum, W.G. 256
Cubitt, James: *Church Design for Congregations*, cited 56
Cuddington, Abbotsford 260
  Overdale 246

Davenham, St Wilfred's 22
Davison, T. Raffles, architect 33, 64, 80, 109, 114, 122, 126, 149, 151
De Tabley, 2nd Lord 242
Deganwy, All Saints 180–1, **181**, 183, 268–9
Delamere, 1st Baron (Thomas Cholmondeley) 1, 2, 212 n19
Delamere, 2nd Baron (Hugh Cholmondeley) 27, 40, 41, 238, 245, 248, 249, 279
Denson, W. 238–9
Denton, J.B.: *The Farm Homesteads of England* 65
Devey, George, architect 77
Dewhurst, George C. 240, 278
Dickson, F. & A. 240
Dickson, S.J.R. 269
Dobie, Dr W.M. 239
Dodleston, cottages at, 269, 271
  Dodleston Farm 269
  Dodleston Lane Farm 260
  Pump House 244
  Reading Room etc 267
  St Mary's **129**, 129–30, 241
  school 88, 101, 241
  shippon 266
Douglas, Elizabeth (née Edmunds) (J.D.'s wife) 4–6

The Work of John Douglas

Douglas, John, architect, birth 1
  book plate **v**
  caricature of, **xx**
  character 13
  children 4–5, 6
  correspondence 14–5, 29–31, 224–5, 230–7
  death 9
  education 3
  in 1890 **10**
  lack of financial control 15–6, 47–8, 69, 179
  marriage 4
  patrons 28
  property ownership 16–7
  pupils and assistants 205–8
  pupillage 19–22
  sisters 1, 3
  will 9
Douglas, John senior (J.D.'s father) 1–2, 3, 211 n5, 212 n19
Douglas, Mary (née Swindley) (J.D.'s mother) 1, 48
Douglas, Sholto Theodore (J.D.'s son) 4, 7, 8, 9–10, 11, 195
Douglas & Fordham, architects 6, 60, 146–180, 236–7
Douglas & Minshull, architects 6, 7, 187–204
Douglas, Minshull & Muspratt, architects 7
Droitwich Cottage Hospital 152–3, 260

Eastham, Carlett Park chapel 173, 186, 254
  St Mary's 42, 139–40, 238, 245, 251, 252, 256, 261, 278
Eastlake, Charles L.: *Hints on Household Taste* 87, 105, *History of the Gothic Revival* 59, 222 n2
Eaton estate 59, 60, 61
  buildings 62–76, 79, 89, **163**, **165**
  management 64, 68
Eaton, Gas Works Cottages 249
Eaton Hall 39, 59, 60, 61, 64, 75, 76, 77, 212 n19, 220 n7, 223 n5
  Aldford Lodge 90, 248
  Belgrave Kennels 242
  Belgrave Lodge 259
  Bruera Lodge 260
  Buerton Kennels 278
  cricket pavilion 264
  Deer Fence 262
  Dutch Tea House 101, **102**, 243
  Eccleston Approach Bridge 263
  Eccleston Hill Lodge **frontisp.** 119, 137, 250
  Eccleston Lodge 69, 161–3, **162**, 242, 263
  Gamekeeper's Cottage (now Eaton Lodge) 97–9, **98**, 241
  garden gates 264
  Gardeners' Bothy 69–70, **70**, 161, 162, 263
  Hatton Heath Lodge 258
  Iron Bridge Lodge 264
  Laundry 263, 275
  Luncheon Room design **35**, 247
  North Lodge 263
  obelisk 166, 260
  Park Keeper's Cottage (now Deer Park Cottage) **79**, 242
    Pulford Approach, cottages at, **158**, 254
  Stud Lodge **35**, 119, 251
  Upper Belgrave Lodge 75, 248
Eaton Lodge *see* Eaton Hall, Gamekeeper's Cottage
Eaton Stud 62, **63**, 74, 80–1, 97, 241, 242, 254, 263, 278
Ecclesiologist 19, 20, 21, 46
Eccleston, Church Cottage 95, 241
  Coach-House 241
  cottage groups 90–2, **162**, 163, 244, 252, 254, 257, 260, 265, 269, 271, 275
  Eccleston Hill 68, 118–9, 120, 147, 251, 262
  Ferry House 75, 165, 257, 258
  Gas Works Cottage 268
  Green Bank Lodge 253
  The Paddocks **xix**, **68**, 72, 119–20, 121, 230–7, 253
    loose boxes 242
  Pumphouse 246
  Rake Farm 249, 265
  Reading Room 262
  St Mary's 60, 71, 75, 76
  school **100**, 101, 124, 134, 245
  Shelter Shed 255
  smithy 62, 67, 165, 267
  stables 268
  Upper Servants' Houses (now Morris Oak) 102–3, 246
  Wrexham Road Farm 65, 93, **94**, **95**, 94–5, 147, 160, 221 n23, 223 n23, 249, 260
Edmonton, St Mary's 200, 278
Edwards, J.C., brick manufacturer 113, 137, 158, 160, standard chimneys **161**, 277

Index

Edwards, Peter, of Dodleston, builder 72, 73, 74
Edwards, Walter, architect 205
Egerton, Sir Philip M. de Grey 244
Egerton-Warburton, Rev. Geoffrey 224–5 n10, 225 nn11 & 14
  Piers 280
Egerton-Warburton, Rowland E., 28, 79, 92, 104, 110, 137, 212 n19, 223 n21, 224 nn29 & 31, 225 n14, 227 n4, 240, 241, 242, 243, 244, 246, 250, 252, 253, 258, 263, 278
Elford House 278
Ellesmere, Earl of, 264, 265, 266, 267, 272, 273
Eltz, Schloss **96**, 97
Eyton (Denbigh) school-chapel 241

Farndon, St Chad's 240
Flint, Cornist Hall 147–8, 254
  Plas-y-Mynydd 253
Fordham, Daniel Porter, architect (J.D.'s partner) 6–7, 15, 81, 146, 147, 153, 156, 170, 171, 187, 214 n61
Frampton, Edward Reginald, stained glass artist 224–5 n10
Frankby, Hill Bark Farm 246
Frodsham Baptist Church (now Union Church) 256
Frodsham, The Bear's Paw 274
  Dunsdale **97**, 247
  Overton School 246
Frost, Mrs Eleanor 152, 179, 267, 269, 270

Garnett, Robert & Sons 238
Gerona Cathedral (Spain) 220 n27
Gladstone family 28, 202–3, 260, 266, 272, 274
Gladstone, Helen 275
Gladstone, W.E. 61–2, 198, 200, 257, 258, 261
Glangwna (Caernarfon) 157, 262
Gloddaeth (Caernarfon), west wing 258
Glossop Hall 278
Glossop Technical School 272
Godwin, E.W., architect 77, 81
Goodhart-Rendel, H.S., quoted 48, 173–4, 175, 194, 200, 204
Gorstella, cottages at 257, 267, 278
  Gorstella Farm 159, 255, 260
  Old Smithy 260
  smithy 257
Grayson, G.E., architect 205
Grayson & Ould, architects 206, 228 n6

Great Barrow, Barrowmore Hall 36, **116**, **117**, 117–8, 252
  Manor House 244
  St Bartholomew's 141, 142, 242, 253
Great Budworth, Budworth Heath Farm 241
  Cock Inn stables 252
  cottages at, 79, 80
  Dene Cottages 240
  design for Dr Willetts' house 35
  George & Dragon Inn **35**, **92**, 92–3, 246
  Goldmine House 278
  High Street, Nos. 54–7, 242
  St Mary & All Saints 185, **186**, 254
Great Crosby Congregational Church 184, 268
Great Saughall, Shotwick Park **114**, 114, 115, 117, 243, 275
Greaves, R.M. 262
Greenfield (Flints) Holy Trinity 203, 276
Gresford, All Saints 249, 265, 276, 277
Grosvenor, Hugh Lupus *see* 1st Duke of Westminster
Grosvenor, Richard *see* 2nd Marquess of Westminster

Halkyn Castle (Flints) 151, 256, 278
Halkyn, St Mary the Virgin **134**, 134–7, **135**, **136**, 138, 139, 248
Halton, St Mary's, gravestone & memorial tablet 258
Hargrave, St Peter's 260, 278
  schoolmaster's house 271
Harrison, James, architect 26, 65, 217 n11
Hart, Son & Peard 137
Hartford, Hartford Lodge (now Whitehall) 1–2
  St John's 130–1, 134, 137, 174, 244, 255
Hawarden Castle 157, 257, 258, 260
Hawarden, St Deiniol's Church 185, 202, 248, 254, 261, 266, 272–3, 274, 276, 278
  St Deiniol's Library 29, 62, 72, 198–200, **199**, 271, 272–3, 274
  The Sundial 203, 275
Haydock (Lancs), St James's 181–2, 261
Heatley *see* Oughtrington
Helsby, St Paul's **54**, 54–5, 56, 81, 240, 276
High Legh, Dairy Farmhouse 278
Higher Kinnerton, All Saints 263
Hignett, Harold, architect 206, 207
Higson, John, of Liverpool 50, 240

285

The Work of John Douglas

Hillside house design (unidentified) **189**, 276
Hinderton Hall (Cheshire) 51, **52**
Hodgkinson, G. 243, 244
Hodkinson, Edward, architect, 60, 206–7, 228 n26
Hoghton Tower, oriel window at, 148, 149, 151, 155
Holkham, estate cottages 278
Holt (Denbigh), St Chad's 139, 243
Holywell (Flints) Workhouse 253
Hope, Alexander Beresford 39
Hopwas (Staffs), St Chad's **127**, 127, 134, 251
Howard, Rev. R.H. 253
Hoylake Congregational Church 202, 274–5
Hughes, Thomas of Aldford, builder 72
Huntington (Cheshire), Cheaveley Hall Farm **99**, 246, 248

Jenkins, F.: *Architect and Patron* 32
Jodrell Hall 151, 255
Jones, John Joseph of Abberley 28, 250, 258, 277
Jones, William 260, 277

Kelly and Edwards, architects 26
Kemp, Edward, landscape architect 47
Kenyon, the Hons. Georgina and Henrietta 104, 109, 157, 248, 252
Kenyon, the Hon. Henrietta 262, 263
Kerr, Robert: *The English Gentleman's House* 51, 53–4
Kirby, Edmund, architect 79, 113, 227 n4, 280
Kirkby (Lancs) cottages at, 255

Largs, house at, 256
Latchford, St Mary's R.C. Church 203, 276
Ledward, Septimus 246
Lever, William Hesketh (later Lord Leverhulme) 28, 168–9, 170, 171, 225–6 n12, 226 n15, 267
Lever Brothers 261, 262, 264, 265, 267, 268, 269, 270, 271
Little Budworth, St Peter's 139, 242
Liverpool, Cope's Tobacco Factory **115**, 115–6, 250
Liverpool, Exchange Station design 29, 116–7, 251
Llanarmon-yn-Ial (Denbigh), St Garmon's 241
Llanfechain, St Garmon's 141, 253

Llanferres (Denbigh), St Berres's 261
Llangefni (Anglesey), Rayner Memorial Clock Tower 273
Lloyd, Lewis 241
Lockerbie (Dumfries), Episcopal Church 274
Lockwood, Thomas M., architect 24, 26, 62, 204, 207
Lockwood, W.T., architect 204
London, All Saints Margaret Street 38, 39
  Grosvenor estate 62
  Grosvenor House 61
Longden Manor (Salop) & cottages 275
Lower Kinnerton, Broad Hey Farm 262
  Wm Parker's Farm 242
  Yew Tree Bank Farm 264
Lower Peover, Colshaw Hall 203, 274
Lymm, farm(s) etc 278
  St Mary's 242, 243
Lyon, Thomas Henry 277

MacGregor, Rev. William, Vicar of Tamworth 127, 155, 157–8, 255, 261
Maentwrog (Merioneth), St Twrog 33–4, 182–3, **183**, 266, 268
  Plas Tan-y-Bwlch 243
Malpas, Cae-li-Cae Farmhouse, Willington 279
  St Oswald's 185, 256
Manafon (Montgomery), Henllys Hall 269
  St Michael's 269
Marbury, St Michael's 185, 261
Marston, St Paul's 131, 245
Memorials of Old Cheshire 7
Minshull, Charles Howard, architect (J.D.'s partner) 6, 7, 75, 81, 146, 187, 197, 214 nn69 & 73
Minshull Vernon, Weaver Bank Farm 241
Mold, British School 246
  Cottage Hospital 248
  St John the Evangelist 131, 173, 174, 249
  St Mary's, reredos 249
Mostyn Hall, entrance gates 266
Mostyn, Lady Augusta 180, 258, 268
Mostyn, Lord 266
Moulton (Cheshire), St Stephen's 131, 247
Muspratt, E.J., architect 7, 197
Muspratt, Richard 254
Muthesius, Hermann, quoted 34–6, 75, 207, 208, 210

Index

Nannerch (Flints), Station Lodge, Penbedw 245
  Tai Cochion 248
Nesfield, William Andrews, architect 222–3 n5, 280
Nesfield, William Eden, architect 77–80 *passim*, 86, 87, 105, 209, 222–3 n5, 280, sketch by, **86**
Netherton (Lancs), cottages at 255
Newton Hall (Lancs) **88**
Norley, Agent's House, Ruloc 245
Northop, St Peter's **140**, 247, 249, 250
  Sessions House 248
  Soughton (Sychden) Hall 240, 243
Northwich, Market Hall 245
  Witton Grammar School 29–32, 56, 89, 240–1, 245

Oakeley, W.E. 243
Oakmere, Abbots Moss, garden ornament 27, 40, 238
Oakmere Hall *see* Sandiway
Okell, George 244
Old Colwyn, St John the Baptist 200, 203, 271, 277
Oughtrington, Burford Lane Farm, Heatley 80, 240
Ould, Edward A.L., architect 24, 169, 205–6, 207, 228 n6
Over Congregational Church (now URC) xix, 43–4, **44**, 81, 119, 239
Over, St Chad's 274, 275
  St John the Evangelist 27, 32–3, 41–2, **42**, 48, 112, 195, 238
Over Wyresdale (Lancs), Abbeystead 33, 36, 149–50, **149, 150, 151**, 188, 199, 255, 261, 264
Over Wyresdale (Lancs), Church 262
Overton (Flints), Bryn-y-Pys 245, 250
Owen, William, architect 169
Owens, Benjamin, contractor 47–8
Oxted (Surrey), Home Place 151–2, **152**

Paley, Edward Graham, architect 3, 19, 20, 21, 22, 39, 48, 110, 128
Paley, Frederick A. 20
Paley & Austin, architects 19, 128, 173, 175
Parker, the Hon. Cecil Thomas, land agent 67, 68, 69, 70, 71, 73, 74, 76, 94, 120, 146, 159, 166–7, 185, 198, 230–7
Peel, Edmund 245, 250
Penbedw *see* Nannerch
Penley (Flints), Llannerch Panna (now Tudor Court) 107, **108**, 108, 109, 249
Penmorfa (Caernarfon), St Beuno's 271
Penson, Thomas M., architect 25, 26, 28, 60, 78
Perrins, Dyson 152, 260
Perrins, Mrs F.S., (later Mrs Williams) 14–5, 16, 178–9, 226 n4
Polesworth Vicarage 97, 242
Port Sunlight 168–71
  Dell Bridge 169, 264
  housing 261, 262, 264–5, 267, 268, 269–70, 271
  school (later The Lyceum) **169**, 169–70, 187, 265
Portinscale, Lonnin Garth 203, **278**
Powles, A.E., architect 206
Poulton (Cheshire), Green Farm 259
  Pear Tree Farm 267
  Wallet's Farm 262
  Yew Tree Farm 255, 257
Pulford, Brookside Farm 159, 255
  Children's Home 274
  cottages at, 244, 257, 259, 278
  The Cuckoo's Nest, 159, 251
  The Elms 68, 242
  Grosvenor Arms 268
  Ironhouse Farm 254
  The Limes Farmhouse (now Green Paddocks) **18**, 101–2, 103, 243, 265
  Manor Farm 242, 267
  Meadow House Farm 278
  St Mary's **72**, 72, 137, 139, 173, 231, 235, 252
  school 250
  schoolmaster's house 266

Rhosllannerchrugog (Denbigh), St David's 262
RIBA 32
  Journal, Douglas obituary 13–4
Rickman, Thomas 20
Rimmer, Heber, architect 206, 228 n21
Roberts, Robert 253
Rossett (Denbigh) Bailiff's House 252
  Christ Church 173–5, **174**, 177, 256
  Coffee House 251
  Mount Alyn Farmhouse 278
  Presbyterian Church 131, 246
Rowden Abbey *see* Bromyard
Ruloe, *see* Norley
Runcorn, Weston, St John the Evangelist 183–4, **184**, 268
Ruskin, John: *Lectures on Architecture* ... 39: *The Seven Lamps of Architecture* 25, 38: *The Stones of Venice* 38–9

The Work of John Douglas

Ruthin, Coetmor, Bryn Goodman 256
   Dedwyddfa, Bryn Goodman 256
   Grammar School 153, 259
   Peers Memorial **154**, 155, 253

St Andrews (Fife), All Saints 275
St Asaph, Bronwylfa 148, 254
   Church House 276
Saighton, cottages at, 242, 244, 253, 264, 265
   Dairy Farm 254
   Grange 242, 265
   House 253, 263
   Mount Farm 159
   Saighton Lane Farm **159**, 159–60, **160**, 258
   smithy 261
   wheelwright's shop 250
Saltney Ferry, St Matthew's 202, 276
Sandiway 1, 2, 8, 9, cottages at, 250, 262, 275
   Chester Road cottage **89**
   Forest Hey 43, 116, 252, 279
   The Homestead 2, 275
   Manor 156, 279
   Oakmere Hall **50**, 50–54, **53**, 81, 82, 105, 240, 278
   Park Cottage (now Littlefold) 2
   Parsonage (now Croft House) 195, 275
   St John the Evangelist 9, 13, 16, **132**, **194**, 194–5, 273, 279
Saunders & Taylor, heating engineers 229 n40
Schloss Eltz **96**, 97
Scotland, Col. David 15, 68, 118
Scott, George G.: *Remarks on Secular and Domestic Architecture* . . . 39, 46, 50, 51
Sealand (Flints), St Bartholomew's 48–50, 134, 239
Sédille, Paul 36, 103–4, 120
Sefton, 4th Earl of, 28, 80, 126, 149, 150, 168, 249, 255, 259, 260, 261, 262, 264, 277
Sefton, St Helen's Well 260
Sharpe, Edmund, architect 19, 20, 21, 22, 216 nn1 6, 15
Shaw, Richard Norman, architect 36, 77, 78, 82, 87, 105, 128, 150, 209
   sketch by, **82**
Shocklach, St Edith's 279
Shotton, St Ethelwold's 200, **201**, 246, 270
Shotwick Park *see* Great Saughall
Smith, C.W. Jervis 262

Smith, George (J.D.'s assistant) 29, 31, 181, 206
Smith, H. Lyle, grain merchant 117, 192, 252
Smith-Barry, A.H. 254
Soughton Hall *see* Northop
SPAB 25, 110, 142
Stockton-on-Teme (Worcs), school 260
Stratton Park 279
Street, G.E.: *Brick and Marble in the Middle Ages* . . . 39
Strong, James, architect 206
Swindley, James, smith 1, 69, 146, 196, 211 n10, 225 n11
Swindley, John, smith 1
Swire, William 275

Tallarn Green (Flints), The Gelli **104**, 104–5, **105**, 108, 109, 157, 248, 263
   Kenyon cottages 262
   Parsonage 109, 157, 252
Tamworth, Bolehall Manor 155, 261
   Young Men's Institute **157**, 157–8, 162, 255
Tarbock (Lancs), smithy 255
Tattenhall, St Alban's 88, 129, 130, 174, 241
Thompson, Jabez, of Northwich 195–6, 260
Thornton (Lancs), Nag's Head Inn 259
Thornton Hough cottages **171**, 171, 189–90, 263
Thornton Hough, Thornton Manor 170, 187, 267
Tilston, St Mary's 141, 248
Torr, Rev.W.E., Vicar of Eastham 173, 186, 254
Trelawnyd (Flints), St Michael's 185, 266
Trelawny, H.D. 243
Tremadoc, The Wern 155, 156, 229, 262
Trofarth (Denbigh), St John's 271
Twemlow Green, cottages at 279

Utkinton, St Paul's 279

Vale Royal, cottages and lodge 279
   south wing 27, **40**, 40–1, 52, 81, 124, 147, 199, 200, 238, 248

Walley, J., architect 204
Wallington, W.J. 277
Warburton, Bent Farm 110, 250
   Church Hall 258
   Mill **103**, 243
   Post Office 263

Index

St Werburgh's New Church 137–9, **138**, 145, 173, 174, 253, 262, 271
St Werburgh's Old Church **142**, 142–5, **144**, 174, 250, 252
school 243
Sunday School 246
Warrington, Boteler Grammar School 3, 42–3, 153, 238
   St Ann's **55**, 55–6, **57**, 81, 82, 88, 126, 220 n27, 240
   St Elphin's 274
   Sankey Street, Nos. 19 & 21 44–6, **45**, 47, 50, 238
Waterhouse, Alfred, architect 39, 51, 61, 64, 76, 77, 87, 209
Watts, T.B. 254
Waverton, Avenue Farm 279
   Brookdale Farm 159, 258
   Church Farmhouse 90, **92**, 253
   Common Farm 279
   cottages at, 244, 247, 259, 269, 271
   Cotton Abbots Farmhouse **92**, 244, 254, 256, 258
   Cotton Hall Farm 262
   Guy Lane Farm 279
   Oak Farm 279
   Reading Room 270
   St Peter's 185, 257–8
   Salmon's House 230, 233, 234
   school **100**, 101, 248
   smithy etc 266
   wheelwright's shop 266
Weaverham, St Mary's 1, 3, 140–1, 248, 250
Webb, Philip, architect 38, 78
Wern, The *see* Tremadoc
West, Col. Cornwallis 256
West Kirby, St Andrew's **176**, 176–7, 202, 259, 275–6
Westminster, 1st Marquess of, 59
Westminster, 2nd Marquess of, (Richard Grosvenor) 24, 26, 28, 59–60, 113, 218 n7, 220 n2, 239
Westminster, 3rd Marquess of, later 1st Duke of, (Hugh Lupus Grosvenor)
   character 60–1
   patronage 24, 28, 60–76, 77, 113, 129, 190, 192, 198, 238–79 *passim*
   politics 61–2
Westminster, 2nd Duke of, (Bend'Or) 76, 198
Weston *see* Runcorn
Wettenhall Hall **93**, 93
Whitchurch, Churton Memorial Fountain 252
   Public Hall 279
   Town Hall design 54
White, Miss, of Chester 42, 238
Whitegate, Cassia Lodge 279
   St Mary's **124**, 124–5, 134, 142, 245
   Vicarage 105, 107, 249
Wigan parish church 22
Wigfair, Cefn Meiriadog **148**, 148, 223 n5, 253
Wightwick Manor 205–6
Wilbraham, G.F. 245, 246
Williams, Mrs F.S. *see* Mrs F.S. Perrins
Williams, T. Alfred **xx**, 11, 183
Williams, Rev. & Mrs T.J. 269
Worsley, Bridgewater Hotel 168, 273
Worsley Hall, West Lodge 265
Worsley, Lady Ellesmere Coffee Tavern 168, 266
Worsley Old Hall, Lodge 265
   Stud Farm, Gatekeeper's Lodge 267
Worsley, Packet House shop 272
   St Mark's lectern 264
   Wardley Hall 168, 264
Wrexham Public Library design 274
Wyresdale (Lancs), Mrs Whitaker's Farmhouse 261

Youlgreave, stables 279

East side of St Werburgh Street, Chester. St Oswald's Chambers, 1